Panics without Borders

NEW SEXUAL WORLDS

Marlon M. Bailey and Jeffrey Q. McCune, Series Editors

Featuring the most cutting-edge scholarship focused on racialized gender and sexuality studies, this series offers a platform for work that highlights new sexual practices and formations within diverse, understudied geographies. The dialectic of race, gender, and sexuality is central to the spine of all books in this series—rethinking the core questions of queer theory, gender and sexuality studies, and critical interrogations of race. With an interdisciplinary scope, authors draw on innovative methodologies, produce novel theories, and accelerate the study of gender and sexuality into new worlds of thought.

Panics without Borders

How Global Sporting Events Drive Myths about Sex Trafficking

Gregory Mitchell

UNIVERSITY OF CALIFORNIA PRESS

University of California Press
Oakland, California

© 2022 by Gregory Mitchell

Library of Congress Cataloging-in-Publication Data

Names: Mitchell, Gregory (Gregory Carter), author.
Title: Panics without borders : how global sporting events
    drive myths about sex trafficking / Gregory Mitchell.
Other titles: New sexual worlds ; 1.
Description: Oakland, California : University of California
    Press, [2022] | Series: New sexual worlds ; 1 | Includes
    bibliographical references and index.
Identifiers: LCCN 2022008335 (print) | LCCN 2022008336
    (ebook) | ISBN 9780520381766 (cloth) |
    ISBN 9780520381773 (paperback) | ISBN 9780520381780
    (epub)
Subjects: LCSH: Human trafficking—Social aspects—21st
    century. | Sports—Social aspects—21st century. | BISAC:
    SOCIAL SCIENCE / Anthropology / Cultural & Social |
    SOCIAL SCIENCE / Women's Studies
Classification: LCC HQ281 .M58 2022 (print) | LCC HQ281
    (ebook) | DDC 306.3/62-dc23/eng/20220404
LC record available at https://lccn.loc.gov/2022008335
LC ebook record available at https://lccn.loc.gov/2022008336

Manufactured in the United States of America

31 30 29 28 27 26 25 24 23 22
10 9 8 7 6 5 4 3 2 1

Para as putas

Contents

Figures

Preface

Many people had never heard of QAnon until the January 6, 2021, insurrection at the US Capitol when Trump loyalists, spurred on by their president, invaded Congress in a spectacular and deadly display that killed five people. Enigmatic images were seared into the national psyche of a bare-chested, tattooed man known as the "Q Shaman" wearing horns and furs as he stood triumphantly inside the chamber. Despite the attack, QAnon conspiracy theorists can even be found among the ranks of elected Republican leaders in Congress. Its ideology has increasingly seeped into the mainstream. Believers claim that there is a cabal of Democratic politicians and liberal celebrities who sex traffic children and then harvest adrenaline from them to create a psychoactive drug called adrenochrome. Their information comes from an anonymous source, Q, who posted cryptic messages on 4chan and 8chan message boards, claiming that Trump had come to save the United States from this threat and would one day reveal himself in a great purge called The Storm. And yet, according to reporting from the *New York Times*, just a year before the insurrection QAnon had been "on the ropes."[1] Having been largely deplatformed by social media, its members were running out of steam, becoming disconnected, and growing bored.

Then came QAnon's "Save the Children" movement, in which QAnon members began hundreds of groups on Facebook and other social media platforms to raise awareness about supposed child sex trafficking. Their membership swelled 3,000 percent in just three months. As the *Times* reports, "It created a kind of 'QAnon Lite' on-ramp—an issue QAnon believers could talk about openly without scaring off potential recruits with bizarre claims about Hillary Clinton eating babies, and one that could pass nearly unnoticed in groups devoted to parenting, natural health and other nonpolitical topics. Typical of the new, understated QAnon style are Facebook videos in which parents sound the alarm about pedophiles brainwashing and preying on children."[2] During the siege on the Capitol, QAnon believers stole laptops of congressional leaders, believing they would contain evidence of their involvement in child sex trafficking.

During the COVID-19 pandemic, wearing masks not only became politicized but co-opted into a moral panic. *USA Today* felt obligated to run a story assuring the public that mask wearing does not make children more at risk for child sex trafficking. This was deemed necessary after the proliferation of viral posts on social media with headlines like, "Did you KNOW That a Child in AMERICA Is over 66,000 X More Likely to Be Human Trafficked than to Get COVID-19?"[3] QAnon supporters and the anti–child sex trafficking social media groups would have members believe that liberals support mask wearing as part of the Democratic cabal's efforts to sex traffic children.

Scholars have long observed how powerfully the rhetoric of sex trafficking can be instrumentalized by those with ulterior motives. This book is filled with examples of corrupt politicians, duplicitous evangelical Christian organizations, anti-prostitution feminist groups, charismatic fraudsters, and profit-mongering corporations who all use exaggerated statistics and sensational claims to spur a moral panic about the supposed proliferation of a vast but invisible tidal wave of sex trafficking engulfing the world. In all of these cases, the people in question—whether they believe their own falsehoods about sex trafficking or not—have other financial motives or are pushing various other policy agendas. The anti-trafficking movement was rotting from the inside out long before QAnon got its hooks into it.

There are now so many anti-trafficking organizations profiting off their own endless "awareness raising campaigns" that social scientists have widely adopted Laura María Agustín's term *the rescue industry* to refer to the way employees and anti-trafficking executives capitalize on the powerful feelings surrounding "sex trafficking" in order to spur private donations, government grants, and corporate sponsorships.[4] Many of these organizations exist purely in the realm of the spectacular—within online campaigns, social media endeavors, "documentary" films, and campus speaking tours—but some attempt to "rescue and rehabilitate" actual people in the sex industry, often against their will. Because the rescue industry relies on sensationalism and uses only the most melodramatic examples rather than deal with the more realistic and nuanced forms that actual sexual exploitation takes, its leaders and their organizations are much more effective at lining their own pockets than at ameliorating the suffering of the exploited women and children who certainly do exist. This phenomenon is an example of what the sociologist Kimberly Kay Hoang has called "perverse humanitarianism," in which the consequences of the "collusion of compassion (the desire to help those in need) and repression (unnecessarily harsh state penalties) and the problems that arise when NGOs, states, and individualize mobilize empathy rather than the recognition of rights."[5]

There are many tropes and motifs in the mythologies of sex trafficking, but one of the most common is the erroneous belief that mega-events such as the Super Bowl, World Cup, Olympics, or other large conventions or gatherings cause major increases in sex trafficking. The most common estimate is that 40,000 women and girls are trafficked at each World Cup, but this is an example of what social scientists call a "zombie statistic": an unsourced number that is recycled by the media, passed along, and retold, like a rumor that just won't die. As I demonstrate throughout this book, there is no correlation between sex trafficking and mega-events. Indeed, the moral panic about sex trafficking and prostitution happening at these events is so pervasive, and so frequently and easily disproven, that it even has its own entry on Snopes.com debunking it.[6] However, when I myself first encountered these claims over a decade ago, I remember thinking that it might make intuitive sense that demand for paid sex during large events would increase, and that this could create incentives for coercion and exploitation. And yet the victims never materialized despite millions of extra dollars being spent on extra police, consultants, and awareness-raising ad campaigns. In the introductory chapter, I reveal the economic reasons behind why sex trafficking does not increase during mega-events, but more importantly I demonstrate that what *does* happen during these events is that all the extra policing and attention result in the prosecution of consensual sex work. Even worse, mega-events correlate not with sexual exploitation but with brutal physical and sexual violence against the sex workers perpetrated by police.

Still, the media cannot seem to help themselves.

Wandering through Moscow, I come upon children playing in a park and sit down. A pack of football (i.e., soccer) fans, many of them from Latin America, barrel through the park, chanting and singing on their way to a World Cup match. I realize that I have just followed the Moskva River down to Gorky Park. With a smirk, I pull out my phone to open Spotify and listen to The Scorpions sing "Wind of Change" (because, come on, how could you not?). Glancing at my phone, though, I see my Google Alerts spewing news headlines proclaiming: "A Stage for Human Trafficking: The World Cup in Russia" and "Sex Trafficking Made Easier, Thanks to the World Cup in Russia."[7] A British tabloid warns that "an army of seductive women, often working with gangs" will be ready to ensnare English fans "in fake Russian bride scams at the FIFA World Cup."[8]

This struck me as odd. I had just spent the day with sex worker rights advocates, who had told me that the government had shut down almost the entire sex industry before the Cup. There was practically nowhere for women to work even if they wanted to. Instead, what women were afraid of was being rounded up and sent to camps for undesirables that they had heard were located outside of cities, where the homeless, drug addicts, and prostitutes were supposedly being sent. Some journalists did maintain that such internment camps existed, though I couldn't verify how many sex workers may have been forcibly relocated to them. The reality on the ground during the World Cup in Russia was women living in very real fear of the state abducting them, not sex traffickers doing so.

Such sensationalistic headlines reminded me of similar news coverage I had seen when I was beginning research for this book in my longtime field site of Brazil. During the 2014 World Cup there, tabloid-mongers like Perez Hilton claimed without any actual evidence: "World Cup Expected to Cause Rise in Prostitution and Sexual Assault in Brazil."[9] For more than ten years, I've been followed by headlines and claims such as these. This book documents my own investigative journey as I tried to map the many hands of the state and how sex workers became collateral damage for the anti-trafficking movement's more sweeping agenda to stamp out sexual exploitation, which for many of the powerful organizations in that movement means the total eradication of all sex work. Using multisited ethnography from my time spent in Brazil, Russia, South Africa, Qatar, Japan, and England, I examine the role of *obsessive quantification* and the media's fetishization of statistics in producing the perverse relationship of the state to nongovernmental organization (NGOs) and religious organizations. These partner groups use bad data science and sensationalistic rhetoric to produce sex trafficking imagery and discourse that is spectacular but fallacious.

The consequences of such fallacious spectacles of sex trafficking are heightened surveillance, the impunity of the police, the further entrenching of a coercive state apparatus, and greater vulnerability of non-white women. Because of their international nature, sporting events act as an amplifier for these effects, expanding these same patterns of state-produced violence across the globe into a variety of political and economic circumstances. Consequently, the confluence of moral panics, global sporting events, and the spectacularization of sex trafficking by moral entrepreneurs and celebrity spokespeople in the rescue industry has morphed into a powerful and deadly force for those working in sexual economies. This book examines the dangerous shifts within the anti–sex trafficking movement to reveal how the changing nature of governance and the increasingly strong bonds of peculiar alliances between groups once divided by politics and ideology (such as evangelicals, radical feminists, corporations, and the police) ultimately perpetuate harm against vulnerable populations despite these actors coming cloaked in the guise of human rights.

Acronyms

APLO	anti-prostitution loyalty oath
CATW	Coalition Against Trafficking in Women
COSA	Children's Organization of Southeast Asia
COYOTE	Call Off Your Tired Old Ethics
FIFA	Fédération Internationale de Football Association
FOSTA-SESTA	(Allow States and Victims to) Fight Online Sex Trafficking Act-Stop Enabling Sex Traffickers Act
GAATW	Global Alliance Against Traffic in Women
IJM	International Justice Mission
ILO	International Labour Organization
IOC	International Olympic Committee
IOM	International Organization for Migration
NOW	National Organization for Women
PEPFAR	President's Emergency Plan for AIDS Relief
SWERF	sex worker–exclusionary radical feminist
TERF	trans-exclusionary radical feminist
TIP Report	Trafficking in Persons Report
TVPA	(Victims of) Trafficking and Violence Protection Act
WAP	Women Against Pornography
WAVPM	Women Against Violence in Pornography and Media
WCTU	Women's Christian Temperance Union

FIFA Men's World Cup and Summer Olympics Hosts (2000–2028)

2000	Olympics	Sydney
2002	World Cup	Japan and South Korea
2004	Olympics	Athens
2006	World Cup	Germany
2008	Olympics	Beijing
2010	World Cup	South Africa
2012	Olympics	London
2014	World Cup	Brazil
2016	Olympics	Rio de Janeiro
2018	World Cup	Russia
2020	Olympics	Tokyo*
2022	World Cup	Qatar
2024	Olympics	Paris
2026	World Cup	United States, Canada, and Mexico
2028	Olympics	Los Angeles

* Postponed in 2021 due to COVID-19.

Introduction

The Myth of the 40,000 Missing Girls

A VERY BRAZILIAN BEGINNING

Pamela, a teenage prostitute who had traveled from the poor Northeast of Brazil to cosmopolitan São Paulo to work, was in the shower when she heard the loud knock. Pamela was a *travesti* (an emic identity somewhat similar to transgender woman) who lived in a small overcrowded building filled with other travesti sex workers, many of whom had experienced housing discrimination or harassment in other buildings.[1] The landlady managed both the building as well as some of the business affairs of the women. Pamela left the steamy bathroom and cracked open the door to see who was there, only to have police shove through and, she later explained, "I was soon getting my head beaten in."[2] This was no criminal raid, however, as prostitution is not a crime in Brazil; it was a "rescue operation."[3] Nearly eighty travestis and transgender women, including six minors in their mid- to late teens, were forcibly rescued from the building and taken into police custody that day in February 2011, many of them physically or sexually assaulted in the process.[4]

Police had to subdue the travestis because they did not want to be rescued. Nor did the minors want to be returned to the more conservative city of Belém. "Here we can ride the bus and go to the mall without being called names," said Daiany. Samantha, age seventeen, agreed, declaring that she and those whose families couldn't stop them would be taking the two-day bus trip back to continue selling sex in São Paulo as soon as possible. Perhaps that's because in their makeshift

I

travesti community, unlike in the families they had fled, they had some semblance of emotional support. Dimitri Sales, the policy coordinator for sexual diversity for the state government, contradicted them and defended the intervention on the grounds that it was merely "difficult for the travestis to recognize their situation [as] sexual exploitation."[5]

When news of the raid came out, I was sitting in a cheap bar in Copacabana in Rio de Janeiro frequented by backpackers, working-class locals, women selling sex, and the occasional travesti while interviewing *garotos de programa* (rent boys) who worked in bath houses called *saunas* that featured brothel-style male prostitution. (These men were the focus of my dissertation fieldwork and first book.) The consensus among these locals was that the police needed to stop barging into poor people's homes and mind their own business. Far from being perplexed about sex trafficking, and equally far from framing the story as an issue of lesbian, gay, bisexual, and transgender (LGBT) rights, the scuttlebutt among the bar patrons was that this raid was just part of a larger crackdown that had included harassment of prostitutes, homeless street kids, and brutal raids on *favelas* (shantytowns) looking for drugs and gang members, which had ended in the deaths of many young Black and brown men. To wit: they were fed up.

I begin with the case of the travesti prostitutes because it encapsulates and represents several pressing problems happening in the period preceding Brazil's hosting of the 2014 World Cup and the 2016 Olympic Games. When one begins tugging at the loose threads of the shoddily woven story about the rescue of the travestis, one finds that state actors acting in bad faith used them (like so many other women in Brazil's sex industry) to simultaneously appease the US State Department and international human rights and women's rights organizations and broaden the power of a corrupt state apparatus. In this analysis, I build on Paul Amar's notion of the *parastatal* (a lexical mirroring of *paramilitary*) to describe "coalitions that can include government policy makers, NGOs, private-security agencies, morality campaigns and property developers . . . performing the public functions of a state that has outsourced its functions into a parallel realm of reduced accountability and unregulated power."[6] Legal scholar Janet Halley describes a related phenomenon from within feminist legal studies: governance feminism, which she describes as "an underrecognized but important fact of governance more generally in the early twenty-first century . . . refer[ring] to the incremental but by now quite noticeable installation of feminists and feminist ideas in actual legal-institutional power."[7] As examples, she cites the deployment of explicitly feminist expertise about gender policy in educational reform, NGO development and management, feminist prosecutors, and feminist cooperation with "sex crimes" units. She also explicitly identifies governance feminism with the institutionalization of anti–sex trafficking apparatuses within the state.

Parastatal tactics that harm sex workers and others on the margins of society are not new in Brazil, but they were intensified as a result of global sporting events and increased public attention. Nor is the instrumentalization of moral panics around sporting events unique to Brazil. As I document throughout this book, there is a pervasive parastatal pattern of governments, neoliberal entrepreneurs, evangelical Christian groups, and allegedly progressive activists who promote a false correlation between global sporting events and sex trafficking. The wildly inaccurate "zombie statistic" that 40,000 women and girls are trafficked for sex before each World Cup has taken on mythic status despite being completely fabricated. Nonetheless, various media outlets dust off this falsehood every four years despite these girls' nonexistence.

The result is a moral panic that extends far beyond feminist, religious, and juridical circles, filtering into popular consciousness. For example, in the case of Brazil, a popular *telenovela* (soap opera) called *Salve Jorge* that aired during the run-up to the World Cup focused on sex trafficking. It seized on the fears of predation and reified a hyperbolic vision into a common, if misguided, conception about what sex trafficking looks like. Such pop culture examples are both born of the moral panic about sex trafficking and contribute to said panic, continually resuscitating its mythologies and breathing life into this discourse in a circular fashion.

Typically, the religious groups and the neo-abolitionist feminist groups in question oppose all prostitution and believe that total abolition of the sex industry is the first step to stopping trafficking, usually by criminalizing the purchase of all sex, voluntary or otherwise, in an approach known as End Demand (or sometimes as the "Swedish Model," "Nordic Model," "Equality Model," or "sex buyers' laws").[8] Meanwhile, global sex worker rights groups and feminist anti-trafficking groups that advocate legalization or decriminalization of sex trades, or that have sex workers as partners in the development of policies that affect them, are not eligible for US funding, which requires a blanket anti-prostitution loyalty oath (known here as APLO, part of the US Leadership Act of 2003). I deal with the neocolonial impacts of APLO in the next chapter, but its primary effect is that for countries receiving United States Agency for International Development (USAID) money, only neo-abolitionists who consider all sex work to be exploitation/trafficking/rape are allowed to participate in creating public policy and laws around sex work and sex trafficking, including how to police and monitor these activities during sporting events.

This book examines the question of whether sports events correspond with increases in sex trafficking and exploitation, and it demonstrates that this seemingly intuitive correlation is baseless. Throughout this book, I document that sexual commerce (forced or unforced) remains stagnant or even decreases during these global sporting events. While commercial sex levels do not increase during these events, police violence against sex workers during such events *always* does.

We are living in a time of panic concerning the idea of *sex trafficking*, the definition of which missionaries, philanthropists, politicians, and law enforcement have expanded beyond any real utility in an effort to exploit the concept for their own individual aims. The near endless growth of what falls into the category of sex trafficking makes it difficult to stop the actual sexual exploitation and forced prostitution that does exist in the sex industry.[9] The powerful people in these alliances provide funding only for NGOs and projects that rescue unwilling victims of prostitution, setting up perverse incentives for marginalized people needing aid to perform particular racialized fantasies of helplessness that appeal to donors while ignoring less sympathetic cases (e.g., those of voluntary sex workers who experience sexual assault, debt bondage, or exploitation). Additionally, overly broad and punitive laws passed in response to the imagined threats of trafficking frequently backfire, resulting in such things as sex workers being placed on sex offender registries, sex workers losing custody of their children, and sex workers being forced into court-approved moral rehabilitation programs run by religious charities to avoid jail time.

Sex trafficking and "modern-day slavery" have suffered from what the legal scholar Janie Chuang calls "exploitation creep" as an endlessly growing army of nonprofits, charities, and government offices join scholars, who operate in what she calls a "rigor-free zone," in pushing for an expansion of anti-trafficking regimes into human rights law, tax law, tort law, public health law, labor law, and even the purview of military action.[10] Therefore, this book examines the development of these coalitions of neoliberal agents, state forces, religiously motivated actors, and NGOs—Laura María Agustín's aptly termed "rescue industry," which I mentioned in the preface.[11] The rescue industry is big business.

In addition to hundreds of millions of dollars from governments, The Freedom Fund (an antislavery organization that tracks spending on antislavery initiatives) reported that from 2012 to 2014 private businesses and foundations gave US$233 million to "combat slavery."[12] As Chuang argues, "this exploitation creep has the compelling goal of widening the anti-trafficking net to capture more forms of exploitation. But close analysis reveals that it is also a technique to protect the hegemony of a particular US anti-trafficking approach—one having broad bipartisan support in US politics—and to fend off competing approaches calling for labor rights and comprehensive migration policy reforms that are particularly contentious in the US."[13] She concludes that exploitation creep allows continued US dominance over a variety of strategic, political, economic, and military areas and to "generate, via 'slavery' rebranding, heightened moral condemnation and commitment to its cause."[14]

The rescue industry operates using principles similar to what Forrest Stuart calls "therapeutic policing," in which the goal is to transform those the state sees as a problem—be they homeless people, drug addicts, or sex workers—into rehabilitated, reintegrated, and self-governing citizens. He writes, "In the end, therapeutic policing can cause more problems than it cures. Such relentless police contact destabilizes the already precarious lives of those . . . [it] views as irresponsible and self-destructive, it actively delegitimates and criminalizes indigenous, self-directed attempts at rehabilitation and upward mobility that may resonate more harmoniously with residents' personal circumstances than the regimes of recovery dictated from above."[15] Even when operating through therapeutic policing, however, the global rescue industry is often hindered by a lack of cultural competence, its moral entrepreneurs failing to understand the complex lived realities and political economic circumstances affecting women in the various societies in which the global NGOs and missionaries operate. Frequently, those on the ground don't even speak the language and may not have ever lived in the countries in which they are launching operations. Consequently, the desired therapeutic policing often fails to move past punitive, corrupt, and violent forms of discretionary and capricious police engagement. In such instances, the humanitarian impulses of the parastatal alliances in question become perverse. As Kimberly Kay Hoang writes, "Perverse humanitarianism also refers to NGOs' operation as dislocated arms of the state that, under the guise of promoting freedom, engage in exercises of rescue that mirror practices of incarceration."[16] The perverse state has many tendrils with which to reach into the lives of those whose sexual lives and practices manifest in undesirable ways. There is what Pierre Bourdieu and others discuss as the (masculinist) right hand, or the hands of the police, carceral systems, and so on. On the (often feminized) left-hand side are the religious partner organizations, allied, nonprofits, and corporate partners of social welfare programs. The left hand grew under neoliberalism, the late capitalist regime that stripped back social safety nets and caused the NGO-ification of traditional state functions. When these hands operate together they form what Jamie Peck refers to as "the ambidextrous state."[17] In its efforts to police sex trafficking (or to at least create a kind of security theater out of the policing of sex trafficking), the state routinely grabs onto sex workers with both hands and won't let go.

I have chosen to focus specifically on how these perverse rescue industry coalitions come together around major sporting events because governments pass broader and more harmful measures during times of nationalistic spectacle and fervor. Jules Boykoff writes about capitalist celebrations like mega-events, arguing that under what Naomi Klein called "disaster capitalism," "neoliberal capitalists unabashedly capitalize on catastrophe" because "disasters create collective states of shock that can soften us up to the point where we hand over what we would otherwise ardently defend. . . . Celebration capitalism is disaster capitalism's affable cousin."[18] Boykoff found that rather than producing a rush toward privatization as in disaster capitalism, celebration capitalism, as ensued in the run-up to the World Cup and the Olympics, "manipulates state actors as partners, pushing us toward economics rooted in so-called public-private partnerships" even though these "partnerships are lopsided: the public pays and the private profits. In a smiley-faced bait and switch, the public takes the risks and private groups scoop up the rewards."[19] What Boykoff has located is the parastatal shift that has become central to the mega-event, a shift that I argue uses spectacle to reterritorialize and remake the erotic landscape of the city in ways that are harmful to sex workers.

SOME NOTES ON TERMINOLOGY

The term *sex worker* has emerged as the preferred term of the global sex worker rights movement. Some in that movement suggest that the word *prostitute* is pejorative (especially when used in a society where prostitution is illegal, therefore making "prostitute" a criminal category.) However, I came up in activist circles working with the Brazilian

Network of Prostitutes, and many of the people in this book are Brazilian activists who prefer to use the word prostitute or to reclaim the word *puta* (whore). (It's worth noting that prostitution is not illegal in Brazil, though many activities surrounding it are, so it is policed indirectly at the discretion of police.) Some of the Brazilian activists I knew subscribe to what they call *putafeminismo* (whore-feminism), a term and mode of feminist thought originating in Argentina but thriving in Brazil. (I discuss *putafeministas* at length in the final chapter.) These women did not find *sex worker* offensive (and some other Brazilian groups do use the term), but many I knew see that term as unnecessary and sanitizing language that they consider a very gringo way of speaking. However, *sex work* is a useful term even in Brazil because it is a much broader term encompassing commercial sexual services beyond prostitution (e.g., stripping, camming). The Brazilian Ministry of Labor also lists "sex professional" (*profissional do sexo*) as an official job title and description, making that the technical term there despite any eyerolling from prostitutes' rights activists and putafeministas. Thus, I move between various terms, particularly sex worker and prostitute, as necessitated by people's self-identification and for purposes of clarity, not to signal a moral value judgment.

Some activists object to using the terms *sex trafficking* and *labor trafficking* as distinct. They reason that because sex work is work, sex trafficking should be considered one form of labor trafficking. However, the media sources, governmental and nongovernmental organizations, and individuals I interacted with and interviewed almost always used these terms discretely. I therefore follow that practice for the purpose of clarity. Sometimes, when it is clear from context that I am discussing all trafficking broadly or discussing a particular form of trafficking already established, I simply say "trafficking" without specifying sex and/ or labor trafficking. In truth, the entire rubric of "sex trafficking" is so badly corroded and so thoroughly corrupted by anti-prostitution activists that social scientists and activists need to work toward developing an entirely new language for the phenomenon that the term *sex trafficking* attempts to describe.

Radical feminism is a complicated term that at one point included a much broader array of positions and ideologies around sexual politics. Historically, radical feminists of the 1970s and 1980s often opposed trans rights (including the mere existence of "transsexuals"), sex work (a term they will never use), pornography in all its forms, and BDSM (bondage, discipline, sadism/masochism). More recent generations of activists have sometimes used the term sloppily or even been completely unaware of the positions that this moniker signaled for those who survived the "Feminist Sex Wars" of the 1980s. Social conservatives often call activists "radical feminists" when they really just mean a feminist who has what the Right thinks of as "extreme views." Many people have no conception of radical feminism as arising in opposition to more mainstream liberal feminists during second wave feminism. Hence, I use the term here in its classical sense from the Sex Wars and because the groups in question use the term for self-identification (e.g., forming "RadFem" groups on social media) and hew very closely to their traditional sex-negative positions. Within sex worker rights circles, to identify as a "radical feminist" means a very particular thing (i.e., total moral opposition to all forms of prostitution and a rejection of the framework of *sex work as work*). So while I am aware that some readers may feel a defensive twinge—"Not all radical feminists!"—I nonetheless am using that term advisedly. I map the genealogy of this version of radical feminism in question at length in the next chapter, lest there be any confusion. There are also plenty of other feminists—liberal feminists, cultural feminists, postcolonial feminists, socialist feminists, and others—who subscribe to anti–sex trafficking ideology and who participate in the rescue industry. While I also object to the feminist and evangelical Christian appropriation of the term *abolitionist* (a co-opting that is racially problematic), I do recognize that this is how the anti-prostitution movement has characterized itself, but in order to distinguish these groups from the nineteenth-century abolitionists who fought against the transatlantic slave trade, I sometimes refer to them as "neo-abolitionists."

Because of the variety of fans and attendees as well as the language used in ads, in news articles, and by interviewees in various countries, I use *futebol*, football, and soccer interchangeably.

METHOD AND SCOPE

Witnessing the devastating brothel raids and violence against sex workers in Brazil led me to consider how this pattern had played out in other recent and upcoming host cities for the Fédération Internationale de Football Association (FIFA) Men's World Cup and the Summer Olympics. The ethnographic heart of this book lies in Rio de Janeiro, my second home for the better part of two decades. Yet as I watched the unfolding violence against female sex workers around me, I began investigating this strange rescue industry coalition and its modus operandi in other host countries. Out of logistical and financial necessity, I chose not to include all the host cities or other mega-event sites where a moral panic in the media about an imagined onslaught of sex trafficking occurs. To keep expanding the purview of the book to encompass such events would have meant trying to do research not only in all Super Bowl host cities every year, but also in host cities for events like the Cricket World Cup, dozens of cities a year hosting Formula One races, the annual Kentucky Derby, large trade shows, political conventions, and even astronomical events.[20]

In what really marked the myth's "jumping the shark" moment, attorneys general and media outlets in Kentucky, Wyoming, and Nebraska reported that sex trafficking would spike during the total solar eclipse that sliced across a thin band of the United States in 2017 for several minutes. Frenzied headlines before the astronomical event proclaimed, "Wyoming Solar Eclipse a Hotbed for Sex Trafficking"; "As Solar Eclipse Nears, the Fight against Human Trafficking Is Ramping Up"; and "Seminars Teach Human Trafficking Intervention ahead of Solar Eclipse Events." One official claimed that in the region of the eclipse, "a pimp will make approximately 1,000 dollars per day per girl."[21] Officials were especially concerned about children being separated from parents and made vulnerable during the two minutes and forty seconds of darkness.[22]

Panicky headlines alone are not sufficient reason to select a field site. I realized I could not run around the world going to hundreds of cities to investigate every spurious claim. I chose to focus on the FIFA Men's World Cup and the Summer Olympics because the international hype around the sex trafficking and sporting event myth is most prevalent for those, and they tend to attract more money for anti-trafficking task forces and rescue industry groups. There is similar domestic hype about the Super Bowl in the United States every year, but the rest of the world isn't very interested in the National Football League (NFL). I was more concerned with panics that extend *beyond* national borders to emerge and mutate within a range of cultural contexts.

It is strange that the anti–sex trafficking movement considers the World Cup and Summer Olympics to be so similar when they actually draw very different audiences. Many more families and children attend the Summer Olympics. The Summer Olympics are also only a couple weeks long, lasting roughly half the time of the World Cup. (The Winter Olympics are so sparsely attended and often held in such cold and unsexy locations that the panic is less potent about those sites.) The World Cup is typically spread over many cities (sometimes more than twenty cities that may even span multiple neighboring countries), so I focused on the most touristed cities during the Cups (e.g., Moscow and Saint Petersburg in Russia, Rio de Janeiro in Brazil, Cape Town in South Africa).

Rather than attempt to do fieldwork in dozens or hundreds of cities in order to offer this book as a rebuttal of an already known falsehood, the real questions should be: Why does this pattern of panic and concomitant police violence persist? What animates the panic? What fantasies undergird it? What motivates its propagators? And why should it be that the panic attaches so easily to nationalistic spectacles like global sporting events?

So began a truly global project as I expanded from Rio de Janeiro and traveled to meet with sex worker activists in Cape Town, South Africa, for several weeks who had conducted their own sex worker–led research on sexual exploitation and police violence during the 2010 World Cup. During the 2018 World Cup, I met with Russian activists in St. Petersburg who told me of camps where sex workers, people struggling with drug addiction, and homeless people were concentrated to keep them out of the view of journalists and tourists. In São Paulo, I met the head of the Federal Bureau of Investigation (FBI) team that travels to global sporting events worldwide to coordinate security with local authorities. During several stints in London totaling a little over two months, I spoke with people from Scotland Yard and the Lord Mayor's Office in London who had led the anti–sex trafficking task force during the 2012 London Olympics to get their side of the story. In the United States, I met with evangelical Christian megachurch leaders who travel to global sporting events to launch anti-prostitution efforts among local churches. And twice I traveled to Doha, host of the 2022 World Cup, for a couple of weeks each time, to learn how Western hotel chains like the Marriott and Hilton apparently make agreements with human traffickers and/or other third parties to allow migrant sex workers to openly and visibly work in their hotel bars. I also went to Tokyo for two weeks to meet with scholars of migrant labor rights and to visit red light districts there. In addition to more than fifty interviews in these countries with sex workers, clients, policy makers, and activists, I also conducted participant observation, spending hundreds of hours in brothels, saunas, massage parlors, and red light areas studying price fluctuations and levels of commerce, monitoring trends in the nationality of clients and sex workers, and examining working conditions. These shorter stints of weeks and months were different than the three-month-long World Cup project and two-month-long Olympic projects in Rio before, during, and after the World Cup and Olympic Games (which were on top of my prior years of research there off and on since 2005).

While parts of this book are ethnographic in the classic sense—particularly those concerning Brazil—other parts used approaches based on performance studies to follow the *discourse* of sex trafficking. This follows the methodological approach of Elizabeth Bernstein, who describes a "theoretically driven *ethnography of a discourse*" as "deliberately mobile and multisited, traveling with its empirical object across varied political and cultural domains."[23] Bernstein's conception of discourse echoes the Foucauldian one with which many readers may be familiar, signaling "a constellation of words, materialities, and practices as they coalesce in historically and culturally situated ways, constructing the empirical object under consideration and the social locations in which it is manifest."[24] Similarly, Jo Doezema writes in *Sex Slaves and Discourse Masters* that "in approaching 'trafficking in women' as a discourse, I am concerned with how certain definitions of the problem become dominant, with whose knowledge is accepted and whose sidelined and with the social practices involved in constructing and legitimating knowledge."[25] The importance of recognizing sex trafficking in this way is that, per Foucault, discourses have material effects in that they are "practices that systematically form the objects of which they speak."[26]

Doing an ethnography of a discourse like sex trafficking does not mean that the voices of my interlocutors vanish, but it does mean that unlike the research for my first book, there was not as strong of a focus on interviewing the same few dozen people for many hours and following their lives over the years. Instead of focusing attention tightly on the human subject, I attempt to follow the sex trafficking discourse, mapping moments at which it touches my interlocutors, but tracing it as it stretches across borders, morphing and twisting into new forms as it creates new harms.

While parastatal alliances have created *sex trafficking* through juridical, legal, social, and institutional means, they have also lent a certain elasticity and malleability to the idea, making it a slippery discourse that can therefore best be understood if mapped, tracked, and investigated in a variety of cultural, social, and historical contexts. Thus, the mixed method and multisited approach of this book is an effort to craft an ethnography of a discourse by looking at it from everywhere and all at once, rather than capturing one highly specific moment of lived experience in just one place and time as is the case for conventional ethnographies of a community or people. In her book *Pedagogies of Crossing,* M. Jacqui Alexander finds it disturbing that "physical geographic segregation is a potent metaphor for the multiple sites of separation and oppositions generated by the state, but which are also sustained in the very knowledge frameworks we deploy and in the contradictory practices of living the oppositions we enforce."[27] In that spirit, I argue that multisited work—often rather snobbily maligned within anthropology as inherently "thin"—actually resists the "products of domination and hierarchy" that Alexander speaks of as fossilizing "deep in the interior, forcing us to genuflect at the altar of alterity and separation," which are experienced as "hypernationalism and empire."[28] Multisited, multidisciplinary research begins to step around that problem and is necessary to ethnographically interrogate discourses.

What these research methods showed is that although a link between sex trafficking and global sporting events may seem intuitive, it is a total and deliberate fabrication that reveals more about the groups concocting fantasies of sex slaves than it does the actual lived experiences of women who sell sex. During these events—when celebrities lend their voices to media campaigns, or when feminist groups rally, or when evangelical Christian missionaries arrive in a country and preach sermons about sex predation and abduction by traffickers—what one does invariably see correlated is not trafficking but rather intensification of police and state violence against sex workers. This violence is also almost invariably accompanied by land grabs, rapid gentrification, and displacing poor people under the auspices of promoting "economic development," a problem exacerbated, as Andrea Cornwall, Sonia Corrêa, and Susie Jolly have shown, by the lack of interest and outright hostility shown by "development theory" experts to issues of gender and sexuality.[29] As the government cracks down on certain forms of sexuality, such as the travestis mentioned previously, it is promoting others, and this shift reveals much about the potentially negative consequences for unreflexive privileging of normative sexual subjectivity and the relationship of the state to forms of subaltern sexuality.

RESISTING RESCUE

In the days that followed the raid of the travestis whom I described at the beginning of this chapter, initial reports of these women's status as "trafficked" became increasingly murky. The prostitutes said the woman who ran the house where they lived sometimes slapped them for breaking house rules and she allegedly held their birth certificates, a red flag for exploitation. Life certainly does not seem to have been unilaterally pleasant for them. Yet not all of them had complaints. They regularly made 400 reais (at that time, US$250) for a good night and still made 80 reais (US$50) on a bad one.[30] One woman quoted said the landlady did take 30 reais (US$19) of each woman's earnings each day for room and board, but that they were, in fact, free to come and go as they wished so long as they agreed to work late into the night. Somewhat surprisingly, unlike most debt bondage schemes in which unmanageably high "rents" are charged, the amounts in this case are not necessarily exploitative. As Hoang has demonstrated in her field sites in Vietnam, those outside the industry often misunderstand the economic relationships of managers and sex workers and fail to grasp the nuances of autonomy and consent from the perspective of the workers.[31] The travestis also reported that the landlady/pimp helped them to arrange and save for the breast implant surgeries that many of them were working toward, that she functioned something like a bank. Holding their money might seem suspicious to law enforcement or anti-trafficking groups that don't actually talk to sex workers, but it is not surprising considering the intimidating difficulties of setting up a bank account as a working-class prostitute in Brazil without proper papers and ID, especially if one's gender presentation does not match one's documents (not to mention when you have to keep what the women often call "whores' hours" rather than bankers' hours). In short, there were abuses in their new home situation, but the rubric of sex trafficking is not an easy match.

Nonetheless, the government broke up this group of cohabiting travestis and shipped the minors back to the conservative Northeast against their will to families from whom they had fled. Thus did the Brazilian state use brutal force to insist on the valorization of the "traditional family" unit ahead of the sexual autonomy of sex workers, the young people's rights to safety and security, and their ability to forge their own forms of kinship among themselves and with others in their new home. This kind of police violence is nothing new, as gays, lesbians, and, in particular, travestis and trans people regularly face extremely high rates of harassment and physical abuse from deeply prejudiced military and municipal police forces.[32] What the government hailed as a human rights victory in self-congratulatory fashion for the news corps was, in reality, a case of the state forcing the women to exchange a potentially (but not altogether) bad situation of their own choosing for a definitively bad one of the state's devising.

Through this action the government added eighty more rescued people to Brazil's government tally in its efforts to make adequate yearly progress in the US State Department's Trafficking in Persons Report (TIP Report). Failing to (appear to) take adequate steps to combat trafficking results in a downgrading and losing esteem in the eyes of the international community, not to mention a significant loss of funding. Each country's progress is monitored by the US State Department and consists of whether the United States feels a country has provided enough evidence of "vigorously investigating" severe cases, whether the country provides for and protects victims whom it does not choose to deport (deportation of victims being a common occurrence), whether the country has supported ample public awareness about the danger and scope of trafficking, and—importantly— whether the country has made serious attempts to "reduce the demand for commercial sex acts" and nationals' "participation in international sex tourism." This latter point includes completely legal and consensual prostitution and sex tourism, a bit of moral imperialism by the George W. Bush administration that nonetheless suited the secular liberal feminist views of the Barack Obama administration and its State Department as well as the subsequent Donald Trump and Joseph Biden administrations. In this way, the US *forces* sovereign states to attack legal forms of sexual work in order to combat "trafficking." It *requires* a conflation of prostitution with trafficking.

Adding eighty cases to Brazil's file with the State Department counts for a lot of TIP Report points. Whether the sex trafficking in question was, in fact, "trafficking" as conventionally understood is of secondary importance because it registers internationally as a human rights intervention. Moreover, Brazil's Luiz Inácio Lula da Silva (2003–2010) and Dilma Rousseff (2011–2016) administrations had been eager to promote the idea of Brazil as deeply interested in human rights issues.[33] Of special interest are women's rights and LGBT rights, which help to bolster its claims to join other "First World" leaders with comparable economic clout with a permanent seat on the United Nations (UN) Security Council. Brazil's anti-trafficking laws, which were overhauled in 2003, are being so abysmally abused that Marina Pereira Pires de Oliveira, the Ministry of Justice official who crafted the legislation, resigned in 2008 and began writing fierce critiques about how those laws were being misused and were actually *increasing* the abuse of women.[34] Much as in the United States, left- and right-wing politicians in Brazil similarly agree on the importance of stopping sex trafficking, with the far-right Jair Bolsonaro regime in Brazil condemning sex trafficking just as the Worker's Party administrations before him did.

Brazilians have an expression: *para ingles ver* ("for the English to see"), referring to laws that were passed against slavery but never put into practice, existing purely for show. Today it's used to describe pulling the wool over someone's eyes to keep up appearances, including in this case public policies that do one thing while pretending to do quite another. I maintain that the crackdowns against sex workers before sporting events happen in order to present an image of a safe and prosperous Brazil to the media (and one can also include poor favela dwellers and the homeless here) and are very much in keeping with this tradition of being "for the English to see."

Brazilians also have another favorite quip about their homeland: *O Brasil é o país do futuro—e sempre será*. (Brazil is the country of the future—and always will be). These sporting events presented the government with a valuable opportunity to erase the ironic tagline in that sentence and to come into its own in the eyes of millions of people who would tune in all over the world. The news media were awash in stories about how far Brazil had come and how far it had yet to go, worries about whether violence or renewed protests during the games (such as those that happened during the Confederations Cup in 2013, which I discuss in the final chapter) would frighten tourists, and debates about whether Brazil's soaring economic growth was merely a bubble that was now popping and sliding into recession. (Indeed, Brazil eventually did have an economic meltdown, which is partly to blame for the rise of an authoritarian right-wing demagogue in the form of Jair Bolsonaro, who is president at the time of this writing.) It simply would not do for prostitutes, drug dealers, and child beggars to come flooding out of Rio's infamous favelas to harass tourists or be captured by journalists' cameras.

But how to obtain the kind of control necessary to pull off such a transformation for the world to see? Beginning in 2009, Rio's evangelical Christian mayor began a militarized version of "broken windows theory" called O Choque de Ordem, the Shock of Order. That same year, the governor of the state hired Rudy Giuliani (New York's architect for racial profiling and "broken windows" policing enforcement, who later went on to serve as President Trump's lawyer) as chief of security for the 2016 Olympic Games.[35] The Brazilian government cracked down with brute and excessive force against small infractions like vagrancy and public lewdness (to target prostitutes), which eventually escalated into massive military incursions into the favelas with armored tanks in a process it calls *pacificação* (pacification).

This intensification is reminiscent of brutal crackdowns during Brazil's military dictatorship (1964–1985), but also of a series of "quality of life" sweeps in the run-up to the UN Earth Summit in 1992, documented by Amar, in which police rounded up prostitutes (especially travestis) in a series of operations with moralizing names like Operation Shame, Operation Sodom, and Operation Come Here Dollbaby.[36] However, the size, scale, and imbrication of intrastatal alliances of feminist, human rights, and evangelical Christian organizations lend tacit moral credence to the government's assault: company is coming, and Brazil's poor had better be on their best behavior.

The parastatal alliances identified by Amar represent a broader depiction of what Elizabeth Bernstein has called "militarized humanitarianism" meeting "carceral feminism."[37] Bernstein explains that what unites neo-abolitionist feminists like the Coalition Against Trafficking in Women (CATW) and Equality Now with evangelical Christians like Focus on the Family is not an apolitical common interest in human rights but a shared commitment to a carceral ideology that advocates state punishment, criminalization, jail, and imprisonment. There is also a new wave of young evangelicals who are willing to set aside hot button issues such as gay marriage and abortion and to embrace the language of women's rights and social justice to garner support for anti-trafficking.[38] Evangelicals and antitraffickers got perhaps their biggest boost from George W. Bush, who expanded Bill Clinton's "charitable choice initiative" that made religious groups eligible for federal funding. As Denise Brennan notes, the rush to talk about sex trafficking instead of other forms of trafficking into forced labor was spurred as much by xenophobia and a desire to avoid comprehensive immigration reform as by a concern with sexuality.[39] In my own analysis, I take up Bernstein's focus on the carceral but expand it beyond the evangelical and feminist camps to Amar's broader array of actors in order to map the repeating political economic pattern related to global sporting events and ultimately to better understand the effects of this carceral feminist parastate on sexual culture in Brazil.

The result of this approach is a renewed attention to how the rescue industry has increasingly turned toward spectacles such as protests, gimmicky awareness campaigns, viral videos, Facebook groups touting conspiracy theories, and urban legends about traffickers marking women's cars at Walmart. The sociological phenomenon of the moral panic goes back centuries, but the parastatal alliances that now constitute the anti-trafficking rescue industry have learned to spectacularize their cause in new ways that have catapulted it into a crowded marketplace of moral entrepreneurs competing for hundreds of millions of dollars. Using the global reach of sporting events, these fallacious spectacles allow the moral panic to extend without regard for borders, producing ever-more state violence against already marginalized women.

A WINDING PATH

Ethnography as a genre of writing has taken on an apologetic tone in recent years as authors struggle to work out their subjectivity, their privilege, and often their liberal guilt as they try to justify why they are qualified to write about people whose experiences are different from their own. This is well-intentioned but often seems aimed at exonerating them of some unstated offense while taking focus *away* from the communities with whom they worked. What matters most is how the ethnographer is interpellated into one's field site by the community in question, not their own feelings about doing the work, per se.[40] Nonetheless, it's helpful to understand where an author comes from because objectivity is a powerful myth in academia, and all research methodologies are informed by one's intersecting identities and one's personal history.

My own subjectivity was received differently in each country where I worked. In most sites, my whiteness was paramount. It was a more overt asset in Qatar, Japan, and Russia, for example, where nonwhite researchers would likely have encountered overtly racist bias accessing spaces that welcomed me. In Brazil, and to some extent in South Africa, it depended what neighborhood I was in and what communities I worked with; sometimes it purely bestowed privilege, and sometimes it rightly aroused suspicion. My long history with Rio de Janeiro and my relationships developed there over the decades also affected my ability to do ethnography there, which is part of the reason Brazil remains the dominant field site in this book.

My status as a US citizen was also very important; it helped in places like Qatar and Japan but made working in Russia difficult. In Brazil, my nationality combined with my male privilege meant that I always read as a gringo sex tourist, making it much easier to do research because women would constantly approach me and strike up a conversation. I was also allowed to enter brothels that female researchers could not. My sexual orientation was a somewhat more complicated factor.

When I was planning my trip to Russia, friends and colleagues practically begged me not to go because they feared for my safety. In Qatar, homosexuality is illegal. But in Brazil, when I would out myself as gay, it convinced female sex workers that I was, indeed, there for legitimate research purposes and not just a shy gringo making excuses about why I was in a brothel. All of my intersecting identities and privileges collided in different ways depending on which field sites and circumstances I was in, opening some doors and closing others but always altering the ultimate shape this book would take.

I never intended to study sex work. I grew up gay in a rural midwestern town, raised in a broken and violent home by working-class parents who had not attended university. I had no idea what professors did or that research on such a thing even existed. I managed to eat in elementary school because my siblings and I qualified for free lunch. When I was a teen, we lost our home to foreclosure. I joined so many extracurricular activities and worked so many hours at the local library that I would leave for school at six o'clock in the morning and often not get home until ten o'clock at night, thus staying out of the house. I realized that there was a thing known as "white trash" and that my grandmother was a little too quick in assuring me that no matter what the other kids said, we were not *that*. (Spoiler alert: we were.) I desperately wanted to escape the cornfields and trailer parks that surrounded me . . . and that meant college.

I applied to one school, Illinois State University, and was able to attend using Pell Grants (back when Pell Grants were meaningful enough to make that possible). I also worked part-time at the career center and at the café inside the Barnes & Noble. I lied about my sexual history with men so that I could sell my plasma twice a week at a for-profit clinic. I took as many as seven classes a semester because anything over five courses was gratis. I studied theater, and my friends and I sometimes fantasized about starting a company one day. If someone had told me then that I would one day move to Brazil, learn Portuguese, befriend and live among prostitutes there, and then travel the world writing about sex worker rights, I would surely have thought them mad.

And yet when I finished school and moved to Chicago in 2002, I found myself living in Boystown. I lacked the self-awareness to realize that this pattern—rural boy moves to big city gayborhood—was a well-worn trope and not an exceptional tale. I worked in a range of jobs as I tried to figure out what I wanted to do, briefly working for a casting agency, then in domestic violence intervention counseling with groups of men seeking to avoid jail time through diversion programs, and taught middle school in what colleagues referred to as a "behavior disordered" special ed classroom. I quickly began to feel uneasy with the gay community around me, which was mostly white and middle class, mainstream in its politics, frequently not-so-subtle in its racism, and organized primarily around consumerism. I also didn't have the language then to describe the fact that within a couple of years, my own white privilege had much more fully begun paying dividends despite my class background. I was climbing the ranks in public policy administration at the Chicago Public Schools, making more money, and able to afford new leisure activities like traveling abroad. However, at work I was asked to participate in the closure and takeover of local schools. At the direction of C-suite bureaucrats, I wasted vast sums of money on do-nothing consultants, taxpayer money that should have gone back into the poor and underserved communities of color from whence it came. I witnessed an endless parade of promotions of abusive teachers and incompetent principals because it was easier to move them up in the system than out.

Fed up with this institutional rot, I went back to school. I matriculated at the University of Chicago, intending to write my master's thesis in cultural anthropology about the growth of gay consumer markets, effectively seeking to critique my own community rather than find some "exotic Other" upon which to direct my newly developing "academic gaze." After doing a paper analyzing the amount of ad space given in gay publications to various categories—pharmaceuticals, alcohol, financial services, and so on—I narrowed my focus to travel, which was a main driver of gay spending and something that fascinated me as someone who had previously not traveled much. My adviser, Stephan Palmié, wisely steered me away from the circuit party scenes of popular places like Mykonos and Ibiza and urged me to spend the summer of 2005 in Brazil—which often topped the lists of best new gay travel destinations—studying Portuguese and talking to gringos and tour operators in Brazilian cities about why they were there. How does a place become the next big thing among gays? What ideas animated their travel? What were their dreams? Their disappointments? Within a day or two of arriving in Brazil, I realized that these aging gringos all had beautiful Brazilian men in their twenties on their arms. *Oh shit,* I thought. I know why they are here. And it's not because there was a focus group or an ad campaign. This is sex tourism.

The more I spoke to the clients and, eventually, to the garotos de programa, the more I became fascinated by how racialized desire and culturally specific affects were being interpellated between the men. I wrote my master's thesis at the University of Chicago about the growth of gay sex tourism among African American men in Bahia and its overlap with diasporic heritage tourism. This then became one chapter in my PhD dissertation in performance studies at Northwestern University, which was an ethnography of garotos and their gringo clients in several Brazilian cities. This, in turn, would evolve into my first book, *Tourist Attractions: Performing Race and Masculinity in Brazil's Sexual Economy*. And that is how it came to pass that I was in Brazil when the brothel raids began.

By 2011, we knew the 2014 World Cup and the 2016 Olympics were coming and that *cariocas* (residents of Rio de Janeiro) were expected to be on their best behavior. Police were closing sex motels and brothels, harassing the women and sometimes assaulting, robbing, or raping them. I had never seen this kind of violence against sex workers in Rio before. The police had no interest in the male sex workers, whose existence was so unthinkable as to keep them off the radar. But women in the city's sexual economy were shaken by this turn of events. I had known leaders of Brazil's prostitutes' rights movement for several years at that point and most of the other researchers living in Rio who studied the heterosexual sex industry. One of the most prolific of these was Thad Blanchette.

A fellow midwestern boy, Thad had moved to Brazil decades earlier, fully emigrated, and married a powerhouse scholar and pioneer of Afro-Brazilian feminist theory named Ana Paula da Silva, who would later work as his co-researcher. One fateful afternoon, Thad told me about a new collective of about a dozen researchers and journalists from Brazil, Portugal, Canada, and the United States who were going to undertake a massive study of Rio's sexual economy spanning from before the 2014 World Cup until after the 2016 Olympics, with an eye toward countering the misinformation that we were already seeing from culturally incompetent foreign activists and missionaries now flooding Brazil. Prostitutes from the prostitutes' rights group Davida were instrumental to its founding and overseeing its ethics (in a reversal of most institutional review board power structures). It was to be called the Observatório da Prostituição (Prostitution Policy Watch, literally the Prostitution Observatory). The group was being given an initial five-year charter at the Metropolitan Ethnographic Lab at the social science college of the Federal University of Rio de Janeiro, he explained—and would I like to join?

CRITICAL ETHNOGRAPHY AS ETHICAL IMPERATIVE

Police entered the house where Isabel and three hundred other women were legally selling sex in Niterói, Rio de Janeiro, on May 23, 2014. (All names are pseudonyms unless they are public officials, researchers, or spokespeople for organizations.) They were acting without a court order and chose to steal the women's money and extort them, and they singled out several of the women for rape. Isabel was one of the women the police beat and gang raped in this operation, which occurred just weeks before the World Cup. When the police were done, they closed the building and labeled the rooms as crimes scenes, which effectively evicted the women and made them homeless. Unlike the other women who were intimidated by police, Isabel pressed her claim and testified against them. On June 21, men abducted her and tortured her by cutting her with razor blades on her limbs and torso. We believed them to be from the *milícia* (organized groups of off-duty and former cops, security guards, and so on who act alongside the interests of the police or sometimes purely for their own benefit). They showed her pictures of her children that they had taken and told her to stop talking to the press. Isabel went from making several thousand dollars a month selling sex legally to being totally destitute and homeless. When I speak of the ways that the anti-trafficking movement and its policy objectives have empowered the carceral right hand of the state and allowed police to act with impunity, it is cases like Isabel's that occupy the forefront of my mind.

When the raid happened, Laura Murray, who was both a member of Davida and a member of the Observatório, arrived on the scene immediately to coordinate a legal response. Members of our collective were united by a common commitment to "critical ethnographic practice," or ethnography that does not pretend to "read culture" "over the shoulder of the natives" in a detached manner (as had once been true of traditional anthropology).[41] Instead, critical ethnography recognizes that ethnographers are implicated by wider social structures and systems of power/oppression and have a duty to do ethnography that is informed by the needs and desires of our interlocutors (who are sometimes even described as or employed as co-researchers). Critical ethnography also maintains that ethnographers have an imperative to advocate for social justice for the people who contribute their insights, stories, and life experiences to our work. Successful academics make our careers, get tenure, earn raises, and garner awards using the experiences, writings, discoveries, and the work of others. In the case of research done with and alongside sex workers, our academic labor rests on their sexual labor. Therefore, great care must be taken to both get it right and give back. And so when Isabel was attacked, my colleagues and I scrambled to find her safe housing, clothes, a secure phone, and access to psychological counseling, and to raise enough money for food while she was in hiding.

While the other women went to work during the Cup in other neighborhoods and venues, Isabel remained hidden, shuffled from house to house by the Observatório members so the milícia would not find and murder her. She still worried about her former coworkers. "They're scared," she told Julie Ruvolo, a journalist and one of the Observatório researchers. "Because, like it or not, they know what's happening. And after all that's happened to me, they're even more scared."[42]

Because she was not a trafficking "victim," neo-abolitionist feminist and evangelical groups were not interested in her case. Laura found that the government's mechanisms for women's rights and human rights protections were unable to turn her into an ideal victim worthy of protection because of her insistence that she was a victim of state violence, not sex trafficking.[43] Eventually, I was able to use connections I had with a lawyer in Rio named João Gabriel Rabello Sodré to get myself a meeting with Amy Radetsky, the chief economic and political officer for the US Consulate in Rio de Janeiro, to discuss Isabel's case. This was a fraught decision for me because Radetsky's office was responsible for generating the TIP Report for Brazil, which I still regard as a neocolonial cudgel of US foreign policy. But Radetsky also oversaw the US State Department's Human Rights Report on Brazil, in which I hoped she might highlight Isabel's case such that it could create international visibility and enough pressure from Brazil's politicians that it would stop the police/milícia from further harming her. In the end, Isabel made it all the way to Brasilia, the capital, to testify before congress. The morning she did so, her father's house mysteriously burned to the ground. Eventually, Isabel fled Rio entirely. The Observatório proved no match for the perverse violence of the parastate.

The raid that brought so much damage into the lives of Isabel and her coworkers was not the last. On the morning of June 12, 2014, the opening day of the World Cup, police arrived with reporters from Globo TV at Balcony Bar, a restaurant popular with sex workers and gringo clients. Police shuttered the venue, placing a sign on the front of the building stating that "the conduct [of Balcony Bar] reinforces a derogatory image of Brazil, which is viewed internationally as a country that permits sexual tourism." They also closed a nearby hotel known to rent rooms to sex workers and clients. That evening, over a hundred women turned up to work at their usual bar but found it closed. They simply moved about ten feet over to stand in the plaza next to it. One woman called out to me cheerfully as she held up her phone, "Balcony is closed, but the wifi is still on!" The women loitered outside the closed bar close enough to keep the signal. Soon hundreds of clients appeared, and mobile venders swooped in with cheap drinks and snacks. A rollicking party ensued outside the closed bar most every night for the month of the Cup. Across the street, viewers left the FIFA Fan Fest viewing area on Copacabana beach. Approximately three hundred police stood around for crowd control. With no media presence, they no longer cared about the prostitution. As I stood in the square, two European tourists asked some police officers in front of me where else they could go to find sex and promptly received directions from the police to Barbarella, another nearby sex tourist venue.

The Observatório had teams of researchers in place for weeks before the 2014 World Cup in Rio, all thirty-two days of the World Cup, as well as after the World Cup. We worked in both indoor and outdoor venues. Of the 279 venues we mapped and visited, we focused on around 75 primary ones that represented a suitable cross-section of the touristy Zona Sul (south zone, which includes Copacabana); the Centro (downtown, including the nearby bohemian area of Lapa); and Vila Mimosa, a large, slum-like red light area where anywhere from five hundred to a thousand women normally work, often charging as little as twenty-five cents a minute. Venues included freestanding brothels that are usually more working class (including what are known as *fast fodas* [fast fucks] or *inferninhos* [little hells]), saunas with brothel-style prostitution and entertainment known as *termas* (ranging from lower middle class to upper class), strip clubs, sex tourist bars, plazas, parks, and streets. We conducted formal and informal interviews with hundreds of women and used one formal survey instrument.[44]

We also did a great deal of participant observation, particularly tallying head counts over time throughout the roughly two-month period (sometimes visiting the same venues multiple times a day to chart the ebb and flow of the commerce). We ascertained not only the number of sex workers in each site over time but also the number of clients, and sought to determine what percentage of men were foreign versus domestic as well as which nationalities were represented. In the formal and informal interviews with sex workers, waitstaff, managers, bouncers, and clients we also collected data on the following:

Migration patterns (e.g., were women coming from other cities in Brazil to sell sex? Other countries?)

Length and nature of work history (e.g., were they sex workers before the World Cup, or did they begin selling because of the World Cup? Were they working in multiple venues? Had they changed venues because of the Cup?)

Pricing (e.g., did they attempt to raise prices for the Cup? Did they charge consistently across client nationalities? When business waned, did they lower prices?)

Levels of commercial activity (e.g., were they making more than usual? Less than they expected/hoped? How many *programas* [tricks] were they doing in a given day?)

Third-party facilitation (e.g., were they working with managers, pimps, boyfriends, or other third parties? Was this new? In brothels, how much was the house taking?)

Working conditions (e.g., were they being fined for missing work during the Cup? Did managers in brothels make them pay for their own costumes, condoms, STI testing, etc.? Were there any minors or people working who looked underage? Were there any signs of abuse such as bruises, fearfulness, or visible distress?)

In the ensuing weeks, it became clear as I visited dozens of venues to speak with sex workers with my colleagues that the women were disappointed. "The Cup should end! It sucks," one opined. Priscilla, a woman in her forties, explained, "I thought I would make money, but no one wants programas! They only want to talk, maybe buy a drink, and then take selfies with me for their Facebook."

Downtown brothel venues resorted to giving out free beer on game days if people would come but still could not coax clients to enter. Eventually, business was so poor they actually closed down during games. Although gringos abounded and women raised prices, the Observatório found that only 16 of 279 venues had an increase in business. [45] Local clients preferred to stay home with their families or friends and to avoid the crowds of gringos. Thus, women moved from downtown venues popular with locals to Copacabana, chasing the gringos but creating a massive oversupply of sexual labor and increasing competition in the process.

Despite the radical feminist group Femen protesting sex tourism top-less outside the Copacabana Palace Hotel and the evangelicals from Exodus Cry touring Brazil preaching about a frenzy of sex trafficking in Brazil, sexual commerce went down overall, and police violence went up. Simultaneously, construction and other development continued in Copacabana even as the state tried to shutter venues and drive out sex workers. The carceral parastate was in full swing, yet the individual parastatal actors consistently revealed that in the Brazilian case it was the optics and not the actual rescue/removal/rehabilitation of prostitutes that was most important.

FALLACIOUS CLAIMS AND PERVERSE EFFECTS

Each time I returned to Rio de Janeiro in the 2000s and 2010s, I saw the ongoing war being waged against sex workers there, so I began to monitor accounts of sex trafficking and popular depictions of the sexual economies in my field sites, which were seldom accurate. After giving a lecture at the Federal University of Rio de Janeiro (UFRJ) about the media's manipulative narrativization of a sex trafficking bust focused on Brazilian male sex workers, I was surprised to be invited by the Office of the Secretary of Human Rights for Rio de Janeiro to meet for a half day to provide feedback privately.

In that assessment, Thad and I both presented our experiences to the government. Neither of us had observed regular underage prostitution in the targeted areas in Copa until the mega-disco known as Help!—the largest safe and legal site for sex tourists and workers to meet and strike deals—was closed to make room for the new Museum of Image and Sound on Copacabana's beachfront in time for the 2014 World Cup. (That museum remains unfinished, long abandoned, but now possibly being resurrected nearly a decade later.) Nonetheless, Help! was shuttered amid sensationalized reports about the horrors of sex tourism and "child prostitution."[46] The scene outside Help!, though, was in fact so thoroughly unshocking that Frommer's guidebook recommended it:

> By the Help disco, the Terraço Atlântico is where johns and hookers hook up in the afternoon and early evening. For those who like people-watching, it can make a fascinating scene. . . . The good news is that [it] isn't dangerous or even overly sleazy. Indeed, it can be interesting observing the hustle and bustle and to and fro, though the atmosphere is not exactly family-friendly (unless you come from a very odd family).[47]

And this is from *Frommer's*, not an edgier title like *Lonely Planet* or *Rough Guides*, but the guidebook for the staid and bougie traveler. Yet as my colleague and I explained to the Office of the Secretary of Human Rights representative—who confessed that no one working on the government's new manual for anti-trafficking had actually been to the red light areas they would target—with Help! gone, the industry had begun spilling into the alleys and streets, with hundreds of sex workers and clients mingling. The handful of other bars in the area couldn't hold the overflow. No longer was there security carding young-looking girls or the ability to monitor what was happening. And so now one *could* find at least a few girls appearing to be in their midteens working outside, as the industry had had to shift outdoors and there were no longer safeguards like doormen, property owners, and sex workers of legal age keeping an eye out for illegal activities and booting transgressors from the premises. By shutting down the safer legal indoor spaces for solicitation, the anti-trafficking crackdown had inadvertently fostered the development of an underaged prostitution market in the area (albeit a very small one), paradoxically creating the very exploitation it purported to abhor.

Nor were we the first or only experts to note that the state uses its anti-trafficking laws to increase extralegal detention of sexually vulnerable populations, raise sentences for vice crimes, and harass single women and travestis traveling across borders—all without satisfactorily bringing actual traffickers or abusers to justice.[48] The media ran similar stories about sex trafficking when Dallas hosted the Super Bowl, causing the Dallas police to go on TV and announce that 50,000 to 100,000 prostitutes, including trafficking victims, could show up for the big game, which the Global Alliance Against Traffic in Women (GAATW) points out would be enough for every fan in the stadium to have their own prostitute.[49] Despite much alarm, an embarrassed FBI representative in Dallas soon had to publicly admit that there had been *no* trafficking as expected.[50] However, the coverage after the fact of the "surprising" absence of sex trafficking at these sporting events was not given nearly the amount of attention as the stories leading up to the event. When such fallacious coverage happens, it creates a kind of "Schrödinger's trafficking victim" in which the victim is somehow "there" (in the public's mind) but not at all there (in reality), leaving readers under the mistaken impression that sex trafficking actually *had* coincided with the Super Bowl.[51]

Seeing a pattern in previous host sites, reporters in Minnesota noted that in Dallas, "in a span of about two weeks, a total of 59 people had been arrested on prostitution related charges. Thirteen were allegedly johns. Three were busted for outstanding warrants and were believed to be pimps. Only one person faced a human-trafficking charge. None of the arrests involved juveniles."[52] They also noted that in 2016, police in Santa Clara County, California, arrested or cited thirty clients, and that in Houston police had made twenty-one arrests involving "vice prostitution" over a ten-day period. Spending large amounts of overtime pay for police to spend weeks looking for trafficking only to primarily end up arresting sex workers is the consistent Super Bowl pattern. The forced prostitution and exploitation they find is minimal and is not related to the event. They could find and prosecute abusive pimps *anytime* if they made it a priority. Yet as the reporters noted, "earlier this month, a Super Bowl Anti-Sex Trafficking Committee was formed to 'elevate the issue and coordinate Minnesota's heightened response before, during and after Super Bowl LII'" and point to the existence of a $1 million campaign to support the anti–sex trafficking efforts.[53] Simply put, the Super Bowl sex trafficking myth is a revenue generator for profiteering police departments and missionaries.

In an interesting example of how exploitation *can* occur around the Super Bowl, but one that illustrates why a labor rights framework for sex work is more appropriate than therapeutic policing or rescue and rehabilitation initiatives, it's worth mentioning Strippergate 2020. Journalist Felicia Kelley was embedded at the so-called Stripper Bowl, a major party put on by the music label Quality Control the day after Super Bowl LIV in Miami. The label represented former stripper Cardi B as well as Migos and other major stars. Cardi B, Diddy, Wiz Khalifa, and many other celebrities attended the party at The Dome, a famous club. According to Kelley's reporting, more than 350 dancers came to perform, many of them flying to Miami at their own expense and paying a house fee of $350 each and 30 percent of the total revenue to the venue. Viral images of women knee deep in a sea of dollar bills circulated online. When customers were told to clear out at 5:30 a.m., some of these people stole money. Dancers were told to stop playing in the money and posing for photos with it, and instead to clear out and not touch it. Eventually, security demanded the women leave all their bags behind and begin counting it all themselves. Security then took away pillows the women had been resting on (as they were exhausted after fifteen hours in the club), telling them they were stealing club property. The only food available was a food truck selling $20-a-plate salmon cakes. At 11:00 a.m., security told them to line up for a head count, but the women became unruly and began to chant "bring our money" and jumped up onto couches. Men with AK47s appeared and demanded order. Eventually, each woman received about $1,100, meaning many of them lost money on the trip overall. Having been held (sometimes at gunpoint, no less) for over fifteen hours inside the club, many had missed their flights and were stranded. Adding insult to injury, Cardi B took to Instagram to blame them and defend her label, saying, "Y'all weren't entertaining" and "you bitches ain't that cute." Instead of defending them, a celebrity known for asserting her own rights to female sexuality and sexual autonomy exploited sex workers and then shamed them for it.[54]

Strippergate 2020 illustrates how irrelevant the hype of Super Bowl sex trafficking is. The rescue industry's framework cannot account for the labor exploitation that occurred even though the situation contained hallmarks of sex trafficking imagery such as women being held captive, men with guns, abusive clients, and luring the women into expensive travel as well as underpaying them. Yet none of the women claimed to have been trafficked. Rather, they wanted their money and reasonable working conditions in which to dance. The rescue framework falls apart in this brief case study, but it does provide compelling evidence for labor protections and sex worker rights to be strengthened, especially during mega-events. Perhaps because they were such imperfect victims, none of the groups who had been spreading panic about sex trafficking took up the cause of defending or assisting the dancers.

PHANTOM NUMBERS

Well-funded evangelical groups such as the Salvation Army—which most people know only as charitable bell ringers but which also operates a powerful and well-funded evangelical antigay political lobby and moral crusade on a number of issues—took out massive advertisements warning of the dangers of sex trafficking and global sporting events, including the South African World Cup. Likewise, the Protestant Church of Germany and the German Women's Council had taken a similar approach when Germany hosted the World Cup, where the media ran sensationalistic stories about "sex shacks" and "mega-brothels" that would be needed to meet the demand.[55] The South Africa Drug Authority warned that "a billion condoms may not be enough," and Great Britain promptly sent 42 million condoms to its former colony for the Cup.[56] During the Rio Olympics, organizers gave out 450,000 condoms specifically to competitors, "enough condoms for each athlete to have sex 84 times."[57] (In a progressive move, 100,000 of those were "female condoms," and they also gave out 175,000 sachets of lubricant.)[58] Local celebrities in South Africa took to television to warn people not to "fall prey" to traffickers. Graphic media campaigns abounded.[59] Human rights and anti-prostitution activists likewise sounded the sex trafficking alarms that South Africa's 500,000 World Cup attendees would cause sex trafficking to skyrocket to 40,000 victims.[60] Similar claims were made in Vancouver, Athens, Berlin, London, and other host cities.[61]

The most common figure bandied about was that 40,000 people would be trafficked into South Africa for the World Cup, but this number may have come from a Swedish anti-prostitution group; after being uttered in a UN meeting, it quickly congealed into a "known fact" for CNN and various other news outlets even though no one knows anything about the methodology behind the claim whatsoever, and we have no actual research study that ever produced that number. In truth, the figure was simply being recycled from the German World Cup in 2006, when, according to the South African social scientist Marlise Richter, "over-heated media reports suggested that 40,000 women and children would be trafficked into Germany to meet the demand for paid sex of three million soccer tourists. Only five people were subsequently found to have been trafficked during that time period."[62] Prior to the German World Cup in 2006, the supposed connection between prostitution and mega-events was not especially prominent. It's also worth noting that Swedish anti-prostitution feminist groups have a long-standing gripe with Germany over that country's legalization laws and seem to hold it in especial contempt, so it is unsurprising that the 40,000 figure began as Swedish speculation about Germany.

The New Internationalist describes the reaction of Dr. Nivedita Prasad from Ban Ying Coordination and Counselling Centre against Trafficking in Persons, who "opened a newspaper and panicked: a new report claimed that 40,000 'forced prostitutes' were coming to Germany for the 2006 Football World Cup. 'I thought, where are we going to put 40,000 people?' Prasad recalls. 'There are eight beds in our shelter, and only about 400 in the whole of Berlin!'" The reporter concludes, "She needn't have worried, since it turned out that the 40,000 was a fictitious number. What was worrying, however was the response: 71 police raids in brothels during the football month, compared to 5 to 10 a month in 'normal' times," which resulted in the arrests of ten undocumented sex workers (not trafficking victims).[63]

The International Organization for Migration (IOM) took special note of the original 40,000 figure and conducted a four-month-long investigation. It concluded that "the 40,000 estimate was unfounded and unrealistic."[64] Moreover, the IOM found that there was neither evidence nor "significant information" indicating any increase in sex trafficking during the 1998 World Cup in Paris, the UEFA championships in Portugal in 2004, or the 2004 Olympic Games in Athens.[65] The mysterious origin of the 40,000 figure vexed the IOM. "Law enforcement and many NGOs were quickly disassociating themselves from this figure as there was apparently no basis for this estimate. However, the media were timely to pick up on the figure and it persistently re-appeared. In the end, few seemed to know where it had originated from."[66] They speculate that an initial figure of 30,000 mentioned by the German Women's Council was the origin and became inflated, or that *The Guardian* had given the estimate of 40,000 migrant sex workers, who were then rendered by the German magazine *Emma* as "40,000 forced prostitutes."[67] Most organizers and activists I spoke to attributed it to Swedish neo-abolitionists who had offered it in the aforementioned UN meeting, with some attesting that it had been offered as an off-the-cuff suggestion and was never intended to be a real estimate even by the Swedes. Regardless of who began the rumor of the 40,000, the IOM noted that many NGOs and police were "disappointed by journalists who were just after 'sex 'n crime' stories, also just searching for further support of the 40,000" and concluded that "the hype around the 40,000 figure proved to be unfounded, which may make it harder for [anti-trafficking efforts and NGOs] to be taken serious[ly] with their cause in the future," thereby actually increasing "potential harm to survivors of [sex] trafficking."[68]

It is also possible that the 40,000 figure stuck because of the religious significance of the number forty and the prominence of Christians in the anti-trafficking panics. In Christian mythology, the Great Flood lasted forty days and nights, Moses spent the same number of nights on Mount Sinai (three times), Lent lasts forty days (for so too did Christ's withdrawal to the desert), and Christ waited forty days after the Resurrection before the Ascension. It's impossible to say why the 40,000 statistic proved unkillable; it may just be that it's a nice round number that happens to be big enough to sound scary.

Despite South Africa being a completely different country with relatively little in common with Germany and the fact that the statistic hadn't even been accurate the first time around, anti-prostitution groups stuck with the 40,000 figure. Calling it "the Cup crisis that never was,"

South African journalist Kashiefa Ajam reported: "40,000: That's how many cases of human trafficking were predicted during the World Cup. Zero: that's the actual number of reported cases."[69] The filmmaker Courtney Campbell documented the entire fiasco of the 40,000-strong sex trafficking myth and its consequences in South Africa in the documentary *Don't Shout Too Loud*.[70] The IOM, which is responsible for running many anti-trafficking programs, derided the whole World Cup sex trafficking thing as a "myth," with director Mariam Kohkar calling it "hype." South Africa, she said, "has had a problem with human trafficking for a long time now. Suddenly, before the World Cup started, it was highlighted as a big problem. . . . The initial figure was 40,000. Then it was 100,000. We don't know where these figures came from. But the problem got attention, and people were made aware of something they may not necessarily have known about. So maybe the hype wasn't such a bad thing."[71] Except, of course, the policies one embraces to combat trafficking are vastly different depending on the size and scope of sexual exploitation in a location, and hype has very real consequences for sex workers, stigma, public health, and public perception—not to mention that laws ought to be based on facts and data, not rumors.

Sex Workers Education and Advocacy Taskforce (SWEAT), a sex worker advocacy group in Cape Town, teamed up with researchers at Wits University, the University of Ghent in Belgium, and public health officials at Stellenbosch University to conduct several studies for the United Nations Population Fund, most notably a large phone survey of sex workers before, during, and after the games, and another study that trained sex workers as field workers to implement a survey of twenty-two hundred sex workers working across the country's major red light districts, including repetitions for before, during, and after the Cup as well as additional methodological components, including participants keeping field notes of their business interactions for the field-workers. Although their findings are painstakingly elaborated, the basic summary is as follows. There was a small increase of women advertising in the run-up and during the Cup. Fewer non–South Africans advertised (or were advertised for) in newspapers and sex trader sites than expected. Domestic client rates went down slightly during the Cup, and foreign clients went up slightly, for an overall *steady level of demand*. There was no substantial demographic shift, including age or nationality. However, reports of police brutality, harassment, and corruption increased significantly.[72]

Some sex workers viewed the World Cup positively. As one woman said, "One of [my clients] bought me a ticket to go to the stadium to watch soccer. It was my first time. . . . I don't even wish for that day to pass, I would like to go back again to watch."[73] Mostly, though, they complained. "There is no business like before the World Cup. The clients are busy watching the ball. The time for sex it's too short." "There were no changes at all. I am sick and tired of the World Cup. I'm sorry to say that, but for me it was bad."[74] Many complained of police violence. "The police officers took my money, they put me in [the car] and drove around with me, on the way they threw me out of the moving car, my leg got injured and I went to the hospital," said one. The tactic of dumping prostitutes in rural or far-flung places surfaces regularly in the accounts. As another woman complained: "I bumped into police and they asked me if I know that prostitution is illegal. . . . [One cop] who was a female hit me with a fist on my face and I bled lots of blood. . . . I spent about three days not being able to talk." Several others complained of being pepper sprayed, including one woman who reported that "police arrest sex workers and take our money. They sleep with us and they don't pay. They take clients' money and pepper spray our vaginas and clients' penises."[75]

Sitting in his office in London City Hall, Councilman Andrew Boff reviewed a post-Olympic research report he had compiled. Boff explained in his report that despite the city throwing $1 million at the anti-trafficking initiative, "I found no strong evidence that trafficking for sexual exploitation does in fact increase during sporting events nor that such trafficking or prostitution had increased in London. In fact my research found a decrease. . . . The data I have however reveals that raids increased significantly in the Olympic host boroughs. This has not led to large numbers of sex traffickers being caught nor victims found."[76]

In my interviews with National Health Service (NHS) manager Georgina Perry, who runs services for fifteen hundred sex workers a year in three boroughs, she explained that the Lord Mayor's Office maintains that all prostitution is exploitation and that all prostitution is therefore forced. "I've seen trafficking," she told me in her East End office. "We've had sex trafficking here before with Thai trafficking victims in the early 2000s. I would tell you if it was happening during these events, but it's not. . . . And most of the sex workers held in debt bondage tell me they don't want rescue. They want to marry or they want to work for themselves. Many do want transition [out of the sex industry], but not rescue." She had been part of the Mayor's Office's coalition on trafficking and the Olympics but had frequently been a dissenting voice. "Everyone saw dollar signs. . . . People wanted to make their careers off of it. They were hiring PR companies, media people. . . . [T]he police got 600,000 pounds extra [then approximately $1 million USD]. . . . I just kept releasing the data, keeping my head down. . . . I work based on evidence and I think in terms of vulnerabilities, not victims."

Perry said she hoped to write a report summarizing the experience. "I'll title it, 'Watch Out, Rio!'. . . But the Policing and Crime Act made it possible to bust brothels; police threatened to tell landlords what the women were doing [selling sex], or they can threaten the landlord and say that they will go after them for 'living off immoral earnings.' Use the trafficking discourse to scare them. . . . We lost contact with many women. And when they got robbed or beaten or raped, they don't report it. Or the police answer a domestic violence call from a sex worker and say, 'Next time, don't call us again. This is a brothel . . .'. But the abolitionist groups accuse me of 'keeping women in prostitution.'" When I ask her why the neo-abolitionists in the anti-trafficking coalition didn't look at evidence before and are only now beginning to focus on research to discover why they found no victims as they expected, she notes that a lot of the people they rely on are religious groups. "The Salvation Army, they don't publish any numbers. They say research takes them away from their core mission. They admit they have no interest in evidence, only faith."[77]

My London interviews with the Lord Mayor's Office representatives who personally headed up the Olympic anti-trafficking efforts under then mayor Boris Johnson revealed somewhat contrite policy makers. They did not have evidence of any trafficking cases during the Olympics, they said, but noted that this "lack of conclusive data" does not mean it didn't happen. They speculated that perhaps they had prevented it because traffickers saw that Johnson's forces were ready for them. (In Brazil, a team of researchers looking into child sex trafficking in the World Cup in the northeast similarly concluded that perhaps the lack of cases meant they had actually prevented it and concluded that "the absence of data" should not be misconstrued as the problem not existing or result in withdrawal of their grant funding.)[78] The folks representing Scotland Yard and the Lord Mayor's Office, however, said they were genuinely sorry about the police exploitation, which they were surprised by and which they admitted happened but said was an unintended consequence and the result of improper police training. Again, one sees that when police are incompetent or operate with impunity, not only are there no consequences, but their departments financially profit from the moral panic clouding the event and obscuring their bad actions.

These leaders assured me that police were supposed to go after organized crime behind the brothels, not the individual women, but local police—as opposed to citywide police overseen by the Lord Mayor's office—weren't as prepared or skilled as the metropolitan police. (Each borough has its own semiautonomous police force, making it hard to have a coherently enforced policy.) As for what they wished they had done differently, both representatives I interviewed agreed that the first thing they would do is not allow anyone a seat at the policy table who was not on board with "the position of this office that all prostitution is exploitation," by which they meant Perry and other social service providers, such as Jane Ayres at the Praed Street Project, who work with sex workers and follow harm reduction models rather than the neo-abolitionism and End Demand approaches.

The emphasis on petty bureaucratic infighting over a desire to reform, and an unwillingness to provide restitution to the women affected by the brothel raids and arrests, is a striking feature of neo-abolitionism. In an analysis of a police raid on an English massage parlor, Annie Hill points out that apart from being a form of violence and harassment, such raids expose women to the media against their will, which "exposes not the horror of trafficking, but a horrifying disregard for their rights. The media and public should not simply accept that police raids demonstrate victim protection. Raids are dramatic, and traumatic, events that incite a cascade of consequences that cause serious and sustained harm to people they purport to rescue. Raids serve the interests of the state, not the victims they produce."[79]

Perhaps most tellingly, when I asked these representatives of Scotland Yard and the Lord Mayor's Office what they had to show for the million dollars spent on anti–sex trafficking efforts, they told me that the accomplishment of which they were the most proud was that although the International Olympic Committee (IOC) would not allow them to put up advertisements or billboards raising awareness about the Olympics and sex trafficking because they damage the Olympic brand, the IOC did let them include information in the welcome kits for the Olympic athletes about the horrors of sex trafficking. When I asked why that was so important, they looked at me quizzically. "Because of the Africans," they said. "You see, the athletes from African countries wouldn't have otherwise known it was wrong to buy a young girl for sex."

The casual but astonishing racism of the anti-trafficking officials illustrates the lack of cultural awareness and the number of ethnocentric assumptions baked into the rescue industry's worldview. The role of white supremacy in undergirding the anti-trafficking movement is a subject I take up in the next chapter, but it is worth highlighting that these officials believed not only that the African male athletes would eagerly participate in child sexual exploitation but also that their own greatest accomplishment was their bit of media outreach to those athletes via the welcome kit. It was this turn to a rather depleted mode of spectacle—the pamphlet devoted to awareness raising—that they pointed rather than any tangible service for victims or betterment of the lives of women or girls.

Other outside observers of the London Olympic task force against sex trafficking, such as the Central America Women's Network (CAWN), which issued a lengthy report on the depictions of sex trafficking during the London Olympics, noted that the British media looked at any migrant woman (especially those seen as "exotic") and "assumed [them] to be trafficked into the capital for the Olympics and to be controlled by criminal gangs," which was a racist trope replicated consistently in the tabloids.[80] (It's also worth noting that there is very good research indicating that informal small-scale networks of known associates are much more prevalent in sex trafficking than organized criminal gangs.)[81] The researchers from CAWN continued that "the ensuing 'moral panic' about trafficking and sexual exploitation was not backed up by any evidence. Indeed, a body of evidence already existed prior to the Olympics demonstrating that major sporting events do not contribute to a rise in the incidence of trafficking for sexual exploitation. It is unclear why no one in government seemed aware of such research. The prediction that London would be 'flooded' with 'sex slaves' proved to be a myth."[82]

Rather than accept claims that the reason there is no evidence of trafficking is that news of anti-trafficking measures scared away the traffickers, the Wall Street Journal points out that the numbers used for the World Cup don't add up: 40,000 sex workers for a few hundred thousand soccer fans, not all of whom are men, and not all of whom would buy sex would just be a preposterously skewed ratio defying basic economics.[83] Moreover, as the GAATW points out, short-term events simply aren't profitable because of costs associated with smuggling, transportation, bribery, and document forgery, instead concluding that while trafficking in various forms is a real problem, the connection between global sporting events and sex trafficking is a fabrication.[84]

NPR's foreign correspondents likewise reported after the 2010 World Cup that the spike in prostitution never happened, sharing an interview from a sex worker named Rose who said: "World Cup, we didn't make money. . . . [E]ven if we go to the pubs, they will all just tell us: No, we are here for soccer not for sex." Another added, "No, I didn't make money, nothing. I only see my regular clients, my local clients." A city councilman in Cape Town noted, "We've not seen international trafficking, certainly not the ludicrous 40,000-figures and stuff that were bandied about. So it is exactly ten at last count."[85] Other managers and pimps said business was "terrible," and sex workers complained that these sports tourists were "boring" and they were "disappointed" when some Mexicans offered one of them US$500, but they couldn't get her through their hotel's security, so the deal fell through.[86]

And yet despite the evidence being painfully clear from South Africa in 2010, when London's turn came in 2012, the Metropolitan Police moved in on five London Olympic boroughs. Although London did not see the same level of rape, abuse, theft, and torture of sex workers by police as South Africa, Russia, and Rio de Janeiro, London police used the Proceeds of Crime Act to seize money, jewelry, and other property. Sometimes the sex workers were found not guilty yet still could not have their money and belongings returned and faced court fees from defending themselves. As one woman told a reporter, "They took my life savings, including money from my mom. . . . I was left with nothing after a lifetime of hard work. I'm not young anymore and don't know how I'll manage. . . . My family found out what job I was doing and that has caused a lot of upset."[87]

As Laura María Agustín documented at length during the pre-Olympic raids in London, the moral panic was not actually rooted in social fact. The areas targeted conveniently happened to be on the cusp of gentrification, with a campaign in the run-up to the Olympics reporting that the crackdown was necessary in order to prevent organized criminal elements (and also, interestingly, the athletes themselves) from sexually exploiting women.[88]

But the outcome was again the same. The bishops of Newcastle and Winchester at the Church of England raised alarm. Volunteers set up a shelter at a local church where they would care for the rescued victims of sex trafficking and greet them with care packages. As the NHS's Perry explained to me, they ended up alone without a single victim brought in to receive their eager care. When the games were over, police had no tangible evidence of trafficking to show, but they did have a lot of arrests of sex workers and had made it much harder for education, outreach, and advocacy groups who do frontline work with sex workers to provide services. It also means that in a time of austerity and budget cuts to schools, hospitals, pension plans, health care, and policing, valuable resources were squandered to appease a handful of evangelical Christian groups and misinformed leftist activists and celebrities. It also de-emphasized other forms of trafficking and exploitation relevant to sporting events, including construction labor. And finally, the panic turned consensual sex workers into victims of physical and sexual violence, both juridically and materially, thereby creating the necessary conditions for the exploitation that these groups claim to wish to prevent.

SPECTACULAR PANICS

The concept of the moral panic has long had importance in sociology and anthropology, and it is central to understanding this book. While earlier social scientists in "disaster studies" had focused on the panicked reactions of crowds during natural and human-made disasters, Stanley Cohen adapted his doctoral work into the book *Folk Devils and Moral Panics* in 1972, therein coining the term "moral panic." Cohen focused on British panics about youth culture (i.e., Mods and Rockers) that resulted in arrests, violence, and persecution of young people in a small seaside resort community in England called Clacton-on-Sear.[89] As Erich Goode and Nachman Ben-Yehuda write in their book *Moral Panics: The Social Construction of Deviance*, "Once a class of behavior, and a category of deviants, was identified, extremely small deviations from the norm became noticed, commented on, judged and reacted to. The Clacton disturbances, minor offenses, or even gatherings which might become offenses, were instantly the focus of press police attention."[90] They note that rather than looking at *why* disturbances occurred, Cohen asked why the mainstream media, the public, and the police *reacted* the way they did. For scholars of moral panics, the actors in a moral panic include (1) the press, (2) the public, (3) agents of formal social control or law enforcement, (4) politicians and lawmakers, and (5) action groups such as activists and NGOs.[91]

There are many examples of moral panics. In medieval times, there were witch hunts. (Similarly structured and similarly deadly panics resulting in the deaths of "witches" also continue to occur today in parts of India, Nigeria, and elsewhere.) In the twentieth century, there were panics about marijuana, memorably resulting in the now cult classic 1936 film *Reefer Madness*. In the 1980s, large numbers of people became convinced that there were satanic cults sexually abusing children (or people who, while working with unethical therapists, became convinced that they themselves had been abused by such nonexistent Satanists). In the 1990s, there were moral panics about rap music, hip-hop, and heavy metal. Tipper Gore, wife of then vice president Al Gore, famously led a censorship campaign after hearing an album by Prince. Around the same time, there was a panic about video games, which were erroneously linked to psychosis, violence, rape, and all manner of social ills. More recently, one might cite fears about terrorism in the United States and the resulting demonization of Muslims and Middle Easterners. Another common example is the widespread fear that has developed about allowing transgender people to use restrooms consistent with their identities and allowing trans kids to compete in sports with cisgender students. As president, Donald Trump continued to stoke fears about immigrants, whom he has famously called murderers and rapists. Right-wing media followed his lead in panicking over caravans of migrants and refugees, which he described as an "invasion" and an "infestation." Aides reported that he had inquired about shooting migrants in the legs at the border and installing a moat filled with alligators and snakes to go along with his infamous "border wall," which he also imagined he might top with electrified moving spikes. What binds all of these examples together?

Following Cohen, Goode and Ben-Yehuda assert that the moral panic is defined by five elements:

1. heightened levels of concern about a perceived behavior, phenomenon, or group;
2. a level of hostility toward the group or category regarded as engaging in the behavior or causing the condition;
3. substantial or widespread consensus that the threat is real;
4. a disproportionate threat level (e.g., exaggerating statistics, maintaining a belief that the numbers of instances or offenders are much greater than they are, fabricating data, circulating rumors of harm, belief that the danger posed is more grave than it is); and
5. volatility (i.e., moral panics come and go, although they become routinized or institutionalized in the form of policies, norms, etc.).[92]

In these panics, it is the folk devil (e.g., the Muslim, the migrant, the trans person) who bears the brunt of the panic. As I argue in the next chapter, to understand the historical panic about "white sexual slavery" and the contemporary panic about "sex trafficking," the folk devil is often the pimp or trafficker. (Pursuit of such folk devils can have deadly results, as in 2017 when a mob in Bangladesh, responding to rumors of child sex traffickers being in the area, seized a forty-two-year-old woman with mental disabilities, then abducted her and tied her to a tractor, where they tortured her for hours before finally killing her.)[93] Historically, in the United States the emphasis on white sexual slavery meant Asian American migrants who were imagined to be sex slavers. Today, laws in place often define a pimp as someone "living off immoral earnings," which can even include parents and children. Actual sex traffickers are, as I noted earlier, almost never found during mega-event panics. Sex workers themselves are not so much folk devils in my analysis as they are collateral damage in the fight against the devilish sex traffickers who are rarely found.

The anthropologist Carole Vance later developed the idea of the moral panic (sometimes also termed a social panic) into a "sex panic."[94] The queer theorist and historian Jeffrey Weeks noted that folk devils are often those deemed to be "immoral" or "degenerate" and that therefore, "sexuality has had a peculiar centrality in such panics, and sexual 'deviants' have been omnipresent scapegoats."[95] In her famous essay "Thinking Sex," the anthropologist Gayle Rubin cites Weeks before writing that "because sexuality in Western societies is so mystified, the wars over it are often fought at oblique angles, aimed at phony targets, conducted with misplaced passions, and are highly, intensely symbolic. . . . [D]uring a moral panic such fears attach to some unfortunate sexual activity or population. The media become ablaze with indignation, the public behaves like a rabid mob, the police are activated, and the state enacts new laws and regulations"[96] Thus, among moral panics, the sex panic has proven to be especially dangerous and of special interest to queer studies and sexuality studies.

Anti-prostitution radical feminists have objected to the use of the term *moral panic*. In her book *Not a Choice, Not a Job*, Janice Raymond inveighs against "longtime apologist for prostitution" Ronald Weitzer, whom she says has been "yammering about moral panics for years, using this term repetitively in many of his articles to create linguistic sensationalism. . . . So now it is feminist abolitionists whose challenge to the sex industry is labeled a 'moral panic' at a time that pimps and brothel owners are welcomed as allies by a UN committee report, and by numbers of academics, NGOs and some governments."[97] What seems lost on Raymond is that even this unfounded claim that "pimps" are being welcomed by the United Nations is precisely the kind of hyperbole that Weitzer has carefully analyzed over the years (i.e., "yammered about") in his sociological research.[98] Remembering that a key feature of defining a moral panic is that there is an inflation of statistics and exaggeration of the threat, Weitzer and coauthor Melissa Ditmore note that despite claims of hundreds of thousands or even millions of sex trafficking victims, the Central Intelligence Agency (CIA) acknowledged that no US or international agency has compiled, or is in the process of compiling, accurate statistics, citing a report that claimed "700,000 to 2 million women and children are trafficked globally each year."[99] A few years later the figure was 4 million; then, two years, later it fell to "600,000 to 800,000" with no explanation or evidence. Claims about domestic cases vary widely, from 14,500 to 50,000, again without ever citing evidence beyond attempting to compile newspaper stories.[100]

The inconsistency of statistics is so striking that they become essentially meaningless. Sally Merry notes that the International Labour Organization (ILO) estimates one million women and girls are trafficked for sex out of twelve million victims of forced labor (despite baseless claims by anti-prostitution groups that sex trafficking is the most common form of trafficking). Yet Merry points out that Kevin Bales, a bestselling author, claims there are "27 million modern-day slaves."[101] In response to claims from Republicans in the House of Representatives that child sex trafficking in the United States is a $9.8 billion industry, the *Washington Post* "Fact-Checker" column concluded, "We also must treat [the] '9.5 billion' [figure] as a fantasy, unconnected to any real data. The State Department should take steps to correct the record."[102] Despite the kind of deep analysis and fact checking that scholars and journalists undertake to refute alarmist claims, Raymond argues that the real moral panic we should be concerned with is that of academics who are panicking about all the success of the anti-prostitution movement. There is another layer of irony in Raymond's objections to the framework of moral panics, considering that previously she was most famous in feminist circles for sowing early moral panics in the 1970s and 1980s about "transsexualism" and predatory "she-males" who were "cross-dressing" so they could assault women.[103] (I return to the link between anti–sex trafficking and trans exclusionary beliefs within radical feminism in the next chapter.)

In 2018, the sociologist Elizabeth Bernstein published her book-length study of the anti–sex trafficking coalition of evangelical Christians, radical feminists, police, and neoliberal actors I've described. She writes that "the theory of 'sex panics' (and its analytical predecessor, 'moral panics')" has been "the most frequent explanation for the recent surge in attention to sex trafficking."[104] She notes that the similarities between these coalitions in both the white slave trade panic and the current sex trafficking panic, especially the presence of evangelicals, "has led many secular observers to a kind of 'aha!' moment in which any presumed complexity of the issue can henceforth be easily dismissed. On this reading 'puritanical' and sex-negative feminist activists have been duped into forging an alliance with sex-panicked Christians, who rally around trafficking as they have other proxy issues (like abortion and gay marriage) in order to reassert a traditionalist sexual politics."[105] Bernstein is also critical of the sex panic theory because she believes it suggests "a cycle of moral combustion that is destined to be endlessly repeated," whereas she thinks the attention to trafficking must also be understood as "not only entrenched and self-replicating, but also quite new."[106] To this end, she offers new ideas for understanding the coalition as rooted in "carceral feminism," "militarized humanitarianism," and "redemptive capitalism." This book relies heavily on Bernstein's monumental work and is indebted to these key terms, in particular, but I am not quite ready to dispense with the importance of the moral panic framework. As Rubin and other queer studies scholars have shown, what is most significant about the sex panic is not that it occurs (and reoccurs), but that it results in the entrenchment of systematic harms to sexual minorities (e.g., homosexuals, sex workers, transgender people). And in this book, I want to provide an understanding of the role of spectacle (e.g., protests, telenovelas, ad campaigns, viral content, nationalistic sporting events) as both contributing to and distracting from the harms that are linked to the panic. So while I concede to Bernstein that moral panic theory is not wholly sufficient, I maintain that it has not yet lost its utility, either.

Bernstein is also more easily able to let go of moral panics because of a phenomenon she observed among the many evangelicals she met while doing her research. She writes that these younger evangelicals in the anti-trafficking movement were more tolerant of the issues of homosexuality and abortion, citing Arlene Stein's work that antigay attitudes among evangelicals correlated with class among those Christians (with more professional and middle-class evangelicals tending to support abortion and gay rights).[107] Bernstein even found that some of the evangelicals considered themselves part of the "Christian moderates" or even "progressives" rather than "the Right." The evangelicals in her study are highly educated and relatively affluent. "Among many left-leaning secular critics of contemporary anti-trafficking campaigns, old stereotypes persist about . . . Christians toward this issue, a group that is frequently assumed to be one and the same with anti-pornography, anti-abortion, and anti-gay right activists of generations past."[108] She concludes that her research on "justice-oriented churches" contradicts that.

Here, I part ways from Bernstein. When I monitor the social media accounts of even the secular anti-trafficking groups, I can't help but notice that when they post anything supporting LGBT rights or indicating the vulnerability of LGBT homeless youth to exploitation, as the behemoth Polaris Project sometimes does, religious followers flood their comments with homophobic and transphobic vitriol. Moreover, the international actors who are most visible in the myth of sex trafficking and the global sporting event are often virulently and violently homophobic, including the Salvation Army and Exodus Cry's larger parent organization and close affiliates. The latter is the anti-trafficking ministry associated with the International House of Prayer (IHOP), a megachurch in Kansas City with branches all over the world. IHOP funds other sex-related lobbying efforts elsewhere in Africa and most notably is linked to lobbying for the "Kill the Gays Bill" in Uganda.[109] IHOP also came to national attention when some members with ties to the "ex-gay movement" were arrested for allegedly ritually raping a woman and then murdering her, causing the church to quickly distance itself from these former ministry members.[110] IHOP's anti-trafficking ministry, Exodus Cry, writes about going on a tour throughout Brazil before the World Cup to show its anti-trafficking film, *Nefarious: Merchant of Souls* to evangelical churches and asking churchgoers to participate in "The Call," an IHOP program organized by founder Lou Engel, who went to Uganda to preach that homosexuality is the result of demonic possession and who maintains that a "satanic tornado of homosexuals" is planning to take over the world and must be converted into ex-gays before they can do so.[111] Exodus Cry became obsessed with doing "rescue" work in Brazil, writing on the website:

> As the eyes of the sporting world begin to turn their gaze toward Brazil for the World Cup 2014 and the Rio de Janeiro Olympics in 2016, a team from Exodus Cry prepares to carry a torch of light, life and freedom to this nation steeped in human trafficking and sexual exploitation. At Exodus Cry, we believe that prayer is the foundation of every move of God on behalf of those most vulnerable. . . . Boasting beautiful beaches and a burgeoning sex industry, this nation sits by as an estimated 250,000 children, usually under

the age of 14, are prey to the appetites of pedophile sex tourists pouring in from both the U.S. and Europe. In fact, the Brazilian Federal Police believe that up to 400,000 children a year are sold in prostitution, especially at resorts and in other tourist areas. Notably, Brazil has seen the exploitation of young boys in commercial sex more than many other places. Therefore, we understand this to be a key launching area from which we can help to reach this nation with the love of Jesus.[112]

This group has an annual operating budget of over $1 million and a very large global presence. It tours churches and campuses with its presentations and films, such as *Nefarious: Merchant of Souls*, to advocate for the global criminalization of purchasing sex. Initially, the group claims to have "partnered" with over five hundred Brazilian churches and "planted prayer rooms in each of the 12 World Cup host cities."[113] It does not mention how many actual sex trafficking victims it found or saved, instead preferring to say that it "reached 1,972 exploited men, women, and children." What "reaching" means is unclear, though the group does stop sex workers and ask to pray with them and does distribute bits of jewelry and other trinkets that it also sells to donors. However, it claims to have "trained over 1,539 international volunteers in outreach and intervention," which means that it found almost as many religious do-gooders worried about exploitation as supposedly exploited people.[114]

It's also not really clear that the people being counted as "reached" actually wanted to be contacted, let alone counted as a statistic for the group's Facebook, Twitter, films, or PowerPoint presentations. As Exodus Cry bemoaned on its Facebook page, "After weeks of planning a beautiful banquet in Natal for women we had been ministering to, not one showed up. But the Lord had a better plan. Five churches united to pack the dinner, flowers, and gifts into cars and deliver them to a brothel with over 30 women. We invaded that brothel with the love of Jesus and the Church came alive by ministering to these women. In our weakness He is strong!"[115] So after weeks of "reaching" the "exploited" women, even free food couldn't convince them to show up. One wonders what the thirty women working in the brothel thought of the "loving invasion" of their totally legal workplace. Yet Exodus Cry continues to produce slick, well-produced media content, documentary films, and other propaganda to show as members travel around the world to churches. The specter of sex trafficking seems to serve the interests of the ministers a good deal more than the ministered.

In *Sex Panic and the Punitive State*, the anthropologist Roger Lancaster notes that "moral panics generate certain well-known forms of political organization. Self-styled leaders of the movement—'moral entrepreneurs'—convince others that containment, punishment, banishment, or destruction of the person or persons designated as scapegoat will set things right. . . . [T]he acute state of fear cultivated by the movement's leaders effaces meaningful distinctions between threats real and imaginary, significant and insignificant "[116] Lancaster's analysis is especially relevant to the case of Exodus Cry, whose moral entrepreneurship places it at the capitalist helm of the rescue industry. Lancaster goes on to say that "what Freudians call displacement is a recurring feature of moral panics: panics often express, in an irrational, spectral, or misguided way, other social anxieties."[117] This is true for IHOP's duet of panics: the Satanic tornado of homosexuals in Uganda and the scourge of sex traffickers on the prowl in Brazil and other host countries for mega-events (which Exodus Cry unfailingly goes to as it is deeply invested in the myth of the global sporting event as a site of sex trafficking).

In Brazil, there has also been a strange relationship between those in radical feminist circles. One confounding but important example of the connections between conservative, right-wing, antiabortion, antigay activists and feminists is the Brazilian politician known as Sara Winter (born Sara Fernanda Giromini.) Winter founded the Brazilian chapter of Femen, an extremist group known for topless protests to draw attention to sexual exploitation of women (which for them includes prostitution, sex tourism, the wearing of hijab, religion in general and Islam in particular, and myriad other forms of "oppression"). I address Femen more fully in later chapters, but they led a number of high-profile protests before the 2014 World Cup, including topless takeovers of the Rio airport and the famous Copacabana Palace Hotel. Winter said she had worked in prostitution for ten months and had also experienced family violence and sex abuse.[118] She eventually founded BastardXs, a probisexuality group. By 2013, she was fighting with Femen's leadership in Ukraine and began to express sympathies toward Naziism and fascism. (Her self-given name, Sara Winter, is the same as a known English Nazi militant in World War II, but it is unclear if this is a coincidence.) Winter left or was expelled from Femen and became a supporter of far-right causes in Brazil, abandoning her pro-homosexuality and pro-bisexuality positions as well as her stated hatred of Christianity. In 2014, she wrote a book about the seven times she had been "betrayed by feminism" and disavowed it. She became an antiabortion activist and converted to Catholicism, allying herself with politicians who were fighting against gay rights and Black social justice groups. In 2018, she ran for federal office in Rio de Janeiro and lost but was appointed by the right-wing authoritarian president Jair Bolsonaro's administration as "national coordinator of maternity policies" at the newly reformulated Ministry of Women, Family, and Human Rights. She then joined a paramilitary group devoted to supporting Bolsonaro and expressing a desire to begin a civil war to put down the Left in Brazil. She gained national infamy in Brazil when she revealed the name and location of a ten-year-old rape victim who was trying to get a legal abortion, causing "pro-life" mobs to chase down the girl.[119] In 2020, the Federal Police seized her computer and cell phone in a criminal investigation into a scheme involving the spreading of fake news through bots and other electronic means to further right-wing causes.[120]

While Winter's journey from anti-prostitution crusader to a right-wing fascist and political appointee may seem anomalous, it illustrates the connections between the puritanical and sex negative mindset of the anti-sex radical feminists and the pro-family, antiabortion, right-wing culture warriors. Moreover, when I consider the amount of resources and the presence of IHOP and similar faith-based groups such as the notoriously homophobic Salvation Army in the panics and observe the ways in which they devote their labor to both "rescuing" women and harming gay people, I cannot help but find myself on the side of the queer theorists who have identified sexual minorities as the folk devils who would suffer as result of moral panics. For whatever reason, many of the groups I encountered around the world are quite different than Bernstein's moderate and modern Christians. Perhaps it's because of their global ambitions and the long history of missionary work in Latin America; perhaps it's because I interacted with many more international groups. I can only speculate as to why and how I encountered so many antiabortion and antigay evangelicals. Therefore, I draw on Bernstein's vital concepts, such as militarized humanitarianism (which is heavily on display in the earlier examples of "invading" brothels with the love of Jesus). Her framework of carceral feminism is reshaping our entire feminist episteme right now (despite few people on the Left crediting her for coining the term). So, while I deeply respect and honor her work, I also cannot write off the power of the moral panic analytic and its role in demonizing LGBT people and sex workers.

OVERVIEW OF THE CHAPTERS

Rather than present a chronology of the forms and effects of panics at each mega-event, I have instead organized this book around important themes related to the rescue industry and how it spreads panics globally through fallacious spectacles. Some chapters focus more on some sites, but I weave my analysis across multiple sites and timelines. I do begin, however, with a history of the sex trafficking panic in the chapter 1, "Sex Trafficking Discourse as White Supremacy." Working forward from the "white slave trade" panic at the turn of the twentieth century and the passing of the White Slave Trade Act (Mann Act) in 1910, I examine how xenophobia has always infused the anti-trafficking movement. This chapter also positions this history alongside sensationalistic journalism about the "yellow peril," the importance of "noblesse oblige" within white feminism, anti-Black invocations in the construction of the highly racialized figure of the "pimp," anti-trafficking's role in policing racial mixing and miscegenation, and concerted efforts to funnel money away from comprehensive immigration reform to focus on a narrow vision of sex trafficking (to the exclusion of other labor abuses of migrants). I then examine how the spectacular discourses emanating from the United States and Europe became entrenched as a neocolonial foreign policy tool that ultimately allowed the myth of sex trafficking and the mega-event to become vividly linked in the public imagination.

In chapter 2, "Panic at the Gringo," I flip the gaze and ask readers to consider how sex workers view clients and seek to exploit them during sporting events. This chapter draws on interviews conducted in red light areas in Rio with sex workers, clients, and football/soccer fans to examine the performance of masculinity among the fans. In particular, I examine competing discourses about hooliganism and the projection of toxic masculinity onto these foreign men. I also examine claims by the missionaries that hundreds of foreigners from Latin America and the United States would come to Brazil, roaming the streets looking for girls to kidnap and sell into sexual slavery, and how this contributed to xenophobia (just as it had in the United States a century earlier). Far from finding the gringos during sporting events to be predatory or dangerous, many of the women described these clients as exceptionally easy marks whom they could overcharge, scam, exploit, and sometimes even rob. I center the voices of female sex workers who describe their own perceptions of "gringo masculinity" and beliefs about the characteristics of masculinity associated with various nationalities in order to understand how the women adjust their prices and expectations and alter their own performances of self in their interactions in order to, as they put it, "exploit the gringos."

Chapter 3, "Fallacious Spectacles and the Celebrification of Sex Trafficking," begins with an examination of the UN Gift Box, a street art stunt that the religious leaders, anti-prostitution feminist groups, and the United Nations brought to Brazil to place in known red light areas before the World Cup. From here, I work outward through the media landscape to examine anti-prostitution media campaigns released by the Vatican, the Brazilian soccer team, the Salvation Army in South Africa, and white feminist celebrities in the United States; in Brazilian comic books and telenovelas; and by US women political figures such as Ivanka Trump, Cindy McCain, and Kamala Harris. I also examine how celebrities such as Ashton Kutcher, Lena Dunham, Emma Thompson, Meryl Streep, Susan Sarandon, Meg Ryan, and Anne Hathaway promoted the conflation of sex trafficking and sex work that inadvertently fuels the stigma and violence perpetrated against the sex workers they fantasize about saving. In this exploration of how sex trafficking becomes a spectacle, I also examine how the panic during sporting events always relies on the elusive figure of 40,000 missing girls who are allegedly trafficked for sex, yet the girls truly are missing because they are part of a white rescue fantasy that is unrealizable. These missing girls, even in their absence, prove to be a kind of spectacle as well, and this hollow, fallacious spectacle lends power and grants authority to increasingly violent systems of policing and surveillance.

I focus in chapter 4, "Eat—Pray—Labor," on the binary relationship between labor trafficking and sex trafficking in Doha, Qatar. I examine how third parties bring women from the Philippines, China, Hong Kong, Ukraine, and Lebanon to openly do sex work in the hotel bars of recognizable Western hotel chains like the Hilton, Westin, and Marriott. I theorize the role of the spectacular in their hypervisibility and read it against the hyperinvisibility of the thousands of male migrant laborers—many held in debt bondage schemes—who travel from places like Bangladesh and North Korea to build the FIFA stadiums as well as satellite campuses for American universities and other construction projects. As I explain in that chapter, more than seven hundred of these men have died, having been worked to death in the heat or otherwise killed by the terrible living conditions in the labor camps. There is a discourse in Qatar that such men "leer" and "gaze" inappropriately at the Arab and white expatriate women and so should be confined by construction firms to the labor camps 24/7. Meanwhile anti-prostitution feminist groups in the United States speculate that white women are being sex trafficked from Russia and Ukraine to meet desires in the labor camps, as if the men making a few dollars a day could afford to purchase services from these high-end white escorts (or that they would even be allowed to enter). I examine the racialized fantasies projected onto these two groups of migrant workers—male construction workers and female sex workers—to critique Orientalist Western feminist assumptions about sexuality in the "Arab World."

In chapter 5, "Let Come the Whore Assemblage," I situate readers within the run-up to the 2014 World Cup and 2016 Olympics in Rio and discuss the sexual terrain of "unruly politics." This argument draws on the Brazilian feminist theorist Sonia Corrêa's work on unruly politics, which she defines as "provocations in exploring the limits, caveats and pitfalls of crystallized notions of citizenship, civil society and justice."[121] These embodied provocations move "beyond conventional state and law centered grammars underlining contradictions, fragmentations and erosion of public spheres."[122] They are not the politics of practicality. They are extraneous to political parties, union formations, wildcat strikes, ballot initiatives, and legislation. They are fundamentally about demonstrations of affect that congeal, becoming events. I apply these theories of affect to the embodied politics and performative moments unfolding in the sexual landscapes of various host cities. Ultimately, I relate these to theories of assemblage to map the relationship between such assemblages and an emerging movement known as *putapolitics* (whore-politics) and/or putafeminismo. This move toward putapolitics and putafeminismo allows for a more hopeful ending to this book than one may initially expect.

Although many activists and social scientists have written articles focused on the host cities in which they work that debunk the correlation between sex trafficking and sporting events, no one has yet taken a global approach to theorizing these parastatal formations in tension with one another or incorporated fieldwork from multiple countries. Social scientists have no broader overarching understanding of this phenomenon, which is why I wanted to write the first book-length treatment of the mega-events–trafficking myth. I expand beyond the realms of anthropology, sociology, and political science (the primary fields represented in these studies) by moving the analysis into the realm of performance studies to open up new lines of theoretical inquiry often ignored by social scientists. In so doing, I hope to follow the spectacle of sex trafficking from the public imagination into the more nuanced lived realities of the women working in sex trades in these countries who are so deeply affected by the sex panics and the moral entrepreneurs that have swept them up in their crushing embrace.

CHAPTER 1

Sex Trafficking Discourse
as White Supremacy

The anthropologist Thad Blanchette and I sit in the lounge of 4 × 4 (Quatro por Quatro), a heterosexual *termas* (bathhouse brothel) in downtown Rio de Janeiro, surrounded by foreigners and locals.[1] At first glance, we must look like any other two gringos out on the town, but we've been in this place enough that many of the sex workers and staff know us as researchers. We watch the sixty or so women flow through the lounge, smiling at the men and sometimes giving potential clients' backsides a squeeze. The women are fishing for *programas* (tricks, or sessions with a client), thus their moniker *garotas de programa* ("program girls"), or simply *garotas*. This week's theme is *festa junina*, the harvest festival when people wear stereotypical costumes of rural backwoods types. Consequently, half the women in the termas today look something like Mary Ann from *Gilligan's Island*, with gingham tops knotted above the navel, while also sporting thongs.

The men at 4 × 4 wear white robes, provided by the house. They mostly sit in pairs and small groups, ignoring the women as they chat. One of the clients, a forty-something Brazilian man, has hands that grow directly from his shoulders in the manner associated with fetuses poisoned by thalidomide, which was a fairly common occurrence in Brazil for his age cohort. He wears wire-rimmed glasses, has a fresh buzz cut, and—despite not having arms—is still able to hold a *caipirinha*, Brazil's national cocktail, for himself, which he sips at as he looks about at the scantily clad women. He is a regular, cheerful and friendly with the women, several of whom are chatting him up, touching him flirtatiously. He beams at the attention. "In keeping with tonight's *festa junina* barnyard theme, I could only describe this guy as looking happy as a pig in shit," I later jot in my field notes. One of the prostitutes sitting at the table with us tells us she really likes this guy. "I probably would not sleep with him without pay, but then again, I wouldn't sleep with hardly any of these guys here without pay. I am strictly sex for money. But he is a nice guy and fun to be in bed with. He's different and he takes some getting used to, but he's not at all bad."

Because 4 × 4 is such a typical Rio de Janeiro brothel, it is worth laying out the scene of what it's actually like inside such a space, given that there is enough feminist and evangelical anxiety about its existence that foreign groups were eager to have the Brazilian military police shut it down. In fact, late in 2019, 4 × 4 burned down in what appears to have been an act of arson; several firefighters died fighting the blaze. It is unclear who set the fire, but rumors abound that the culprits were off-duty, retired, or former police and their affiliates called milícias, who extort brothels for money. If so, the corrupt police state finished off what the radical feminists and missionaries hadn't been able to during the World Cup and the Olympics some years before.

It's important to know that because 4 × 4 is lower to-middle class, the women tend to be *morena* (mixed race, literally "brown"), although some white women and a few Black women work there as well. Many of the women have thicker bodies and large tattoos, which are much more common in this brothel than in the higher-end venues of the touristy Zona Sul beachfront, which tend to feature slimmer women and fewer tattoos. The women in the Zona Sul are also lighter skinned and often straighten and dye their hair blonde, even if they are from the same favelas and poor neighborhoods as the women working in 4 × 4. Here in 4 × 4, the music is also *baile funk*, the distinctive rat-tat-tat-rat-tat music of the favelas.

An employee walks by whom I haven't seen before. "A new floor manager? Zé Carlos [the owner] hired a *sapatão* [butch lesbian or "dyke"] to run the floor?" I ask.

"No," says Barbara, one of the women. "He's a trans man," she says, leaning into the masculine pronoun *ele* for emphasis. "And he's in charge of security now."

The other women nod approvingly. Despite stereotypes about working-class Brazilians being more homophobic and transphobic, the clients don't seem the slightest bit fazed, and the women seem to like this new guy. "I can't even begin to imagine the fancy places in Zona Sul making a hire like that," Thad says to me, and I nod in agreement.

Most clients here are Brazilian, but there are always a few gringos. The Brazilians are usually friends from work, typically lower-level employees who work in offices downtown, but most are not members of the managerial class. This means most of them are *morenos* or *pardos*, Brazilian terms for mixed-race people. Very few are outright *brancos* (white), and none of them are *negro* (Black).[2] Black men in 4 × 4 were usually gringos; groups of African American men visiting Brazil for sex tourism has been a steadily increasing phenomenon since the mid-1990s.

Along come some young guys who look out of place as they ogle the women, giggling and slapping each other in disbelief, looking incredibly immature and overwhelmed by the space. All of these boys are unambiguously white. Unlike the rest of the patrons, who perform studied nonchalance about their brothel surroundings, these teenagers gape and giggle, still draped in puberty, all knees and elbows.

One among our group of researchers and prostitutes looks at the boys and chuckles. "Sexual exploitation of children is a crime," she remarks, referring to the posters prominently displayed all over Rio de Janeiro as an anti–child prostitution measure. "I'll denounce you!" declares Thads, quoting the next line from the posters, which urges citizens to report suspected sex criminals. Everyone laughs. These women—all morenas from the favelas and the periphery of the city—enjoy such humor because they have long known what researchers have been saying: the realities of prostitution in Brazil are out of sync with their depiction in the global mediascape.[3] It is next to impossible to find innocent, coerced, underage girls lured away from their families by predatory sex traffickers—at least in the primary red light districts in Rio. This mocking of official discourse is consistent with what James Scott analyzed as "hidden transcripts," weapons of the weak that allow those on the margins of society to resist dominant discourses through humor.[4] Cariocas such as these women are experts at this form of resistance.

One of the morena women at our table shakes her head as the boys stumble about the lounge. "I heard it's one of those boys' eighteenth birthday," she says. "His schoolmates are buying him a programa to celebrate."

"Good news for us," says another tablemate, eyeing the group. "The young ones (os jovens) finish quickly. They're easy money and easy to please."

The time for humor and camaraderie has ended; it's time to work. She stands up and glides toward the boys like a lioness stalking a band of spindly-legged gazelles who have no idea what is about to happen.

SEXUALITY IN A HOTHOUSE

The myth of the 40,000 and the false linking of mega-events and sex trafficking began during the World Cup in Germany in 2006. But to really understand this relatively recent invention, it's imperative to examine the origins of the anti–sex trafficking movement in the late nineteenth- and early twentieth-century women's movements. That means tracing a white supremacist, xenophobic, and openly racist vein in these movements and watching it snake ever outward until it coiled around the heart of the US government and gained the ability to alter the policies of foreign governments. It is at that moment that the racist discourse emerged fully formed into xenophobic anti–sex trafficking policies deployed by foreign governments at the behest of the US and European parastatal alliances. Very shortly after that, the mega-events were co-opted as powerful sites of signification to further enact militarized humanitarianism, bolster gentrification and land grabs, and entrench laws harmful to sexually vulnerable women. We will return to the global sporting events in the next chapter, but it's impossible to understand the anti–sex trafficking movement without a thorough understanding of its roots in white supremacy.

Like a hothouse containing a tropical ecosystem in miniature, masculinity in a termas is clearly identified as such when one is outside looking in. Seen from the center, however, it becomes clear that one is dealing with an internally segmented, highly diversified system, one so chaotic that one might say there is no discernible pattern at all. There are many social norms and rules one must abide by in termas, if performative displays of masculinity are to be legible. One can also witness, however, innumerable reminders of masculinity's precarity, and indeed its fractal and constructed character.

Although media reports about brothels filled with sex tourists fuel anti-prostitution fantasies, the reality is more complex. As attested by the presence of young, sexually inexperienced men and people with disabilities, carioca brothels are environments where all sorts of masculinities can be cultivated. Men do not have a *right* to sex in these venues; on the contrary. Termas do not provide a *right* of access to the women's sexual services or bodies.[5] Women do not have to accept anyone's advances.

This doesn't mean that the women working termas don't complain about management. Mostly, they gripe about stuff the way workers at any job do: about fines for tardiness, inept supervisory staff, irritating coworkers, and bad clients. They also have complaints specific to sex work: being compelled to work shifts during menstruation, for example, or needing to buy outfits for the ever-rotating theme nights. The house takes its cut, but the money the women earn is theirs, and they are not known for tolerating foolishness, be it from clients or termas employers. Managers at 4 × 4 are likewise intolerant of nonsense from clients. They also take seriously the women's health and that of their clients, as business depends on men not bringing home any unwanted surprises to their wives, so 4 × 4 requires mandatory and frequent sexually transmitted infection (STI) and HIV screenings. Mandatory testing is a controversial practice and is opposed by many sex worker rights advocates and public health officials, who see it as a violation of rights and privacy.

We never saw any signs of sex trafficking in 4 × 4, which was one of the few venues to have reasonably steady business during the World Cup and Olympics. Almost all of the women were longtime workers, and many of them were people we had known for years and had interviewed in the past. The house usually takes about half the money of a programa, which the women consider a fair price for paying security, bartenders, janitorial staff, bookkeepers, and so on. It's hard to estimate earnings because the Brazilian currency, the real, has fluctuated from 1.5 BRL to the US dollar to more than 5 BRL to the dollar over the years I've done research in 4 × 4. As a rough approximation, women in 4 × 4 make about seven to ten times what their family members and other women from their communities make working as maids, as nannies, or in the service industry. Women working in the higher-end venues in the South Zone can make significantly more.

Meanwhile, prostitutes in Rio usually control their own hours (though 4 × 4 does mandate shifts), spend significant time with their children, and report a lot of autonomy. They also frequently point out that unlike their friends and relatives who work as maids in middle-class homes, they themselves are not sexually assaulted at work. (It's not uncommon in Brazil to hear some variation of an old "joke" from white men that goes: "I can't be racist; there's no Black girl working in my house I haven't fucked.")[6] At one point, I sat down to lunch with a leader of Exodus Cry before the organization went to Brazil and explained that while the sensationalized version of sex trafficking was a myth, there is a very real problem with young Black girls pressed into live-in domestic servitude who are abused and exploited. Perhaps the organization's vast wealth and media influence could improve the lives and working conditions of these girls who are all too often exploited? A similar but exponentially more extreme situation for live-in help can be found in Qatar, host of the 2022 World Cup. This line of dialogue went nowhere. The leader acknowledged that this was sad but said the group's ministry is focused on sex trafficking (especially during mega-events) and abolishing pornography.

Commercial venues are a normalized part of Rio de Janeiro's sexscape in the Durkheimian sense of a "normal social fact."[7] In other words, they can be found throughout the city and are largely seen as unexceptional by the people who work or live near them. Every region of Rio has one or more brothels. In carioca life, they are readily apparent, "grounded in the nature of things" and intimately "related to the general conditions of collective life in the social type under consideration."[8] It is only from the perspective of wealthy white gringos that the commercial sexual landscape seems "exotic" or even noteworthy.

Until 4 × 4 burned down, women over the many years I conducted research reported that they generally liked working there. It was, they would often remark, *tranquilo*, "chill." Sometimes, they lamented, it was downright boring. Whenever I read panicked screeds imagining how awful it must be to be a prostitute working in a brothel, I think about 4 × 4 and how utterly banal it actually is for the women. Certainly none of them have ever described it as the kind of sex trafficking hellscape that the evangelicals and radical feminists setting up shop in Rio seemed to think it was.

During a class trip to Rio for a seminar called Race, Gender & Sexuality in Brazil, I actually took seven of my undergraduates to Vila Mimosa (the red light slum area), Mab's (a gringo sex tourist bar in Copacabana), and 4 × 4 to show them a cross-section of the city's sexual economy. After the manager gave them a tour of 4 × 4's many floors (including steam rooms, a whiskey bar, the showroom, a rooftop patio, and various other spaces), they settled in while the women began to do pole dances to drum up business for clients. While one of the women danced to Adele's "Someone Like You" (an admittedly odd and heartbreaking choice for a seductive pole dance), one of my students remarked, "This is so much more boring than I thought it would be. When can we leave?" She then added, "How can you stand it—sitting around here all the time?"

Nearby, another woman was coming back from the bathroom clad in a G-string and stilettos, and she crawled across the booth's seat on her hands and knees to cozy up to an aging Brazilian client. As she nibbled on his ear, she kicked her leg up behind her, and I saw that she had accidentally impaled some toilet paper on her stiletto heel. 4 × 4 could be boring for the women and for us researchers alike, I told the students, but as I sat there with them, I also reflected that it was full of funny moments, too. And sometimes it was also full of moments of disappointment, sadness, or regret for the women or the clients, moments that can only be described as pitiful. But also, 4 × 4 was full of camaraderie and connection. I caught the eye of the woman and gestured to my own heel while looking at hers until she noticed the toilet paper on her shoe, which she knocked off with her other heel while giving me a wink of thanks. Why were moral entrepreneurs in the United States so obsessed with the idea that places like 4 × 4 were some kind of very special hell on earth? Why was it worth spending tens of thousands—or even hundreds of thousands—to fly dozens of mostly white people across the world to stay for months to protest this place? To starve these women out of business, to persecute the clientele or owners? Why were these people who were so on fire with evangelical ecstasy and feminist fury determined to see 4 × 4 and every other place like it shut down forever?

Neo-abolitionists often try to link prostitution, sex tourism, and sex trafficking to race. As I discussed previously, there are interlocking systems of race, class, gender, and sexuality operating in the brothel space. Brazilians have their own racial classification systems and ways of discussing race. They have many more categories of race than Americans, and the doctrine of "self-identification" prominent in the United States holds very little sway.[9] They also sometimes use *color* and *race* interchangeably, leading to complicated discourses and categories. In Brazil, one's race is a question of interpellation: How do others read you, and how do they treat you based on that? Theirs was never a society that followed the "one-drop" rule. In fact, the government encouraged racial mixing because it feared the Black population of freed slaves would overthrow the white people if white men did not begin diluting Black bloodlines in Brazil. In *Nem Preto, Nem Branco, Muito Contrário*, Lilia Moritz Schwarcz describes this effort to diminish the Black population through *embranquecimento* (racial mixing, literally whitening) as an illogical adaptation of the ideas about eugenics popular at that time.[10] Thus, Brazil shifted toward a much-mythologized narrative of "racial democracy" despite the fact that anti-Blackness and racism still thrive there and that color, in some ways a proxy for race, correlates strongly with income and other demographic data.

Brazil has a large porn industry with a lot of non-white women working in it. Many feminists have decried racial fetishization in porn—or rather, the imagined racial fetishization experienced by gringo viewers even though Brazilians also consume an awful lot of Brazilian porn.[11] Indeed, it's important to remember that sexual tourism is a small fraction of overall commercial sex, and that most commercial sexual exchange globally is happening locally in racially and ethnically homogenous settings. Lin Chew, a reformed anti-trafficking activist, writes of the way she and her fellow activists viewed sexual tourism, in particular, as "imperialism, sexism, and racism rolled into one."[12] While it's true that wealthier and whiter Westerners are often the ones engaging in sex tourism in places like Southeast Asia and Latin America, radical feminists almost always impose Western understandings of race and gender on others, effectively re-racializing them rather than centering the emic and culturally specific understandings of race that the "wounded third-world prostitutes" have already established for themselves in their own lives.[13] Western radical feminists have cast their own neocolonial notions of what race is (along with many attendant suppositions about agency) onto the narratives of victimhood they construct for prostitutes elsewhere in the world. As Carole S. Vance has noted, the narratives compelled by the rescue industry follow the very particular literary form and conventions of melodrama, a subject I take up later in this chapter.[14] By instrumentalizing global sex workers in this way, the anti-trafficking movement has failed to grapple with its own problematic history of white supremacy and racism.

THE WHITE SLAVE TRADE

The anti–sex trafficking movement has always had a fleshy white underbelly. Its secret vulnerability to critique is that historically it wedded itself to white supremacy ideologically and white supremacists individually. The contemporary anti–sex trafficking movement has, instead of confronting these past entanglements, attempted to whitewash its anti-Blackness by adopting the language of "abolitionism" and "modern slavery," a rhetorical move that is in and of itself a worrying deracialization of these historically situated terms.[15] When we read the history of anti-trafficking, however, we are reading a history of white supremacy that has always intertwined itself knottily within white US feminism. It is necessary to fully elaborate the history of white US feminism in order to understand how the anti-trafficking movement that emerged in the United States came to enact a neocolonial agenda that sought to shutter 4 × 4 and other venues in Brazil before the World Cup.

The story of white supremacy in the anti-trafficking movement begins with the moral panic about "white slavery" and the eventual passage of the Mann Act or White Slave Trade Act in 1910.

During the early twentieth century, a disparate coalition of prostitution abolitionists eerily similar to the one today coalesced into a crusade against white sex slavery. These groups included the Women's Christian Temperance Union (WCTU) movement, early feminists, the Ku Klux Klan, police commissions, socialists, anarchists, and wealthy philanthropists.[16] Although Jo Doezema argues that the initial white slave panic began in England in 1885, and that it served as inspiration, the panic in the United States also had its own unique etiology rooted in anxieties about female sexuality, racial mixing, urbanization, and the demise of US American manliness.[17]

In the early twentieth century, Hearst- and Pulitzer-owned newspapers ran salacious stories about "Asian conspirators who kidnapped young, vulnerable, small-town and farm women across the United States and forced them into lives of prostitution."[18] According to historian Mark Thomas Connelly, these melodramas replaced another similar genre, "Indian captivity stories," in which natives carried off white girls.[19] Public fascination with these news stories about white slavery was intense and linked to the theory of the "yellow peril," a belief that Asian immigrants were supposedly going to flood the United States and destroy white hegemony. Central to this conspiracy theory was that the Chinese had opium at their disposal, which they could use to drug white women into submission. Although the Chinese featured prominently in the white slave panic, some versions of the myth were anti-Semitic. According to Doezema's *Sex Slaves and Discourse Masters,* muckraking journalist George Kibbe Turner frequently accused a cabal of Russian Jews of trafficking women and girls for prostitution in Chicago and New York.[20] This claim was echoed by Samuel Paynter Wilson's *Chicago and Its Cess-Pools of Infamy* (1910), which referred to "brutal Russian Jewish whoremongers."[21] And in still other accounts, the traffickers were immigrants from Italy, sometimes from France, or occasionally from elsewhere in Southern and Eastern Europe—that is to say, Catholic "ethnic immigrants" who were not yet seen as truly white in 1900.[22]

That the white slave trade panic was xenophobic in its origin is easily seen in evidence. Donovan points to an especially revealing quote in *White Slave Hell* (1910), in which Lehman and Clarkson said of the United States: "A great deal of this evil is done by foreigners, and I do believe that the root of the trouble is laziness. They come from countries where the highest good is just to lie in the sun and sleep. They do not, they cannot, understand the love of work, the dignity of labor, the joy of accomplishment."[23] One of the more famous books from that time was Ernest Bell's *Fighting the Traffic in Young Girls; or The War on the White Slave Trade* (1910).[24] The book is filled with lurid accounts and photos depicting the downfall of good young white women.

The accompanying illustrations show just how early contemporary tropes about sex slavery began. Many of the narratives shown in popular media coverage about sex trafficking still emphasize scenarios such as unwitting women who do not understand that the job ad they are answering for a dancer is actually a path into sexual slavery. Similarly, the idea that migrant women traveling alone will be ensnared the moment they arrive at train stations remains ubiquitous. The stories from this period followed the formulas of melodrama, a pattern that would continue when white slavery stories eventually morphed into pulp fiction novels in the mid-twentieth century. Melodrama does not refer merely to exaggeration, but also to a specific narrative/dramatic structure characterized by strong appeals to emotion at the expense of character development. Dialogue is rendered with great sentimentality, and plots are kept simple, relying on easily recognized character types to tell stories that often deal with morality, love, fidelity, marriage, and virtue. Because the stories often have a strong moral lesson, the fates of characters at the end are clear, and there are linear consequences for characters' actions. Vance writes that "the ubiquitous antitrafficking melodrama displaces modern concepts of extreme labor exploitation and rights violations, replacing them with scripts of male lust endangering innocent women. It also replaces the trafficked person's claim to multiple rights with a single remedy, the right to be rescued. Melodrama is a very flexible narrative form, and the anti-trafficking drama can be and is set in any global location—Nepal, Moldova, Nigeria—with small changes in costumes, background scenery, and names, which nevertheless lend local color and 'authenticity.'"[25] Thus, structural conditions and complexity fade away, and we get the usual cast of brutal pimps, evil sex traffickers, mobsters, unwilling prostitutes with hearts of gold, reluctant mothers abandoned by lotharios and left with hungry mouths

THE FIRST STEP

Ice cream parlors of the city and fruit stores combined, largely run by foreigners, are the places where scores of girls have taken their first step downward. Does the mother know the character of the place and the man she is with?

FIGURE 1. Illustration from *Fighting the Traffic in Young Girls* depicting a man of ambiguous ethnicity ensnaring a young white woman in an ice cream parlor. *Source:* Ernest Bell, *Fighting the Traffic in Young Girls; or, the War on the White Slave Trade* (n.p.: publisher unknown, 1910).

THE LURE OF THE STAGE—ANSWERING A WANT AD
Disreputable Theatrical Agents sometimes act as white slave traders,
alluring positions on the stage being the net used to catch young girls.

FIGURE 2. Illustration from *Fighting the Traffic in Young Girls* warning of the dangers of answering fake job advertisements in the entertainment industry. *Source:* Ernest Bell, *Fighting the Traffic in Young Girls; or, the War on the White Slave Trade* (n.p.: publisher unknown, 1910).

"DANGER"

Meeting young girls at the Railway Depots is one of the methods of
the white slave trader. They promise to take the strangers to their friends;
in fact, anything to get them to accompany them. Once in a closed car-
riage, they are lost.

FIGURE 3. Illustration from *Fighting the Traffic in Young Girls* showing a young
woman arriving at the train station, where a white slaver disguised as a gentleman
awaits. *Source:* Ernest Bell, *Fighting the Traffic in Young Girls; or, the War on the
White Slave Trade* (n.p.: publisher unknown, 1910).

to feed, and fallen women who dare to enjoy sex work and therefore meet grisly ends.

In her analysis of investigative journalists who double as "slave hunters, brothel busters," and "anti-sex-trafficking humanitarians," Roxana Galusca links the melodramatic form of sex trafficking narrative propagated by contemporary swashbuckling journalists to what Michel Foucault termed a "popular regime of truth," characterized by "specific visual tropes and narrative genres" wherein "the types of statements and discourses perceived in a society" are taken as true and "the mechanisms that produce and propagate truth narratives" ultimately uplift those "who are celebrated as truth-bearers."[26] She chiefly analyzes media depictions such as the memoir by Aaron Cohen, *Slave Hunter: One Man's Global Quest to Free Victims of Human Trafficking* (2009), and a documentary of his that aired on CNN called *Innocence for Sale* (2010). However, activists follow similar tacks. Jenn Tyburczy argues that in the case of Mexico's anti-trafficking industry, prominent activists such as Rosi Orozco depend "on highly saleable, scripted narratives of violent spectacle and sexual torture. To garner media attention, donations and, celebrity activist status, she populates these stories with heteronormative configurations of cunning, sex-crazed men and gullible women desperate for love. Her rhetoric foments a melodramatic form of empathy that invents (and not only reflects) a category of 'woman' as always cisgender and heterosexual, typically brown and racialized as 'other.'"[27] Such reliance on empathy, she says, flattens "colonial and neocolonial histories and covers over the damaging influences of free trade, particularly on rural and agrarian economies," sneakily erasing neoliberalism from the discourse of empathy.

All of these contemporary tropes originated in early twentieth-century melodramatic narratives, including dozens of best-selling books, hundreds of newspaper stories, and a popular film called *The Traffic in Souls* (1913). Despite this, "for the period during which this scare erupted, no one managed to turn up a single case of kidnapping for forced prostitution."[28] Nonetheless, in 1910 Congress passed the White Slave Trade Act, or Mann Act, making it a crime to entice or to facilitate the passage of "any woman or girl for the purpose of prostitution or debauchery, or any other immoral purpose." (The Mann Act was later amended in 1978 and 1986 but remains law.)[29]

A contemporary reader, steeped in media coverage of the policing, assault, and degradation of Black bodies by the state, will no doubt have noticed with some trepidation the ambiguity of the phrase "any other immoral purpose" in the Mann Act. Such a reader will likewise be unsurprised to learn that the law was not used to prosecute the non-existent sex trafficking of white women in 1910, but rather to prosecute adultery, premarital sex, racial mixing, and miscegenation. Then, as now, the crusaders did not consider the women in question to be capable of giving consent, or at least did not maintain that their consent mattered when society needed to be defended against the twin threats of female sexuality and racial mixing.

The white slave trade panic and the anti-trafficking pioneers who began it did more than sow the seeds of racism, anti-Semitism, and xenophobia. They also had a special relationship to lynching and to anti-Blackness specifically. Authorities believed the White Slave Trade/Mann Act was necessary for combating the rise of another threat: the hypersexual Black male or, in the parlance of the time, the "Black beast rapist." As Donovan writes, "stories of animalistic African Americans raping white women provided a powerful rationale for racial violence in the New South. Although the idea that African American men were unable to control their sexual desires was a staple of white racial thinking throughout the nineteenth century, the myth of the Black rapist gained wide acceptance only in the late 1880s."[30] As Doezema points out, at this time "sex between a Black man and a white woman became that which by definition could not be consented to."[31]

The false belief and widespread fear that "Negroes" were raping white women was instrumental in establishing the terroristic Jim Crow regime. Prior to the 1880s, most lynchings were not in the South but on the Western frontier, and most lynching victims were Mexican, Chinese, and Italian immigrants.[32] After the shift from targeting immigrants in the West to targeting former slaves and their descendants in the South, lynching reached its apex in 1892, when 161 Black people were lynched.[33] With the advent of photography, "spectacle lynchings" emerged as festive gatherings, facilitated by special train routes for the occasion, that included the ritual torture, castration, and mutilation of Black men along with souvenirs (including body parts), postcards, and photographs for the white attendees.

In the context of Brazil, Christen A. Smith notes the similarities in the ways that the Brazilian police and death squads spectacularize the torture and killing of Black men today.[34] There are striking similarities (violence that she calls palimpsestic) in the chaining of Black bodies together in lines, the popular circulation of photos of police in mid-kill, and the display of mutilated bodies of alleged criminals (e.g., tying them to poles or trees, sometimes even using U-shaped bicycle locks to hold the victims in place.) Luciane de Oliveira Rocha argues that such anti-Black violence has a profound impact on women, particularly the mothers of the young Black men killed. The experiences of such women "are either invisibilized or not taken into consideration in traditional analyses of violence"; by neglecting them, scholars have failed to understand how such violence contributes to Black women's radicalization and activism.[35]

In the United States, the idea of the "Black male brute" is necessary in the current moment for police to justify excessive violence against Black bodies as well as to rationalize as "reasonable" their fear of unarmed Black men. Contemporary news accounts and two hundred or more years of literature are too full of examples of bestial comparisons to even begin to list, but the figure of "the pimp," popularized in hip-hop and rap music but also instrumentalized by the anti-prostitution industry as a racialized boogeyman, belongs to this same archive of deadly white fantasies. In a study of sex trafficking prosecutions, anthropologists Kathleen Williamson and Anthony Marcus found that the US criminal justice system shows strong racial bias when it comes to selectively identifying black men to prosecute for sex trafficking–related offenses.[36] As Linda Tucker-Smith argues, "The return of the Black brute in rap raises the specter of racialized and sexualized violence that governed the relationships between white and Black men both prior to emancipation and during the Jim Crow era. The specter of the Black brute recalls the trauma wrought by both the imagined figurations of violence and the literal violence that defined the axis around which turned and around which were negotiated the practices that governed how Black and white men were to behave and thus their relationships to each other."[37] In its obsession with cartoonish pimps exploiting women, the anti–sex trafficking movement continues to rely on racist imagery that hearkens back to the white slavery panic.

Lest it seem that I am unfairly laying the horror of lynching at the door of pioneering white advocates for women's rights, it's instructive to recall the words of Rebecca Felton, a leader within the WCTU movement, when she spoke in 1897 of the danger of Black male rapists preying on white women: "If it takes lynching to protect women's dearest possession from drunken, ravening beasts, then I say lynch a thousand a week if it becomes necessary."[38] She later became the first woman sworn in as senator in the US Congress.

Meanwhile, Frances Willard, head of the WCTU, said "the grog-shop is the Negro's center of power. Better whisky and more of it is the rallying cry of great, dark-faced mobs. The colored race multiplies like the locust of Egypt. . . . [T]he safety of women, of childhood, the home, is menaced in a thousand localities at this moment."[39] As Donovan notes, the anti-lynching activist and Black feminist journalist Ida B. Wells took deep umbrage and referred to Willard's prejudice in her own speeches. Scoffing publicly at Wells, Willard retorted that white women would rarely if ever be capable of willingly having sex with a Black man. Eventually, the WCTU would go so far as to bar all Black women from its ranks and intensify its racist admonitions of Black men and immigrants, whom it believed were raping and sexually enslaving white girls and women.[40]

The WCTU was not alone in its racist approach to (white) women's rights. Indeed, first wave feminism itself dripped with white supremacy. Leaders such as Elizabeth Cady Stanton and Susan B. Anthony turned on the antislavery movement after initially working toward shared objectives and cooperating with abolitionist leaders such as Frederick Douglass because they believed that the same principles of liberalism— bodily autonomy, inalienable rights to liberty, property rights, self-determination, and eventually suffrage—would emancipate enslaved Black people as well as grant equality to women. When the Fifteenth Amendment passed in 1870, Black men (theoretically) got the right to vote. White feminists who had fought tirelessly as part of the antislavery movement were dismayed that Black men were being given rights over and above white women. To that end, Elizabeth Cady Stanton said Black men would be much worse voters than white women. She asked, "What will we and our daughters suffer if these degraded Black men are allowed to have the rights that would make them even worse than our Saxon fathers?"[41] She even said that Black women would be even worse off with their Black male husbands acting as new masters than they were under white slave masters.

Susan B. Anthony argued that "ignorant" Black men and immigrants (remembering that these immigrants were not properly white yet) could not be trusted with the vote, especially when more educated white women like herself were denied the right that was being given to these non-white men.[42] So Stanton and Anthony said that from then on, they would support no other cause but the cause of (white) women, and they were not going to deal with race any more, cutting off a growing cadre of Black women's rights advocates—a strain in the movement that would alienate Black feminists such as Ida B. Wells, Frances Harper, and Anna Julia Cooper.[43] In recent years, Twitter and other internet platforms have seen a host of hashtags and online complaints about "white feminism." Yes, Black feminism has always existed and has been intertwined with the feminist movement, animating its core. Black feminists deserve recognition as part of any genealogy of feminism, but ever since the moment that feminism emerged in the United States, white supremacist thinking within feminism has not only systematically de-privileged the needs and experiences of Black women but actively sought to denigrate and harm them, perhaps never so much as it did in the name of combatting "white slavery" and "sex trafficking." In truth, feminism qua feminism was not only predominantly white, but white supremacist.

The contemporary anti–sex trafficking movement has not reconciled itself to the fact that it began as racist. And I mean "racist" *not* just in the garden variety, racism-is-the-water-we-all-swim-in sort of prejudice, but as an overtly white supremacist movement for whom the degradation and death of Black bodies was foundational, not incidental. Nor has the anti–sex trafficking movement's predominantly white leadership today recognized that this ideology—from racist invocations of pimps to neocolonial foreign aid policies to the condescending desire to "give voice to the voiceless" victim prostitutes in the third world whom it seeks to rescue and rehabilitate—continues to undergird its assumptions and actions, thereby causing harm to non-white sex workers globally.

The so-called abolitionist movement of today sprang forth from the pro-lynching white women of the temperance movement and the xenophobes of first wave feminism who spread lies about the "yellow peril" and the imagined epidemic of "white slavery." The common thread among all of the groups (both religious and secular) in the modern coalition against sex trafficking, which for them encompasses all prostitution, is that they are invested in a particular fantasy that positions themselves as able, willing, and even "called" by some moral purpose to rescue, to uplift, and to empower. This orientation toward suffering is also a long-standing aspect of liberalism with its own racist underpinnings, that of *noblesse oblige.*

Noblesse oblige (literally "nobility obliges") refers to the concept that those with wealth, power, and status have an affirmative obligation to help their social inferiors. Early feminists such as Jane Addams, the founder of Hull House and crusader against "white slavery," advocated a feminist version of this position in calling on middle- and upper-class women with leisure time to devote themselves to philanthropy and volunteering to help less fortunate women. At a glance, this may seem like not only an obviously good thing but an easily granted ethical requirement. (Men no less than Winston Churchill and Spider-man's Uncle Ben have, after all, observed that with great power comes great responsibility.) And yet the attitude of noblesse oblige was also rooted in ethnocentrism, colonialism, and white supremacy. Rudyard Kipling became closely associated with this tradition due to his 1899 poem, "The White Man's Burden: The United States and the Philippine Islands," which made the forceful racist argument that the United States had a duty to colonize and rule over Filipinos.[44] Colonial projects across the Global South were rationalized using the idea that white people had, by virtue of their more "advanced" civilizations and levels of education, an obligation to rule. Noblesse oblige has not only served as a mantra for anti-trafficking policy but has spawned all manner of liberal rescue projects, a subject I return to at length later in this chapter.

Moral panics, by their nature, come and go. Yet they leave long-lasting and harmful laws and policies that are deeply entrenched. The moral panic about the sexual enslavement of white women led down a path where noblesse oblige was the guiding light, and that eventually led us to the neocolonial rescue policies and missionary activities harming sex workers today.

As the First World War erupted, the public lost interest in the white slave trade panic. Prostitutes went from being unwilling victims to predatory vectors of disease who were undeserving of sympathy. The "white slave trade" idea did not die completely, however, and it regularly appeared as a sexual fantasy in salacious pulp novels. Once society relegated it to a pornographic trope, the specter of white slavery visibly ossified at long last into what it had always been: a sexualized plaything invented for the purpose of white titillation. And there it remained—dormant and waiting—to be dusted off by a new generation of self-styled "abolitionists" eager to reanimate the rhetoric of stopping sexual slavery and rescuing women from prostitution.

THE SEX WARS: PRETRAFFICKING FEMINIST BATTLEGROUNDS

Second wave feminism emerged as a critique of prevailing social conditions that excluded women from political, cultural, economic, and educational opportunities. Central to its aims was to assert bodily autonomy: to have reproductive choice, freedom from domestic violence, and the right to walk freely without fear of rape. The movement was successful in a series of landmark legal cases brought by the National Organization for Women (NOW, founded in 1966), but this "change from within" approach for the mainstream "liberal feminists" of NOW was deemed insufficient by "radical feminists." Radical feminists wanted to think structurally about women's oppression (thus their introduction of the concept of "patriarchy," which they believed was transhistorical and universal). Although we often think of the 1980s as the period of the "Sex Wars" within feminism, the contentious question of sexuality was at the forefront early on in second wave feminism. As Nan Hunter notes in her chronology, New York Radical Women protested Miss America and *Playboy* in 1968. In 1973, COYOTE (Call Off Your Old Tired Ethics), a sex worker rights group advocating for decriminalization of prostitution, was founded. That same year saw not only *Roe v. Wade* but also *Miller v. California*, which downgraded the threshold for violating obscenity laws from material needing to be "utterly without social value" to merely lacking in serious artistic or social value.[45]

By 1975, rape was especially central to the cause, and Susan Brownmiller published *Against Our Will*. But her critique of pornography was central to her analysis of rape. "There can be no equality in porn, no female equivalent, no turning of the tables in the name of bawdy fun. Pornography, like rape, is a male invention, designed to dehumanize women."[46] While Brownmiller's work was fundamental to feminist understandings of rape as being about power, it also helped to establish the idea that under patriarchy all men *benefit* from rape, even if they themselves individually do not commit the act.

Although there is some debate over which anti-violence march should officially be called the first Take Back the Night, in 1978 Women Against Violence in Pornography and Media (WAVPM) held a conference in San Francisco under this name and held a march of five thousand women. Andrea Dworkin and her fellow radical feminist activists led their followers through San Francisco's Tenderloin district past sex workers, strip clubs, and porn theaters to demand an end to pornography. As Dworkin wrote, "Pornography is the orchestrated destruction of women's bodies and souls; rape, battery, incest, and prostitution animate it; dehumanization and sadism characterize it; it is war on women, serial assaults on dignity, identity, and human worth; it is tyranny."[47] For radical feminists, to be tolerant or celebratory of pornography was to support rape. As Robin Morgan famously proclaimed, "Pornography is the theory, rape is the practice."[48] Catharine MacKinnon similarly noted that "pornography, in the feminist view, is a form of forced sex, a practice of sexual politics, and the institution of gender inequality" and that "if pornography is part of your sexuality, then you have no right to your sexuality."[49]

Following the conference, Laura Lederer published an anthology of anti-porn essays (mostly from the meeting in San Francisco) entitled *Take Back the Night: Women on Pornography.*[50] Lederer later remarked that "pornography is a brilliant social marketing campaign for commercial sexual exploitation."[51] Given this view, it's unsurprising that Lederer would later shift her focus from the lost cause of banning pornography to banning prostitution/sex trafficking, even serving in the administration of George W. Bush as his anti–sex trafficking czar. The same year Lederer's book came out, NOW passed a resolution unilaterally condemning both prostitution and BDSM.[52] BDSM came to be a particular preoccupation of radical feminists, including Audre Lorde, whose own sex negativity has often been overlooked by scholars and activists eager to celebrate her many contributions to queer and feminist histories and theories. Lorde says in an interview that "S/M is not the sharing of power, it is merely a depressing replay of the old and destructive dominant/subordinate mode of human relating and one-sided power, which is even now grinding our earth and our human consciousness into dust."[53] She goes on to argue that "sadomasochism is an institutionalized celebration of dominant/subordinate relationships. And it prepares us either to accept subordination or to enforce dominance. *Even in play*, to affirm that the exertion of power over powerlessness is erotic, is empowering, is to set the emotional and social stage for the continuation of that relationship, politically, socially, and economically. . . . Sadomasochism feeds the belief that domination is inevitable and legitimately enjoyable."[54] Lorde also links this vision of sex to pornography. "The s/m concept of 'vanilla' sex is sex devoid of passion. They are saying that there can be no passion without unequal power. That feels very sad and lonely to me, and destructive. The linkage of passion to dominance/subordination is the prototype of the heterosexual image of male-female relationships, one which justifies pornography. Women are supposed to love being brutalized. This is also the prototypical justification of all relationships of oppression—that the subordinate one who is 'different' enjoys the inferior position."[55]

Part of why the Sex Wars felt so intractable is that radical feminists and sex radical feminists had completely different worldviews when it came to what constituted autonomy, pleasure, agency, resistance, oppression, harm, and danger. This is why such a constellation of issues—porn, BDSM, prostitution, sex trafficking, rape—became inextricable from one another. For radical feminists, porn, sadomasochism, and prostitution either *were* rape or at least promoted it.

This framework of sex negativity—of always prefiguring sex as a site of danger and trauma and violation and oppression—led many of the movement's leaders to the extreme decision to ally themselves with people who held a similar view of sex and who had recently come to have enough power to do something about it. Laura Lederer was not the only radical feminist to hop into bed with conservative Republicans, though. Women Against Pornography (WAP), whose founders included Gloria Steinem, Andrea Dworkin, Adrienne Rich, and Robin Morgan, were instrumental in testifying before and furthering the Meese Commission on Pornography, a major inquest into porn ordered by President Ronald Reagan. In 1986, this commission published an infamous two-thousand-page report filled with falsehoods and fearmongering. During her testimony to the New York attorney general's Commission on Pornography, an impassioned Andrea Dworkin explained, "Pornography is used in rape—to plan it, to execute it, to choreograph it, to engender the excitement to commit the act."[56]

Race has proven to be a particular sticking point for the Sex Wars. Radical feminists often emphasized that the sex industry disproportionately harms women of color and that porn often relies on racist stereotypes. As Black feminist theorist and scholar Mireille Miller-Young writes in *A Taste for Brown Sugar: Black Women and Pornography*, Black feminist authors following the radical line "are not wrong," but she notes that "the story is more complex, and Black women's performances deserve a more nuanced analysis. Not only do Black women's representations in porn include portrayals that sometimes undermine stereotypes, Black actresses often try to capture something quite different from the meanings normatively attached to their bodies."[57] Miller-Young's analysis contends that Black women in porn remake their image, that they work to control their products, and that they see themselves as mirrors for Black viewers and fans.

Similarly, in *The Color of Kink: Black Women, BDSM and Pornography*, Ariane Cruz describes her struggle with Black radical feminist critiques of porn. She argues for a "politics of perversion to critically interrogate the historically contentious relationship between Black feminism and pornography ... in my personal attempt to reconcile Black feminism and pornography as a Black feminist scholar of pornography who does not view it as wholly oppressive, inimical and definitely at odds with a kind of Black feminist political agenda."[58] She describes her struggle feeling distanced from people like Patricia Hill Collins, Jewel D. Amoah, and Alice Walker, the latter of whom saw porn as "an impossible tool of sexual intimacy."[59] Cruz likewise recounts struggling as a Black feminist to reconcile herself to Audre Lorde's view of S/M and porn, given the profound admiration she has for Lorde in so many other regards.

Black feminist scholar Jennifer Nash writes that "nowhere are the dangers of fantasy more apparent than in racialized pornography, a representational site that antipornography feminists have been particularly invested in critiquing. . . . [T]his body of scholarship treats race as an 'intensifier' which demonstrates the severity of pornography's gender-based injury." She concludes that "despite their interest in using race to bolster claims about pornography's sexism, antipornography feminists have been inattentive to pornography's mobilization of particular racial and ethnic differences. They conflate the variety of racial and ethnic representations within pornography under a theory that the deployment of *any* racial or ethnic trope always renders pornography pernicious sexist representation."[60] Nash devotes particular attention to MacKinnon and Dworkin's arguments that porn is not a representation of violence against women, but rather *is* violence against women. Summarizing their views, she writes, "Eliminating pornography entirely, then, is the only way to ensure that women are not subjected to the violent production of pornography—conditions which MacKinnon sees as analogous to prostitution and rape—and that women are not subjected to the continued circulation of images which normalize male violence against women."[61]

I previously described how radical feminists' ideology collapses BDSM, porn, and prostitution into rape. They believe that all of these phenomena are to be opposed, because even if one *imagines* one is consensually (and even enjoyably) participating in the sexual act in question, it ultimately harms women *everywhere* overall. Even their obsession with "transsexualism" is often expressed in the language of rape, as in Janice Raymond's famous 1979 book, *The Transsexual Empire: The Making of the She-Male*, in which she proclaimed, "All transsexuals rape women's bodies by reducing the real female form to an artifact, appropriating this body for themselves. . . . Transsexuals merely cut off the most obvious means of invading women, so that they seem noninvasive."[62] She concludes her polemic by declaring that "the problem with transsexualism would best be served by morally mandating it out of existence."[63]

It should come as no surprise that in this reductionist view, when the anti-pornography movement reinvented itself as the anti–sex trafficking movement in the 1990s, Lederer and other radical feminists would similarly conflate all prostitution with sex trafficking and sexual exploitation and therefore render it reducible to rape. The link between rape and pornography has now been reframed as a link between sex trafficking and pornography.

In 2020, Exodus Cry launched a highly successful campaign against Pornhub, alleging that the site included videos of rape and sexual exploitation, which eventually resulted in the site taking down a majority of its content. Melissa McCarthy and HBO Max planned to gift Exodus Cry with $20,000 and to feature it as one of their organizations in their 20 Days of Kindness Campaign. The *Daily Beast* and other organizations promptly published stories detailing the anti–sex trafficking ministry's ties to anti-LGBT and anti-abortion efforts.[64] McCarthy immediately rescinded her support and apologized, saying "We backed a charity that . . . stands for everything that we do not."[65] In response, Exodus Cry called the journalism "false and defamatory" and stated that the group is inclusive and works with many different organizations. It emphasizes that various leaders have expressed their own opinions about "protection of life in the womb," but that Exodus Cry officially has no political views on anything other than sexual exploitation.[66] The group says that "Exodus Cry exists to help every person, including those who identify as LGBTQ+, be free from the harms of commercial sexual exploitation" and respects all people, but it does not actually denounce or repudiate IHOP leaders preaching about homosexuality and demonic possession, satanic tornados of homosexuality, or gay people "facing flaming missiles from the evil one."[67] Its website has a list of myths circulating about the organization that announces "Myth: Exodus Cry 'is a racist' organization," though the group does not respond to the specific allegations circulating about its racism.[68] The site also offers some testimonials from women of color. Exodus Cry's response to the HBO Max kerfuffle about its anti-abortion and anti-gay ties is not just a non-apology apology; it's a non-apology non-apology.

Even after HBO Max and McCarthy rescinded their donation, none other than Nicholas Kristof jumped on the bandwagon, referring to Exodus Cry's TraffickingHub campaign in a piece called "The Children of Pornhub" and linking to its leader's Twitter account for *New York Times* readers to follow. (I discuss Kristof's role as a key figure in the celebrification of sex trafficking more in chapter 3.) In response,

Melissa Gira Grant wrote in the *New Republic*, "There is no question that Pornhub sits at the crux of two bad ideas: a race to the bottom gig economy and a tech-determinist business model that values stickiness and seamlessness over content moderation. . . . [T]o confront them with a religious crusade is not only useless but dangerous."[69] She denounces Kristof, saying, "Kristof is exactly the kind of gatekeeper a group like Exodus Cry—seeking to establish its credentials, elevate its name, and attract liberals to its cause—wants on its side. His track record of using traumatic stories to draw readers in is a perfect fit. . . . [W]hat made Kristof the perfect pitchman for the tent revival wing of the sex trafficking movement is now turned toward its new cause: porn."[70] Exodus Cry is not alone. The journalist Drew Fox notes that the anti-pornography group Morality in Media changed its name to the National Center on Sexual Exploitation without actually changing anything about its membership, mission, or funding sources except that it offers itself up to mainstream press as an expert on "subjects such as sex trafficking, child exploitation and the dangers of decriminalizing prostitution."[71] While Pornhub users certainly upload exploitative videos that it needs to take down, there remains little interrogation of this new reincarnation of the Sex Wars or why secular liberals are so eager to crawl into bed with groups so intimately tied to antiabortion and anti-LGBTQ+ causes.

THE WHITE FANTASTIC

Throughout this chapter I have traced a history of the anti–sex trafficking movement that exposes the fragile and condescending whiteness at its core. This mode of whiteness that relies on the Western (usually white) savior is comprised of the liberal notion of noblesse oblige. The idea that the privileged, educated, and civilized know what is best for the less fortunate and have a moral obligation to help still creeps into popular liberal human rights projects such as voluntourism, NGOs focused on "empowering" or "uplifting" locals, micro-lending initiatives, and study away programs wherein students from wealthy countries receive course credit at home for helping unfortunate souls abroad. Many such projects are religious in nature and combine mission trips with voluntourism. Such initiatives may have positive outcomes and provide some meaningful experiences (probably more profoundly for the helpers than the "helped"), but they must be understood in light of the history of ethnocentrism in whose lineage they reside.

In 1899, when Rudyard Kipling penned his passionate call for colonization in "The White Man's Burden," he wrote:

Take up the White Man's burden—
And reap his old reward:
The blame of those ye better
The hate of those ye guard—
The cry of hosts ye humour
(Ah slowly) to the light:
"Why brought ye us from bondage,
"Our loved Egyptian night?"[72]

Here, Filipinos are described as resisting their rescue. They blame their "betters" and hate their "guards," crying out against them and protesting their own liberation, longing to be left in their suffering because they do not know better. The "reward" of ruling over the lesser dark folk, according to Kipling, is really a burden. What a rueful and noble thing: to be called upon to rule over those who do not appreciate it. When I read Kipling, I cannot help but remember the protests of sex workers in the Global South: workers in India and Thailand carrying signs saying "Rescue us from the rescuers!" and images of sewing machines with big red Xs through them protesting Westerners' obsession with "retraining" sex workers in sweatshops. But when I read Kipling's bone-chilling words today, I also think of the proliferation of voluntourism; human trafficking tours; study abroad programs; and anti-trafficking businesses that urge "rescued" women to handcraft little items that church groups, NGOs, and boutiques can sell to consumers eager to feel good about their "proceeds going to help sex trafficking victims."

Today, there are perhaps hundreds of anti–sex trafficking programs that have grown out of this tradition of noblesse oblige. Houston, Texas, offers not one but two driving tours: Children at Risk's Human Trafficking Bus Tour, which focuses on learning to spot the signs of trafficking, and Elijah Rising's van tours, which also offer a Human Trafficking 101 class with visual aids. Destiny Rescue charges US$3,500 (not including airfare) to join its two-week trip in Thailand and Cambodia to "see the issue of child sex trafficking" and to "visit Red Light districts to see what the commercial sex industry looks like."[73] But it also includes trips to "Destiny Café and other quaint coffee shops" and an opportunity to "visit local tourist interactions." Destiny Rescue has thirteen trips slated for the next year, some in private partnership with religious universities.

Rahab's Rope charges US$3,450 (not including airfare) for an eleven-day trip to Mumbai, India, to "travel with us to our center in the heart of the Red Light District," urging customers to "come help us on the front lines as we work to rescue those trapped in sexual slavery by [. . .] sharing the love of Christ." It also informs them: "You will also enjoy shopping and taking a tour of Mumbai's historical sites."[74] The same organization also does a trip in Bangalore, India, where it provides opportunities for sightseeing outside of the sex industry. "You will join with our aftercare programs and help these women and children learn their identity is in Christ alone, and that they can do and be anything with Him by their side. You will have the opportunity to shop and visit Bangalore's ancient palaces or gardens."[75] Other mission trips are on offer from various groups going to Guatemala, Zimbabwe, and Ethiopia, as well as to Thailand and Cambodia.

Also in India is Crossroads Church's anti–sex trafficking program, which charges $3,400 to "be on the relief team" for the church's outreach workers, giving them "space to retreat and kick back, and bring some extra hope from the other side of the world."[76] It also informs them that they will "take part in an immersive prayer walk through the red light district" as they tour the area, interrupting the working women to see if they would like to pray.[77] The program also promises that "you'll introduce the girls to playing in the wild, rappelling/rock climbing, rafting rivers, and finding meaningful new levels of friendships."[78] Never mind that rafting and rock climbing are commonly featured leisure activities for Western college students and tourists and probably not what mental health professionals would list as top priorities for newly freed and traumatized children rescued from boundless rape and torment. For customers who prefer to remember the "victims" they traveled halfway around the world to see in a more "natural habitat" than, say, whitewater rafting, there is a See Human Trafficking Photography Expedition available in Thailand.[79]

Global sporting events have likewise been incorporated into the anti-trafficking tourism industry. I AM Freedom, a nonprofit organization, sent its members on a trip to Brazil during the 2014 World Cup to "spread the word against human trafficking for three and a half weeks" while some other members spent only eight days. "Recife is one of the original transatlantic slave cities, so it has a long history of slavery. . . . That's one of the reasons we chose that city and felt like the Lord was leading us there," explained its cofounder, adding, "It will be an incredible adventure and journey for us."[80]

Not to be outdone by Christians, on the secular liberal side is the University of Wisconsin–Madison, whose College of Agricultural and

Life Sciences offers a study abroad course called the Global and Human Rights Training in Spain and Morocco to Combat Sex Trafficking. The program description insists that of the "hundreds of women and girls" who make the dangerous trip from Nigeria to Spain via Morocco, "most [. . .] are already caught up in sex trafficking networks."[81] The program, which costs US$6,450 (including airfare), purports to teach students to do things like "understand and analyze the demand side" and "through collective narratives (visual arts, theater, music, body movement among other techniques) assist staff of organizations, and also victims and survivors to find their previously silenced voice."[82] One imagines what the Nigerian woman and ostensible sex trafficking survivor must think after her rescue when she is handed over to a fresh-faced college student from Wisconsin bidding her to lift her voice in song and trippingly dance, that she may be "silenced" no more. I suspect she would rather the student had just sent her the six thousand dollars instead.

Armed with a minimum cumulative GPA of 2.0, some with an optional elective selected from a list of courses approximate to global health prior to their visit, these intrepid students "will arrive in one of the major trafficking and migration transit cities and, using a theory of self and mutual care, we will gather voices, narratives, and discourses from a variety of stakeholders involved in the migration-trafficking process at the destination country."[83] The outcome is that "we will take these messages to organizations and individuals in the transit settings, gathering more information and take it back to the destination country closing the circle of communication and care."[84] The mix of social justice terminology (*self-care*, *silencing*) and neoliberal idioms (*stakeholders*) is remarkable. So, too, is the peculiarly condescending notion that what the "stakeholders" in Morocco and Spain really need is students from the United States to "close the circle of communication" by relaying information back and forth between groups in Morocco and Spain in some sort of NGO-ified game of telephone.

All of the churches, organizations, and programs described here are part of a common rescue industry. The migrant women become a product in this chain, while the universities (alongside student loan providers) and NGOs make money, get grants, pay professors' salaries, and professionalize themselves in relation to the women. The sociologists Elena Shih and Elizabeth Bernstein, intrigued by the increasing popularity of such voluntourism, mission trips, and "service-learning" programs focused on sex trafficking, traveled to Thailand (Shih's long-time field site) to take part in one. Their tour cost US$1,200 per person (excluding airfare); had fifteen participants; and was run by two organizations, the secular Global Exchange and the Christian Not for Sale. Citing Kimberly Kay Hoang's work on sex tourism in Vietnam, they note that Western tourists enjoy the sense that "virtuous third world poverty" is appealing to visitors because it highlights their own helping capacities, which are fundamental to the encounter. Ironically, this instrumentalization of virtuous poverty—spectacularized and performed for the traveling Westerners—is just as essential to the experience for the "anti-prostitution activists" as it is for the sex tourists.[85]

Bernstein and Shih describe the other participants as having been inspired by popular movies about sex trafficking such as the Oscar-winning white savior documentary *Born into Brothels* (2004), about a woman who gives cameras to the children of sex workers in India to photograph their daily lives in the red light district. Another popular source of inspiration was the Liam Neeson action-thriller *Taken* (2008), in which a courageous father and former black ops agent must punch, kick, and torture his way through endless Albanian baddies to rescue his daughter before her honor is besmirched at a sex slave auction. The tour organizers reported to the sociologists that visitors were frequently disappointed by the realities they saw, feeling both unimpressed with the level of suffering and also "not feeling needed."[86]

I contend that this savior-based tourism model is rooted in the same logic and genealogy as the white feminist volunteerism that early leaders of the movement positioned as a matter of noblesse oblige. While the exact racial makeup of these well-off foreigners is unclear, the phenomenon of fighting sex trafficking as a leisure activity vis-à-vis tourism is rooted in whiteness no matter the race of the participants. (The same is true of all European and US colonial endeavors regardless of the complicity of some smaller number of people of color.) The tourists and students must imagine their presence as somehow beneficial to the locals, and consequently they experience disappointment when they are not made to feel enough like the rescuers they imagined themselves to be and the lives of sex workers do not adhere to the expectations set by media like the popular and well-received films identified earlier. In short, what the visitors long for is more melodramatic titillation in the spectacle they have come to behold.

This titillation is often marked by racialization, Othering, and Orientalism. Galusca's study of the documentary *Innocence for Sale* (2001) notes that the journalist-protagonist Aaron Cohen busts brothels in Cambodia but pauses to make connections with the girls on camera.

"On finding himself in a hotel room with a 'karaoke girl,' Cohen is heard exclaiming 'Oh, she's so shy!' Cohen's remark becomes especially flirtatious when counterposed against the young woman's silence and anxious bearing."[87] White savior narratives also rely on the titillating prospect of the sex encounter denied but still brushed up against. Galusca notes that *New York Times* reporter Kristof admits that he poses as a sex tourist looking for young girls in Cambodia. Moreover, Cohen confesses "in *Slave Hunter* (2009) that he sometimes has to make out with women in brothels to distract the pimp," which she says is "suggestive of the erotic exchange that becomes integral to the interactions between humanitarian journalists and alleged victims."[88]

Readers of anthropology will already have noticed similarities between the documentary brothel busting and spectacle-laden sex trafficking tourism and the oft-remarked-upon histories of safaris, exhibitions, and World Fairs popular around Kipling's time. Indeed, anthropology itself (often nicknamed "the handmaiden of colonialism") contributed toward the popular display of indigenous peoples, whom the scholar-adventurers presented as spectacles. This mode of display also helped to birth "natural history" museums that portrayed anthropological items collected through colonial conquest.

The spirit of noblesse oblige, when fused with adventure travel, owes thanks in part to cultural anthropologists in the nineteenth century. Travel writers and ethnographers had wowed Western readers with tales of exotic natives and "the sexual lives of savages."[89] Safaris to see animals in Africa emerged in the 1850s, in part popularized by famous travelers such as Sir Richard Burton. Soon, intrepid white travelers were visiting not only animals but also native people. The safari "came home" during World's Fairs, which famously included people of various indigenous heritage living in enclosures similar to zoo exhibits whom guests could observe.[90] Later in the twentieth century, affordable and mainstream companies came to offer a variety of related activities such as amateur wildlife photography tours, cultural tourism, voluntourism, diasporic heritage tourism, and forms of ecotourism that involve visiting natives to watch or even participate in indigenous rituals. Another popular form of modern safari is the "favela," "slum," or "township" tour, in which tourists visit poor neighborhoods, orphanages, and schools in places like Brazil, India, or South Africa.[91] When these kinds of tours are understood as descended from the tradition of the safari, it is easy to understand why activists accuse them of the "zoofication" of poverty.[92]

Nonetheless, organizers of sex trafficking and poverty tours point to the idea that such tours uplift the local community and raise awareness about social inequality among the foreigners' privileged peers, though this rhetoric is nearly identical to that heard from adherents of noblesse oblige. Whether traveling the world to snap pictures of giraffes, poor people in favelas, or "sex trafficking victims," the tourists and their gaze are fundamentally united by the scopophilic pleasure of beholding the Other and imagining themselves in a relationship with it that feels socially uplifting for the helper. Central to this imagined relationship is the concretization provided by photography of the encounter: the transformation of suffering and redemption into spectacle.

Kimberly Pendleton, writing about the sex trafficking narratives that result from the commingling of radical feminists and evangelical Christians, argues that these groups "link sex work, pornography consumption, and forced prostitution, all of which constitute a site through which gender norms are negotiated."[93] For Pendleton, it is "masculinity itself" that "is imagined to be the central victim within the evangelical fight against sex trafficking," and evangelicals have absorbed radical feminists' "emphasis on the ways that men harm women" even if the evangelicals utilize radical feminist ideas to anti-feminist ends.[94] To prove this, she examines the role of evangelical men in the anti–sex trafficking and anti-pornography movement who minister to other men about stopping porn consumption or urge fellow men who serve in the military overseas not to patronize "prostitutes" or "sex slaves" and to see them instead as women who were abused by their fathers, sold by their parents, and coerced by pimps, and who otherwise would be "traditional wives" and mothers. Good Christian men must therefore stop sexual slavery (which they believe is perpetuated by the porn industry) because this will restore traditional family values. There is also a racist tinge to such anti-trafficking discourses, as Shih points out, in that they suggest "that human trafficking can be explained by bad family values, or cultural norms that consider girl children to be disposable" and "facilitate the heroic, paternalist, and 'caring' interventions that have now been well-documented."[95] Yet to do this, evangelicals today rely on the form of melodrama with all the familiar tropes of fallen women and rescued girls, villainous pimps, and good white crusaders that read like something out of the "white slave trade" stories of the early twentieth century.

Titillation—the arousal from beholding the oblique sexual possibilities of another person's activities and their situation from a somewhat removed state—has always been an important aspect to spectacle. Gone are the days when women's rights advocates—even the whitest of them—advocate for the scopophilic pleasure of watching the lynching of Black men. Yet what binds together the racist nineteenth-century advocates for women's rights and the contemporary twenty-first-century anti–sex trafficking movement is their mutual fixation on the carceral: the appeal to violence, punishment, imprisonment, and shaming.[96] Lock up the pimps. Lock up the johns. Lock up the traffickers and third-party facilitators. Lock up the taxi drivers who take women to clients. Lock up the motel owners who turn a blind eye. Their continued recourse to the carceral framework is disturbing for its consistency.

Self-righteousness is a pleasurable feeling. The evangelicals and anti-prostitution feminists are not just sex negative but are titillated by the salacious spectacle of anti-trafficking. This is why their documentaries, Hollywood movies, TV specials, and talk shows always focus on the most melodramatic examples, in which victims are innocent and unsuspecting, are kidnapped, are raped, and suffer unspeakable horrors. This is why Trump improvises long, rambling, and vivid (but unrealistic) accounts of women taped up in blue electrical tape with arms and legs behind their backs, tossed atop one another in white vans. There is no distance between the pornified visions of sex trafficking put forward by Donald Trump and those of Exodus Cry or the Salvation Army. Neither is rooted in reality, but the tellers of these tales take peculiar pleasure in embellishing the finest of sexual details. In terms of sensationalism, they have not progressed an inch since the yellow journalism that produced the white slave trade panic nor from the pulp fiction of the mid-twentieth century. For the anti-trafficking movement, there is often a fetishistic enjoyment in recounting and circulating imagined sex trafficking scenarios, which they paint in their videos, documentaries, and speeches with lurid detail. And yet the radical feminists, evangelical missionaries and right-wing Republicans can revel in the intellectual distancing provided by self-righteous disavowal of the sex act and positioning of one's own erotic subjectivity as firmly opposed to—but always curiously alongside of and inseparable from—the sexual depravity they spend their days obsessing over. The neo-abolitionist's dwelling on the most lurid details of violence, the endless descriptions of bruised genitals, the placement of tape or chains or ropes, the graphic recounting of every act of penetration becomes an obsession and fetish. For people who claim to deny other forms of pornography, these hypersexualized and fantastic scripts take on the perverse form of sex negative erotica.

SLAVERY DISCOURSE

The anti-trafficking movement was quick to co-opt the terms *sexual slavery* and *modern slavery*. There is also a deliberate attempt by the anti-prostitution movement to brand itself as "abolitionists" and an effort to invent a genealogy that they can trace to antislavery advocates like William Wilberforce, the British politician who led the campaign against the British slave trade, championed the Society for the Suppression of Vice, and advocated for Christian missionary work in the colonies. For feminists and evangelical Christians alike, Wilberforce and the abolitionists are both an inspiration but also a moral smokescreen that allows them to carry out their own anti-prostitution, anti-pornography, and anti-vice moral crusades.

The anti–sex trafficking movement's attempt to narrativize itself as an outgrowth of abolitionism is false. The truth is that the movement is not anti-racist at all, but rather white supremacist in its past and present incarnations. The attempt to co-opt the abolitionist movement is a rhetorical flourish that is, in and of itself, a sign of the racism of the movement. Moreover, the fact that the movement eagerly seizes—of all the possible vantages available—the viewpoint of the white saviors of enslaved Africans is the most revealing of all the movement's affective attachments to slavery discourse.

As Tryon P. Woods has argued, "antiblack racism underwrites the contemporary movement against 'modern-day slavery.' The anti-slavery movement is haunted by the specter of racial slavery even while it feeds off of it parasitically."[97] He goes on to explain that the movement "deploys non-racial language to define the racialized realities that it addresses, an approach that solidifies the existing racial regime." Moreover, what is lost when this discursive deracialization happens is the lesson from Black history that rescue movements "are always self-referential: they aim at the salvation of the rescuer, not the rescued."[98] He also has little patience for the constant comparisons the movement makes between modern-day slavery and old "racial slavery" in an effort to "emphasize how much worse the situation is today."[99] He is right that such claims are rampant in the anti–sex trafficking movement. For example, Gospel for Asia stated in a press release that "in this century, more young women and girls are enslaved in brothels each year than were shipped to slave plantations at the height of the slave trade in the 18th and 19th centuries."[100] Finally, Woods drives home the point: "While slavery is evoked to cloak contemporary abolitionism with a political saliency and emotional urgency that only memory of *the* foundational institution of the modern world can sustain, there is a decided absence of solidarity with actual black suffering today."[101] Lyndsey Beutin echoes this in her analysis of curatorial exhibits that use images of Black suffering to position the Black Atlantic slave trade as part of a genealogy that culminates in "modern day slavery," thereby appropriating Black historical experiences and co-opting that trauma and memory for the rescue industry's own ends.[102]

Julia O'Connell Davidson names Kevin Bales, the best-selling author of several books on "modern slavery," as one of the people who has popularized the idea that "old slavery" was race-based but "new slavery" is "colour-blind," with the "common denominator in vulnerability to slavery today" being "poverty, not color."[103] She objects to this line of reasoning on the grounds that "according to the global slavery 'indexes' produced by the new abolitionists, including Bales himself, the overwhelming majority of those dubbed slaves are found in the places once colonized by Europe and America. To suggest that their poverty has nothing to do with 'colour' is to forget both that they are predominantly drawn from populations historically subject to the exclusion clause of the racial contract and the centrality of that exclusion clause to patterns of economic development and underdevelopment in the contemporary world."[104] Julieta Hua has also examined the rhetorical appropriation of transatlantic slavery by the contemporary trafficking movement. For example, she notes that the behemoth NGO Polaris Project takes its name from the North Star because of its "significance in slave narratives as the nighttime guide for slaves attempting to escape the South" and that the NGO has described itself as "fighting 'trafficking and slavery in the spirit of a modern-day Underground Railroad.'"[105] Hua argues that that "framing trafficking through transatlantic slavery helps construct a national project and projection of 'the universal force of American norms and institutions,'" such that America then presumes to speak on behalf of the world.[106] And, indeed, this is borne out when one considers how this discourse has, in turn, been adopted by governments.

After shifting her focus from her work with WAP to helping George W. Bush fight sex trafficking, Lederer worked as a consultant for the sensationalistic sex trafficking films *The Day My God Died* (2003) and *Trade* (2007). She commented, "For the past few years I have been calling human trafficking . . . a contemporary form of slavery. When I first made the comparison, I took some heat. Critics said . . . that it referenced a particular period in our country's history."[107] She went on to say, "In a previous century, Africans labored in the tobacco fields, and slaves were bred for strength and endurance. The fields have been replaced by brothels and sex shops, and the new trade is in young women and children."[108] She argues that just like enslaved Africans, today's sex slaves are tricked, deceived, lured, kidnapped, and coerced. She notes that they are taken from their native homelands to foreign countries where they do not know the language or culture. "They are forced to do someone else's bidding for someone else's financial gain," she concludes.[109] Such comparisons appeal to emotion easily enough, but they elide the complexity of migrant women's agency, their constrained choices, and their varied experiences of sexual labor, as well as other forms of labor under late capitalism. Her comparison to chattel slavery also demeans those who were captured, murdered, or killed in the transatlantic slave trade and reinforces anti-Blackness by erasing the particularities of those experiences and co-opting them to administer the policies of the Bush administration.

Read against Woods's essay on anti-Blackness, Lederer's words exemplify the rhetorical deracialization of the movement and the ineptitude of the anti-trafficking movement when it comes to Black history. Instead, the contemporary antislavery movement has drawn more or less arbitrary lines around what constitutes "slave" conditions without ever reckoning with what "work" means under capitalism or allowing that exploited workers engage in "various modes of self-authored activity, including armed resistance" all the time, as Woods notes.[110] Black history teaches us that "the best way to preserve the racial *status quo* is to simply re-present it in non-racial terms."[111] The anti-trafficking movement seeks to appropriate the rhetorical force and emotional heft of the language of slavery, but without seriously considering the consequences of this strategy for anti-Blackness and for the effects that their policies and programs will have on the surveillance regimes that govern the lives of migrants and people of color.

RACISM AND THE NEOCOLONIAL
INSTITUTIONALIZATION OF ANTI-TRAFFICKING

It is not only at the rhetorical and symbolic level that the anti–sex trafficking movement aligns with white supremacist goals. Specifically, the narrow focus on sex trafficking diverts much-needed resources from comprehensive immigration reform, labor trafficking abuses, and sexual abuse that happens to migrant workers outside of the parameters of the sex trafficking imaginary. As Kamala Kempadoo notes in "From Moral Panic to Global Justice," those who seek to limit immigration have co-opted the discourse of trafficking to argue for tougher laws using the smokescreen of human rights language.[112] In 1996, Bill Clinton introduced the Charitable Choice Initiative, which allowed the government to directly fund religious organizations to provide social services. It was expanded in 2000.[113] This allowed anti-trafficking groups to take government money, but religious conservative groups have no taste for comprehensive immigration reform that would require addressing systematic racism and xenophobia in society (including in states with Republican elected officials). But the one thing that gets bipartisan support in the sphere of anti-trafficking is anti–sex trafficking. What politician wants to be seen voting *against* an anti–sex trafficking bill? Who is *for* sex trafficking? This privileging of resources for anti–sex trafficking at the expense of addressing the fundamental exploitation of migrants furthers the xenophobia and racism that migrant workers already face. Ironically, it may even increase the sexual exploitation of migrant women, who may experience sexual assault, sexual harassment, and rape while working in domestic, agricultural, or other non–sex work sectors.

The US State Department also uses anti-trafficking policies to stop other countries from decriminalizing prostitution. This has two main forms: the APLO and the TIP Report. APLO was an amendment to the 2003 President's Emergency Plan for AIDS Relief (PEPFAR), which required an explicit statement from NGOs and other organizations that do global health work asserting that they oppose prostitution and sex trafficking and that, more specifically, they do not support legalization or decriminalization of prostitution. It expanded from being one of Bush's "global gag rules" to a policy affecting US-based groups as well.[114] This frustrated many groups who supported decriminalization or legalization of sex industries or who worked in countries like Brazil, where sex work is a legal profession appearing in labor laws. Many of these organizations wished to have sex workers as members of policy task forces or wished to center sex workers in peer education, peer outreach, and peer research.

Thus, in 2005 Brazil lost US$40 million in USAID money owed through PEPFAR because it would not sign a statement condemning prostitution, which is not illegal there.[115] In 2013, the Supreme Court decided 6–2 on free speech grounds that APLO was unconstitutional, with Chief Justice Roberts writing that APLO sought to force nonprofit organizations to "pledge allegiance to the [U.S.] Government's policy."[116]

But the ruling only applied to US-based groups. As Sonia Corrêa and José Miguel Nieto Olivar point out, "less than a month after of the suspension of the USAID agreement in May 2005, the Federal Police raided a boat party at the Rio Marina after receiving a tip that drugs and minors providing sexual services were aboard. Twenty-nine American male tourists, most of them Black, and 40 sex workers were apprehended. The police realized that neither minors nor drugs were involved and, consequently the women were freed."[117] Interestingly, they point out that the police confiscated the men's passports, and "the Federal Police publicly announced that the men were accused of the (non-existent) crime of 'sexual tourism' and would therefore be deported. The case was extensively publicized by anti-trafficking organizations as a major policy 'victory'" despite there not being any actual allegations of sex trafficking.[118] Similar episodes in which sex tourists were arrested and harassed for having legal commercial sex with adults before being released continued to occur, and anti-trafficking activists continued to use those numbers to further inflate the sense of severity and scale of sex trafficking.

As a result of situations like this, George Soros's Open Society Foundation fought its way to the Supreme Court again, hoping it would further strike down APLO because US NGOs working abroad are financially entangled with and logistically inseparable from the foreign groups. However, in 2019 the Supreme Court found against Open Society and ruled that APLO would be enforced on foreign soil.

APLO is a tool for dictating morality to other governments, but it also has allowed anti-trafficking groups who conflate all prostitution with sex trafficking and who support End Demand (sometimes known as the Swedish Model) to not only suck up vital USAID resources but establish themselves firmly within the funding structures, making them more likely to continue to receive funding even after the 2013 ruling. End Demand, as I discuss later, is a "sex buyer law" that effectively decriminalizes the sale of sex but seeks increased penalties for consumers of sexual services. There is growing evidence that not only does End Demand not work, but when its policies are in place, violence against sex workers increases, especially among street-based women and the most vulnerable.

End Demand is also the preferred policy model for nearly all anti–sex trafficking organizations in the evangelical Christian movement and the radical feminist movement I have described in this chapter. (There *are* many anti-trafficking organizations, including those affiliated with the GAATW, that support full decriminalization and do distinguish between sex work and sex trafficking.) Scholars have also noted that in addition to APLO, each reauthorization of the Victims of Trafficking and Violence Protection Act (TVPA) by Congress has further narrowed "the focus of anti-trafficking efforts toward voluntary prostitution and to turn attention to the 'demand' for prostitution," making the TVPA a thin entering wedge for End Demand.[119] The TVPA and APLO are neocolonial, deeply moralistic, and also deadly. Their effects on Black and brown people worldwide are part of the racist policies of the US state apparatus, yet they remain central to the anti-trafficking movement's strategies.

A second neocolonial policy takes the form of the US TIP Report. It was Lederer who initially began issuing such a report, although it did not take its current name until after the TVPA was authorized in 2000. The TIP Report ranks all countries as either Tier 1, Tier 2, Tier 2 Watchlist, or Tier 3. If a country drops in the ranking, it risks losing foreign aid. Unsurprisingly, a quick Google image search reveals a color-coded map that looks suspiciously like what a map of friends and foes of the US State Department would.

In an op-ed in the *Philadelphia Inquirer* in 2007, the anthropologist Laura María Agustín wrote of the TIP report:

> Having named sexual slavery as a particular evil to be eradicated, the United States grades other countries on how they are doing. On the one hand, it sounds like an obvious way to do good: Describe the ghastly conditions you as a rich outsider observe in poor countries. Focus on places where sex is sold. Say all women found were kidnapped virgins and are now enslaved; announce to the world that you will liberate them. Organize raids. Denounce anyone who objects—even if their objection is that you are intervening in their country's internal affairs. Ignore victims who resist rescue. Use lurid language and talk continuously about the most sensational and terrible cases. . . . It is easy to haul out sensationalistic language (sex slavery, child prostitution), but it is much harder to sort out the real victims from the more routinely disadvantaged and trying-to-get-ahead. Those who know intimately the problems of the poor in their own cultures rarely deny that they can decide to leave home and pay others to help them travel and find work, in sex or in any other trade. Victims are "protected" rather than granted autonomy. At the Empower Center in Chiang Mai, Thailand, signs written by migrant women "rescued from" selling sex include: "We lose our savings and belongings"; We are locked up"; "We are held till deportation"; "We are interrogated by many people"; "Our family must borrow money to survive while we wait."[120]

Rescue organizations suck up grant money to advance their causes and set up "diversion" and "rehabilitation" programs for "rescued" sex workers, often billing the state for providing these services. A common symbol in the global sex worker rights movement is a picture of a sewing machine inside a red circle with a line struck through it, a reference to the number of rescue industry do-gooders whose solution is to essentially force women out of sex trades and into sweatshops. Even anti–sex trafficking advocate Kristof—who has live-tweeted brothel raids and purchased girls from traffickers to liberate them—has written passionate defenses in the *New York Times* of sweatshop factories as an overly maligned industry that should be the solution to, rather than a continuation of, abject poverty. The fact that one kind of work—sex work—is considered irredeemably exploitative while the other is not says a great deal about the capitalism and sexual puritanism of the anti–sex trafficking movement.

For Agustín, however, the biggest problem with the TIP Report isn't even its racism and neocolonialism, but its utter lack of a research methodology or any social scientific validity. There are, she notes, fifty-two employees at the Office to Monitor and Combat Trafficking in Persons. She urges readers to

> imagine that such a report could be of great use to many people. In that case, I want to know how the data was gathered, which sources were consulted, who was allowed to give information, whose estimates were deemed authoritative and *how data were confirmed.* I want to know precisely how researchers handled the considerable international muddle over definitions, since the fact that people mean different things when they say the word *trafficking* is a notorious source of conflict and confusion, not to mention that a lot of the English keywords *cannot be reliably translated* into all other languages (for example, abuse, exploitation, force, coercion). Yet every year since the beginning the Report has fudged explaining how it's compiled. Instead of concrete information on methodology we get the vaguest of statements, really worthy of a Cold War spy operation.[121]

Local sex worker rights and anti-trafficking activists chafe against the US imposition of its prescriptions for trafficking. Writing of challenges in South Africa, Kadakwashe Vanyoro complains the that TIP Report categorizes South Africa as Tier 2 but provides "little to no empirical evidence to support this claim."[122] The policies imposed from outside the United States also influence the creation of laws from within South Africa that "perpetuate and build on stereotypes of vulnerable women without agency or choices, and draw on ideas of sex work as an activity that should be prevented and criminalized . . . [failing] to understand the complex realities that migrant women face" and construing all migrant women as "trafficked women, inherently vulnerable, and in need of rescue and protection."[123]

Agustin notes that the US Department of State consults various US and foreign officials, NGOs, and reports published in each country.[124] Essentially, the TIP Report compiles vague anecdotes and uncited references from nameless institutions and groups. There is no information on how the groups are chosen or whether the slightest bit of fact checking, verification, or gatekeeping has been done. It also used to be the case that at least one hundred cases of trafficking needed to be documented before a country was forced into being ranked for the TIP Report, but in 2008 this requirement was done away with, and now the United States simply ranks whomever they want. This may sound minor, but if sex trafficking is so ubiquitous that it is happening all around us in plain sight—as virtually every "consciousness raising" ad campaign in every airport and bus station would have us believe—then why would it be so difficult to find a mere one hundred victims per country that the threshold must be lowered to literally zero cases? It is almost as if the NGOs and dozens of US State Department employees making their careers in this rescue industry have a vested political and financial interest in the promotion of the idea that sexual slavery is endemic and that they should be given money to combat and prevent an invisible threat that is somehow everywhere and nowhere all at once.

END DEMAND

The final tool in the neocolonial policy toolbox is End Demand, the rescue industry's unanimously preferred approach. Sometimes known as the Swedish Model, Nordic Model, Equality Model, or sex buyers' laws, End Demand effectively decriminalizes the sale of sexual services while increasing penalties for the purchase of sexual services. For would-be progressives, this is an intoxicatingly clever bit of perceived good governance. Under End Demand, women are no longer charged with crimes for exercising bodily autonomy. In theory, when they are raped or exploited or violated, they can go to the police without fear of being arrested and charged with prostitution. They don't get placed on sex offender registries, and they shouldn't lose custody of their children under this system. Granted, End Demand aims to (often literally) starve women out of the sex industry and into the arms of rescue groups by putting them out of business for their own good. It is still paternalistic, just not as visibly violent.

End Demand doesn't work. It is the policy equivalent of a Whack-A-Mole game. When End Demand laws are passed—as they have been in Sweden, Norway, Ireland, France, and many other places—sex workers who can afford to move some of their business indoors or on-line quickly do so.[125] Visible street prostitution goes down. Taxpaying homeowners in gentrifying areas love it because they think the prostitution went away and their property values go up. Constituents and donors are pleased with their locally elected representatives. Liberals pat themselves on the back for having made the streets safer for children and other community members. Meanwhile, sex workers have to go to more hidden locations instead of the usual motels and parked cars: abandoned buildings, wooded areas, remote and isolated places. Sexual assault and violence against sex workers goes up. End Demand creates a secondary market for security, pimps, and third parties as women need to be protected. People who get left behind when End Demand hits are usually street-based women working in survival sex and working with addiction issues. These are often women of color and trans women. Disproportionately, the clients being scooped up in this carceral approach are men of color, furthering the racist prison industrial complex. End Demand makes mostly white middle-class folks feel good about "stopping exploitation" while consolidating their financial privilege precisely *at the expense of* women of color (often trans women of color) and the most vulnerable sex workers. It is impossible to institute an End Demand approach that is not fundamentally rooted in white supremacy.

End Demand is becoming popular because of the visible "improvements" it provides, but it is not actually successful at reducing prostitution or harm. As the sociologist Niina Vuolajärvi argues, End Demand disproportionately harms migrants, who often face eviction and deportation in what she terms "punitive humanitarianism." Vuolajärvi spent two years interviewing 113 sex workers and 82 officials, police, and health-care workers in Sweden, Finland, and Norway, noting that a particular problem faced by sex workers under the law is housing because landlords are afraid they themselves will be charged with pimping or trafficking.[126] As Boglárka Fedorkó explains, "In June 2019, two sex workers, one of whom was pregnant, were jailed for nine months in Ireland. The two Romanian women were selling sexual services from a flat they shared for safety when they were raided by the police. Selling sex is legal in Ireland, which has implemented the so-called Swedish model . . . but because there were two of them the police were able to charge them both with brothel keeping, which isn't legal."[127] She goes on to note that "in Sweden, the mere assumption that a migrant person will not support themselves by 'honest means' is sufficient grounds for denial of entry. As Swedish policies openly declare that victims of trafficking should not be reintegrated into society in Sweden, but rather in their country of origin."[128] When functioning at its best, the Swedish Model aims to drive sex workers out of business by making clients afraid of arrest and prosecution. Starving women out of the sex industry is the best-case scenario. But instead, even under the Swedish Model, migrant sex workers are denied entry, targeted, arrested, monitored, and deported.

In the context of Nigerian migrant sex workers, Sine Plambech has described a "deportation economy" in which the "state-funded deportation for migrants has emerged as a business opportunity for private companies worldwide since 2001," noting that private corporations "have been investigated by the UK's Serious Fraud Office for allegedly charging for tagging migrants who were dead or did not exist" in order to "pay attention to efficiency and the cost of not filling up the charted planes heading to Nigeria."[129] The money fueling this xenophobic deportation economy comes from religious congregations as well as USAID, UN offices, European Union (EU) offices, the Ford Foundation (normally a progressive darling of academics), and European governments that prefer to repatriate them rather than grant asylum.[130] End Demand approaches that push migrant sex workers into parastatal processes that earn profit for deporting people demonstrate that the current policy rush toward the Swedish Model is predicated on xenophobia, racism, and collaboration with the carceral state.

In *Criminalising the Purchase of Sex*, Jay Levy writes that "this trafficking panic in Sweden occurred in spite of levels of prostitution in the country having never been demonstrably high and in spite of the existence of little evidence of escalating trafficking in the 1990s."[131] Instead, he attributes the panic in Sweden to widespread fears about immigrants. "A concern over an influx of foreign bodies through sex work in migration and human trafficking was coupled with associations with organized crime, drugs and HIV, with broader fears and racisms surrounding immigrants generally, and with the prospective influence of liberal, strange and *foreign* ideas and values."[132] But regardless of its unintended consequences and spurious motivating factors, has the Swedish Model succeeded in decreasing prostitution? "There is no convincing evidence demonstrating that overall levels of prostitution in Sweden have declined since the *sexköpslagen* [sex law] was introduced in 1999."[133] In a somewhat different vein, Yvonne Svanström argues that the consensus in Sweden that now exists around End Demand was "enabled by the embedding of the question in the larger issue of human rights, rather than the issue of male demand," which had been central to the original 1999 law.[134] (The co-opting of human rights rhetoric is a subject I take up in chapter 5 in my analysis of "femonationalism.") Anita Heber's research on Sweden found actual sex trafficking there to be an "elusive crime," noting that over a ten-year period the number of annual cases reported to the police increased from fifteen to eighty-one, while actual convictions ranged from zero to six.[135] This shows heightened awareness and concern about an issue but provides little evidence of the existence of said crime. And this is in a country whose well-funded and sympathetic political establishment is highly focused on rooting out sex trafficking and takes as broad a definition of the crime as possible.

New Zealand, on the other hand, has followed the decriminalization route. Lynzi Armstrong, a lecturer in criminology in Wellington, New Zealand, writes that "myths abound regarding New Zealand's model, including unsubstantiated claims that the sex industry has expanded, with pimps emboldened in the wake of the new law, and that sex trafficking is rife."[136] She says that when the law took effect, one condition of its passage was that its effects must be studied. "Researchers from the University of Otago's School of Medicine, highlighted many benefits: more than 60 percent of the 772 sex workers who participated reported feeling more able to refuse to see certain clients, and 95 percent said they felt they had rights after decriminalization."[137] Despite this evidence, neo-abolitionists continue to proselytize on behalf of racist and ineffective polies such as End Demand. Moreover, they also continue to bolster neocolonial policy tools such as APLO and the TIP Report without adequately reflecting on the racial dimensions of these approaches.

CONCLUSION

The anti–sex trafficking movement relies on the deployment of racialized spectacle to enact neocolonial policy agendas and capitalize on "third world" suffering to justify the rescue industry's continued existence. The abolitionist movement's turn toward the scopophilic explains why something like the anti-trafficking safari I described earlier is an ideal form of activism. It is rooted in an economy of affects—outrage, disgust, indignation, pleasure, guilt—that requires no meaningful intervention beyond looking. For the Christians, the rhetoric of "bearing witness" to the spectacle of suffering provides strong cover. The gaze of these safaris is crafted from a white Western standpoint and actively constructs the "third world" Other as an object for visual consumption, to be gawked at, furtively glanced at, photographed, or videotaped. The travelers can leer freely in ways that would be antagonistic if the locals returned the gaze. This allows the recreation of the colonial encounter in which the tourist of sex trafficking can return home to their church or university with documentary evidence of suffering and the ability to narrativize their travel, socially misremembering it as somehow equally meaningful to the object of their gaze while simultaneously furthering demand among their Western peers to go and witness such spectacles of suffering for themselves.

The World Cup and the Olympic Games are their own kind of safaris. They invite tourists to come and behold the local marvels of the host countries and the visiting delegations. The Olympics even has "hospitality houses" in which various countries host themed food, drinks, games, and activities representing their countries. But these mega-events are also political events. They do not simply happen; they must be negotiated and sought after. Countries compete with one another to see who can seduce FIFA and the IOC. Just as they are occurring amid particular political and economic contexts, they are also occurring within what Denise Brennan referred to as "sexscapes": the sexual terrain of that place's political economy.[138]

I began this chapter with a thickly described snapshot of a real-world brothel snapped during the World Cup in Rio de Janeiro, but I have traced in this chapter the long history of the anti–sex trafficking movement that ultimately led up to the moment when that brothel and the other Brazilian sex venues came to occupy the full attention of the anti-prostitution alliance that sought to close it. The arrival of Exodus Cry in Brazil for the World Cup and the Olympics and its visits to brothels around the country and rallies to pray away the trafficking must be understood within a history of antislavery activities that began with the xenophobic and racist moral panics over "white slavery" and that now function as part of a neocolonial effort to spectacularize sex trafficking in an effort to eradicate all prostitution, which is, de facto, sexual slavery.

In order to understand the political and symbolic significance of Western anti–sex trafficking groups descending on a "third world" country to do battle with traffickers and rescue women, we must be able to position that activity within the history of the anti-trafficking movement. And that means acknowledging that the history in question is rooted in white supremacy: from the white slave trade panic to anti-miscegenation laws, from xenophobia to the suppression of comprehensive immigration reform, from its fixation with the racialized figure of the pimp to the deracialization and dehistoricization of histories of Black slavery, from noblesse oblige to the founding of a white savior rescue industry, from the anti-prostitution loyalty oath to the TIP report, the anti–sex trafficking movement is rooted in anti-Blackness, neocolonialism, and white first world narcissism that it feeds at the expense of sex workers. The raids and rescue operations that I've described in this book to this point are just examples that can go into this damning list of positions and activities, yet they are important ones. Framed within this genealogy, the supposed interventions during these events must also be understood as occurring within a particular *racial* context and a *racist* history, not only a political and economic one. The mega-event is a relatively new battleground in an old conflict. And it's on this battleground that the war against sex trafficking has found its greatest weapon: the spectacular.

CHAPTER 2

Panic at the Gringo

As I stood in Rio de Janeiro's Praça do Lido, immediately adjacent to the shuttered Balcony Bar, among the hundreds of sex workers and clients, I noticed two Iranian men in their forties. The two men looked like a Persian version of what Brazilians call O Gordo e O Magro, or what people in the US know as Laurel and Hardy. One of them was short and fat and loud, the other tall and skinny and shy. It was easy to deduce their nationality as Iranian because they wore matching clothes, including T-shirts emblazoned with the word IRAN. They each wore a matching white tank top undershirt underneath, visible by its ribbed outline, and black socks with Iranian flags on the shins pulled up to their knees. A few centimeters of hairy knees appeared between the men's socks and their matching khaki cargo shorts, which were obscured by their fanny packs, which bulged with wads of money, maps, guidebooks, and electronics. They both wore nearly identical watches, which were also enormous and looked far too expensive to wear out in Copacabana at night. It seemed impossible to me that these gringos would still be in possession of all these belongings in the morning.

O Gordo and O Magro tried to negotiate with a Brazilian prostitute. She was a *branca* (a white woman) with black hair, maybe thirty years old, wearing a short dress that, by design, didn't quite cover her *bunda* (butt). O Gordo was doing the talking, asking her how much. She wanted 300 reais (then about US$100), but he offered 200 (then about US$67). He struggled to speak English, and they had some difficulty with one another's accents. He took out his iPhone and used it to type the number 200. He pointed at it emphatically. Then he said, "for both of us."

"Both of you?" she asked. "Together?" She looked confused at this request.

"No!" he said, looking disgusted. "First me. Then him." O Gordo smiled in satisfaction at this plan. She looked from O Gordo to O Magro. O Magro gave a sheepish look, lowering his gaze and shrugging.

The woman looked back to O Gordo, rolled her eyes at the pair of them, and walked away. She approached another gringo. This one was younger, around thirty years old, muscular and handsome. But this guy didn't have a lot of money. The women's prices were higher than he expected so he only wanted a blowjob, hoping it would be cheap. She gave him a dirty look, looking unimpressed at the prospect of losing prime time for programas doing cheap blowjobs. They began to move off together, though, so she seemed amenable enough to acquiesce to what would at least be a fast bit of cash. O Gordo and O Magro watched her leave with the beefy guy. They stood there a moment, a brief ring of empty space encircling them. There they were, alone together and unable to get laid even in a crowd of prostitutes. O Gordo huffed, refusing to look at O Magro, then appeared to steel his nerve to talk to another woman.

Two young white women in their early twenties approached him before he could move. These women wore their blonde hair in the kind of straight style of Zona Sul garotas (and women who want to look like they are from the touristy Zona Sul.) They seemed to be friends and to know each other well. They were clearly travestis to my eyes, but at that time I interacted with travestis and transgender women nearly every day. I felt they could easily "pass" as cisgender for most people not familiar with the particular nuances of gender performativity among Brazilian travestis, which is a different gender subjectivity than transgender, but adjacent to it. Typically, travestis do not seek out any kind of genital surgeries, and those who sell sex are most often *ativo*, or "tops" who take the penetrative role. (Usually this is part of the appeal for their clients, who identify as straight men.) I thought the Iranians had not noticed. They barely looked at the women before O Gordo began his haggling, punching numbers into the phone's calculator screen.

One woman kept O Magro busy while the other berated O Gordo for his unrealistic bargaining attempts. The women kept exchanging glances and muttering in Portuguese to each other about these stingy gringos ("*pão duro*," literally "hard bread") even as one of them also struggled to communicate her displeasure to O Gordo in English.

"Where you stay?" she asked, not even bothering to flirt or be seductive.

O Gordo lit up. He understood something! "Barra! We stay Barra da Tijuca! Very nice hotel!" O Gordo proclaimed, using improper English in an effort to be more legible though he spoke it fluently. Barra da Tijuca is a famously expensive area for rich cariocas and tourists who want to stay far from the city's noise (or don't understand how far it is from the main attractions).

More meaningful glances between the prostitutes. A nod.

One woman agreed to the price on the phone: 200 reais.

"200 for her. 200 for me," she explained.

"200 total!" O Gordo said.

"No," the woman said slowly, patiently, as if speaking to a child. "200 for her. 200 for me. One hour."

"OK," agreed O Gordo.

"We take taxi now to Barra. We go to hotel with you," she explained, dragging him to the curb to hail a cab. His enormous watch reflected in the street lights. "First you pay. You pay us now."

O Magro walked nervously along behind O Gordo, who was looking very excited about the impending sexual escapades now that the financial discussion was finished.

I wondered what would happen when they arrived in the wealthy neighborhood at their fancy hotel and attempted to take the women back to their room. I imagined the receptionist trying to explain to O Gordo that his travesti friends could not accompany him and that they would need to find a *motel* for such things. In Brazil, one typically is not allowed by management to bring unregistered guests to *hoteis* (hotels). *Moteis* (motels), by definition, rent by the hour and are where many Brazilians, including young people who may live at home until marriage, unashamedly go to have sex. Of course, the women knew this already—but by then they would already have their money, or they would be able to ask for more money for the extra time. O Gordo did not ask when his hour began. Barra was a long way away, perhaps forty minutes. Of course, if they got to the hotel and he did not want to pay, the women could make an *escandalo* (scandal). The anthropologist Don Kulick interviewed Brazilian travesti prostitutes extensively about their tactics for extracting additional money from clients by "making a scandal" in public to call attention to the men's sexual congress with them.[1] I wished I could be in the lobby to see the performance.

Or perhaps the Iranians would somehow succeed in getting the women past the receptionist to their room. I wondered what would happen when they realized one of the women was a travesti. Would O Gordo be surprised? Angry? Excited? Or perhaps he was savvier than I thought, and he knew all along. I wondered if the men were as careless with their valuables in the hotel room as they were with the valuables they carried on the street. And I wondered what other *jeitinhos* (tricks, clever little ways) the women might have in store for them tonight. I made a note to look for the women the next night in the plaza and to ask them how it went, but I never saw them again. I hoped they had vanished from the commercial sex scene because the night had such a happy ending for them and not a bad one, but I never learned what happened. Such is the nature of ethnography sometimes.

GOOD GRINGOS AND PHARISEES

In the run-up to the Brazilian Cup, there was a great deal of media hype about predatory foreigners and the idea that gringos were coming to kidnap children, exploit women, and cause harm. What follows is an examination of the ways in which poorly conceived ideas about "gringos" contributed to the development of this situation. I juxtapose this ill-conceived figure of the predatory gringo with interviews, participant observations, and ethnographic data about gringos to argue that the World Cup and Olympics in Brazil did not bring predatory gringos, as imagined during the panic, but actually brought unusually naïve gringos whom prostitutes saw as easy prey. Rather than clients exploiting prostitutes, prostitutes routinely described how easy it was to rob, pickpocket, bamboozle, and even beat up and mug clients during major sporting events. This is not to say, of course, that all sex workers did this or that sex workers are prone to criminality, especially not those who are professionalized as full-time workers with reputations and long-standing relationships with clients. Yet the World Cup presented women with the opportunity to take advantage of an especially clueless bunch of clients, and many proudly did, even if it didn't extend to outright robbery.

Despite the fact that neither prostitution nor sex trafficking increased during the Cup, US media continued to run sensationalistic headlines such as one in the *Huffington Post* that proclaimed: "Children Sold for Sex at World Cup for Few Dollars, Pack of Cigarettes."[2] Meanwhile, Human Trafficking Search (a project of the peculiarly shadowy OLP Foundation) claimed, "In the year prior to the FIFA World Cup, girls from the impoverished areas of Brazil began to go missing. . . . Many of the young women were kidnapped from the slums of Brazil

FIGURE 4. Poster hanging near Balcony Bar showing a member of the Brazilian World Cup team encouraging people to report the exploitation of children and adolescents. Photo by Amanda De Lisio.

by sex traffickers and taken to the FIFA World Cup sites where they were used to service the construction workers building the soccer stadiums."[3] As evidence, the project links to a story in a British tabloid referring to unsourced, unsubstantiated rumors, told second (or possibly third) hand, that the Russian mafia was trafficking girls within Brazil and also bringing sex slaves from Africa to Brazil. This claim is highly dubious considering that our team of a dozen highly trained social scientists from top universities with decades of experience in Rio's sexual economy spent thousands of hours collectively examining all manner of situations and levels of prostitution occurring in hundreds of venues, including the lower-end ones frequented by local construction workers in Rio de Janeiro, and we found very few Brazilian women who had traveled from anywhere outside Rio for the Cup and only one non-Brazilian: a Peruvian woman working at 4 × 4 who complained that she was used to making more money working in Lima than she was getting during the Cup. We found not a single migrant woman from anywhere in Africa and no evidence that any of the brothels had suddenly been infiltrated by Russians. And yet foreign tabloids that didn't even bother to send a reporter to the field were quick to panic locals with stories of foreigners engaging in heinous acts.

All of this fearmongering about gringos and recruitment into sex trafficking for the World Cup and then Olympics in Brazil came to constitute what we might call the Great Gringo Panic of 2013–2016. In thinking about the uneasiness and fear surrounding the arrival of large numbers of gringos, it's important to understand that in Brazil, *gringo* is not really the quasi-racialized epithet that it can be in the United States, Mexico, and the borderlands area between the two. Rather, in Brazil, it is a much more neutral term meaning "foreigner," and a gringo may be of any race. (I've even heard Brazilians from one part of the country refer to their fellow countrymen from farther away as gringos.) Yet whenever the subject of sex tourism comes up in Brazil and especially during the moral panic preceding the sporting events, the term gringo could quickly take on a lot of additional connotations. Despite prostitutes' own feelings of agency, evangelicals and radical feminist groups staged protests to warn of the coming surge of gringo sex traffickers and buyers. Femen had its topless protests in the airport and Copacabana Palace Hotel in Rio (which I return to in the next chapter). But a group of Brazilian and foreign missionaries also chained themselves to the front of the Golden Tulip Hotel in the Brazilian city of Recife, demanding to "break the silence" about sex trafficking.[4]

The 2014 World Cup in Brazil was a success in terms of numbers for the tourism industry. In Rio de Janeiro, the host city with the most number of visitors, there were 471,000 gringo tourists and 415,000 domestic Brazilian visitors during the Cup, with an average expenditure of a couple hundred dollars per day.[5] Thus, it's no surprise that the prostitutes in Brazil thought they would make a lot of money and began making preparations such as taking English classes to prepare for the influx.[6] There are a lot of strange beliefs about football fans looking for sex. As Melissa Gira Grant puts it: "The fantasy asks us to imagine the visiting packs of excitable men, engorged by victory or deflated by defeat. Who will celebrate with them? Who will soothe them? Worse, all that running and ball-chasing (or just watching it) is said to stoke a demand for sex so high that it would exhaust a city's native sex industry."[7] She goes on to argue that "like all fantasies, the 'roving sporting sex workers' trope should be mostly harmless. It tells us about our culture's deeply held myths and fears about sex work . . . it's an innocuous fantasy—until seized upon by those who find it threatening or politically useful."[8]

True to Grant's warning, the "reforms" in Copacabana justified during this time of "gringo panic" created conditions that made women selling sex in Rio de Janeiro *more* vulnerable and marginalized—not less—and highlight that the real dangers for these women come not from gringos but from police. The state was able to act with impunity in part because parastatal alliances of missionaries and NGOs and feminists are so hyper-focused on their gringo watching. But their understanding of the gringo was misinformed, and it's important to critically interrogate the nature of the gringo client. Studying gringo interactions also creates an opportunity for analyzing performances of masculinity and how they are interpellated cross-culturally into new social contexts and, indeed, how gringo masculinity functions as a polyvalent signifier.

O Gordo and O Magro were typical tourists purchasing sex during the World Cup in several ways. As the earlier ethnographic description illustrates—rendered from my field notes—they were not experts in the sexual economy; in fact, they were quite naïve. They did not know the appropriate prices. They lacked any linguistic facility with Portuguese and had difficulty understanding the women's attempts at English. They did not understand how the mechanics of a programa work or what details they should have negotiated: *How long is it? Where does one go for the programa? Which acts exactly are included? Will condoms be used and, if so, who should provide them? When should one pay? How much should one pay based on the answers to these questions?* In fact, the Iranians were such poor sex tourists that they were shy about approaching and negotiating with multiple women. They eventually each got their own prostitute, but only because the women were working together. They almost ended up in a threesome with one another, but it seemed that would have been because of the awkwardness of the negotiation and not because they actually wanted to share a woman or have some homosocial or homoerotic bond. These gringos bungled their attempt to pay women for sex so badly that they almost ended the night in bed with each other.

In fact, members of the Observatório and I saw this pattern again and again. Some tourists during the World Cup had not come to specifically purchase programas. Many of them came to the Praça to look at the titillating scene but did not want to pay for sex, though some considered it or eventually would be persuaded by the women's sales pitch. Women complained that the gringos wanted to chat, maybe buy them a drink, and that they all wanted to take selfies with them for Facebook or Instagram but did not want to buy. They were *bad gringos*. They wasted the women's time and took them away from clients who might actually pay. Or they took so long to give in to the pressure that they were a waste of time. Overwhelmingly, gringos during the Cup overpaid for programas. Regular sex tourists who come to Brazil frequently know how much a programa in a given venue with a given woman should cost. The gringos during the World Cup were easily taken advantage of financially. Thus, there was something of a paradox in that many of the gringos were cheap—*pão duro*, as the women called them—and yet many of them also overpaid in the end. That both of these things could be true of the gringos is a testament to the shrewdness and performative competence of the sex workers.

Like the Iranians, I saw many instances of gringos becoming flustered and asking if they could share a woman. In fact, *immediately* after the Iranians left, I heard two Italian men who were in their mid-twenties approach a young morena woman in her late teens or early twenties and ask her to have sex with both of them. They hoped to get a discount by doing this. She responded in Portuguese, saying she was too tired for something like that. It was the beginning of the night, before most women had even caught their first programa, so it was more likely that she wanted to make more money and not give discounts. The men kept asking, and she offered to find them a second woman, but they really wanted the threesome with the discount. Just as with the Iranians, the first woman walked away dismissively, and a pair of women working together stepped up immediately and solicited them so they could each have their own. But again, they didn't want to pay double.

The Italians imagined themselves to be shrewd negotiators. They acted as if they would walk away but then turned back to negotiate again. Then they really did try the tactic of walking away, looking over their shoulders to see if the women would relent and call them back rather than lose the programa. It wasn't a very convincing act. The women just let them keep walking. Of course, anyone with experience would know that no prostitute is going to give a 50 percent discount for the very first programa of the night and certainly not for the opening night of the Cup, when they all still expected to make a small fortune. At the *end* of a slow night, prostitutes certainly might do this, and some will even give free programas for the opportunity to sleep over and save themselves a long commute or expensive taxi ride back to the Zona Norte (North Zone) where many live. (Taxi drivers know this and sometimes appear at the end of the night with offers to exchange rides for oral sex.)

The Italian guys eventually stopped walking and, looking forlornly back at the women they desired, pulled out their wallets. They put their heads together, whispering, and began counting their money to see if they had enough reais to meet the women's price. The last I saw them, they were walking slowly back to the women with empty wallets offering all the money they had for the chance at a programa. The women smiled. These were good gringos.

According to the anthropologist Thad Blanchette, the women have various nomenclature to describe gringos.[9] Their understanding of gringos is different than the imagery of gringos used by the government and even by popular media. The prostitutes speak of "good gringos" (*gringos bons*). According to Blanchette, "For the prostitutes in Copacabana, the 'good gringo' is a newcomer who speaks little or no Portuguese and pays for *programas* without haggling."[10] As women collectively explained to me in the field: good gringos pay well, much more than Brazilians. A good gringo uses a condom, is polite, doesn't attempt to have anal sex or engage in other activities he did not negotiate, and cums quickly. A good gringo can become a regular customer and often be landed for longer periods of time so that the woman can do multiple programas with him over the span of his visit(s). Sometimes a good gringo takes her as a girlfriend or presents immigration opportunities. Many prostitutes reported to Blanchette and Ana Paula da Silva that when they found a good gringo, they would try to get pregnant so as to leverage the man into immigration or providing monthly remittances.[11] This is also a phenomenon studied at great length by the Brazilian social scientist Renata Melo Rosa, whose research shows that love and emotional attachments spur transnational migrations of Brazilian women in complicated ways that blur edges of constructs such as "sexual tourism."[12] Alternatively, this strategy of impregnation could also end quite badly for women carrying any disowned children of gringos, of course.

Prostitutes in Rio also speak disparagingly of gringos whom they refer to with the slang word Pharisees (*fariseus*), a term that reflects the evangelical Christian background of many of them. Pharisees are gringos who feel they are morally above buying a *programa*. The gringos who wasted women's time offering them drinks and wanting to chat and take selfies for social media but who would not buy a *programa* because they believed that they should not "need" to pay for sex were Pharisees. As one prostitute explained to Blanchette in the Observatório's field site, "A Pharisee is a gringo who thinks he is better than us. He speaks Portuguese and knows how to act like a Brazilian. He doesn't fuck or get off: he just likes to have a girl around at his table, serving as scenery, making him feel good, but when it's time for the *programa*, he doesn't want to pay."[13]

It's also worth noting how thoroughly heterosexual the gringo subject is. During the World Cup, business in the gay saunas dropped to almost nothing, and the male sex workers could sometimes go entire days without a *programa*. The straight gringo fans crowded the touristy neighborhood of Ipanema, which historically has a big gay contingent and a famous gay beach. Some venues on the beach and surrounding areas removed their rainbow flags because the gringos would stand at a distance and refuse to enter. The moment the flags came down, the gringos rushed the new sections of beach and the venues. The Olympics, which last a much shorter time, have a somewhat gayer and more family-oriented fan base. (Somewhat true to type, gay tourists I spoke to during the 2016 Olympics were especially excited about men's diving, men's swimming, men's volleyball, and men's and women's gymnastics.) The male sex workers did decent business, although there are many hundreds more heterosexual commercial sex venues in Rio. The heteronormativity and homophobia of the FIFA fan base, however, is undeniably real.

British tabloids even ran stories about the desirability of heterosexual English lads. The *Mirror* proclaimed, "Brazilian Women Turning to

Prostitution for World Cup—and England fans are their biggest goal: The working girls of Rio's Vila Mimosa red light district are offering cut-price 'specials' for England fans because 'they have travelled so far.'"[14] The reporter in question did not understand the logic of the prostitutes, who did not want to target gringos because they had come so far, but because they had more money than most Brazilians and Latin American visitors and could more easily be taken advantage of. Far from being given a discount, these good gringos were going to be ripped off while being made to *think* that they had gotten a good deal.

In her research on tourism in the Bahamas, M. Jacqui Alexander points out that the state remakes itself for tourists, even going so far as to attempt to educate or train locals how to adapt to large influxes of tourists "even if the tourists annoy them," as one public service announcement put it.[15] "A major symbol in the state-organized system for the tourist depended on the organization and creation of paradise, with all of its comforts and contents," which included attempts at imposing order, cleanliness, and tidiness to appeal to gringos used to "hard-nosed, high pressure North American management techniques" that were otherwise at odds with island culture.[16] "Ultimately, tourism as a metasystem makes it possible for the state to circumscribe boundaries around the nation while servicing imperialism. The evidence for this is that the state simultaneously reenacts the dissolution of the nation through these political economic gestures, which it ideologically recodes as natural, as (super)natural, or as savior of the people."[17] During mega-events such as the World Cup and Olympics, the state's performance and reenactment of hypernationalism similarly recodes all participating countries in essentialist and nationalist terms with great emphasis on patriotic imagery, flags, and discourse about the "essential characteristics" of particular nationalities. This even manifests in the Olympics in the form of cultural houses in which each participating country gets to display various ephemera deemed quintessential by the organizers. (Disturbingly but somewhat predictably, when I visited these in Rio, all the African nations had to share a house and present as a single culture.) Yet the gringo tourists catered to by the parastate may not always behave or live up to the expectations of the host country working so hard to "create paradise" for them.

The anthropologist Erica L. Williams conducted a book-length study of sex tourism in Bahia, in Brazil's northeast, a place known for its high concentrations of African American and Italian clients. She notes that the Brazilians had particular disdain for the Italian gringos, whom they commonly "described as men from lower-class backgrounds who took advantage of the privileges of their foreign currency" and whose presence and behavior prompted the tourism minister to say "we don't want this type of visitor in our country."[18] Locals complained that they spent as little as possible and provoked disagreements. Often, the tourists in Williams's study were factory workers, security guards, and laborers in blue-collar positions. These "second-class" visitors were known in Williams's field site as "C and D class foreigners," "*turistas* McDonalds," and "*duristas*"—which Williams points out is a Portuguese pun combining the words for "broke" (*duro*) and "tourists" (*turistas*).[19] In other words, the locals saw the Italian gringos in Bahia in terms similar to how the carioca prostitutes described Pharisees, including the Italians and Iranians in the earlier ethnographic description.

The women I interviewed also spoke at length about *gringos latinos*. The countries with the most number of attendees were (in order): Argentina, Chile, Colombia, Ecuador, the United States, France, Mexico, England, and Germany, with a total of 192,000 gringos latinos and 60,000 other gringos from those top countries.[20] "There are gringos and then there are gringos latinos," Priscilla explained. "Gringos are good. They are much better than Brazilians! But gringos latinos are horrible. . . . [T]he gringo latino never wants to pay. He has no money but he thinks [he] should get sex anyway! Ridiculous!" When I asked who among the gringos latinos was the worst, she quickly singled out two nationalities. "The Chileans!" she said, rolling her eyes. "Always these little guys biting at your ankles! They want pussy, pussy, pussy but they have no money! Oh, and Argentines, of course." Women often complained about having sex with Argentines, but this also reflected general football and sociopolitical rivalries. There were also many caravans in Rio from these two countries. "They come here and they think that pussy is going to be 20 *reais*!" Priscilla laughed. "Take that down to the Centro, go to the *fast fodas* (type of brothel) where it's a *real* per minute. For an hour long programa? I expect you to come to the street in Copacabana and bring me 250, 300. Sometimes I get 400. My friend made 500 from a good gringo once." Groups of gringos latinos would stay with six or seven men in a van or car, sleeping in the parked vehicle. These large groups of Latino gringos were an irritation to Brazilian police and to other businesses, not only prostitutes. In an interview I conducted with an FBI agent from the United States who was working with the military police and civil police in Brazil on World Cup security issues, he explained that the police were always dealing with misbehaving bands of

Chilean gringos who were partying in the streets, getting drunk, getting into fights, and generally causing trouble.

There are expert sex tourists who participate in message boards and leave reviews and updates on brothels and on individual women. They refer to themselves as "mongers" (from the term *whoremonger*) and have extended debates on the finer points of sexual tourism in Brazil and sometimes elsewhere, depending on whether they are specialists in Brazil or are generalists who purchase sex in other countries and regions. They pride themselves on never overpaying and on being as cheap as possible. They often speak Portuguese, or at least enough to negotiate effectively. They fancy themselves connoisseurs of Rio's sexual economy. The women dislike such gringos, finding them irritating or at least disappointing, but can respect them because they are essentially gringos who know something of Brazil and behave more like a Brazilian client.

There is a disjuncture between the government's portrayal of gringos, which casts them as predators, and the prostitutes' understanding of gringos. The government is always concerned about gringo sex tourists who may exploit women or children, but to emphasize the predatory nature of gringo sex tourists during major events relies on stereotypes of football fans as hypermasculine, sexually aggressive, and immoral. This reliance combines sexist ideas about masculinity with assumptions that sports fans will be more likely to harm women and children. There is, in fact, no evidence whatsoever that a sports fan would be more likely to sexually exploit someone than a gringo who doesn't like sports. In fact, it would make more sense that the gringo coming for a sporting event would be there mainly for the soccer and would find sex incidental; he's not likely to go out of his way to find some underground, less visible brothel with underage girls. He is not knowledgeable enough to access the darkest parts of an underground economy. If he purchases sex, he is likely to get it in the most touristy venue possible, which is the highest paid zone for women to work in, namely the area around Balcony, which was also the *least* likely to have underage prostitutes—at least until the government closed Balcony Bar and prostitution spilled into the backstreets and dark alleys.

POLICE RESPONSES IN GRINGO SPACES

I briefly described the morning raid on Balcony Bar (which was shuttered the opening day of the World Cup) earlier in this book, but it is worth giving a fuller account of the raids on that venue and the surrounding area. It's important to understand how the police behaved in touristy areas that were densely populated with gringos—many of them looking to patronize the prostitutes—and how police officers' behavior changed depending on whether or not they were policing in front of cameras (crafting the spectacle of policing and putting on a show).

The military police arrived at Balcony Bar in Copacabana the morning of the opening day ceremonies for the 2014 World Cup.[21] They brought cameramen with them from O Globo, a major news network that at that time was roughly in the same vein as Fox News. Balcony Bar was infamous as a restaurant/bar on the *orla* (beachfront) where gringos could meet prostitutes before leaving to complete *programas* off-site. However, prostitution is not illegal in Brazil, and prostitutes working in the area are within their rights to frequent whatever bars or establishments they wish, so long as they do not disturb the peace. On slow weekdays, one could still find a few dozen women working at Balcony, and on weekends one could find a hundred or so women inside, on the patio, or standing just outside. Balcony was a family-friendly establishment during the day, but around 10:00 p.m. prostitutes would begin to arrive. Balcony profited from the prostitution only inasmuch as they sold food and drink to the patrons. Unfortunately, Balcony was also located across the street from the FIFA Fan Fest viewing area on Copacabana beach, the central viewing area (with an enormous screen) and the most visible part of Rio during the World Cup in the eyes of journalists. Balcony and its hundreds of clients and prostitutes were right at the heart of Rio's World Cup festivities. Balcony and the women who sold sexual services there were thrilled at this placement, imagining this would be great for business. They were wrong.

On that first day of the Cup, the police shuttered Balcony Bar, hanging a sign on the door that said it was ordered to suspend all economic activity and being charged with "*favorecimento da prostituição ou de outra forma de exploração sexual de criança ou adolescente ou de vulnerável*" (roughly, encouraging prostitution or other forms of child, adolescent, or other exploitation of the vulnerable). There was never any formal charge or conviction. Facing endless expensive legal battles, the owner eventually stopped fighting.

That evening, I went with colleagues to watch what would happen when the women came to work and found it closed. Clients came too. People began jovially chanting, "Open! Open! Open!" in Portuguese. They laughed and stood next to Balcony. Someone inked the police sign with a little stamp reading "FUCK FIFA." That night, around two hundred garotas de programa and another two hundred potential clients partied in the Praça do Lido right outside of Balcony and on the patio area of the now closed venue. The prostitutes clung close enough to Balcony Bar to continue using its Wi-Fi signal. *Ambulantes* (mobile venders) seized the business opportunity to sell beer and snacks.

That night, I saw three girls standing between cars on the edges of the scene who looked to me to be clearly underage. This was the great irony of the raid. Balcony had never had underage girls. My colleagues and I were there hundreds of nights doing fieldwork over the years and never saw a single case of a minor working inside the venue. On rare occasions, there would be underage teenage girls working in the surrounding area on the streets and beaches, but not inside the Balcony. In 2012, O Globo ran an exposé in which the interviewer spoke to two underage girls (sixteen and seventeen years of age) who had fake IDs and were working in the area. In sensationalistic fashion, O Globo made it seem as if Balcony Bar itself were a den of child prostitution that needed to be closed immediately. Two years later, on the morning of the World Cup opening ceremony, O Globo was there to film the final raid that shuttered the venue for good. In truth, managers were vigilant about keeping such girls out—and so were the working women—out of not maternal instincts but capitalist ones, as they loudly and angrily directed girls to go get themselves fucked elsewhere rather than on this particular patch of beachfront. Now with Balcony closed for only a few hours, suddenly underage teenaged girls were able to work the main sexual marketplace in Praça do Lido where all the women of age were working.

During the Cup, I observed on a nightly basis that there were almost always three or four younger teenagers working in the street among the revelers at Praça do Lido. They would usually not stand in the heart of the plaza itself but rather loiter between parked cars where they were less visible and could easily pretend not to be part of the scene if police hassled them. (This is in contrast to the older women, who wanted maximum visibility in the center of the action.) Other researchers observed the same thing, and we recorded in our field notes that there were always a few foreign men who would go over to chat with the girls and leave with them, presumably for programas. To be clear, it would be a gross misinterpretation of these data to say that the World Cup caused a statistically significant spike in underage prostitution in Rio de Janeiro. However, the forced closure of Balcony Bar, at least one hotel in the area, and eventually several other nearby clubs known for facilitating sex work in the area certainly corresponded with the appearance or relocalization of a small amount of consistent underage prostitution in an area where it had not had an opportunity to flourish before. It is also worth noting that the girls in question were not prepubescent children. I've spent over fifteen years watching these spaces and interviewing the women and girls, and I would estimate they were probably between fifteen and seventeen years old. That is, I believe they were old enough to legally consent to *have sex* with such men (age fourteen in Brazil) but did not appear old enough to legally consent to *sell sex* to them (age eighteen in Brazil).

When outside groups refer to child prostitution (*prostituição infantil*) they usually are referring to teenagers who are often *above* the age of consent for sex, but the use of the word *child* intentionally conjures up images of much younger children. The discourse of sex trafficking requires the circulation of particular mythologies rooted in the Victorian "cult of the child," which is why anti-prostitution groups rely on imagery of children (usually white girls) that emphasizes innocence and purity. Such appeals to emotion rest on the assumption that children are unagentive. In fact, in-depth ethnographic research by Anthony Marcus and Amber Horning shows that no real prototypical pimp exists and that anti-trafficking activists vastly overestimate the presence of pimps or market facilitators and their role in recruitment, observing that the relationships such people have with minors can seem surprisingly flexible and dynamic as described from the teenagers' perspectives.[22] Because those in the anti-trafficking movement don't understand the experiences of the minors, they develop interventions that either don't work or are rejected by the underage sex workers, which results in the continuation of sexual exploitation within the underground sexual economy.

The initial observations by the Observatóio in Rio don't reveal whether this underage teenage prostitution was a redistribution of labor that simply made girls already working elsewhere in Rio de Janeiro more visible or whether the girls in question turned up for the World Cup like so many adult women, looking to make some money off the gringos. However, what is clear is that had the sexual commerce been allowed to continue safely and legally at Balcony Bar, then it would have been very difficult for underage girls to work that area of the beachfront with easy access to the World Cup tourists. There is no evidence that there was an actual increase overall in underage sex workers related to the World Cup.

The sexual commerce also extended down the block and reconcentrated at a similar place called Mab's, which effectively has become the new Balcony Bar. There are also numerous other venues on the side streets extending out from the Praça do Lido, which continue to flourish and had the good fortune of not being in the direct line of sight from the FIFA Fan Fest. Police were all over the orla that night, keeping the peace in case anyone got robbed or a tourist got too rowdy, which sometimes happened. More than fifty police officers were visible along the edges of the Praça do Lido where the prostitutes worked next to the shuttered Balcony Bar. These police were standing only a few meters from the underage girls described earlier. I personally observed sex tourists asking these police for directions to commercial sex venues in the neighborhood and heard the police give them directions to Barbarella, a venue that had also been subjected to police raids before the World Cup. Even though the police had closed Balcony for allegedly encouraging sexual exploitation that very morning, the police no longer had any interest in any of the women or girls selling sex in front of their eyes. Sexual exploitation didn't matter. O Globo and its cameras, which had been alongside them that morning, were now long gone.

Prior to Balcony, the largest bar on the orla for sex tourism was the Help! discotheque, which the government closed in 2009 and spent years tearing down so that it could build the Museum of Image and Sound there. As Britain's *Guardian* put it in a headline: "Rio nightclub closure leaves prostitutes Helpless: Notorious venue to make way for museum in city clean-up ahead of World Cup, raising concerns over its 2,000 patron prostitutes."[23] This was one of the largest and most obvious visible of the land grabs that sought to turn the most visible part of Rio's entire sexual economy into a shining, modern marvel of the state. At the time of this writing—seven years after the World Cup and twelve years after the closure of Help!—the Museum of Image and Sound is hopelessly behind schedule, over budget, and still not open to the public. It is a shuttered construction site, open to the elements, abandoned partway through building with uncertain plans to finish it.

Just before the World Cup, O Globo ran a special report on the coming scourge of gringos and sexual exploitation, saying, "With fewer than 50 days before the World Cup begins, 600,000 foreigners should land in the country and add to the three million people who, according to the Ministry of Tourism, will move between the 12 host cities for the event. The championship will boost the economy and change the routine of the country, but will also leave Brazilian children and adolescents more vulnerable to sexual exploitation. In several cities in Brazil, there are already signs of people enticing minors—people willing to mobilize small armies in order to satisfy the demand for sex."[24]

More damaging than discourse, though, were the actual raids on venues. In 2012, the Brazilian police raided twelve legal establishments in Rio on the grounds that they were supposedly guilty of "encouraging prostitution." In Brazil, prostitution is lawful, but virtually everything surrounding it is not. Brothel venues operate in a legal gray zone and, according to various sex workers and managers, invariably pay the police to exercise discretion. Most of these venues are not hidden at all and operate in plain sight, advertising themselves in as visible a manner as possible with large signs, flyers, T-shirts, and other paraphernalia. However, police went after Centaurus (in the posh Ipanema neighborhood of Rio), which is perhaps the most exclusive and expensive termas in the city and caters to high-ranking politicians and celebrities (as one example, Justin Bieber was photographed by the tabloids leaving Centaurus in 2013). Approximately one hundred agents worked together to close Centaurus temporarily and raid eleven other similar venues, including L'uomo, Café Sensoo, La Cicciolina, Barbarella, Don Juan, Nightclub Calabria, and other destinations popular among sex tourists and locals alike. Their warrant justified the raids by stating that "one cannot forget also that there is a certain tolerance and indifference to the brothels, but, in most cases, these establishments are used not only for the purpose of sexual exploitation, sexual encounters, but also for sexual exploitation of adolescents, mafia groups money laundering, drug trafficking, firearms possession, police corruption, among others."[25] Although this made for good press at the time, all of the venues reopened and continued business as usual. The police left them alone, and nothing came of the allegations. The general belief of the employees and sex workers is that the police decided it was more lucrative to go back to the old system of bribery and discretionary policing.

When looking at this pattern of raids, one sees another form of fallacious spectacle. Just as the left arm of the state with its anti-trafficking groups, official religious partners, and so on spectacularizes sex trafficking through nonsensical awareness-raising campaigns, the right arm of the state with its police and corrupt security apparatus also spectacularizes sex trafficking by propagandizing about its sting operations, circulating images of police raids, and issuing misleading press releases. It is through this parastatal turn to fallacious spectacle that one sees the ever-increasing boldness of the police actions and impunity of law enforcement that ultimately harms sex workers in the name of "human rights" and "women's rights."

Despite O Globo and the police targeting the touristy zones filled with gringos, there was no evidence of significant sexual exploitation in Rio during the World Cup by gringos, traffickers, or pimps. In fact, the prostitutes working in the area were furious at the presence of journalists' cameras, fearing that family and friends might see them on the news. Over in Vila Mimosa, a gringo-led anti–sex trafficking NGO, Menina Dança, printed up a "menu" of sexual services and corresponding prices in English claiming to be offering "an hour of sex for 60 *reais* (US$18) down from the normal price of 90 *reais* (US$27) with a threesome costing 40 *reais* ($12) per girl for every half hour and 80 *reais* (US$24) for an hour."[26] According to prostitutes I spoke to in the area, the NGO had passed these out to the prostitutes and then photographed them, putting their faces online in a sensationalistic news story about the menus (which the women said the NGO itself had created, paid to print, and then planted on the prostitutes).[27] After an outcry from the women, the NGO blurred their faces in the photos that appeared in the story online. The exploitation in red light areas came from police and NGOs and the journalists there poking around trying to get sensational stories, not from the much-feared hordes of gringos, 600,000 strong, whom parastatal alliances had warned were coming to exploit, kidnap, rape, and enslave the girls and women of Brazil.

In truth, most gringo sports fans I spoke with were Pharisees. Sometimes they would get talked into a programa by an aggressive prostitute, but they had not planned for this eventuality. They were what social scientists of sexual economies sometimes refer to as "accidental sex tourists." Many of these gringos had hoped to hook up with a Brazilian woman, but when this opportunity did not present itself at a bar or on a dating app like Tinder, they would settle for a prostitute at the end of their trip. (They couldn't go back to their home countries with no sexual conquests to brag about, so they became more amenable to prostitutes as time passed.) There were also some gringos who took the Pharisees' tendency toward titillating modes of spectatorship to whole new levels, such as a small group of English soccer fans who set up foldable chairs and a beer cooler along the edge of the praça to watch the sexual commerce there as if it were a show. None of them bought a programa, but they kept a running commentary and irritated the women to no end. These gringos were obnoxious, but they weren't actually hurting anyone.

Studying the sexual economy of Rio de Janeiro before, during, and after the Cup, it became clear that sports fans who came to Rio—whether Pharisees or good gringos—during this mega-event were neophytes. Far from being predatory men who would exploit women, the sex tourists during the Cup were cherished by the women as the easiest marks to come along in years. As another woman, Pamela, explained as she and I looked out from our table at the crowds of men beginning to appear in the praça nearby. "*Nossa!* (Oh my!) Look at all these gringos!" She laughed and swung an arm out, gesturing at them. "It's like it's raining in my garden! (*Chovendo na minha horta!*) Come here! I'm ready!" she said, clucking at them like they were chickens running around mindlessly in need of corralling. As she clucked, she kicked one leg up on a chair, making a right angle with her knee, and made fanning motions at her crotch, as if shooing these little gringo chickens toward her vagina.

Blanchette writes, "Gringos, as strangers, also contain something of that which Lévi-Strauss labeled the *floating signifier,* in that they represent an indeterminate value of signification."[28] The gringo can be mercurial and can change over time, even adopting some of the features of the host culture, such as the good gringos who may turn into "mongers" and begin to treat the prostitutes like Brazilian men do. Blanchette goes on to elaborate how the category of the gringo developed over time into its present state as an empty canvas onto which individuals may project whatever they like according to their own ideologies. In the case of the World Cup (and also the Olympics), the "gringo" is merely a socially constructed boogeyman, but he's still a useful one because he allows the government, the evangelical Christian and Catholic groups, the anti-prostitution feminist groups,- and others to enact their own agendas under the cover of a moral panic. The significations projected onto the idea of the gringo reveal more about the sexual obsessions of those doing the projecting than about the actual reality of the sexual economy. There are certainly some number of gringos who would purchase sex from underage girls in Rio in any given year, but overwhelmingly the prostitutes understood the gringos who attended the World Cup to be prey, not predators. This was true not only in the primary outdoor area next to the closed Balcony Bar across from the FIFA Fan Fest—where one might expect to find accidental sex tourists stumbling out of the match and into the street party scene not realizing it's the longtime heart of prostitution in Copacabana—but also in the indoor brothel scene.

GRINGOS ON A FENCE

Thad and I sit inside a termas in Copacabana, wearing white bathrobes and flip-flops, sipping caipirinhas, and jotting down notes. This is our assignment from the Observatório because only males are allowed in termas, and the majority of researchers on our team are female. Termas are bathhouses with brothel-style heterosexual prostitution. A sauna is a gay version of this.[29] A sauna can come "with garotos" (meaning sex workers are available) or "without garotos" (meaning male clients have sex with one another for free), but a termas always involves prostitution. A client wears a wristband and upon leaving pays an entry fee, room rental, any food or bar tab, and the cost of a programa. Programas in a high-end venue like this usually run around 300 reais, including the room/entry fees. The house may take up to half of this. Women find this to be acceptable because even though they make the same or perhaps even slightly less than they might on the street, here they have privacy and also security to deal with any police, clients, or other dangerous elements.

This particular termas is several stories tall, which is typical. It has a steam room and a dry sauna, neither of which the women can enter. (In places with male prostitution, garotos are allowed in these spaces, which are much more sexually charged than in heterosexual termas.) There is a whole floor filled with *cabines*, which are rooms available for rent for programas. There is also a rectangular room with a full bar at one end. There are seats and little tables along the periphery, and there is a DJ playing club music. The floor is reserved for dancing, but at the moment only a few women are on it. Almost all of the forty women in this Zona Sul termas are white, with hair that has (usually) been dyed blonde and chemically straightened. Each stands alone, scattered across the space, staying in one spot doing a vague little dance that involves shaking her bunda. Each woman wears a very short skirt that rides up when she does this, so most of the dancing also involves yanking her skirt back down every few seconds. The benches are filled with men in bathrobes, chatting with one another and sometimes with women who have come by to join them, flirt with them, and perhaps let the client buy them a drink (usually not alcoholic ones because, as the women invariably point out to me, most do not want the calories or the health problems from nonstop nightly drinking).

Two women have joined our table. They are very interested in the research of the Observatório and in hearing more about the prostitutes' rights group, Davida, that we mention. We watch a group of young gringos from the United States enter the bar area and sit down directly across from us. They sit in a perfect row, like four birds perching on a fence, their hands folded neatly on their laps. We all agree that they appear uniformly and completely terrified, and that this is adorable.

These men look barely out of college, in their early to mid-twenties. They are all white and seem very clean-cut, with closely shaven faces and neat hair. They tug and adjust their robes nervously, laughing awkwardly and whispering in one another's ears as they watch the garotas on the dance floor. It's like a middle school dance in a gymnasium: bashful boys hugging the wall afraid to ask a girl to dance. Suddenly an old Black man who looks to be almost seventy takes the floor and begins to dance a very deft little samba with one of the women. He's so good that the whole bar stares at him, enraptured. The woman positively beams with joy as she throws aside her little dress-grabbing dance and gets to really show off. They move into some other style, a sort of ballroom dance, and he twirls her. At various times, people applaud and shout approval. Diane, one of the women sitting with us, explains that this guy is a regular. He's an expat, and all the women love him. To them, it doesn't matter that he's old. Nor do they care that he is Black. (Indeed, the racism of "racial preferences" in the brothels usually flows from client to prostitute, not the other way around.) He is a good gringo: charming, generous, respectful, and a good dancer, too!

After they finish, the two dancers move to sit on one of the benches. No one wants to follow this act. We continue to watch the white boys. One of the women approaches and sits, whispering in the ear of one of them. He is the one who entered the room first and chose their seats, and he seems to be braver than his friends—at least brave enough to chat with the prostitute. After a minute, she grimaces and moves away. Diane goes to this prostitute to investigate. She reports back to our table: "They say they are only here to look. They are only curious. They don't want a programa." Everyone laughs at this.

After about ten minutes, several more women have made forays. And of course they have also told all the other women in the bar about these gringo boys who only want to look. The game is on. The women come by to torture the boys, doing their skirt-tugging dances in their faces, chewing on the boys' earlobes, and playing with the rope belts of the boys' robes. They tease them and make fun of them.

The lead gringo is the first to *subir*, as the women say, or "go upstairs" for a programa. Once he is gone, the other boys do not scoot apart to fill out the space. If anything, they seem to scrunch closer together as if huddling for protection. Another woman comes in and sits where the leader was. She works on the next guy. He is broad shouldered, like a football player. This one has a wedding ring, I notice. He even fiddles with it, perhaps a Freudian expression of guilt. I remark to my tablemates that he looks so young he couldn't possibly have been married very long. The woman continues to wear him down. The broad-shouldered boy keeps blushing, keeps shaking his head, keeps declining, and keeps pushing her hands away from him. But after another five minutes, she is pulling him by the arm, towing him across the floor like a little tugboat dragging a heftier ship. Up they go to their cabine.

The third to go is red haired and freckled. Diane leaves our bench and grabs this ginger. She tousles his hair and whispers in his ear. Whatever she says works, because soon he is walking out the door holding her hand. He mumbles some kind of apology to his friend, whom he has now abandoned all alone on the bench.

I turn to my colleague and say, "5 . . . 4 . . . 3 . . . ," but I don't get to finish. A woman—one of the few with black hair—walks past the bench. She doesn't say a word. She doesn't even look him in the eye. She simply strides past him without stopping, sliding his hand into hers as she passes, and takes him upstairs. By now, he just looks relieved to not be left out.

A couple hours later, my colleague and I have left the termas and are back outside of the shuttered Balcony Bar to do some interviews with the women working there and to see how business is that night. Suddenly, in the distance I see four figures approaching. They are laughing and clasping each other, shouting and jumping, and talking over one other. I am dumbstruck and slap my colleague on his shoulder.

"*Olha!*" is all I can say. *Look*. We watch as our four little birds on the fence thunder past us, now ecstatic. We can hear snippets of their stories as they regale one another with talk of their prowess during the programa, full of nothing but bravado now. All traces of their timidity have vanished. We can't help but wonder how the women's versions of events would compare to theirs, but as the prostitutes always say, the details of a programa stay "entre quatro paredes, querido" (between these four walls, honey).

GIRLS AT PLAY

It was not only foreign reporters, tabloids, missionaries, and neo-abolitionist radical feminist groups spurring the moral panic about sex trafficking during the Cup. Brazilian media also participated. I discuss *Salve Jorge*, a telenovela, in the next chapter as one example of this phenomenon. But another interesting piece was a full-length graphic novel, *Meninas em jogo* (*Girls at Play*), produced by Pública, an investigative journalism agency. In it, intrepid journalists discuss the children who will be abducted and sold into sexual slavery, particularly in the northeast of Brazil. They claim not only that there are increases in trafficking in the run-up to the Cup, but also that the girls are getting younger, especially in places where there are many foreigners.[30] The characters didactically explain that the predicted child sex trafficking hadn't occurred quite as expected during the Confederations Cup the year before because of the complication of sudden mass political uprisings, a series of protests I describe in chapter 5. The gringos who appear in the graphic novel are portrayed as boorish hooligans. It singles out Italians as the biggest offenders (consistent with what Erica L. Williams, cited earlier, observed in the Northeast). In one frame, a gringo urinates on the street, moaning incoherently as a Brazilian onlooker folds his arms under a thought bubble simply saying, "*These gringos . . . .*"

As the graphic novel progresses, the theme of gringos comes up repeatedly. At one point, two prostitutes, Juditi and her "little sister" Bruna, are chatting with a client. "Want to do a programa?" Juditi asks him.

"Not now. I only just arrived," he responds.

Bruna chimes in, saying of Juditi. "She lived for five years in Europe with her gringo ex-husband," as if this will be a selling point.

"I'm Brazilian. Why are you talking like this?" the client says.

Bruna exclaims, "Oh! I forgot we were speaking Portuguese."

Just then, a white blonde gringo with Teutonic features inserts himself between the women, ignoring the Brazilian. "Hey! Wanna go talk?" he says to Bruna.

After she's alone, Juditi says to herself, "I hate gringos now. But I need to get food for my children. So here I am."

Meanwhile, the gringo has sent Bruna off on an errand. "This worthless (*fuleiro*) gringo wants to give me a hundred dollars to buy cocaine!" she exclaims, looking irritated.

What this rather clumsily laid out scene reveals is very much in keeping with the prostitutes' discourse about good gringos and Pharisees. At first the women in the graphic novel are excited that they may have landed a gringo but then are disappointed when he turns out to be Brazilian and also not interested in closing the deal quickly. The women offer as a selling point the fact that Juditi knows her way around gringo

FIGURE 5. Page from *Meninas em jogo. Source:* De Maio and Andrea Dip, *Meninas em jogo* (Brasília: Agência de reportagem e jornalismo investigativo, 2013).

culture, having married a gringo and lived in Europe. A gringo who provides immigration opportunity and long-term stability is the definition of a "good gringo." But the "worthless" Teutonic interloper is a Pharisee. He is rude, interrupting them, and then wastes Bruna's time by asking her to go buy him drugs instead of agreeing to a programa quickly. Meanwhile, the authors portray Juditi as noble. We know she is noble because she is only turning tricks "to feed her children," which positions her as a victim of circumstance and sets her outside the realm of "putas" who enjoy their work and actively choose it. Brazilians refer to such a person as a *moça de família* (family girl). Ensuring readers understand her as the *good* kind of prostitute, this character is adamant that she "hates gringos" even while they remain her primary target.

The journalists behind the graphic novel have a clear agenda when it comes to exposing the gringos whom they believe drive the demand for prostitution, and in particular child sex trafficking. The choice to develop the story as a graphic novel is presumably to make the information they are conveying more interesting and accessible to laypeople, potentially to sex workers or those who work with them. Yet all *Meninas em jogo* really does is portray gringos as flattened out stereotypes without individual personalities. They are rendered as uncultured and insensitive even as they are the most desirable clients. In this sense, the journalists do seem aware of the "good gringo versus Pharisee" distinction that exists for many prostitutes in Brazil, but they also use the idea of the gringo as a kind of boogeyman to further their anti–sex trafficking morality tale, thereby contributing to the sex panics that seized the country in the same year that the graphic novel was released. Similarly, the "meninas" in the story are also rendered as lacking complex motivations and rich interior lives. The variety of feelings toward gringos is lost in this morality tale so that the graphic novel can push a Manichean agenda that divides the prostitutes into those with good reasons who are in bad circumstances versus fallen women.

OF HOOLIGANS AND PISHTACOS

Perhaps because so many anthropologists are not natives of their field sites and have therefore all had the experience of arriving as outsiders, the question of how different ethnic groups think about, talk about, and treat foreigners has been a frequent subject of research for more than a century. In the case of the World Cup and Olympics, authorities in host nations emphasize cultural exchange. As I have mentioned briefly, the

Olympics features host "houses" from different countries, which offer activities—some are filled with games for children and adults, some have live music—themed for the country in question. Local businesses are excited about the extra income they hope they will get, though often they are disappointed. Because people inside the Olympic venues are forced to buy the (generally terrible) food inside the venues, local restaurants immediately adjacent to the venues often sit empty, and business may in fact decrease as regular customers avoid the congestion caused by the events.

There's also a lot of discourse about the bad behavior of football fans, building on a long-standing trope about "football hooligans," or groups of aggressive fans. Although male football fans' behavior patterns, intensity of actions, and subcultural identities vary somewhat from culture to culture, Ramón Spaaj notes certain transnational characteristics, including pleasurable emotional arousal from doing violence, performing hypermasculinity, collective management of group representation as fans of a team, territorial identification of public space, communicating threats to rival hooligans, and a sense of solidarity and belonging.[31] This last element arises from the perceived differences between self and other (i.e., rival hooligan groups, the in-group and authorities, the in-group and non-hooligans) as they cling to "what Freud described as the 'narcissism of minor differences.'"[32] Fears about Russian hooligans, which emerged in Russia in the 1990s and adopted much of English football hooliganism's clothes and terminology directly, also clouded the Russian World Cup.[33]

Despite official rhetoric about cultural exchange, the World Cup also sows fears about foreigners and shores up jingoism. Because football fans are closely associated with misogyny and displays of hypermasculinity, it makes intuitive sense that members of the media and host countries would imagine them as likely to engage in prolific bouts of drinking and sex seeking, which are stereotypically masculine behaviors. Attendees at the Olympics, which draws more families and children, do not prompt these same associations. Many Olympic sports are also not coded as masculine, despite the enormous endurance and strength required, and do not draw hypermasculine displays from supporters. (Men do not paint their faces or bodies, chanting and hollering in the stands, for gymnastics, men's diving, sailing, or volleyball, to say nothing of certain "feminized" winter sports like figure skating and ice dancing.) Unlike during the Olympics, fear of the marauding foreigner is practically built into the World Cup.

In the case of South America, there is a genre of "gringo stories" with an especially long and bloody history. Known variously as *pishtacos*, ñakaq, and *kharisiri*, these tales refer to a white foreigner, a "terrifying boogeyman who waylays" travelers in order to drain the fat from their bodies and sell it to the other whites.[34] In her work on pishtaco tales, the anthropologist Mary Weismantel notes that "the pishtaco initially appears to be friendly, handsome—indeed, irresistibly attractive to men and women alike" before engaging in gruesome acts such as rape (including sometimes raping men), castration, the eating of infants, and the removal of organs.[35] As Weismantel notes, these legends seem much more like the plots of slasher flicks than they do romantic folktales. The pishtacos sometimes ride horses, sometimes drive fancy gringo cars like Mercedes Benzes (or, in one account from Lima, a Nissan Patrol), and are always looking for native flesh.

These stories of foreigners are explicitly racialized. In these tales, the outsider is white and often remarkably pale. And the victims are explicitly of indigenous or mixed heritage. In these frightening folktales, the white man comes to consume dark meat. Despite their Andean origins in Peru, Ecuador, and Bolivia, pishtaco tales resemble any number of contemporary urban legends about organ traffickers.[36] In an inversion of the genre, 2006 saw the release of the breathtakingly bad US horror movie *Turistas*, which focused on a group of gringo backpackers in Brazil who are tormented by a trafficking ring out to harvest their organs. While modern cosmopolitan audiences in the West might scoff at the tales of pishtacos that natives in South America tell, those same audiences are the ones feeding clicks and likes and shares to sensationalistic media reports like the *Huffington Post UK*'s "Rio Child Sex Trafficking 'Epidemic' Could Rocket During the 2016 Olympics—Here's Why."[37] The idea that gringos are coming to rape, seduce, kidnap, and destroy women and children is an old genre in South America.

Whether pishtaco tales, football hooligan stories, organ harvesters, or sex traffickers, the folk devils in these stories always make good fodder for telenovelas and bloody leads for the nightly news. However, central to all of these myths are fantasies about gringo masculinity. They all rely on the idea that the gringo is violent, hypermasculine, sexually seductive, wealthy, and cunning. The whiteness of the gringo hooligan is emphasized not only because of the strong traditions of soccer hooliganism in Western European countries but also because of the wealth, power, and privilege associated with getting away with such behaviors. Of course, during the World Cup people came from all over the world. The reality was that there were thousands of Middle Eastern and Asian men in attendance. Shortly after O Gordo and O Magro left with the travestis,

I watched a very drunk tourist strip completely naked and shout in slurred Japanese at the sex workers and football fans until the police arrested him, dragging him across the pavement into their car. The gringos outside Balcony Bar could hardly inspire fear in anyone. It's a pity the evangelicals and the women from Femen didn't bother to come in person to behold the reality of fragile and broken gringo masculinity. In truth, as the sex workers and Observatório researchers observed, the gringos who stumbled about during the Brazilian Olympics and especially during the World Cup were, by and large, slovenly, drunk, sexually insecure, perpetually lost, linguistically incompetent, and easily fooled. And that's just the way the sex workers wanted it. Their only gripe was that there weren't a few hundred thousand more just like them.

CONCLUSION

The gringo holds a special place in carioca culture. Tourism is the life-blood of the carioca economy, and gringos are a constant presence for anyone who lives in the Centro or Zona Sul. Cariocas may find gringos exasperating, silly, offensive, naïve, cosmopolitan, or even sexually desirable. Cariocas know gringos intimately. In a reversal of the anthropological gaze, they study them and their behavior, motivated not by intellectualism but by entrepreneurialism. Yet Carioca constructions of the gringo are not the ones that dominated media coverage of the World Cup, nor are they ones the government had in mind when it began designing advertising campaigns for the public. The Catholic Church certainly did not show any great familiarity with cariocas' more nuanced feelings about gringos when it used its considerable heft to start scaring Brazilians. When Femen arrived and took over the airport at Rio de Janeiro, staging naked protests to draw attention to "sexual exploitation," they weren't using carioca sex worker understandings of gringos; instead, they held an ideologically driven position forged by international radical feminists. And when evangelical groups from the United States came into Brazilian churches to show horrifying movies about "sex trafficking" in an effort to "raise awareness" about the thousands of gringo predators supposedly coming to carry off Brazil's daughters, they were not using cariocas' complex understandings of gringos.

Instead, all of these groups projected their own fantasies, fears, and prejudices onto the idea of the gringo. In so doing, they created a mythological narrative about Brazil that imagines Brazilian women as vulnerable and already in a state of becoming victims to predatory foreign men. This narrative renders impossible any idea of agency for Brazilian women who sell sex because it promotes an ideology of moralizing neo-colonial forces that collapses all prostitutes into the category of trafficking victims. In so doing, it rejects Brazil's autonomy as a country where prostitution is not a crime and surrenders instead to outsiders' views of Brazil as somehow backward, incompetent, and unable to protect its own citizens. In truth, the prostitutes in Rio found that the gringos who came during the Cup and purchased sex were especially "good gringos" who were susceptible to the little tricks and jeitinhos of prostitutes, paid what was asked, were polite and generous, and didn't make trouble. Far from bringing misbehaving or violent soccer hooligans, the World Cup brought (as far as the prostitutes of Rio were concerned) perhaps too many Pharisees who didn't want to buy sex, but the gringos who did buy were the best kind of gringos possible.

The reactionary period I have described—the aforementioned Great Gringo Panic—may seem relatively unimportant. Who cares if these privileged gringos are misunderstood or maligned? My purpose here is not to instill sympathy for gringos, nor is it to make some kind of "men's rights" claim that radical feminists have maligned "lad culture" and ought to let boys be boys. Instead, what is important to understand is that the Great Gringo Panic was a moral panic. As the feminist anthropologist Gayle Rubin has argued, during periods of moral panic, conservative powers who believe sexuality is fundamentally sinful are able to enact legislative changes and take other actions that have long-term consequences in restricting the sexual choices and freedoms of others, especially those already on the sexual margins of society.[38] Gringo panic also has these kinds of consequences, including for the women in Niteroi I mentioned earlier in the book whom police beat, robbed, evicted, and raped.

I do not believe evangelicals and anti-prostitution feminist groups would condone such a raid, but their fearmongering and contributions to gringo panic make them complicit in its execution. Subscribing to an ideology of gringo panic because one is repulsed by men who purchase sex allows anti-prostitution forces to construct the gringo as they need him to be in order to justify their own moral imperialism. It allows social cleansing campaigns and brothel raids to happen in red light areas. Gringo panic provides an opportunity to seize this land, gentrify areas like Copacabana, and abuse women who sell sex. In so doing, it erases these women's rights to safety and security and restricts their ability to move through their own city spaces of their own free will. Indeed, it is a grim irony that the anti-trafficking movement's mythologies would ultimately foreclose the free movement of women.

Fostering gringo panic around major sporting events in Rio has the effect of ripping these women out of the sexual landscape of their city in order to cleanse the city so that it may be reborn without sin. In a telling final coda, the space that once housed Balcony Bar reopened under new ownership in time for the 2016 Olympics. It is now a shining, well-lit, expensive beachfront restaurant with not a single puta to be found on the premises.

And the name of this fancy new restaurant? Imaculada. The immaculate one. Conceived without sin, indeed.

CHAPTER 3

Fallacious Spectacles and the Celebrification of Sex Trafficking

The UN Gift Box came to the red light slum district of Vila Mimosa in Rio de Janeiro shortly before the World Cup in 2014. "Originally launched by STOP THE TRAFFIK, ECPAT-USA [formerly End Child Prostitution and Trafficking], and the United Nations Global Initiative to Fight Human Trafficking [UN.GIFT] at the 2012 London Olympics, the 10-foot-high structure functions as a metaphor for the techniques used by sex traffickers," the ECPAT-USA website explains. "Visitors are lured into a big, colorfully wrapped box, only to be confronted—through photographs and survivor stories—with the harsh realities of sex trafficking."[1] Vila Mimosa was an infamous brothel district where a thousand or more women worked at any given time, often selling sex for as little as thirty cents a minute—surely a pitiful site in need of Western intervention and the kind of "sex trafficking awareness" that a spectacle like the Gift Box could bring.

In one sense, the Gift Box is almost perfectly conceived. A coalition of charities and governmental organizations from across the "left arm of the state" has come together and worked to reduce the complicated realities about trafficking into simplistic narratives of perfect victims. To do this, they must spectacularize the exploitation and "produce" sex trafficking for a global audience. The box provides no benefit to survivors or tangible solutions. It exists to "raise awareness" but only in the vaguest of ways. And while thousands of people have seen it as they passed by its various locations in Rio and its other incarnations on

FIGURE 6. UN Gift Box ribbon-cutting ceremony in Vila Mimosa. Photo by Amanda De Lisio.

college campuses and cities around the world, the effect of the Gift Box is merely to give people a sense that an unseen danger—trafficking—is out there somewhere. It encourages a kind of constant vigilance, which means it is no surprise that people now look for telltale signs of trafficking everywhere.

Yet when the Gift Box came to Vila Mimosa, the women there were confused. "There was a little ceremony," explained Juliana, a fifty-year old longtime resident and prostitute. "Some official-looking people gathered and made speeches. We didn't know what was happening. Then they left. But they forgot their box . . . so now it just sits here. I don't know why." In fact, the organizers had made an effort to explain to the women what it was and had even hired some prostitutes to work as docents, training them how to explain the box and to talk about sex trafficking to anyone who came by. (In Vila Mimosa, there are almost no passersby as almost everyone in the neighborhood is either a prostitute, a client, or a business manager/vendor in the sex industry.) The organizers seemed to have imagined that Vila Mimosa, which is close to the big Maracana stadium, would see a big spike in business. And so

FIGURE 7. UN Gift Box after having been moved to a main thoroughfare in downtown Vila Mimosa near a number of other brothels. Photo by Amanda De Lisio.

did the prostitutes, many of whom were already planning all the major purchases and splurging they would be able to engage in with the influx of gringo cash that was coming.

I couldn't help but think, though, that even if there had been thousands of clients, as the women had hoped, the men looking for programas would not have been able to visit the box and feel whatever it was they were supposed to feel inside the display. It was locked up and ignored most of the time. The only exceptions I saw were once when some women were using it as a place to play cards and drink and another time when I noticed a woman (possibly a docent) settling in for the privacy of a quick nap. It certainly wasn't educating any clients or passersby, and it wasn't preventing the prostitutes from being sex trafficked by teaching them about the possible lurking dangers of sexual exploitation.

So what *was* the purpose of the Gift Box? I'm convinced that the box was never *for* any of the people in Vila Mimosa. Nor was it even for Brazilians at all. What the box really did was allow the NGOs to tell other donors—back in the United Kingdom and United States and at events like "Traffik Free Easter" and "Freedom Sunday" religious services at churches spanning twenty-one different religious denominations—that they had taken the Gift Box all the way to the brothels of Brazil, where prostitutes and clients had beheld its transformative power.[2] The Gift Box became what I call a fallacious spectacle, making its false claims based on a mistaken belief and encouraging others to do the same. Spectacles are a form of visual rhetoric; they make an intentional claim about the world. And fallacious spectacles are an exceptionally powerful type of spectacle, causing deep harms.

According to the logic of the Gift Box, just as sex trafficked women and children are attracted by the false promises of shiny objects and opportunities, so too are passersby intrigued by the odd spectacle of this big box on the street—only to become entrapped. The Gift Box traveled around several locations in Rio de Janeiro known for prostitution during the World Cup and the Olympics. It also travels around various college campuses and other locations to demonstrate that trafficking can pop up anywhere, anytime, in any community and is not something confined to faraway locations. (It does seem that there are multiple boxes in multiple languages, but its creators always refer to it as a singular unique entity.) Inside the box are black-and-white portraits of sad-looking people of various races and short narrative blurbs. The Gift Box is not really for victims so much as it is about providing an emotional experience to the passersby who enter. It's unclear how they are meant to feel, though. Horrified? Sad? Guilty?

The Gift Box is an example of what Lisa Chouliaraki calls a negative appeal, which creates "a logic of complicity" in which the viewer feels that "failure to act" is a "failure to acknowledge our historical and personal participation in human suffering."[3] This is part of the rhetorical force of sex trafficking: when faced with the horrific stories and images associated with it, who wants to deny the imagined victims, raise questions, or refuse aid? As Chouliaraki says of such negative appeals, this leads to a political externalization in that the viewer *must* join the "solidarity of revolution."[4] This is part of why it's so easy to pass well-meaning but enormously harmful anti–sex trafficking legislation (such as Fight Online Sex Trafficking Act-Stop Enabling Sex Traffickers Act [FOSTA/SESTA] in the United States). What kind of person refuses solidarity to a sex trafficking victim? What politician wants to be known as an apologist for sexual exploitation or as "pro–sex trafficking," especially given the powerful imagery and language available in sex trafficking discourse?

As I walked into Vila Mimosa, I saw people cooking *espetinhas* (skewers of grilled meat) over coals on the sidewalk to sell. While they smelled delicious, the familiar sight and smell of raw sewage trickling along the curb meant that I took a pass. On my right was a biker bar, which was most often a rowdy, energetic place but was dead that night. I poked my head inside just to confirm that it was open. The grizzled bartender didn't even look up from the colorful bubble-popping game he was playing on his phone. Continuing down the main drag, I could hear the loud funk music of the favelas, but all of the balconies and bars were empty except for some bored women in skimpy outfits sitting on plastic chairs, smoking cigarettes. I decided to head to a bar managed by Graciela, a self-described *sapatão* (bull dyke), with a few cabines or rooms for rent for sex upstairs. Like most places in Vila Mimosa, it was deafeningly loud in there, but Graciela was friendly, watched out for "her girls," and was always good for some local *fofocas* (bits of gossip). Also, unlike many places in Vila Mimosa, Graciela's bar was clean.

But then there it was: just on my left sat the Gift Box. I had heard about it but not seen it until that night. The sex workers who were being paid to mind it were absent, though. It sat unattended and alone. I approached the box, circling it and touching it gingerly as if encountering an alien ship in a science fiction movie. It was shut tight and locked. (Only later, when I found it downtown sitting in a plaza, would I finally get to wander inside and suddenly have the wrenching experience of becoming a sex trafficked woman.) I continued down the road and found a few women watching the match on TV with varying degrees of enthusiasm. After the match ended, everyone began to shift about, restless. They checked the time and adjusted their clothes. After another twenty minutes passed, they began to complain, cursing first the sports fans who had failed to materialize, then FIFA, and finally for good measure President Dilma Rousseff herself for the shitty economy. Just then, a lone taxi began to cruise down the usually crowded thoroughfare, and the women turned to watch, hopeful. Some men with Argentina jerseys and blue/white paraphernalia rolled down the window and stuck their heads out. The Argentine men's smiles and laughter vanished as they saw the prostitutes staring back at them; perhaps they expected a livelier party atmosphere, or maybe they didn't like the look of the women. They muttered something to the driver and rolled up the windows. The taxi picked up speed and left. "*Filho de puta!*" one woman shouted after it. (Sonofabitch, or more literally—if ironically—son of a whore.) Another prostitute tossed a beer can at the car. The can missed the bumper and clattered on the pavement, leaking its sudsy innards.

This scene happened very early in the World Cup. After a couple more days of boredom, the prostitutes took to kicking soccer balls around the street. Business was down by more than half, and the street was totally dead for long stretches. Soon everyone had to admit to themselves that they were not going to make any of the money they had imagined, and so many of them left and tried to work the downtown brothels, but found those dead inside or closed outright. The women from those downtown venues had likewise experienced the drought and left.

Consequently, hundreds of prostitutes from all over the city began to reassemble in the one location that had significant *movimento* (movement, prostitutes' term for brisk sexual commerce): Copacabana, the touristy beach area and longtime sex tourist haven. Copacabana was also the location FIFA had selected to place its jumbo-sized screens for watching games at the FIFA Fanfest. There, the logic went, the prostitutes would succeed in finding the elusive clients—although still not as many as they had hoped. Moreover, too many of the time-wasting gringos there would want to buy them drinks and feel them up and take selfies with them for their Instagrams but not pay for a programa. The prostitutes from Vila Mimosa would also find the women who regularly worked Copacabana furious at them for interloping on their turf. There, they would fight with one another and price gouge for the next thirty days of the Cup in a dismal race to the bottom, and would subsequently experience the disappointment and dashed hopes of making a fortune from "gringo chasing" (*caça-gringos*). But the women did not know that yet. And so the exodus from Vila Mimosa began. The prostitutes left, more and more each day, abandoning their usual places of business and pressing their way onto heaving, rickety buses and sleek subway cars, leaving behind in Vila Mimosa the big strange box the gringo officials had brought them, whatever it was.

In the case of the UN Gift Box and the widely circulated rumors that 40,000 girls and young women would be sex trafficked for the Cup, there were many fallacious spectacles, ranging from telenovelas to "consciousness-raising" ad campaigns to topless feminist protests by Femen in Copacabana and in the Rio airport. Examining how these parastatal alliances shift toward spectacularity in the way they produce sex trafficking discourse is useful because it opens up a space for discussing the real-world effects of the fallacious spectacle of sex trafficking. Although there is sexual exploitation in Brazil, there were no sex trafficking victims found in Brazil related specifically to the World Cup. Yet there were hundreds of images contained within spectacles *about* trafficking and the Cup. The spectacle of the 40,000 trafficked women and girls exists even though they themselves do not; they are merely specters of sex trafficking. In this chapter, I try to discover who these spectral victims are: how they are generated in meetings and focus groups and conference rooms of NGOs, how they are produced and marketed, and who exactly is harmed by these fallacious spectacles of sex trafficking.

SPECTACULAR REASONING

Much contemporary scholarship on spectacle and its deployment in human rights work is derived from the school of critical theorists known as the Frankfurt School and from that group's intellectual offspring, the Birmingham School. Guy Debord's 1967 book *Society of the Spectacle* has been especially useful as a point of departure for scholars such as Chouliaraki and Wendy Hesford, whose work focuses on celebrity, spectacle, and human rights. For Debord, however, "the spectacle" is composed of accumulated capital, which here takes the form of an image.[5] Debord is critical of the spectacle, which he maintains is an ongoing production of society that also circulates images. The spectacle is a distraction. Debord's notion of the spectacle is wrapped up in his critique of late capitalist post-Fordism and the rise of consumerism. It's therefore quite different than what most people—lay folks and scholars alike—think of when they hear the word *spectacle* (i.e., a more general term arising from a more Aristotelian orientation that spectacle is something that the masses can behold and regard). The anthropologist and queer theorist Marcia Ochoa notes that Debord's conception is not very useful in getting to the subject of the body, however.[6] That is, it's better suited for media studies than it is for ethnographic reality. Ochoa is therefore more interested in the *spectacularity* of gender, including all of the processes that go into producing the spectacle: casting, rehearsing, discussing, focus grouping, and so on.[7]

Debord is especially interested in the relationship between spectacle and celebrity. "The celebrity, the spectacular representation of a living human being, embodies . . . banality. . . . Being a star means specializing in the seemingly lived. . . . Celebrities exist to act out various styles of living and viewing society unfettered, free to express themselves globally. . . . A star of consumption gets elected as a pseudo-power over the lived."[8] Here ones sees both the vapidity of the celebrity, consumed by their own wealth and status, and their power to influence others. In the case of celebrities who produce sex trafficking discourse and seek to advance fallacious spectacles about it, they exert profound influence not only over the consumers of these spectacles but also over the actual sex workers affected by sex trafficking as a cause célèbre.

Debord, the Frankfurt School, and the Birmingham School had much to say on spectacle, particularly those Birmingham scholars like Stuart Hall who were pioneering media studies and struggling with questions and theories of representation. Yet, as is so often the case with a mostly male foundational vanguard, these authors did not account much for gender or sexuality in their work, leaving it to feminist and queer studies scholars struggling to update this body of literature if they wanted to apply it to questions such as how organizations and governments use spectacle in the name of human rights and women's rights, including in campaigns around prostitution, sexual tourism, "sexual slavery," and "sex trafficking."

In the case of the World Cup and the Olympics, it is ironic that even as some sought to use "feminist spectacles" to improve the condition of women in the sex industry, they actually ended up changing the women's relationship to the state and allowed the state to bring harm to the women in question. For example, topless protestors from the feminist group Femen took over the airport and the Copacabana Palace hotel with messages on placards like "*Compre aqui sua garota brazileira*" ("buy your Brazilian girl here," though "Brazilian" was misspelled).[9] Femen is an international organization founded in Ukraine but now headquartered in Paris. Its US branch declares on its website: "FEMEN female activists are the women with special training, physically and psychologically ready to implement the humanitarian tasks of any degree of complexity and level of provocation. FEMEN activists are ready to withstand repressions against them and are propelled by the ideological cause alone. FEMEN is the special force of feminism, its spearhead militant unit, modern incarnation of fearless and free Amazons."[10]

Core to Femen's goal, which it states plainly as "complete victory over patriarchy," are several aims, among them the "complete extermination of prostitution as an egregious form of exploitation of women by criminalizing the clients, investors and organizers of slave-trade. To recognize that sex-industry is the most large-scale and long-term genocide against women."[11] It also requires members to be atheists and to work for the destruction of religion within the state, especially where "Shari'ah and other forms of sadism" are concerned. To that end, Femen has frequently fought to outlaw hijabs, burkas, and other forms of Islamic female dress, which has put it at odds with many other feminist groups, especially those led by women of color.[12] Femen's activist work in Rio used the spectacle of the naked and painted bodies of women to call attention to the perceived injustices of the sexual economy. Primarily, however, the disruption was about "raising awareness."

Indeed, "raising awareness" is a stated goal of nearly all anti–sex trafficking activism. The budgetary emphasis on "awareness" campaigns—producing viral infographics for social media, billboards on highways, and signage in airports and ports of entry—is so prominent because so few of the organizations that produce these campaigns actually provide shelter or services to survivors. At a conference for sex worker advocates and service providers I attended, sex worker rights groups routinely described losing the funding they needed to maintain beds and shelter for sexually exploited women. As groups supporting decriminalization, they lost these funds to major anti-trafficking NGOs with multi-million-dollar budgets, only to find that two-thirds of their referrals were then coming from those same anti-trafficking NGOs because those groups only do awareness raising and lobbying, not service provision. Anti-trafficking NGOs, many with no real concept of effective policy or even a good operational definition of trafficking, leach resources away from sex worker–led organizations that seek to improve conditions and stop sexual exploitation from within the sex industry.

"Raising awareness" thereby becomes another fallacious spectacle, with slick campaigns advertising the existence of "invisible victims" and "missing girls" who are "hidden in plain sight," forcing these feminized subjects to perform by way of their absence. As the anthropologist Laura María Agustín pithily observed on her website in 2015, "One [assumption] holds that certain social problems are 'hidden', and 'hidden populations' are great favourites amongst sociologists (who can then claim to have located and revealed them). Of course, most of us do know marginalised groups exist; we see them every day and may belong to them ourselves. But the idea that we cannot see social ills creates the need for self-identified experts to inform us about them."[13]

The fetishization of "awareness raising" and the tendency to play out these campaigns in spectacular ways is certainly not unique to Brazil. Indeed, they seem to be most prevalent in the United States or among US-based groups who do these campaigns in the developing countries they have targeted, perhaps because the United States is where most of the funding is. The discourse of the "hidden" victims about whom we must all be made aware has trickled down from government agencies and large-scale NGOs to all manner of college campus student groups and local churches. A typical example is the SOAP (Save Our Adolescents from Prostitution) Project, which describes itself as "a hands-on outreach to fight sex trafficking at large events and in communities . . . founded by author, advocate and survivor, Theresa Flores. On her worst night, after being auctioned off to nearly two dozen men in a dingy, dirty, inner-city Detroit motel, Theresa recalled the only item that would have reached out to her, a bar of soap. With that in mind, she created The SOAP Project."[14]

Thus, the group began putting labels on bars of soap. Its first outreach event was in Dallas 2011 for the Super Bowl—the one I described in this book's introduction, wherein anti-trafficking groups alleged that 100,000 women and girls would be victimized, and also the one wherein an embarrassed FBI admitted that it had not found any cases despite spending significant resources looking. Alongside all manner of T-shirts, bracelets, and other awareness-raising items, the group sells cases of soap (labels are shipped separately) for customers who would also like to share all this awareness raising. As its website explains, "After founder Theresa Flores would speak to a group of people at awareness events, she noticed the attendees were in shock, frustrated and yes, even angry. They demanded to know what they could do to stop this crime and protect their children. . . . Kids as young as 9 years old, fathers with their sons, and an 83 year old nun have put labels on bars of soap. There *is* something you can do about this! The beauty of SOAP is that it is simple and easy and can be customized to your wants, needs and abilities."[15]

In Ohio, anti-trafficking activists and local law enforcement collaborated using the soap to prepare for the Major League All-Star Game that was soon to be held in Cincinnati. Local reporting states that activists and law enforcement gave 15,000 bars of the specially marked soap to as many as one hundred hotels in the area. Media quote a program coordinator for the Salvation Army and End Slavery Cincinnati as saying that "we know with any big event or big sports event, there is always an increase in demand for commercial sex (prostitution) . . . and that will no doubt mean an increase in human trafficking. The data is there."[16] Except, of course, the data are not there. The groups in question give no sources and provide no evidence of any sex trafficking related to this sports event other than a vague citation of an unspecified number of arrests during the All-Star game in Minnesota and Kansas City, without providing details about actual apprehensions or convictions, whether the arrests were of women soliciting or men trafficking them, or whether any of these cases were actually linked to the event. SOAP's founder, however, made clear to *The Christian Perspective* that the stakes are dire. "When you're trafficked, if it's for a weekend, if it's for two years or five years, it doesn't matter, you're really broken forever."[17]

Meanwhile, for over a decade the Calgary Polar Bear Ice Dip has urged people to "take a stand against sex slavery" by jumping in the icy water at Mahogany Homeowner's Beach Club. Its website warns (with no sourcing) that there are more slaves today than at any point in human history and that "79% of victims are trafficked for sexual exploitation." It asks, "what will you do to end human trafficking?"[18] Apparently, a cold swim with a US$60 registration fee will do, the proceeds of which are turned over to a religious anti-trafficking charity in the United Kingdom. Similarly, there are "justice runs for freedom" in which you can run five kilometers to fight trafficking, although the money raised appears to be given to the county "family services" department and doesn't seem on the website to be legally earmarked for anything to do with survivors of trafficking per se.[19]

More spectacular still is the Red Sand Project. An artist seeking to raise public awareness about human trafficking sends red sand to any group or person who wants to participate. She writes, "Today, 40.3 million people are in slavery. Take part in raising awareness for those affected by modern day slavery. Join the movement by filling sidewalk cracks with red sand and document your sidewalk transformation on social media using #RedSandProject."[20]

Red seems to be a theme among those obsessed with raising awareness. The Red X project, which urges people to "Draw a RED X on your hand and tell the world about #ENDITMOVEMENT."[21] One might wonder why putting an X on your hand would help to stop trafficking and not just confuse people or let them think that you had been to a nightclub the night before, but the folks at Red X explain that "drawing a RED X on your hand may seem simple at first, but you'll be amazed at the conversations it prompts with everyone from your boss to your barista; conversations that educate and inspire the people in your circles one by one. After all, action starts with awareness."[22] Red X claims that donations, along with proceeds from the extensive array of apparel and other merchandise from its online store, "help fund projects on the ground and around the world, as our partners bring RESCUE, RESTORATION, PREVENTION and AWARENESS."[23] There is, however, little information about who is getting rescued and restored by whom, what precisely is being prevented, and why it fits anti-trafficking best practices for an organization built to "raise awareness" to give its money to other organizations also meant to "raise awareness." But then again, as Red X's website proclaims in large bold typeface: "**Awareness is doing the work.**"[24]

In one of the more confounding versions of the "awareness raising" trope, CNN (an ostensibly apolitical news organization) teamed up with the McCain Institute, a conservative-funded institute at Arizona State University founded by late Republican senator John McCain and his family to tackle various issues, chief among them "counterterrorism" and "human trafficking." As CNN explains, "The CNN Freedom Project continues to excel at raising awareness of the anti-trafficking movement. The #FlytoFreedom Campaign is an interactive and thought-provoking way for many to engage the fight against human trafficking. This campaign invites the public to create a paper airplane and write a plead [*sic*] on it as to how they will contribute to the fight against modern day slavery; record the paper airplane in flight and it could potentially be played on CNN live."[25] Perhaps the most "thought-provoking" thing about this way to raise awareness is what it means to "write a plead," perhaps it is how on earth the people making the plane are supposed to even know "how they will contribute to the fight," or perhaps it is what good all this litter could possibly do to help someone experiencing actual exploitation on the other side of the world.

So how do CNN's partners over at the institute actually address the problem of trafficking? According to their website, "The McCain Institute for International Leadership combats human trafficking through an educational and advocating Human Trafficking Conversation Series. The Conversation Series highlights many different facets of human trafficking by hosting experts in these specific fields in a panel discussion. These discussions are highly beneficial to the anti-trafficking community. They shed light to some areas of human trafficking that are not as well known and also create a space for a call to action."[26] More awareness raising, though how the speakers who constitute McCain's "anti-trafficking community" benefit from such "conversations" other than through their speaker fees isn't exactly clear. However, the McCain Institute defines itself as a "do-tank" and not just a "think tank," citing its partnership with Ashton Kutcher's anti–sex trafficking initiative, Thorn, a high-profile celebrity effort that I analyze more fully below.

Much like the spectacle of the UN Gift Box at sporting events, the point of an "awareness-raising spectacle" is to help communities feel that they have done something. The need to do something is predicated on creating a panic—a sense that there is a vast threat—and then providing a way to ameliorate that feeling. In the logic of the awareness-raising spectacle, the thing to be done about the vast and complex problem of global labor and sexual exploitation should ideally be something simple and short term: jumping in the water, pouring sand on the sidewalk, flying a paper airplane, or labeling some soap.

However, according to the anti-trafficking scholar Samantha Majic, a major change in the anti-trafficking movement happened in the early 2000s; this was the era when anti-trafficking became celebrified.[27] If one wants to "raise awareness," one needs people who have major platforms, drive internet traffic, and reach people through social media. Celebrities get the anti-trafficking message out, rendering the supposedly invisible now hypervisible. Yet as Dina Francesca Haynes has shown in her research on celebrities and anti-trafficking, celebrities most often "veer from mere awareness raising into giving policy recommendations," relying on superficial and uninformed narratives and, unlike actual experts and elected officials, have no accountability for the ramifications of their poor solutions and unintended consequences of policies they help to implement.[28] And so we have entered an age when actors, models, and other celebrities with only a cursory understanding of trafficking and forced migration have become sought-after spokespeople by organizations such as the United Nations, which is teeming with actual experts at its disposal. More than any other trend in anti-trafficking, this shift toward spotlighting celebrities reveals how the state has outsourced humanitarianism and deprioritized entitlement to meaningful assistance for vulnerable populations. Eventually, the celebrities would also come around to furthering the mega-event myth.

CELEBRITIES AND THE PARASTATE

Critical to understanding the proliferation of awareness campaigns is the fact that they are often cooperative ventures between NGOs, religious groups, and the state. As essential areas of government services receded under neoliberalism beginning in the 1980s, NGOs, faith-based groups, charities, and corporations began rushing in to fill the gaps, providing everything from food drives in Ethiopia, to microloan programs to women in South Africa, to voluntourism in orphanages in Southeast Asia. Undoubtedly, many good outcomes have resulted from some of these efforts. However, culturally incompetent and meddlesome foreigners with an outsized sense of their own expertise and ignorance of local customs and actual community needs have also done no small amount of harm.

Spectacles are an increasingly important part of the parastate, especially for NGOs seeking to "help," "raise awareness," and "give voice to the voiceless." The reason for this is that, as Chouliaraki notes, there has been a political-economic shift toward "the marketization of humanitarian practice" as a result of an increase in international organizations and NGOs.[29] "Aid agencies, for instance, expanded their operations by 150 per cent in the 1985–95 decade whereas in the USA alone, their numbers rose by a hundred in the 1980–1990 decade . . . and almost doubled in the subsequent one."[30] The explosion of NGOs directly correlates with the rise of neoliberalism, Thatcherism, and Reaganomics. The state receded and withdrew funding, leaving private entities, charities, and religious groups to pick up the slack despite often having no expertise in effective management, research methods, or even the subject matter—but having plenty in the way of overconfident moralistic agendas.

This shift also meant that funds needed to be raised through an increasing emphasis on appealing to the emotions of comparatively wealthier (and often religious) laypeople in the United States and Europe. Naturally, certain topics and images are better suited for stirring up emotional responses. As Denise Brennan argues, one major reason sex trafficking is both privileged and conflated with other forms of trafficking (despite being a small proportion of all forced labor) is that the George W. Bush administration had sought to turn attention away from the question of immigration reform and migrant labor, which would reveal the failings of the government.[31] Instead, a parastatal alliance was formed that focused on sex trafficking and gave ample federal dollars to faith-based initiatives purportedly working on this issue. Because these organizations believe all prostitution to be sex trafficking, they have a financial incentive to count prostitutes and women who are "at risk for sexual exploitation" as already sexually exploited.[32] Hesford explains, "Opportunistic alliances continue to exist today between neo-abolitionist feminist and right wing groups" that make as a condition for their success the condemnation not only of forced prostitution, but sex work as a whole.[33] According to the US State Department's senior adviser on human trafficking, this has given what she calls "a Biblical mandate to the women's movement."[34]

This conflation has been greatly fueled by the entrance of a number of celebrities, mostly established liberal movie stars known for their stances on feminist issues. In 2016, Amnesty International released a report and statement that its official position on prostitution and sex work was to advocate to "decriminalize consensual sex work." It also called for countries to "include sex workers in the development of laws that affect their lives and safety" and ensure they are "protected from harm, exploitation and coercion."[35]

Anti-prostitution groups were incensed. So, too, were many celebrities. CATW penned a letter denouncing Amnesty's decision, and movie stars rushed to sign on.[36] Among those actresses opposing the decriminalization of consensual sex work were familiar names: Meryl Streep, Kate Winslet, Anne Hathaway, Emily Blunt, Emma Thompson, Angela Bassett, Lisa Kudrow, Mira Sorvino, Jada Pinkett Smith, Jeannie Mai, and Lena Dunham.[37]

The stars did not claim to have any real expertise, but they noted that their awareness had been raised and that they had strong feelings. As Meryl Streep said, "It's never been as urgent as it is today to dismantle the lies perpetrated by the sex trade profiteers: that decriminalization of buying and pimping somehow benefits women and girls."[38] Emma Thompson has been a longtime anti–sex trafficking advocate, at one point putting on an art exhibition on Long Island (which she chose because she heard that Long Island had a lot of sex trafficking). In the exhibit, media coverage reported, "a filthy bedroom, pungent with the smell of sex and cheap perfume, is recreated for the curious. There is peeling wallpaper, soiled condom wrappers littering the floor and a dirty sink filled with half-used lipstick tubes and cigarette butts. Along one wall, a stained bed heaves under the weight of invisible, moving bodies engaged in rough sex."[39] The exhibit was staged in seven chained railroad box cars with their outsides covered in what journalists described as "degrading graffiti meant to stigmatize the captives portrayed inside."[40] She explained that she had seen a TV documentary series as well as *Lilya 4-Ever*, a Swedish-Danish drama infamous in sex worker rights circles for its sensationalistic, melodramatic, and stereotypical depiction of migrant sex work and sex trafficking.

Anne Hathaway explained that she had learned about sexual slavery by playing the role of a prostitute named Fantine in the movie musical *Les Misérables*, a role for which she won an Academy Award in 2013:

> In my case there's no way that I could relate to what my character was going through—I have a very successful, happy life and I don't have any children I've had to give up. . . . And so what I did was I had to get inside the reality of her story as it exists in our world. To do that I read a lot of articles and

watched a lot of documentaries and news clips about sexual slavery, and for me, for this particular story, I came to the realization that I had been thinking about Fantine as someone who lived in the past. And she doesn't. She's living in New York City right now—she's probably less than a block away. This injustice exists in our world, and so every day that I played her, I thought—this isn't an invention, this isn't me acting, this is me honoring that this pain lives in this world and I hope in all of our lifetimes, like today, we see it end.[41]

Amnesty International knew how controversial its policy would be. It had spent over two years analyzing research and data to determine which approach—decriminalization, legalization, or End Demand—actually reduced harm. As Amnesty explained, "We looked at the extensive work done by organizations such as World Health Organisation, UNAIDS, the UN Special Rapporteur on the Right to Health and other UN agencies. We also looked at the positions of others such as the Global Alliance Against Traffic in Women. We conducted detailed research first hand in Argentina, Hong Kong, Norway, and Papua New Guinea and consulted more than 200 sex workers from around the world."[42] The organization had worked with sex worker groups, survivors of sexual exploitation, LGBT groups, HIV/AIDS activists, organizations that favored outright criminalization, and others. In short, they had done their homework. The movie stars had not, but that did not prevent them from using their position in the media to attempt to sway the public, not to mention to sway governments to enact their preferred policies—approaches that would influence sex workers' health and safety on the ground without input from any actual sex workers (Fantine's ghost not withstanding).

Occasionally, a celebrity does turn up on the side of sex worker rights. Having witnessed the raids and evictions happening in London's Soho neighborhood, the actor Rupert Everett became active with the English Collective of Prostitutes. Observing that sex workers working consensually were becoming casualties in a war on trafficking that never seemed to produce any traffickers or victims, he argued vehemently, "There is a land grab going on!"[43] Comedian Margaret Cho also has spoken about sex worker rights and has discussed engaging in sex work in her past, although her scheduled keynote at a Desiree Alliance sex worker–led sex worker rights conference was later canceled for unspecified reasons.

Perhaps no anti-trafficking celebrity has been more active, though, than Ashton Kutcher. In 2009, Kutcher's then wife Demi Moore saw a television documentary about child sex trafficking in Cambodia. She told reporters that she began to look into the issue and discovered it happened in the United States as well.[44] The couple then formed the DNA Foundation ("DNA" was an acronym of sorts of their first names). The next year, they launched their Real Men Don't Buy Girls campaign against child sex trafficking, enlisting a long list of male celebrities to appear holding signs with the campaign's slogan on it. These included Kutcher himself, Justin Timberlake, Jamie Foxx, Bradley Cooper, and Sean Penn (here rather improbably reinventing himself as a feminist protector despite his longtime reputation as an allegedly brutal domestic abuser).[45] In 2012, Kutcher and Moore divorced. Kutcher renamed DNA; it became Thorn: Digital Defenders of Children. Just as thorns protect delicate flowers from would-be predators, so too would Kutcher protect the children of America.

Kutcher testified before the Senate Committee on Foreign Relations in 2017, choking back tears as he described rescuing six thousand children from sex traffickers with his digital solutions and software. Claiming that "internet trolls" told him to "stick to his day job," he defiantly proclaimed, "My day job is as the chairman and co-founder of Thorn. We build software to fight human trafficking and the sexual exploitation of children."[46] He claimed to have met victims all over the world; participated in FBI raids; seen child pornography from Cambodia; and used his technology, called Spotlight, to save the children. Regarding this miraculous software, he demurred, "In an effort to protect its capacity over time, I won't give much detail about what it does, but it's a tool that can be used by law enforcement to prioritize their caseload. It's a neural net, it gets smarter over time, it gets better and it gets more efficient as people use it, and it's working."[47] He went on to claim that law enforcement agencies using it had reduced their investigation time by 60 percent.

The truth of Kutcher's success is more complicated. Although media reported that he had "saved" or "helped save" almost six thousand children from sex trafficking, the software actually merely *identified* six thousand *possible* cases.[48] Of these, 103 children were rescued. That is laudable. We also don't know much about them, including whether they were children abducted and raped on camera by sex tourists (as he claimed in the beginning of his testimony), or teenagers engaging in survival sex who would therefore be classified as trafficked, or children in foster homes being abused, another type of case that Kutcher mentioned. In his testimony, he bemoaned the fact that over and over again, rescued girls ran away and went back to selling sex. "The recidivism rates are through the roof. It's astonishing because when Maslow's

Hierarchy of Needs are (*sic*) not being met, people will resort to survival. And if this is their means of survival and the only source of love that they have in their life, that's what they go for. So, we have to address the pipeline out and we have to create support systems on the other end. It's not an entitlement, it's a demand to end slavery."[49]

Kutcher then requested more money from Congress and, in a parastatal move par excellence, cited his bona fides as a venture capitalist and entrepreneur: "We need money, we need financing in order to build these tools. . . . [I recommend continuing] to foster these private-public partnerships. Spotlight was only enabled by the McCain Institution and the full support of Senator McCain. . . . We got the support of companies that oftentimes war with each other—from Google to Microsoft to AWS [Amazon Web Services] to Facebook. And some of our other technology initiatives include many, many other private companies."[50] According to Forbes, Thorn was one of eight recipients to share in an over $280 million grant from TED (of the famous TED Talks series, in which people present compelling narratives for laypeople about simple solutions to complicated problems).[51]

The public-private cooperatives Kutcher advocates for are already a feature of the anti–sex trafficking landscape, which also includes collaborations between Polaris Project and Palantir Technologies, a data analysis firm known for working with the CIA, US military, and major banks. The "dashboard" of the platform Thorn developed "doesn't just aggregate data according to geographical location, but also culls other relevant information—age, immigration status, language needs, shelter requirements."[52] This well-intentioned data mining also scraped up sensitive information on vulnerable populations and gave it to a company that not only sells data but partners with parastatal actors who can enact grievous harm.

Sex workers were skeptical of such partnerships, including the question of why taxpayer money should be diverted when the wealthiest tech companies in the world are involved, but also about Kutcher's claims and Spotlight specifically. Spotlight uses algorithms to analyze escort data in order to attempt to spot advertisements that are secretly for sex trafficked children. Consensual sex workers complain, though, that the software is profiling and tracking them without their consent. Moreover, Thorn shares its data with police and law enforcement. This parastatal cooperation both fetishizes statistics and data and creates a surveillance state that can act with impunity because its cause is ostensibly just. In the United States, selling sex is a crime, so this surveillance puts women at risk for further harassment, arrest, and violence from police. Writing for Engadget, Violet Blue points out that despite Thorn's CEO saying that the organization is only looking for child sex trafficking, "Of Thorn's 31 nonprofit partners, 27 target adults and vow to abolish consensual sex work under the banner of saving children from sex trafficking."[53] So while Kutcher says he is only out to save children, almost all of his partners are neo-abolitionists pushing End Demand agendas.

Kutcher also has a history of ignoring complaints from sex workers who said that websites such as Backpage.com allowed them to work safely, screen clients, and better manage their own affairs without needing to turn to third parties or pimps. In 2011, Kutcher waged a Twitter war on the *Village Voice*, which owned Backpage and had run a story about the Real Men Don't Buy Girls campaign called "Real Men Get Their Facts Straight."[54] In it, three *Village Voice* writers debunked the wild statistics Kutcher and his celebrity cohort had circulated, noting that Kutcher reported that 100,000–300,000 children would turn to prostitution that year when in fact the research he was referring to said that many were "at risk" of entering prostitution. (The *Village Voice* put the actual number at 827.) Kutcher responded to the *Village Voice*: "Find another way to justify that YOUR property facilitates the sale of HUMAN BEINGS . . . if you ever want 2 have a productive conversation about how 2 end human trafficking as opposed to belittling my efforts lmk" and "REAL MEN DON'T BUY GIRLS and REAL NEWS PUBLICATIONS DON'T SELL THEM."[55] The feud was all downhill from there. The federal government shut down Backpage several years later and, largely because of this, the *Village Voice* went out of business in 2018. Kutcher had the last laugh. Meanwhile, Thorn reports an annual revenue of about $5 million a year to further its digital monitoring of sex workers and suspected sex trafficking and has now added other celebrity affiliates, including Sofia Vergara, Eva Longoria, Zachary Quinto, David Spade, Ben Stiller, Drake, and Ludacris.[56]

Kutcher's appeals for public-private funding solutions, his desire to partner with Congress and conservative think tanks, and his eagerness to share his data with law enforcement around the world epitomize the rescue industry's dependence on parastatal alliances. And it's in work such as that of Thorn that one sees both hands of the state—the humanitarian left and militarized carceral right—working together ambidextrously.[57] Thorn also illustrates the powerful turn to celebrity and how celebrification of anti-trafficking intensifies the role of fundraising and the desire to maximize fund-raising capacity. What is more subtly hidden in this turn to celebrification is how the role of "raising awareness" and the instrumentalization of moral panics can further empower police, who are an enormous source of violence and abuse for sex workers.

THE SUSCEPTIBILITY OF CELEBRITIES TO FRAUD

I do not contend that sex trafficking doesn't exist, but I do think the anti-trafficking movement has made the term itself so intentionally meaningless that scholars and serious activists need new frameworks for studying and understanding the confluence of sexual exploitation and migration. The numbers are disingenuous, and there is a pervasive pattern of corruption and fraud in the rescue industry. This is especially true when there is big money on the line from celebrities, foundations, and donors. The move toward the parastate—and the influx of NGOs, celebrities, law enforcement, and social media influencers that has arisen as a result—has created opportunities for dishonest actors who know how to craft narratives. This happens because there is a voracious public appetite for such spectacles—live-tweeted raids, heart-wrenching movies, viral posts—and a desire to stand in solidarity with the saviors who are doing good work, thereby signaling one's own virtue to one's community and social media followers. Yet what is most important is that this happens at the expense of people who are *actually* being exploited for labor and/or sex. When society takes its cues from celebrities and misdirects its public and private resources toward scam charities or nonsensical "awareness campaigns," the actual victims—whose stories are more complicated and don't fit into memes and sound bites—are revictimized.

The rescue industry's turn toward relying on celebrities to be spokespeople, partners, and donors has resulted in a diminishment of the role of experts with deep local knowledge and a devaluation of expertise more broadly. The need to chase celebrities and the dollars that come with them has created a perverse incentive for anti-trafficking NGOs—especially those in underresourced nations—to serve up only the most pathos-driven and sensationalistic accounts of victims even if they are atypical. There remains much more interest on the part of celebrities in involving themselves with awareness campaigns than in actually helping victims, as seen in the recent sex trafficking cases against Jeffrey Epstein, who was a known and convicted trafficker with many celebrity connections. Thus, celebrity campaigns promoting awareness spur the public to panic but provide no relief.

As I describe later, the celebrification of the anti-trafficking industry has also resulted in several high-profile cases of outright fraud in which celebrities were fooled into supporting charismatic activists who had, in fact, bought local children from parents or orphanages and passed them off as sex trafficking survivors, even going so far as to force them to rehearse monologues and songs about abuse that never actually happened. In some instances, the "rescued children" accused the charismatic activists who had garnered Western media attention and foreign money of keeping them as prisoners or of abusing and molesting them. There is a danger in resorting to the celebrification of human rights causes and of moving to donor models that consist of Western donations flowing to camera-friendly activists turned entrepreneurs.

The Cambodian activist Somaly Mam rose to fame largely due to the work of the Pulitzer Prize–winning *New York Times* journalist Nick Kristof, who highlighted her work in his best-selling book *Half the Sky*, which he coauthored with his wife and fellow journalist Cheryl Wu-Dunn. (Somaly tends to go by her first name, rather like Beyoncé or Bono, so I follow that convention here in deference to her own branding.) Alongside Somaly, Kristof live-tweeted all the action. "Girls are rescued, but still very scared[.] Youngest looks about 13, trafficked from Vietnam."[58] And "Social workers comforting the girls, telling them they are free, won't be punished, rapes are over."[59] Then later, "I've been told to rush out of town for safety. That's what I'm doing now."[60] And "I'm safe & my live-tweeting of the raid on brothel in northern Cambodia is over. You can see them all on my Twitter page."[61]

As *Salon* noted, "Kristof's novel approaches to international women-rights reporting have previously included purchasing two Cambodian underage prostitutes for the purpose of liberating them and [publicly] naming a 9-year-old Congolese rape victim. After those generated criticism from victims' advocates, Kristof shouldn't be surprised that not everyone was cheering along his recent outing."[62] In the film version, Kristof is accompanied on his visit to see Somaly and her rescued girls by the actress Meg Ryan. The young Cambodian girls rush to greet and hug Ryan upon seeing her. Ryan says, "Each of their little hugs is such a success," remarking on how broken the girls had been before Somaly rescued them.[63] (Somaly points to one of the girls—perhaps in her early to mid-teens—and tells the actress laughingly that the girl kept running away from her to go back to the brothel where she worked, requiring multiple rescues.)

But why should these girls run to embrace Meg Ryan the moment she steps into the compound? While it is possible these girls growing up in Phnom Penh in 2011 had previously found great comfort in watching *You've Got Mail*, the effusive display toward the foreign actress gives the viewer an unsettling feeling that the children had been well prepared and coached for the cameras prior to the star's arrival. It only gets creepier when Somaly has the girls perform for Kristof and Ryan, singing songs about their rapes. "Who is brave enough to come up and sing their song?" Mam asks, as Kristof and Ryan sit before them expectantly. In a voice-over, Kristof explains, "It's often hard for these girls to put their past into words. But somehow in a song it's a little bit easier. And most of the girls have their own song that they have written to express their story. And other girls know them by heart and they sing together."[64]

One might even say they've rehearsed. The girls sing in Khmer, "It's difficult to breathe. Life is unfortunate."

Somaly begins to translate for the girls. "[My] heart is breaking. I'm just four years old and they sold me in the brothel. And I don't know nothing about the life here. And they destroy my life. They're beating me, beating me all the time. They force me to have sex like I'm an adult. I want my mother to come and help me. Where is she, why did she leave me alone?"[65]

One wonders what would possess someone to rehearse such a show with small children, asking the girls to perform on camera for two Western celebrities, ultimately to be shown to millions of Westerners. This commodification of third world suffering for an audience of armchair humanitarians truly boggles the mind.

In the film, Kristof explains that while he has been covering sex trafficking since the 1990s, "The wonderful thing about having Meg Ryan with us is that this is her first time in meeting victims of sex trafficking. My hope is that she can amplify those voices and help carry these kinds of stories to the world."[66]

As Ryan says, "Somaly is one of those charismatic people who you are thrown into the air with how impressed you are with their heroism and their dedication and their grace. And she's everything all at once."[67] Ryan is not the only celebrity to fall under Somaly's spell. As *Condé Nast Traveler* described in a feature, "In a flower-filled compound half an hour from Cambodia's Angkor Wat, several dozen women and girls are gathered around Susan Sarandon and Somaly Mam, telling their tearful stories. One woman was raped, then sold to a brothel, where she toiled for 12 years until she was freed in a raid orchestrated by Mam. 'Do you know you are safe now?' Sarandon asks, stroking the woman's hair. . . . Sarandon is a fund-raising powerhouse (she also supports Heifer International), landing a donation for a new dorm for the girls."[68]

Ryan and Sarandon weren't alone. In 2011, Sheryl Sandberg shared the stage with Somaly at *Fortune* magazine's Most Powerful Women summit. "Queen Sofia of Spain has for years promoted Mam's cause and even visited her in the hospital last year when she fell ill. Mark Zuckerberg's former PR guru, Brandee Barker, whom *The New York Times* recently described as 'perhaps the most sought-after image consultant in the startup world,' is a board member for the Somaly Mam Foundation, and Facebook Chief Operating Officer Sheryl Sandberg is an advisory board member."[69] As Mam made the round of cocktail parties in Manhattan and Beverly Hills, went on the *Tyra Banks Show*, and fundraised millions of dollars, she attracted increasing attention from journalists, and with that attention came more scrutiny.

Although Somaly claims to have saved thousands of girls from sex trafficking, reporting from *Cambodia Daily* and *Newsweek* began to unravel her many lies. In 2009, Kristof had reported on a girl named Pross, who features in the film and who also appeared with Oprah on her television network, who stated that she had been tortured, been electrocuted, endured abortions, and had an eye gouged out by a pimp. Unfortunately for Somaly, the girl's family, neighbors, and doctor contradicted this account. Most damningly, her doctor said that he had performed surgery on her eye for a tumor and had before-and-after photographs of the girl's eye (with its tumor).[70] Alas, no eye-gouging pimps after all. As *Newsweek* explained regarding another girl, "Late last year, Ratha finally confessed that her story was fabricated and carefully rehearsed for the cameras under Somaly's instruction, and only after she was chosen from a group of girls who had been put through an audition. Now in her early 30s and living a modest life on the outskirts of Phnom Penh, Ratha says she reluctantly allowed herself to be depicted as a child prostitute: Somaly said that . . . if I want to help another woman I have to do [the interview] very well.'"[71]

More inconsistencies about Somaly's own story and the stories of the girls followed. The teachers and local officials in her home village contradicted the details in her book. She was never forced to marry a soldier; she was never sold by her grandfather. Her childhood friends assert that she graduated high school with them, although she has variously stated she was sold into sexual slavery at age nine or ten, but other times has said she was sixteen.[72] In 2012, she was forced to admit she had lied to the UN General Assembly when she told them that army soldiers had killed eight of her girls at the shelter. Her former husband has said he helped her find a ghostwriter to sell her tales to Hollywood but claims he didn't know about the fraud. It also turned out that her fourteen-year-old daughter was not kidnapped and gang-raped on camera as punishment for Somaly's anti-trafficking work, which she had previously claimed. She made the whole thing up.[73]

Even local missionaries doing anti–sex trafficking work in Cambodia remarked that none of Somaly's stories about child exploitation had ever made sense to them, people who rescued actual girls (but failed to make millions of dollars in the process). Patrick Stayton, the head of the evangelical Christian group International Justice Mission (IJM), said the group saw teenagers aged fourteen to seventeen exploited, trafficked, and raped with horrifying frequency, but asserted that it was essentially unheard of to find clients who wanted to have sex with three-, four-, and five-year-old girls, as Somaly had claimed. "We've never seen prepubescent girls, or very very rarely," he explained.[74] (Psychologists distinguish between groups of adults who report sexual attraction to minors based on their attraction to particular age sets. It is, indeed, extremely rare to find people who wish to have sex with toddlers and young children, but common for men to find teenaged girls sexually arousing.) Yet the shocking tales of baby rapes made Somaly a fortune in Hollywood, while no one remembers the names of the other, scrappier local activists working with sexually exploited women and children in Cambodia.

It is unclear how many of the girls in Somaly's care were sex trafficked or abused (almost certainly some of them) and how many Somaly purchased from poor parents or orphanages after they passed their auditions and screen tests. Eventually Somaly was brought up on criminal charges and banned from ever operating an NGO in Cambodia again, and Kristof had to print an apology in the *New York Times* for believing her "lies" and said he wished he'd never met her.[75] Despite all this, PBS has not retracted or even added a disclaimer to the episode of *Half the Sky* devoted to Somaly Mam and Meg Ryan. Good TV is good TV, even if it's dishonest journalism.

Adding even more complexity, like many anti–sex trafficking organizations, Somaly worked closely with fast fashion apparel industry leaders such as Janet Rivett-Carnac, the vice president of global sourcing for Gap Incorporated. Somaly, along with other organizations like IJM, train "rescued" girls to work in the textile and garment-making industry, including brands that are infamous for running brutal sweatshops.[76] Perhaps it should come as no surprise that none other than Kristof is a famous defender of sweatshops, a position he articulated in the case of Cambodia in a controversial *New York Times* piece called, "Where Sweatshops Are a Dream." In it he writes, "The best way to help people in the poorest countries isn't to campaign against sweatshops but to promote manufacturing there. . . . Among people who work in development, many strongly believe (but few dare say very loudly) that one of the best hopes for the poorest countries would be to build their manufacturing industries. But global campaigns against sweatshops make that less likely."[77] It's a good thing that Somaly, the woman Kristof described as his "hero," can provide labor for the sweatshops after Kristof and Ryan rescue them, at least in the case of the girls who don't pass Somaly's auditions and monologue coaching and make it onto her international celebrity tours.

Journalists just can't seem to get enough of these rescue organizations, however, and are unable to learn the lessons. As detailed in their 2017 documentary film *The Wrong Light*, filmmakers Josie Swantek Heitz and Dave Adams set out to make a documentary in Northern Thailand about the swashbuckling Mickey Choothesa and his organization, Children's Organization of Southeast Asia (COSA).[78] Choothesa describes himself as a war photographer turned anti–sex trafficking crusader who engages in daring raids and rescue missions to save young girls and bring them to his center even as bullets rain down on him.

As in Somaly's case, there are red flags galore. COSA guidelines prohibit anyone from asking the girls about their past (supposedly to avoid traumatizing them). Even the staff and volunteers followed this rule, believing the girls to be survivors of sexual exploitation. But when the filmmakers tracked down the girls' parents and stopped allowing Choothesa to translate (which he had being doing inaccurately), the villagers described Choothesa offering them money for girls (but never boys) in the village, essentially purchasing the children and taking them away to be "educated." Once the filmmakers were able to ask the girls directly about their pasts, the girls were shocked and horrified to see the COSA website and to hear that Choothesa had wholly fabricated their personal histories of sex trafficking, using them to market his group for profit. They had no idea that the staff and volunteers had been told they were survivors of sex trafficking. Choothesa also seems to have lied about his own past, having passed off another (rather famous) war photographer's photos as his own even as he charged tourists to go on photo tours in Thailand with him. A representative from Hands Across the Water, COSA's biggest donor, further explained that "Mickey was transferring tens of thousands of Australian dollars to a bank account in Australia. Where else the money was going, I don't know. The original fraud was three quarters of a million dollars that he committed against us as a charity."[79]

More girls—seventeen total by the film's close—came forward to contradict Choothesa. He expelled them from the organization and from their schools. A young girl named Fon, one of his former charges, explained, "When Mickey found out that we knew the truth, that he lied about us being trafficking victims, he had to get rid of us. I thought, what do I do with my life now? It's a feeling of fear like I've never had before."[80]

Another girl explained, "They brought us together for a meeting at COSA. They wanted to know who we were talking to. . . . They asked if anybody had told the westerners that COSA is not about human trafficking. . . . They were pounding the table, very aggressive. We were shocked . . . because we believed this was our home."[81] What Choothesa didn't know was that the evicted girls had secretly recorded the meeting on one of their phones, confirming COSA's deceptions.

Even worse, several of the girls eventually disclosed that Choothesa had molested them. "We stayed in the same room as Mickey, just the two of us [girls and him]. Before the incident happened, Mickey took a shower. . . . He asked us to give him a massage," one explained, describing an incident that occurred when she was fourteen. "After the massage, we both went to take a shower. When we came back, Mickey had already turned off the light. Around 2 am, he started by taking my hand and touching his penis. I tried to pull my hand back. I wanted to tell my friend, but I was so afraid that Mickey would do something."[82]

Another girl went on: "Mickey has a behavior that is very nasty. . . . That night, we wanted to watch a movie in the house. At first, he only took off his shirt. And then, he asked us to give him a massage in the other room. The thing that we never thought he would do, he was trying to pull my pajama skirt. He put his hand in it. . . . I didn't know what to do. . . . I couldn't believe he did that. Why is [he] hurting children like this?"[83] Choothesa declined to comment on the new allegations and moved on from the NGO, apparently still pursuing his business venture of photo tours for foreigners.

Like Somaly, "Uncle Mickey" had cultivated celebrity status within the NGO world. People functioning at that level of fundraising and social media prominence eventually can become celebrities in their own right because they're able to connect with tech entrepreneurs, movie stars, filmmakers, and journalists, and sometimes have the same public relations managers. They are highly skilled in creating public spectacle, but the actual suffering and exploitation of children and women is rendered invisible by the rescue industry's commitments to celebrification and the fallacious spectacles that attend to that process.

In yet another high-profile case, a woman in the United States named Chong Kim was eventually found to have invented a fanciful tale of her own sexual slavery, which was the subject of a book and movie. As *Salon* explains, "the nightmare of human sex trafficking was famously exposed in the 2012 film *Eden*, wherein a Korean-American high school student is kidnapped and forced into a life of sexual slavery along with dozens, or even hundreds, of other young women. The based-on-a-true-story narrative uncovered and explored a 'horrible underworld' according to reviews, raising awareness about a scourge of exploitation targeting the innocent."[84] The film, which starred Beau Bridges as the main antagonist, was a critical success (82% on Rotten Tomatoes) and garnered several awards and accolades. As film critic Noah Berlatsky explains, "There was only one problem: The film was a lie. There was not, in fact, a massive kidnapping ring dragooning New Mexico teens into sexual slavery. The person on whom the film was supposedly based, Chong Kim, did not commit multiple murders in the course of a daring escape because it never occurred. Trafficking in real life has about as much to do with *Eden* as a real-life infectious disease has to do with *The Walking Dead*."[85]

According to David Schmader in the *Stranger*, the anti-trafficking charity Breaking Out, which had worked with Kim, conducted a year-long investigation and concluded that Kim was not a survivor of sex trafficking as she claimed. "After thorough investigation into her story, people, records and places, as well as many interviews with producers, publishers and people from organizations, we found no truth to her story. In fact, we found a lot of fraud, lies, and most horrifically capitalizing and making money on an issue where so many people are suffering."[86] Schmader also describes Kim defrauding various other charities by "collecting money in their name, using their 501(c)(3) status for her benefit while none of these organizations have seen a dime. I ask if anyone has sent money or goods to Chong Kim for another organization to please contact us as we are leading the legal pursuit of the issue."[87]

Salon writer Berlatsky, responding to the news, notes that Hollywood really should have seen it coming.[88] He says that *Eden* feels familiar not because it is factual, but because it relies on the same tired tropes of other exploitation films "which are clustered about so densely and insistently that it's hard to believe anyone missed them. There are women-in-prison shower scenes (more sedate than the norm, it's true, but recognizable nonetheless). The trope of giving prisoners kittens to love is straight out of *Caged* from 1950, one of the most important films in the genre. There's also some S&M fetish (again a staple of the genre), and inventive tortures involving semi-nudity (here victims are chained in a bucket of ice). The arc of the film is by-the-numbers rape-revenge, and the meth-smoking assistant bad guy seems like a thinly-disguised lift of *Breaking Bad's* Jesse Pinkman."[89]

Nor are such frauds limited to large-scale, high-profile cases. According to the Asia Pacific Regional Correspondent for the Network of Sex Work Projects, in 2017 a Swedish NGO called Love and Hope (formerly Love Nepal) allegedly collected donations from Swedes under the false pretense that it was "saving children from brothels" and even posted before and after photos on social media that went viral, depicting three Nepalese "girls around the age of 8. Prostitutes and total destruction. Three girls 6 years later. Full of hope and faith in a future they never thought were there. They laugh, they smile, their eyes are full of life again. It's this one that is LoveNepal. Thanks for joining and making it possible."[90] However, Håken Gabrielsson, of a Nepalese human rights NGO, claims he had shown the photos to Mikael Alfven in 2009, who then used them with a made-up story.[91] Hannah Badi, a local Nepalese woman, reported that Alfven had instructed her to lie and coached her on how to make up a "better story" to increase donations. "Even though Hannah was not a sex slave in the brothel, she was persuaded to say so. She spoke of how nervous she felt lying, but Mikael would give thumbs up and say 'remember remember' asking her to cry when telling parts of the story."[92] The group received about US$3.4 million in donations the year of the faked viral photos, double the previous year. The Swedish government has begun an investigation.

According to NBC, "San Diego-based 'Saved in America' has made dozens of television appearances over the years, touting its contributions in the fight against sex trafficking. With the help of former Navy SEALS and police officers, the group says it assists law enforcement and parents in locating missing or exploited children."[93] However, the group was yanked from a $2 million plan to run a group home by the county. Its main funder, the Lynch Foundation for Children, cut all its ties amid allegations that the executive director of Saved in America had used bogus statistics and lied in his efforts to garner funding. (The Lynch Foundation later launched an investigation into the background of Saved in America's executive director.) There were also dubious expenses, including almost a quarter of a million dollars in taxpayer-funded expenditures related to a tricked-out RV for the Christian group. Saved in America claimed to have rescued 223 children since 2014, but it's unclear what exactly constituted "rescue," as the group of ex-military and former cops is short on details about any actual children and says it merely serves as "a liaison" among law enforcement agencies.

In another case, Courage House, located on fifty-two acres of property in Northern California, claimed to "[promote] a grand vision of local and global expansion in the fight against sex trafficking. For a time, its founder and CEO, Jenny Williamson of Granite Bay, was catapulted into celebrity orbit."[94] But it abruptly closed, facing citations for inadequate staffing and violations of clients' rights. Even after the facility was shut down, the organization continued to hold fundraisers and opened another home in Tanzania. It took in millions of dollars from individual donors as well as from churches, corporations, and other foundations that the *Sacramento Bee* described as a "who's who" list of names. "The state was contributing $9,100 a month per girl."[95] Williamson planned to expand the home to sixty girls. Unfortunately, the *Bee* was left asking, "Where are the victims?" The money dried up, and the four girls in the house were moved. Williamson said the organization had plans to move to different states and to shift its focus to adult victims, adding that California's requirements were "in conflict with our Christian values/beliefs."[96]

Congressional money also flows into groups with little training or effectiveness, shutting out more experienced and legitimate anti-trafficking organizations that support decriminalization of sex work or use peer-based, sex worker–led approaches to anti-trafficking. For example, in 2020 the US Department of Justice ignored advice it had requested from staffers and spurned the recommendation that federal grants totaling over a million dollars be given to Chicanos Por La Causa in Phoenix, Arizona, and the Catholic Charities of the Diocese of Palm Beach, California, and instead gave over half a million dollars to Hookers for Jesus, which is a Christian anti-prostitution group that operates a safe house that is only available for women willing to leave the sex trade. Safehouse rules include a ban on all "'secular magazines with articles, pictures, etc.

that portray worldly views/advice on living, sex, clothing, [and] makeup tips and [include] mandatory attendance [at] the organization's religious services."[97]

In 2016, a member of the FBI's human trafficking task force and some overzealous officials prosecuted thirty immigrants for child sex trafficking, alleging that a Somali Muslim gang had been forcing young girls into prostitution in Minnesota and Tennessee. A dismayed Sixth Circuit Court of Appeals found no evidence whatsoever that such a ring existed. "If the prosecution proved any sex trafficking at all (and we have serious doubts that it did), then at best it proved two separate, unrelated, and dissimilar sex trafficking" cases, the judges wrote.[98] *Reason* magazine, covering the story, reports that the prosecutions grew out of convoluted statements made by an alleged victim who was mentally ill and who had been coached into fabricating the story by a police officer and the FBI agent.[99] The officer was caught lying to the grand jury, and the court called the prosecution's witnesses "unworthy of belief." Here again, one sees the same sex panic that fueled the white slave trade panic, but in this instance, the folk devils in question are dozens of Muslim immigrant men, who were prosecuted and some of whom, despite not being guilty of sex trafficking, were deported as a result of having come to the attention of the authorities.

The desire to play hero can be quite strong, especially for men, as evidenced by actions of the hypermasculine Navy SEALS, the overzealous FBI agent, NGO leaders like the leader of Love Nepal and COSA's Mickey Choothasa, and journalists like Kristof. In the summer of 2016, New York City councilman Andy King claimed that fourteen "attractive girls" had gone missing in the Bronx between 2014 and 2016, blaming their disappearance on an imagined sex trafficking ring that he intended to bring down. The tabloid *New York Daily News* seized on the story and began stoking fears about teen abductions, even as the New York City Police Department quickly confirmed that eleven of the fourteen were long since back at home.[100] "At King's press conference, he and other demonstrators held signs featuring photos of the girls (photos that have since been spread widely by the media) and information about their disappearances. Apparently, however, King hadn't bothered talking to the families . . . before sounding the alarm about them" and therefore hadn't realized they were actually already home, never having been victimized by the ring of sex traffickers about which he had held his press conference.[101]

The obsession with sex trafficking and willingness to believe fabrications that stretch all credulity can have dire consequences. In 2016, a viral conspiracy theory by the far-right conspiracy group QAnon erupted during the presidential election, claiming that the emails of Hillary Clinton's campaign manager, John Podesta, had secret messages encoded in them about a vast sex trafficking ring run by high-ranking members of the Democratic Party, including Clinton herself.[102] Alt-right media outlets fueled this idea. Eventually, a man drove from North Carolina to Washington, D.C., to Comet Ping Pong, a pizza joint. (QAnon believed the words *cheese pizza* in emails between Democratic staffers were code for "child pornography.") Believing there were child sex slaves held in the basement, he entered the restaurant and opened fire with his rifle.

QAnon is particularly taken with the notion that liberal Hollywood actors such as Tom Hanks and Oprah Winfrey are working with people like Barack Obama, Hillary Clinton, and George Soros to traffic children. They believe that the military recruited Donald Trump to dismantle the vast child sex trafficking ring—a clandestine organization that also secretly runs world affairs. In 2020, QAnon members ran for Congress in fifteen states. One, Marjorie Taylor Greene from Georgia, won a seat in the House of Representatives, and another, Lauren Boebert, a vocal sympathizer and proponent of known QAnon leaders, won a seat in the House from Colorado. Precisely because the media speak about sex trafficking as a vast but invisible threat, the concept is easily corrupted and incorporated into moral panics and conspiracy theories. This combination of vagueness and hyperbole on the part of media and anti-trafficking groups is now having very real consequences.[103]

THE MEGA-EVENT

Celebrification has likewise become a dominant mode for anti-trafficking awareness campaigns vis-à-vis global sporting events. Athletes increasingly have taken up the cause. Baltimore Ravens tight end Benjamin Watson and his wife flew with other NFL players to the Dominican Republic on a trip sponsored by IJM, which touts itself as the world's largest antislavery organization. IJM promised to "take them to see a rescue of women and children and visit field workers to hear their stories. Watson also plans to host a sports day with the children."[104] Following the 2012 London Olympics, a trio of charities in England—The Jubilee Campaign, Happy Child International, and the A21 Campaign—teamed up with the support of Britain's National Crime Agency to arrange for

Brazil-bound flights from the United Kingdom during the 2014 World Cup to show public service announcements (PSAs) about child prostitution featuring players asking fans to "help protect our kids." The campaign (and attendant organization) was called It's a Penalty. In order to get and keep people's attention, its creators used Olympic and World Cup athletes as spokespeople.[105]

It's a Penalty makes the now-familiar claim that "more people [are] enslaved today around the world than in all the 400 years of the trans-Atlantic slave trade" and asserts that "During high profile and sporting events with the influx of hundreds and thousands of people, exploitation can increase." It initially focused on the World Cup and the Olympics but has now added the Super Bowl in the United States (despite saying it is focused on Commonwealth countries), the Commonwealth Games in Australia, and the Rugby Sevens in Hong Kong. The group makes the following incredible, if alliterative, claim:

OUR GLOBAL CAMPAIGNS DURING MAJOR SPORTING EVENTS PREVENT HUMAN TRAFFICKING BY:

- EDUCATING about the global issues of abuse, exploitation and trafficking, penalties for offenders, and the signs to look out for #knowthesigns
- EQUIPPING sporting fans, tourists and the general public with mechanisms to report such crimes, both whilst at home and abroad
- ENCOURAGING people to make a report and stand up against human trafficking

Here again is an emphasis on awareness rather than action, though for It's a Penalty the main actions available include making reports on suspected cases of sexual exploitation. A lot of its campaigns are based on "knowing the signs" of sex trafficking:

An adult could be being sexually exploited if they . . .

- Are isolated from their family and friends
- Are unable to explain injuries, possessions or income
- Have strange markings/brandings/tattoos (e.g., ways for exploiters/pimps to identify them)
- Are being controlled by another person
- Display paranoia or lack of trust
- Have untreated health or dental problems, particularly sexually-transmitted infections
- Display a lack of self-esteem with feelings of shame and humiliation
- Avoid making eye contact and interacting with others[106]

While it is certainly possible that an exploited person would exhibit these signs, so do all manner of other people. (As someone surrounded by university students, I might venture to say that perhaps a majority of them meet more than a few of these criteria, to say nothing of the socially maladjusted academics teaching them.) In raising awareness and urging people to report one another in suspected cases, It's a Penalty encourages a paranoid reading of strangers, particularly foreigners.

Many airlines and associations in the travel industry (including truckers, flight attendants, and airport employees) have been involved in similar "know the signs of trafficking" training and campaigns. This has led to individuals, mostly women of color, being detained. For example, in 2017, US immigration authorities questioned and detained twenty-six-year old Stephanie Ung for over an hour upon her return from a vacation in Cancún because they believed she was a victim of sex trafficking. According to NBC, a tearful Ung recounted, "I just kept telling them that I wanted to go home for my family Thanksgiving dinner, and that they were making me late, but they just didn't care.... They just laughed.... The fact that I missed dinner with my family—you can't take that back."[107]

This is part of a larger trend in the travel industry. Airline Ambassadors, just one of several organizations that trains airline personnel to "spot the signs" of sex trafficking, tells flight attendants to look for passengers who appear "frightened" or "nervous," people who are traveling with someone who is not a parent or relative, or people "who appear drugged."[108] (As a very frequent flyer myself, I've seen an awful lot of nervous passengers who are uncomfortable flying, and as someone who usually pops a full dose of Ambien or Klonopin on any transatlantic flight, I'm sure I've looked pretty well drugged on a few of my journeys.) These well-meaning attempts by vigilant laypeople to surveil one another and to be constantly on the lookout for everyday things that could be construed as trafficking are similar to post-9/11 campaigns to be constantly on the lookout for potential terrorists in airports and on airplanes. The media abound with stories of people attacking fellow passengers for speaking Arabic, for example. Sometimes the consequences of such paranoia extend beyond mere inconvenience and into the stuff of nightmares.

In a truly horrifying case, NPR's *This American Life* reported extensively on a Cambodian immigrant to the United States, Yong Xiong, who was detained by US immigration representatives at the airport when she landed on a flight from Laos. The officers felt that she looked young, despite her presenting them with legitimate documents verifying she was nineteen. She explained, "I just told them it was my choice. That I was not being trafficked, and it was my decision to come to the US to be with my fiancé [a Cambodian man]. Because it was my choice."[109] But as NPR's Nadía Reiman explains, "The officers go through a checklist of eleven questions to determine whether Yong is being trafficked; stuff like, is she missing any documents? Does she appear scared? The answer to 10 of them is no. But then there's one about whether or not she's been coached on what to say. And that one the officers write down, quote, 'Appear to be.' That, plus the fact that she looked so young, seemed to make the officers believe that, yeah, she's probably trafficked."[110]

Reiman goes on to explain to listeners that "this checklist is just normal procedure. It's what officers have to do if they think something's going on. But then they did do something unusual. They wrote a new birthday into her file, January 1, 2000, making her a minor, 17 years old." The officers detained Yong overnight and then the next day they subjected her to a dental exam known for its highly inaccurate results and the fact that at best it is accurate within a range of about five years. In the end, the officers used the exam to declare Yong to be a minor. They then sent her to a juvenile detention facility. "Yong is assigned to a room with four other girls. There are 13-year-olds at the shelter, but also babies. She spends her days doing all these kids' things, like she has to vote for which kids movie to watch during movie night. She goes on trips to the zoo. She does math worksheets."[111] Immigration officials kept moving her birthday back, keeping her at seventeen and then lowering her age to fifteen. She could never age out of the system.

Finally, after fourteen months in the shelter, just after her twenty-first birthday, authorities released Young as a minor into the custody of her aunt, telling the woman, "You need to be aware that she is only 15. We've given her multiple birth dates, but that's the birthday that she's coming home with. It is the birthday that [says] she is 15 years old. You need to keep an eye on her. You must know that [if] anyone who is 18 or older comes and takes her to go get married, you will go to jail for it." As a condition of her release, she had to attend high school with the "other children." In an ending to the story that is as ironic as it is Kafkaesque, according to Reiman, "Everyone was just afraid to miss a trafficking case. And then her passport, her visa, all her documents from Laos just didn't matter anymore. Yong's still here under a fiancé visa, so she has to get married. If she doesn't, she has to go back to Laos."[112] And so Yong had to wait to become an adult again—and hope her fiancé would continue to wait for her, too.

The obsession with knowing the signs of the invisible victims of trafficking leads to the policing of the movements of women of color, particularly migrants. While many of the awareness campaigns prominently feature white girls, there is also a special fixation on Southeast Asian women and girls, whom the rescue industry imagines as especially gullible and easily recruited by traffickers and also especially unable to exercise agency or make self-interested calculations. Racial stereotypes about Asian passivity are deeply embedded into radical feminist, evangelical, and governmental groups. The constant search for signs of victimization also leads to the profiling and tracking of sex workers, whose agency would-be saviors deny. Everything seen in the airport—a tattoo, someone fatigued by travel, too many bags, too few bags, dressing too well, dressing too poorly, introverted people who don't like chatting to the nosy strangers sitting next to them— becomes a flag for potential sex trafficking.

The groups behind It's a Penalty encourage everyone to be on the lookout for "the signs." They are awareness-driven groups, after all. And so, those flying to cities where sporting events are happening are treated to a mandatory video that comes on their seatback screens and over the airplane's speakers automatically. British footballer and sports broadcaster Gary Lineker appears, proclaiming, "The World Cup is an incredible event and Brazil promises to be one of the greatest host nations ever. But sadly, some people will use this opportunity to sexually exploit children. . . . Remember, 17 or under, it's a penalty."[113] Then several other football players individually echo, "It's a penalty!" over and over. On the ground in Rio, football players appear in ubiquitous posters in a similar campaign referring to sexual exploitation as a "red card" (i.e., a severe football penalty).

It's a Penalty's website proclaims, "It was set to be the greatest sporting event in the world, however, many unscrupulous people would use it as an opportunity to traffic children, dress them up to look older and exploit them in order to make money." It encourages the gringos: "IF YOU SEE SOMETHING, SAY SOMETHING by dialing the Brazilian child protection helpline."[114] As I documented earlier in this book, the Brazilian police are notoriously brutal toward marginalized populations, including prostitutes, street children, and beggars. The idea that foreigners should take it upon themselves to "look for signs" and go about calling the police on Brazil's most vulnerable women and children crosses from the realm of arrogance to mortal danger.

The other PSAs from It's a Penalty look much the same from event to event, although they change the athletes in question, who each take turns reading their short lines. For the 2019 Miami Super Bowl, for example, the speakers were US American football players urging people to call to report anything suspicious. Unlike in many of the countries where It's a Penalty operates, in the United States all prostitution is illegal. People selling sex, even if they are underage, can often be charged with prostitution-related offenses and suffer serious consequences, including arrest, fines, imprisonment, loss of child custody, and even placement on sex offender registries. The public has little sympathy because of a general sense that criminals (whatever their crimes, but especially crimes involving sex, including prostitution) get what's coming to them. Here, raising awareness slides into the realm of potential harm. And yet It's a Penalty is quick to report its measurable "impacts," which it does with bulleted points like "reached 307 million people throughout the 2014 World Cup period."[115] (No method for arriving at this number is shown.) It claims that every British Airways flight for three months showed the film, reaching 80,000 travelers. The organization also gave out awareness-raising wristbands at airports and at sports matches. Tellingly, it claims that over 11,000 calls were made throughout the World Cup period reporting crimes against children.[116] (It's a Penalty does not stipulate what the crimes were or whether a crime was found to have been committed, whether those suspected crimes were related to the Cup, or how many more calls this is than are normally received.)

In my own research during the 2014 World Cup in Brazil, NGOs doing outreach work routinely reported to the Observatório da Prostituição when they encountered incidents with minors, but these were almost never sex related and had to do with children being pressed by poor families or gangs into selling snacks and souvenirs. It's a Penalty proudly reports that during the World Cup, the government received reports on twenty-nine foreign nationals.[117] Out of 11,252 calls that it received, that's .0025 percent. It's also not clear how many of those twenty-nine reports were duplicates or even about legitimate cases of exploitation. All those millions of unique views and all that hype for a handful of possibly unfounded complaints. And yet there is no evidence that any of those minuscule number of cases involved a consequential figure in any kind of larger organized criminal network. Moreover, It's a Penalty offers no actual information on whether charges were brought as a result of these calls. Such a total failure sounds like a rather inefficient use of time, money, people power, and other resources for all that "awareness" raised. It might just be that awareness raising is an overhyped and unreliable strategy that primarily benefits content creators, social media influencers, celebrities, and rescue industry personnel rather than people experiencing exploitation working in sex trades.

The Brits were not the only foreigners getting in on the action, though. A group of nuns from seventy-nine countries, led by Sister Gabriella Bottani of Italy, warned not only about the usual threat of child sex trafficking during the World Cup but also about the kidnapping of children to sell in illegal adoptions. In her defense, there are some awful failings in the adoption system in Brazil, though why child adoptions would increase during the World Cup is beyond me.[118] The awareness-raising campaign was called Play for Life, Report Trafficking and consisted of leafleting at airports and touristy areas, urging people to call the police.[119] "Without awareness," said Sister Carmen Sammut, "without acting together in favor of human dignity, the World Cup finals may turn out to be a terrible shame instead of a feast for humanity."[120] As news reports noted, "the umbrella group organizing the campaign is called Talitha Kum, an Aramaic expression that the Bible says Jesus used when commanding a young girl to rise from the dead" in the Gospels.[121] This imperative, and its assumptions about the interior state of minors involved in prostitution (i.e., as already dead and lifeless), may be as telling as anything else.

Before Brazil hosted the World Cup and the Olympics, it first had to host a number of other major events spanning several years to prove that its bid could be successful. Thus, it hosted the Pan-American Games in 2007 as a sort of audition and, after being awarded the right to host the World Cup in 2014, hosted the Confederations Cup in 2013 to show that it had made the necessary preparations. During this period in the early 2010s, there was an increasing amount of concern in the Brazilian media about sex tourism and child exploitation. And so in 2011, a former children's television program star named Xuxa (who is something of a national treasure in Brazil) brought together a group of approximately twenty Brazilian celebrities to produce and sing a song called "Carinho da verdade" (meaning something like "Truth's Affection") to help combat the sexual exploitation of children and adolescents.[122]

"Carinho da verdade" is a celebrity-charity song produced in the same video format as the widely circulated "We Are the World" and "Do They Know It's Christmas?" Celebrities sing individual lines in a recording studio, often with a hand to their ear or headphones, swaying a bit, and then belt out a lumbering, sentimental, and uncomplicated refrain together. The celebrities singing against child exploitation included popular stars such as Beth Carvalho, Preta Gil, Luan Santana, and Ivete Sangalo, the latter of whom would become a UN spokesperson for Brazil a few years later on the subject of sex trafficking. Sangalo would also later actively campaign against prostitution during the World Cup and Olympics in Brazil.

The sense of pending danger from sex traffickers was also boosted in Brazil for the World Cup by a wildly popular telenovela filled with popular actors. *Salve Jorge* (translated nonliterally as *Brave Woman* when released internationally) ran for 179 episodes from 2012 to 2013 in the Brazilian network Rede Globo's prime spot.[123] In the opening scene, an eighteen-year-old woman named Morena ("brown," which is also a colloquial racial term and term of endearment for mixed-race women in Brazil) is in Istanbul at a sex slave auction. She stands on an auction block in a gorgeous but revealing Turkish gown, looking both radiant and terrified as men in tuxedos circle her, inspecting her like a prized heifer. She is sold for US$3,500. Then the audience sees Morena running terrified through the streets trying to find help before a flashback brings us back to eight months earlier. Viewers learn how she found herself sex trafficked from the violent Complexo do Alemão favela in Rio de Janeiro. Morena is an unemployed single mother down on her luck, but she is blessed with an adorable four-year-old son. Wanting to better her life and provide for her son, she accepts a job working in a café in Istanbul. Except, of course, it's a scam. The devious women who recruit her are actually running an international billion-dollar sex trafficking ring. By the end of the series, many adventures and twists later, she has struggled to bring down the sex traffickers and return to her lost love in Brazil.

The telenovela is a dramatic form built on the melodrama genre. It would be a disingenuous academic critique to call it out for being unrealistic. Indeed, trafficking narratives are practically synonymous with melodramatic plot structures, as Carole Vance and Jo Doezema have both noted.[124] In telenovelas, as in melodramas, good and evil come in only Manichean varieties and, in the end, the universe metes out justice, bestowing happy and sad endings generally aligned with one's virtue.

As with the white slave trade panic and its racist invocation of the "yellow peril" and caricatures of sex slave masters, *Salve Jorge* trots out similar racist tropes in its depictions of Turkey, complete with harem imagery, flowing silks, and a slave auction block. It invokes the aesthetics of the Orientalist artist Jean-Léon Gérome's (1824–1904) famous paintings of sex slaves in the Middle East. And like the pulp novels about sex trafficking that I briefly mentioned in chapter 1, wherein consenting prostitutes are punished in the end while nonconsenting victims can be rescued and rehabilitated, so too do melodramatic narratives depict sex trafficking today. In fact, this is essential to the myths produced by the rescue industry, which emphasize incredibly rare examples of sex trafficking that meet high moral criteria while ignoring the much more common and complicated question of migrant sex workers who experience varying degrees of exploitation, but who may want better work conditions, freedom from violence, more control over their sexual labor, and more money—but not "rescue."

So, in the run-up to the World Cup in Brazil, there came to be an increasing amount of sex trafficking "awareness" in the country. In fact, there was so much discourse about the pending onslaught of predatory foreigners that there was a growing sense of moral panic about their arrival. Then came the protestors and the missionaries and the NGOs, passing out leaflets and hanging up posters: Brazil's women and children were no longer safe. And then the raids began, complete with brothel closures followed by those very same police beating and raping the prostitutes who worked there, then evicting them from their homes. All of this "awareness raising" is not just ineffective at stopping sexual exploitation. It actually contributes to the sexual violence experienced by women in Brazil's sex industry. Despite the ineffectiveness of celebrified awareness-raising campaigns, these celebrities and their partner organizations continue to drive the anti-trafficking industry financially.

BEYOND BELIEF

I have leveled some very serious accusations against the rescue industry, including widespread allegations of fraud worth many millions of dollars spread across individuals and institutions on multiple continents. The anti–sex trafficking movement has begun using a hashtag— #believesurvivors—to inoculate itself against any sort of skepticism from the sex worker rights movement, activists, journalists, or academia. Activists have taken to calling those people who question the veracity of sex trafficking claims and statistics the "pimp lobby." Anti-prostitution activist Julie Bindel has alleged a widespread conspiracy among academics and anthropologists to keep women in prostitution and deny their claims of abuse.[125] Raising the ire of a trans-exclusionary radical feminist/sex worker–exclusionary radical feminist (TERF/SWERF) like Bindel tells me that the growing chorus of social scientists described throughout this book who have reached consensus on the harmful ways that trafficking discourse has been deployed may be doing something right. But what of this maxim to "believe survivors"?

As Alison Phipps writes, "in place of the sex worker, sex industry opponents usually insert the 'survivor.' In the debate over Amnesty's policy, it was claimed that the organization had failed to hear or prioritise the concerns of sex workers who had experienced trauma and exploitation, and that these survivors had been 'strategically sidelined' by a movement for decriminalization headed by clients and 'pimps."[126] She notes that this strategy goes back to the anti-pornography efforts of Andrea Dworkin and Gloria Steinem. According to Phipps, most of the survivor tales include childhood sexual abuse, domestic violence, and references to HIV, as well as their hallmark feature: graphic descriptions of rape. "All these experiences became 'investment capital' in the political campaign against decriminalisation."[127] The obsession with vividly detailing or sometimes showing the most lurid and provocative depictions of sexual violence, particularly when it takes the form of a survivor asked to perform their tale live as a kind of storytelling at fundraisers, raises serious ethical questions about the (mostly white) consumer's appetite for racialized trauma. Phipps also presents another important point: "'Survivors' are used as a proxy for currently marginalized sex workers who are 'voiceless,' but the implication is that if they were not, they too would support an end to commercial sex. This enables sex workers advocating decriminalisation to be rejected as 'unrepresentative' on spec. Again, this sleight of hand is cruel: for current sex workers, the condition for dismissal is being able to speak at all."[128]

Claudia Cojocaru, a survivor of sex trafficking who is now a professor and researcher, describes her own conflicts with neo-abolitionists when she serves as a guest speaker on campuses. She claims that the neo-abolitionist movement has "created a new genre of 'modern day slavery' that shares and recycles the narrative structure of the seventeenth century Indian (Native American) and nineteenth century slave testimonials that fascinated and titillated the public with images of degradation, rape, suffering, and prurient violence and sexual misconduct."[129] She goes on to explain that "to be one of the faces of the anti-human trafficking movement, a survivor must go through a conversion experience that has much in common with the Quaker or Puritan conversion rituals of the seventeenth and eighteenth century New England colonies, where 'Indian captivity narratives' involved testimonials of rescue by white settler women who had been taken by indigenous men," noting that these testimonials became best-selling books.[130]

She herself found her own presentations on her experiences as a survivor of forced prostitution and sex trafficking in Japan hijacked by SWERF faculty members eager to prompt and coax her into amending her wording and reframing her complex and nuanced narrative of exploitation into the conventional survivor narrative. She contends that the neo-abolitionists use "sexually explicit, violent, and traumatic imagery in their campaigns" and sought to foist that on her. She concludes that the "survivor narrative" and "awareness raising" approaches employed by NGOs in order to obtain funds reinforce the myth of the perfect victim. "This perfect victim is compelling in a policy environment that valorizes innocence and fetishizes the titillating spectacle of the sexually objectified and battered vaginas of women who cannot think, act, or make decisions for themselves. The perfect puppet-like targets of patriarchy—the exchange of freedom for protestation—the rescue salvation performance mirrors the trope of human trafficking, but involves a legitimate owner of the woman, in the form of the rescuer, rather than one is who is polluted by the dark reality of sex work."[131] The oft-stated desire of the neo-abolitionist movement is to "give voice to the voiceless," but Cojocaru searingly describes her time being displayed by NYU Law School as a situation of contested authorship that erased her experiences as a survivor. To the anti-prostitution feminists in the room, her own more nuanced experiences as a survivor of sex trafficking were beyond belief.

As Christine M. Jacobsen and May-Len Skilbrei write in their analysis of Russian migrant sex workers, "Migrant women involved in prostitution do not speak with one voice. . . . The accounts of the same person may also be ambivalent and unsettled, containing 'several voices' that speak differently in different contexts."[132] They note that individual voices may be informed by various beliefs about freedom, tradition, modernity, and the self that are, in turn, taken from popular cultural representations of various phenomena. Instead they found that the Russian sex workers' "self-representations . . . are not unmediated by or independent of existing regimes of representation, thus rendering the idea of 'giving voice' problematic."[133] "Giving voice" is a lot different than "representing oneself."

I have never met sex worker rights advocates or leaders who believe that survivors of sexual assault should not be believed, or that all survivors of sex trafficking are lying. However, virtually everyone in the anti-prostitution movement believes that all prostitution is inherently harmful not just to individual women but to all women everywhere, that sex work is not a job, and that what women do with their bodies (when it comes to this question, anyway) is not their choice. Only one side in this debate is predicated on the wholesale disbelief and exclusion of the experiences of the other side.

This is not a question about which there can be "both sides-ism" pandering. I have no personal interest in the morality or immorality of prostitution. I've never hired a sex worker of any gender identity, and I have no sexual interest in women. As I outlined in the introduction to this book, I stumbled into the study of sexual economies more than fifteen years ago by accident and only got pulled into this project when I began to see violence being done under the thin fog of "women's rights" discourse at the behest of foreign evangelicals and radical feminists parachuting into Brazil who were too incompetent to understand the complex cultural milieu or the effects of their actions. As a faculty member with the protection of tenure, I do not have any financial incentive to side with the sex worker rights movement in forming my critique of the anti-trafficking rescue industry. What the rescue industry folks may not realize is that a majority of leaders in the sex worker rights movement wish that academics would go away altogether. Academics wishing to "study them" take up sex workers' time and pull them away from their core objectives (e.g., street-based outreach or service provision), often giving them nothing in return other than a vague proclamation that research might yield better public policies somewhere down the line. At some sex worker activist meetings, such as the large biyearly Desiree Alliance conference, academics are banned from certain events. This is hardly how one treats one's supposed lobbyists.

Even as I write this, I am aware that I could bugger off right now, enjoy my sabbatical by *not* writing this book, and thereby also save myself a lot of hate mail and threats in the future. But if I really am part of some "pimp lobby," my stealth payout is many years overdue, and I wish they'd hurry up already. In the end, the sex worker movement has replied to the charge that they do not believe trafficking survivors with a hashtag of their own: #believesexworkers. But this battleground will never be level: one side has the money and power and legislative momentum, and that side cannot even bring itself to utter the term "sex worker." It not only doesn't believe sex workers but actively works to suppress their voices, ban them from public discourse, and prevent them—using legal action if necessary—from participating in government outlets for shaping the policies that affect their lives. I've never known a sex worker rights activist who has sought to do the same to a survivor of sex trafficking who was merely seeking to share their own experience of sexual violence.

The anti-prostitution groups in question who use the rhetorical flourish "believe survivors" are invoking a central tenet of feminism and attempting to tap into the current #MeToo movement and renewed debates about Title IX and campus sexual assault. This is a cynical appropriation of the actual injustices suffered by survivors of sexual assault who are met with disbelief by law enforcement, university officials, and others. I do not maintain that all, or even a majority, of sex trafficking stories are false. I do maintain that corruption and fabrication are widespread. This is not because hundreds or thousands of victims are independently filing false claims, but rather because moral entrepreneurs in the rescue industry must continue to justify their own existence, their jobs, their donations, their celebrity sponsors, and their government grants. They have, with their voracious Western appetite for third-world suffering, set up a system of perverse incentives that pays poor women and girls to perform suffering at their behest. For a group of people who profess to hate pornography so much, the evangelical Christian and radical feminist rescue industry certainly seems to gulp down an awful lot of this particular genre of made-to-order trauma porn.

CONCLUSION

The spectacles I've discussed here—the Gift Box, telenovelas, awareness campaigns, protests, and so on—are all tangible rhetorics that one can behold. Fallacious spectacles, though, are hollow, based on falsehoods. And many of the spectacles I'm concerned with in this book are fallacious spectacles that represent something that is absent and intangible: the "invisible victims" of sex trafficking, the girls "hidden in plain sight," the millions and millions of the missing. These fallacious spectacles make rhetorical claims, but they are rooted in the fantasies of would-be rescuers who have imagined whole alternative worlds inhabited by invisible girls. The spectacles are representations of the elusive and unseen. They presuppose woundedness and are fundamentally about imagining hurt.

This brings me to the question of the relationship between spectacle and fantasy. The sociologist Colin Campbell, whose monumental work

The Romantic Ethic and the Spirit of Modern Consumerism anchored a generation of scholarship on the topic, firmly linked imagination to consumption.[134] He argues that a transformation has occurred in modern capitalist society in which we no longer seek pleasures directly through stimuli and emotional experience (traditional hedonism) but consume images of experiences and derive pleasure. In what he calls "modern autonomous imaginative hedonism," he says "individuals employ their imaginative and creative powers to construct mental images which they consume for the intrinsic pleasure they provide, a practice best described as daydreaming or fantasizing."[135] This mode of fantasy is part of the great neoliberal turn that led us not only to consumerism and the recession of the state, but also to the NGO-ification of humanitarian causes, public-private "partnerships," and the rise of parastatal alliances in which supposedly "radical" feminists happily climb on board with homophobic Christians and corrupt racist cops.

Campbell tells us that "the contemporary hedonist is a dream artist. . . . [C]rucial to this process is the ability to gain pleasure from the emotions so aroused, for when the images are adjusted, so too are the emotions."[136] I believe this is why the Gift Box has enough affective power to get sent around on tour through red light districts and college campuses. It has no usefulness on its own in these locations, but it allows the people who summon and behold it to imagine an entire world of the missing and exploited girls inside that box. So, too, do the red sands and paper airplanes. "As a direct consequence, convincing day-dreams are created, such that individuals react subjectively to them as if they were real."[137] And in our denuded and modern world, where everyone is simultaneously connected and yet utterly disconnected, feeling emotions—even if they are negative ones, like sadness or pity or fear or righteous anger—is powerful. Even addictive. "This is the distinctive modern faculty," Campbell writes, "the ability to create an illusion that is known to be false but felt to be true."[138]

These fantasies become successful bridges to public policy, crowding out the lived realities of migrant sex workers, at the moment that they become shared by others who are willing to participate in the conjuring of the invisible girls. "The individual is both actor and audience in his own drama," which the dreamer has constructed and stars in.[139] This is the (white) Western savior fantasy. But if the fantasy is compelling enough, others can be convinced to take part—and that is where the awareness-raising spectacles come into play. Take fistfuls of red sand and fill in the cracks in the pavement, a cascading web down your street or across your quad representing sexual exploitation and hope for redemption. Now anyone who wants to share in a feeling of shared awareness can join in this fantasy with just a flick of their wrist. This kind of joining up with a group of similarly "aware" people is not unpleasurable. It can even be ecstatic, as evidenced by the swaying megachurch parishioners praying away sex trafficking at Exodus Cry rallies.

Yet these spectacular fantasies are based on an inversion of harm: Who is imagined to be hurt, and who actually gets hurt, in these sex trafficking rescue fantasies? In *Casualties of Care: Immigration and the Politics of Humanitarianism in France*, Miriam Ticktin describes "regimes of care"—including humanitarianism, some human rights movements, and networks fighting violence against women—as "a set of regulated discourses and practices grounded on this moral imperative to relieve suffering."[140] Ticktin concludes that even though (or perhaps because) these regimes of care include various parastatal actors, they "ultimately work to displace possibilities for larger forms of collective change, particularly for the most disenfranchised."[141] The fallacious spectacles I've described create a "moral imperative to act," as Ticktin would say, and the actions they have inspired have had terrible consequences for the most vulnerable populations in both her field sites and my own.

Parastatal alliances must produce spectacles to raise awareness about the missing, hidden, and exploited girls of the world. The Western humanitarian and celebrity sphere is obsessed with "missing girls" globally—not only sex trafficking but gendered infanticide and sex-selective abortion. These are serious problems, to be sure, but one must ask what the West's preoccupation is with missing girls in the Global South, particularly in Southeast Asia. Social scientists feel compelled to find them, put them into typologies, study them, and give voice to these supposedly voiceless souls—even if they are dead, are unborn, or never existed at all. This desire to create spectacles and communities around invisible subjects reveals a great deal about the West's desire to consume these girls and their imagined pain, to incorporate them into shared ideologies and dreamscapes. But there are real people—sex workers, especially—who are excluded from these fantasies because their experiences and choices are impermissible; they do not provide the right kind of pleasure for the Western dreamers. Yet I believe these sex workers have an active entitlement to care even as the parastatal alliances of the anti-trafficking movement exclude them.

It's hard to debate with someone who is missing. Responding to the figure of the missing girl is like trying to wrestle with a ghost. When the fallacious spectacle makes the rhetorical turn to the absent victim, it becomes the most dangerous spectacle of all. It can be neither reasoned with nor reckoned with. And because this kind of spectacle functions solely at the level of awareness raising, it is accountable to no one even as it drains the financial and affective resources from progressive programs working on the margins. Because they depend on disembodiment—the invisible, the missing, the hidden—fallacious spectacles of sex trafficking are able to drift ever farther from material reality and accountability.

CHAPTER 4

Eat—Pray—Labor

The flight from India to Qatar was crowded and chaotic before board-ing even began. Dozens of Indian men in their early twenties wearing nearly identically cut but differently colored wool sweater vests over buttoned shirts crowded around the gate. The men looked confused and disheveled—overwhelmed. Their clothes were threadbare but not dirty. As agents ordered us all to line up by group number, the Indians continued to press in a throng as if planning to storm a castle rather than walk down a jet bridge.

A particularly stern gate agent stood on a chair and began scolding them: "Stop this. You will line up." As her colleagues joined in impos-ing a moment of order, something resembling a queue, however limp and serpentine, began to form. Suddenly a woman in a sari who looked comfortably middle class, certainly wealthier than the men, stealthily cut in line. "You! I saw that!" bellowed the agent on the chair. "Back of the line! You board last. Anyone else going to try me today?" She then got off her chair to physically shepherd the woman to the back, receiv-ing a wave of abuse in Hindi tossed from over the interloper's shoulder. Around her, the men continued to look confused and weary.

Once we had boarded, the men's inexperience with air travel caused delays and frustration for the flight attendants. The men fumbled with the overhead bin latches, and the seatbelts seemed to mystify them. When the plane took off, several men seated in the middle section jumped up and ran to the windows to look out at the ground shrinking away, causing panicked directives from the loudspeaker. Once airborne, I watched as one of the men fumbled around the galley until a flight attendant eventually showed him where the lavatory door was and how to open it. He quickly summoned his friend, who stuck his head in the door as well; the two of them pushed the faucet buttons and flushed the empty toilet, startled by the sudden whoosh it made, then laughed. The middle-class Indians on board rolled their eyes, muttering in disgust and condescension about all of this.

What I was witnessing on this flight were dozens of men on a plane for the first time. They were flying from an extremely poor country to one of the world's wealthiest—and they were certainly not on their way to Qatar for tourism. I highly doubt any of them had bought their own tickets. They were migrant workers coming to join the approximately 500,000 mostly Nepalese, Sri Lankan, and Indian construction workers building the nine stadiums and numerous other buildings before the 2022 World Cup. At the time of this writing, the estimated death toll for these men is twelve hundred, with another seven thousand deaths expected by 2022.[1] Most of the deceased were essentially worked to death in the heat or kept in squalid or unlivable conditions. (These numbers do not account for the fact that in 2020, COVID-19 arrived in Qatar. The resulting lockdown turned the labor camps into death traps.)[2] Preposterously, the government says the death toll for the World Cup is three people, a figure echoed by Al Jazeera, the state-owned media company.[3] Human rights organizations applied considerable pressure to stop Qatar's egregious and fatal labor trafficking, but the government persisted in jailing foreign journalists who reported on it, seizing their equipment and destroying the footage and photographic evidence.[4]

Tens of thousands more workers such as those on my flight were necessary to build various hotels, high-rise buildings, and university buildings. Spanning fourteen square kilometers, Education City is home to six satellite campuses for US universities (along with one British and one French) that sold off their brands, along with their academic freedom, when the Qataris offered to foot the bill and dangled oodles of cash besides. As the *Washington Post* reports, the US universities with campuses in the Gulf stand "accused of benefitting from migrant labor exploitation," but it notes that "many details about operations of Education City are shrouded in secrecy."[5] The universities turning a blind eye toward the human rights abuses and embracing this enterprise included Cornell (medicine), Texas A&M (engineering), Virginia

Commonwealth (arts and design), Carnegie Mellon (business and sciences), Georgetown (foreign service and government), and Northwestern (communications).

When I visited the Qatar campus of Northwestern, my doctoral alma mater, I asked a dean there about government censorship; he assured me, "I worried about that at first, too, but it's fine as long as you don't write too much about Israel." When I told him my first book was about gay sex tourism, he quirked an eyebrow and wryly added, "or that." Homosexuality is illegal in Qatar, and Qatar removes LGBT content from local editions of publications such as the *New York Times*.[6] Meanwhile a student debate about God and gender at Georgetown in Qatar was canceled in 2018, and in 2020 Northwestern University in Qatar canceled an event featuring Mushrou' Leila, a Lebanese indie rock band whose lead singer is openly gay. A spokesman for the Qatar Foundation, the state-linked nonprofit partnered with the universities, said that while it placed "the highest value on academic freedom," it was necessary to operate within "Qatari laws as well as the country's cultural and social customs."[7]

During my visit, I could see the camps for laborers nearby. My university-provided driver shuttled me from building to building because the distances are unwalkable even without accounting for the heat. I heard from professors there that the school had recently passed a controversial rule that students could no longer bring their servants to class to take notes for them. Instead, the servants dutifully carried the wealthy Qatari students' books to the desks and waited outside for class to end so they could retrieve them. Chauffeurs in Mercedes-Benzes idled outside in a line. I asked my driver if we could drive to the laborers' camp, but he politely and firmly declined. He likewise demurred when I asked questions about the conditions there for the men building the universities. Eventually, he agreed to take a slow roll past the perimeter so I could get a closer look at the labor camp, or what the locals often referred to euphemistically as the "bachelors' compounds."

North Koreans seemed to have it particularly rough. "First to leave [the construction site] are the Vietnamese, then the Indians, followed by Nepalese and Thais," writes the *Guardian's* Pete Pattison. "But late into the evening, after everyone else has left, one group of workers toil on. . . . These men are North Korean; an army of labourers from a tyrannical dictatorship, working on perhaps the most high-profile development in Qatar: Lusail City."[8] Sometimes they were not even allowed back to the camp and had to sleep on site. They received as little as 10 percent of their salary during their three-year contract: "Their earnings are expropriated by a chain of North Korean state-run bodies, overseen by Office 39, a department that reportedly controls a fund to bankroll Kim Jong-un's lifestyle."[9] Lusail City, which included a nineteen-story tower, four swimming pools, and apartments renting for about US$12,000 a month, was set to host teams and fans during the 2022 World Cup. The workers made about US$500–$600 a month (US$17–$20 per day), with 50–80 percent of that being sent back to workers' families, and after the company took a hefty fee for doing the remitting. North Korean defectors reported that 85–90 percent of the worker's money actually went to North Korean government officials or the ruling party.[10]

On the plane, I had watched as the South Asian men settled in and became transfixed by the in-flight entertainment system. Looking to my left, I saw one entire row of migrant workers watching the same film, having all started it within a minute or two of one another, so the same scene would burble up, bouncing from screen to screen. I craned my neck to see what they had chosen. They had not selected any of the Bollywood movies on offer, nor a blockbuster action movie, as most of the other men on the flight had. The image was of Julia Roberts enjoying pasta with that big wholesome grin of hers. I realized that the film was *Eat, Pray, Love.*

Over the next couple of hours, the five migrant men watched Julia Roberts (playing the memoirist Elizabeth Gilbert under the direction of that master of camp Ryan Murphy) as she finishes her spaghetti and moves on to consuming India, where she finds all her missing spirituality in an ashram before quickly leaving India behind so she can find love in Indonesia (with a Brazilian, though, and not with an Indonesian, because this is a movie about white lady privilege and, well, let's not be absurd). Whether they agreed with critics that the story was a "narcissistic New Age reading" representing "the worst in Western fetishization of Eastern thought and culture" or that it is was steeped in "unexamined privilege" and "the idealization/exotification of all places east," I will never know.[11] Maybe such critiques are the reserve of "coastal elites" and academics. Perhaps the migrant workers found Julia Roberts gallivanting around their home country and praying to some unspecific version of their gods meaningful in some way I could not.

I hope so. Because like it or not, *Eat, Pray, Love* was the last movie these migrant laborers were going to see for a long time. Possibly ever.

LABOR TRAFFICKING IN QATAR

In this chapter, I want to compare competing discourses about labor trafficking and exploitation in Doha, Qatar. Specifically, I investigate the gendered and racialized nature of migrant male construction workers (mostly of South Asian origin) and migrant female sex workers (mostly of East and Southeast Asian origin, with a small number of Eastern European and Lebanese women working at the very high end). I examine the hyperinvisibility of the men and the Qatari desire to erase them from public view even as the men build the impressive structures that erupt spectacularly from the earth for which the Qatari elites, foreign investors, and US universities claim credit. I contrast this with the status of the migrant sex workers—whom I was surprised to discover work quite openly in the hotel bars of five-star Western hotels. Although Qatar is ostensibly a place where alcohol, prostitution, gay sex, and other vices are heavily policed and severely punished, the truth is that the myriad Western hotel chains there operate in a zone of exception for all these things—not only for foreigners but also Qataris. so long as they obey signs to remove their "traditional dress." These women are not hidden; they are extremely visible. I argue that these Western chains—recognizable brands like Marriott, Westin, and Hilton—help facilitate sex worker migration. That is to say, even while running sex trafficking awareness campaigns and "spot the signs" employee trainings in the United States, the hotels are complicit in what their own awareness campaigns and trainings would call sex trafficking. Or more precisely, I observed hotel management and staff facilitating the introduction of sex workers to Arab and Western male clients, and multiple hotel employees explained to me that the hotels had "an agreement" whereby migrant sex workers (brought into Qatar by third parties) would engage in sex work with hotel guests with the assistance and knowledge of hotel staff. While I cannot claim direct knowledge that these major hotel chains facilitated the migration process of the sex workers or "sex trafficked" the women, employees repeatedly told me that the Western hotel chains work with the sex-working women and their managers for the "benefit of the guests." Therefore, this chapter examines the racialized fantasies projected onto these two groups of migrant workers and critiques Orientalist liberal feminist assumptions about sexuality in the "Arab World."

Although migrant sex work is very visible in Qatar, it is not a widespread phenomenon. As Haley Christenson writes, "When human trafficking is discussed in relation to sporting events, most people of think of sex trafficking before labor trafficking. Yet, no hard evidence confirms sex trafficking increases during sporting events. Conversely, there is empirical evidence to show a link between the World Cup and increased labor trafficking."[12] This gendered bifurcation of visibility is one flaw of human trafficking as an overarching framework. Writing in the context of the neighboring United Arab Emirates (a country with many social, political, and economic similarities to Qatar), Pardis Mahdavi argues that there is also a misguided assumption that domestic work and sex work are mutually exclusive, and that women migrating to the UAE choose to enter sex work because they find the working conditions better than those endured by domestic workers.[13] Mahdavi and Christine Sargent write that "conceptualizations of trafficked persons seemed to hinge upon gender. From speaking with activists in the Philippines, Emirati hospital administrators, or expatriate women working to build a private shelter for women in Dubai, the authors learned that many, if not all, of these interlocutors indicated that 'women and children' were more likely to be trafficked than men," with "women being seen as especially vulnerable to sex trafficking."[14] These groups believed that men were "stronger" and smart enough to be able to avoid being tricked into labor trafficking. The researchers also found that these groups expressed racist views that women (who often came from Asia or Africa) were less valuable to their families than they would presumably be in the West.[15] Similarly gendered and racialized assumptions are a reoccurring theme in much of the anti-trafficking world, as the sociologist Rhacel Parreñas has demonstrated.[16] Despite such beliefs about the relative invulnerability of men, the scale of labor trafficking in the construction industry in the Gulf, and especially in Qatar, is almost unimaginably vast.

Analyzing the media reports, peer-reviewed research, and available data, it's reasonable to predict what may have happened to the men on my flight. According to reporting from the *Guardian*, they're likely to discover that their employer will seize their passports.[17] They will be charged around 36 percent interest on the price of those plane tickets and other transportation costs.[18] They will not be paid, as their employer will withhold two months of salary as an incentive for them to cooperate. They will be made to sleep twelve people to a room in squalid conditions and poor sanitation. They will not be given enough food and sometimes will be given nothing at all for the entire day, be made to work twelve hours on an empty stomach, and then go to bed hungry. They may be denied access to free drinking water despite being made to work when it is 122 degrees Fahrenheit (50 degrees Celsius). They or others in their cohort may die from heat or sanitation-related causes. Their death certificates will not give a cause of death or will say "natural causes."[19] There is nothing natural, however, about teenagers and twenty-somethings having heart attacks. Paul Renkiewicz tracked just such a story in recounting the tale of Iok, a sixteen-year-old boy from Nepal who died of a heart attack two months after his arrival.[20] Of course, if they die quickly, they'll never have to be paid at all. As Sarah Hamill puts it, Doha is "an oasis in the desert, but a graveyard for migrant workers."[21]

In 2013, an average of twenty Indian migrants died each month. By 2014—four years after Qatar won its World Cup bid in a corrupt process full of bribery and other crimes that would result in the ouster of the FIFA head and the imprisonment of several of its top officials—thousands had died.[22] Hamill explains, "The root cause of these deaths is the squalid living and working conditions. Whether a work accident, a heart attack caused by heat stress, or diseases caused by the living conditions, employers could prevent these deaths."[23]

The system that allows so much exploitation is called the *kafala* (sponsorship) system, and it binds a worker to their employer. Under kafala, they cannot quit, they cannot change employers, and they cannot form unions to seek improved conditions. In 2014, the UN called on Qatar to abolish the kafala system.[24] In 2016, Qatar said it would do so, but as Haley Christensen points out, even under the new law, "workers remain within their employer's control and may not, without their employer's permission, change jobs during contracted periods. Additionally, exit permits are still required, and employers can block employees from getting these permits."[25] Part of why it's so hard to stop the abuses is that the construction companies are organized in a labyrinthine web of contractors and subcontractors. As Claudia Müller-Hoff and Zarah Baur argue, "The longer the chain of subcontracting, the higher the risk of labour rights infringements somewhere along it."[26]

Workers like these men are expendable because they are so easy to replace. As Sarath Ganji notes, Qatar needed 1.5 million foreign workers for the Cup in order to complete the US$200 billion worth of development projects related to it.[27] What is most remarkable about all this is that foreign workers are by far the majority of the population. The total population of Qatar, including the migrant workers, is only 2.5 million. A full 94 percent of the population in Qatar is not Qatari citizens.[28] The skilled migrants, foremen, engineers, and businessmen who are overseeing construction, as well as nearly everyone working in any sector of the economy—academics, teachers, marketing executives, bankers, consultants—are noncitizens. Yet the native Qataris, comprising the 6 percent who rule over the population, are incredibly wealthy. As Sunkara Bhaskar notes in his reporting for *In These Times*, "Qatar has the highest concentration of millionaires in the world—more than 14 percent of households in the tiny monarchy hold one million or more dollars in assets."[29] Despite football fans seeing a dazzling skyline boasting an enormous array of opulent towers erupting out of the desert, 60 percent of Qatar's total population actually lives in labor camps.[30]

The ruling elites are quick to squash any form of dissent; Qatar has a vague law carrying prison time and levying huge fines for anyone found to be distributing "false news" about Qatar online. According to Freedom House, the government sentenced a poet to fifteen years in prison for reciting a poem about the Arab Spring on YouTube.[31] In 2015, the BBC's Mark Lobel and a team of journalists who had been invited by the government to come to Qatar for a tour of the labor camps were dismayed to find themselves being arrested and their equipment seized. As he explains, "Suddenly, eight white cars surrounded our vehicle and directed us on to a side road at speed. . . . An hour into my grilling, one of the interrogators brought out a paper folder of photographs which proved they had been trailing me in cars and on foot for two days since the moment I'd arrived. I was shown pictures of myself and the team standing in the street, at a coffee shop, on board a bus and even lying next to a swimming pool with friends. It was a shock. I had never suspected I was being tailed. At 01:00, we were taken to the local prison."[32]

The government had initially invited a dozen reporters to see a variety of labor camps, including substandard ones, but also to show off some new "labor villages" that had gyms and pools—a handful of specially created showpieces built for propaganda purposes. These were part of a disinformation effort by a London-based PR firm hired by Qatar's World Cup organizing committee, which answers to FIFA and which helped to run the tour. Lobel says of his interrogator, "In perfect English and with more than a touch of malice, he threatened us with another four days in prison—to teach us a lesson. I began my second night in prison on a disgusting soiled mattress. At least we did not go hungry, as we had the previous day. One of the guards took pity on us" and sent out for some food.[33] Eventually, they were released. "Bizarrely, we were allowed to join the organized press trip for which we had come. It was as if nothing had happened, despite the fact that our kit was still impounded, and we were banned from leaving the country."[34] In a separate incident, a German TV crew was also detained and had a similar experience.

When Qatar won the bid to host the Cup, football fans were shocked. Players could not possibly play in summer heat like that. Eventually, Qatar moved the tournament to the winter, when temperatures will max out at around 80 degrees Fahrenheit (27 degrees Celsius), but this caused an outcry from fans as it disrupted the seasonal schedules of their various other leagues. Moreover, there were concerns about Qatar's ban on alcohol and how it would handle the sale of beer. As they had done with Russia, gay rights groups repeatedly decried the country's ban on homosexuality, fearing that it would be unsafe for fans to travel to Qatar. Qatar's World Cup organizing committee blithely retorted that gays needed to "respect the culture of Qatar."[35] Then FIFA chief Sett Blatter similarly dismissed concerns by saying of gay fans (not to mention gay players), "I would say they should refrain from any sexual activities."[36] (He later apologized for his "joke.") All this emphasis on the players and fans, though, betrays a lack of interest in the welfare of the migrants who died to make the games possible. The scholar Chris Gaffney once referred to stadiums as "temples of the earthbound gods."[37] If footballers are gods and stadiums the temples where disciples come to worship, what does this make the workers? In the case of Qatar, these gleaming temples are places where humans unlucky enough to be born in poor countries are taken by people in rich countries to be sacrificed at the altar of FIFA.

The abuses and deaths raise the thorny question of whether it is even possible to ethically attend—or even watch—the World Cup. Most football fans are well aware of FIFA's corruption, mismanagement, and criminal activities; it's hard to find anyone who likes FIFA. And FIFA has improved, albeit marginally, since the arrest of senior officials and the ousting of Sett Blatter, the corrupt official who had been at the helm during successful bribery schemes by Russia and Qatar. Of course, there are no governments or organizations spending hundreds of thousands of dollars on awareness raising campaigns or attempting to rescue and rehabilitate male laborers. Any dismay on the part of fans at FIFA's well-documented corruption does not change the fact that thousands of non-white migrants died horrible deaths, and that hundreds of thousands suffered for this spectacle. Fans are literally sitting astride migrants' graves when they choose to attend a World Cup match. When Nepalese workers attempted to sue FIFA, the case landed in a Swiss court, which ruled against them, saying that only Qatar could bring direct change; FIFA could not be expected to apply pressure to sovereign countries for inhumane treatment of the workers building its stadiums.[38] (Never mind that FIFA applies all sorts of pressure, demanding infrastructural changes, changes to local laws, and brand monopolies for its sponsors.) Hence, the only place left from which change could come must be the fans.

When "fast fashion" clothing companies make changes to labor conditions in supply chains (e.g., getting rid of sweatshops), it is almost always because of public pressure. When people see the horrible conditions of workers or learn of violence against the children and adults who make their branded clothes, it generates outrage on social media, and boycotts are threatened. Football fans need to ask themselves if they would still buy clothes if they knew that people had died in the process of making them. Would they consume pornographic content if they knew it had nonconsensual sex in it? Dyed-in-the-wool leftists who object to all manner of labor exploitation and abuses nonetheless dutifully tune in every four years, and Qatar in 2022 will be no exception. But the scale of exploitation in Doha is totally unlike the labor abuses at other recent Cups (which have seen a troubling, but much smaller, number of construction-related deaths) because of its deadly heat, its political and economic conditions, and its kafala migrant labor system. It therefore poses a whole new set of ethical dilemmas for fans.

WE TREAT YOU RIGHT

When you walk into the lobby-level bar at the Hilton in Doha, you are greeted by a sign advising that one cannot enter wearing traditional dress, meaning clothing observant of Islam. This is a Western establishment, and it serves alcohol. The first time I entered I was with a Ghanian American woman colleague who was in law school (and had been a member of the Observatório in Brazil) currently living in Europe who came to catch up with me in Qatar. As a dark-skinned West African woman sitting with a white man, she immediately attracted a few sideways glances. As an expert in sexual economies who was also used to being mistaken for a sex worker herself, she was also the first to clock the actual sex workers turning tricks in the Hilton's bar. "Olhaaaa . . . ," she said, raising an eyebrow. *Look*. (We tended to speak Portuguese to mitigate other's eavesdropping.) Among all the Western and Arab businessmen were a half dozen East Asian women circulating, chatting up the men and nursing fountain drinks.

Intrigued, we resolved to spend a lot of time in hotel bars. My colleague left after a couple of days, and I stayed on. The next year, I returned for a longer stretch and changed hotels as many times as I could, hopping from the Westin to the W to the Marriott and so on. Most of these hotels also had multiple bars and clubs inside them. Because of the significant dangers to both the sex workers and myself, I did not do formal, recorded interviews. Instead, whenever I sat alone in such a bar, I would immediately be approached by a woman who would ask if I was staying at the hotel and if I would like to go upstairs for a "massage." When I would explain that I was not interested and that I was, in fact, conducting research on migrant workers and matters of gender/sexuality, they usually found this confusing at first but were eager to continue the conversation, offering details about their homelands, their children and families, and their experiences in and impression of Qatar. They all spoke English fluently, if sometimes with a heavy accent. I avoided asking them direct questions about sex acts, costs for their services, and other things that might get them in trouble with either the authorities, third-party managers (e.g., traffickers), or the bar staff, who were always keeping an eye on the women (but never hovering over us).

One day Pei-Chun, a thirty-year-old Taiwanese woman, approached me during happy hour and began the usual small talk, asking where I was from and what I did. Her English was quite good, and she was a fast talker; she was not overweight, but a little plump—meaning that she did not have the stereotypical body features and slender silhouette of the Filipina women I would soon grow used to seeing working in higher-end bars. She returned to the subject of a "massage" a few times despite my being upfront about my aims. (In my fifteen years of experience in Brazil, many sex workers initially understood my claiming to be a researcher as a cover I was using because I was embarrassed to say I wanted to pay for sex.) She gave up on the financial element and resolved to simply chat about her life, which she said her clients rarely asked about.

The bartender, a Filipina woman the same age as Pei-chun, approached and, right in front of her, said to me, "If she's bothering you, you just tell me. We have an arrangement with them. I can make her go away. But if you want her here, then it's all good."

"You have an . . . arrangement? With her?" I asked the bartender.

"With the women's bosses," she said. "But I can send her away if you like." She made meaningful eye contact with me for a second or two and smiled courteously, then slapped her hand twice on the table, staccato, before she turned and strode away to pour a double whiskey for a businessman at the end of the bar.

"Pei-chun," I said, flummoxed. "The hotels let you work here? Your bosses arrange it?"

"They arrange everything with the managers," she said simply. I furrowed my brow and snapped forward like I'd been stuck with a hatpin.

Pei-chun was not a free agent who had simply decided to leave her children in Taiwan, bought herself a plane ticket, and shown up at the Hilton looking for paid sex. Men had arranged this situation for her. The Hilton was working with those men. The Hilton employees were trained how to manage the scene and when to look away.

This did not mean that she was being exploited or forced, per se, but she was in a much more vulnerable position than the sex workers I had interviewed in Brazil, South Africa, London, and even Russia. By most legal definitions, Pei-chun had been trafficked. Theoretically in cahoots with the Hilton. The same Hilton that runs "spot the signs" trafficking awareness workshops in the United States.

Pei-chun told me about her two small children, both girls. She worried about them. But her mother was taking care of them. She sent them money regularly, and they were in school. They were smart, and she had high hopes for them. "One of them is smarter than the other," she admitted. "The younger one. She will take care of all of us." Pei-chun's mother thinks she works in the hotel as a bartender—just like the one who was keeping an eye on us.

When I ask if she regrets the decision to come, if she's happy in Doha, she laughs. "I can't answer that. For me, it's no choice."

"You had no choice?" I ask, concerned.

"Yes, yes, I *choose* to come. But it is no question. I provide for my family. I meet people from all over the world. This is the only life for me."

When I ask if she will go back, she tells me, "I already been back twice. I will do this until my daughters can finish school. Unless they forget me."

The prospect of her daughters forgetting their mother strikes me as impossibly sad, but she laughs. "If they forget me, I go home. Then they know who is their mother."

And so began my tour of hotel bars and clubs across Doha. I was shocked to find that almost all of them had similar arrangements. The ethnicity of the women varied by hotel, suggesting that (a) the managers who worked with the hotels had regionally based supply chains of sexual labor (e.g., recruiters working on the ground in a particular area) and (b) the clientele of the hotels, which inherently price-sort by class, had racialized preferences. In the Gulf, African migrant women are at the bottom of the sexual hierarchy; West African and Moroccan migrant sex workers are sometimes kept out of hotel nightclubs. Women from East and Southeast Asia were next up in the hierarchy. My Black feminist theory professor from grad school had come to Qatar to teach at Northwestern's campus for a few years before retiring, and she invited me to a drink at the W. She quickly pointed out the blonde women at the bar, informing me that Russian and Ukrainian women were known to work there as sex workers. They were at the top of the food chain. By far, however, the most common ethnicity I encountered were Filipina women, who seemed to fall just below the white women but above the East Asian women. Filipina women also make up many of the service industry staff, nannies, and domestic workers in Doha.

Night after night I watched as wealthy Arab and white men would settle into a bar and motion for the manager or hotel concierge. After whispering for a moment, the male staff member would leave and return a few minutes later with one or more Filipina women on their arms. (Sex tourist forums online confirm their origin and also give breakdowns of percentages of sex workers in various hotel bars by ethnicity.) No place had more sex workers working there, however, than the nightclub Radisson Blu, which was said to be almost all Filipina sex workers. As one man explained to me, "When things there shut down, everyone goes to the Dairy Queen across the way. They get cheeseburgers and stuff. Expats soaking up the alcohol. . . Plus, Qataris love junk food. Everybody knows that place. . . . On Thursday nights, it's like a whorehouse." (Weekends in Qatar are Friday/Saturday rather than Saturday/Sunday.) I imagine all the Filipina sex workers and their clients striding into Dairy Queen, ordering their Blizzards, negotiating prices, and coordinating their sexual escapades for the evening. Although I heard about this mythic bordello of a Dairy Queen just as I was leaving Qatar and wasn't lucky enough to pay it a visit, the scene looms large in my mind. I had hoped to make one final trip to Qatar and to investigate, but by then COVID-19 was in full swing.

OUT OF SIGHT

The question of which migrants in Qatar the state allows to be seen is a gendered one. As I've argued, migrant sex workers are hypervisible. They may not have freedom of movement, but they are out in public view. So, too, are the nannies and caregivers who push the baby strollers through the mall and take toddlers out. Because Qatar is so hot, it is impossible to be outside for very long. There are no public parks or outdoors spaces where people go to play or stroll or picnic. Instead, a great deal of public social life takes place inside shopping malls. These malls are quite different than the ubiquitous center of teen social life that Westerners might recall from 1980s and 1990s pop culture (and distant memory). For starters, malls in the Gulf Arab countries are massive. The Dubai Mall, for example, is twelve million square feet and has twelve hundred shops as well as an ice rink, twenty-two movie screens, and one of the largest aquariums in the world. It is in the Burj Khalifa complex, which is the tallest building in the world. Other Gulf malls boast roller coasters and indoor ski slopes complete with ski lifts. People host birthday parties in malls, go there for exercise, entertainment, recreation, and socializing. Although they are sites of consumption, the malls are also (and perhaps primarily) places to see and be seen.

The malls in Doha are also built by the migrant male construction workers. Yet there is ongoing tension about the presence of these workers in the spaces. In *The Workers Cup*, a 2017 documentary, one of the South Asian migrant construction workers on a major building whose lower levels consist of a mall explains: "A mall is not a place people like me can go. On our site we aren't allowed downstairs in the mall while it's open. We can only be down there until 10 am. Then we aren't allowed at all. The people who come here are all VIPs. They are big people with high standards." The camera shows the gleaming but still closed shops, top-tier fashion brands with impossibly expensive items. "We could be wearing dirty clothes. Maybe we're dusty and smelly. And that's bad no? Like them—for them to see sweat and dirt? We don't want a disturbance. Or to disgust them. There's no reason to go anyway. So that's why our foreman told us not to go down there at all."[39]

The presence of migrant men in malls (which often they themselves have built) inspires discomfort and anger on the part of many locals. I met one young Qatari man, Abdullah, at the Marriott. He was stylish and smart. He identified himself as an artist and had shown me photos on his phone of some of his work. He explained, "The workers are supposed to get one day a week off. Many don't get that, but they are supposed to. When they have this time off, the foreman puts them all in a shuttle bus and sends them to the mall. They can't buy anything but they just stand around, loitering and looking at people. Just staring. It's uncomfortable. And they stare at the women, especially. And you just can't do that with Muslim women. It's not appropriate behavior."

A thirty-something expat from Belgium who had lived in Doha for several years explained to me that the problem was leering. "These men are not subtle. They leer. Just leer at women. The nannies, the Arabs, even the women in burkas and niqabs. When Arabs say women need to be covered so as not to excite men, it's bullshit on many levels, of course. But the Indians, the Nepalis—they get *so* excited just from looking that it's really uncomfortable. This is why the locals are trying to make a push to have the malls ban the migrant men, which is sad when you think about it."

"Sad why?" I asked, deciding not to be pedantic and point out to him that Qatari women typically wear abayas, not burkas.

"Because they're only allowed out every so often. It's like taking recess away from a kid. . . . But they *are* very aggressive with the leering. It makes the women afraid."

Much has been written about the subject of the flaneur, or the strolling gentleman invoked by Baudelaire who makes an art of perusing the modern city. Walter Benjamin found this urban connoisseur an almost heroic spectator.[40] But in Qatar, there is a desire to police flanerie as it is an act reserved for the middle and upper classes. Even the nannies are allowed to engage in it, but this is because they are women; they are allowed visibility even though they are also in the kafala system. Locals not only want the migrant men out of sight, they also want to deny them the ability to even look. Over and over again, the word *leering* came up as I chatted with bartenders, businesspeople, expats, and academics living in Doha.

Pavithra Prasad and Anjana Raghavan have written about how South Asian men deploy a "haptic gaze as a prosthetic for physical touch" as they leer at women.[41] Drawing on feminist film theory about the gaze, they argue that "to be looked at as woman is to be constructed as an object of pleasure" for men.[42] This scopophilia means that "women's bodies are paradoxically constructed as objects to be looked at while simultaneously being expected to repel the optical touch. . . . [T]he implication [is] that touch cannot be far behind the gaze."[43] To return such a gaze is a provocation. While I do not dispute their accounts of how leering may function in the context of cities in India, transferring the idea of the haptic gaze to the malls of Qatar presents a different conundrum. The men allegedly leering (and who may be merely looking or even glancing) are already considered unwelcome in the shopping mall. Here, the rare entrance of workers into the mall is already an act of physical invasion in the eyes of the elites, and the wealthy women experience the haptic gaze as an assault because it means they are being psychically touched and contaminated by these brown(er) bodies. The desire to render the workers invisible may also contain a psychological element of wanting to repress the knowledge and guilt about the abuses that everyone knows are happening. When the workers gaze back, it implicates the shoppers and, in this way, unmasks the chasms of inequality between groups in this Qatari society, thus "soiling" the experience of the mall.

"Leering" has also become a contentious term in the era of #MeToo and renewed attention to Title IX and sexual assaults. In 2019, Uber issued a long-awaited report on sexual misconduct related to its ride hailing app.[44] It said that in the previous year, 3,045 sexual assaults had happened during its rides in the United States. (That's .0002 percent of its 1.3 billion rides.)[45] While their move toward more transparency and accountability is laudable, the way they have construed "sexual misconduct" is disturbingly broad. In much of the media and reporting, the term in use is "sexual assault," but Uber's actual typology speaks of "misconduct." In its disclosures, Uber included twenty-one categories of sexual misconduct including "leering" and "flirting or inappropriate comments."[46] While aggressive leering can be intimidating, it is interesting to note that the majority of Uber's drivers are immigrants. In New York City, for example, over 90 percent are immigrants, and work as a driver has long been associated with South Asian men.[47] Since at least the Jim Crow era, there is a racial element in who is allowed to look at whom and at what point a look is construed as "sexual misconduct." It is possible to both respect the right of women to not endure intimidation and to recognize that when immigrants and men of color are concerned, there is a long history of fatal paranoia on the subject of "leering."

When Black and brown migrant men in Qatar look at women, whether white expats or Arab women in whatever attire, the mere act of looking gets misconstrued as a mode of misconduct or assault. This is part of the danger of a totalizing discourse of sexual misconduct that collapses acts as different as rape and leering into a single chart or places them on a one-dimensional spectrum. The paranoid reading of the leering migrant is amplified by the fact that he is *out of place*. He is inside the mall rather than under it, above it, or within its walls, building and repairing and expanding it from behind the scenes or after hours. He is, as Mary Douglas would say, "matter out of place"; that is, he is just like dirt.[48] As the famous anthropologist noted in her study of purity and perceptions of social danger, people reject what is dirty because when matter gets out of place, the established order is contravened. Dirt is, as Phyllis Palmer wrote, "a principal means to arrange culture."[49] But dirt is also gendered, as Carol Wical has written in work that builds on both Palmer and Douglas. "Normative white femininity traditionally eschews direct contact with dirt thus bringing into play interactions between work and gender."[50] The "dirty" brown man's body reminds the women of the uncomfortable truth behind the façade of their luxurious mall. In this way, he also "dirties" it. He soils the mall goers' (and evidently especially the women shoppers') sense of the mall as a pure, pristine place. Echoing Wical's comment about normative white femininity, it's clear that although the women in the mall are not all white, they stand in for whiteness to the extent that they advance xenophobic and white supremacist horror at the migrant men's brown and Black bodies.

The idea that the migrant men are a threat to women was also echoed by some of the anti-prostitution radical feminists I encountered. Several of them told me that the construction boom was fueling sex trafficking from Russia and Ukraine to satisfy the demand for sex created by the migrant men in the labor camps. They had never been to Qatar and had no evidence for this claim, but they earnestly believed that this was the case. As an example of this, Mahdavi and Sargent reported on a lecture about sex trafficking in the Gulf given at Scripps College wherein the speaker proclaimed that "to end trafficking we must decrease [male] migrant laborers' wages so they cannot afford to solicit sex work."[51]

The idea that the migrant men who may be making thirteen dollars a day could even afford to pay for sex is preposterous, even more so when one considers that the Eastern European women are at the very upper echelon of Qatar's racialized sexual economy and are able to command hundreds or even thousands of dollars per hour. Even if the radical feminists' fantasies were not rooted in an imperiled white femininity, the idea that the foremen overseeing the brutal kafala system that is killing thousands of migrant men would care enough about the sexual wants of these laborers to import sex workers into the camps is just bizarre. Surely, these men in the camps are not celibate. I have no doubt that, as in prisons and naval ships and other all-male environments, sex happens—including sex for fun, commercial sex, sex as barter, and rape—but the idea that labor trafficking in Qatar is fueling sex trafficking is a white Western feminist fantasy.

There are similar feminist concerns over traditional Islamic dress for women and what it says about visibility in Qatar and other Islamic countries. Femen, the topless feminist group, which protests sex tourism at world sporting events and seeks to abolish all prostitution, holds special contempt for Islamic women's attire. In 2012, Femen had gone to a predominantly Muslim neighborhood in Lavoir, France, wearing burkas that they then pulled off to reveal their naked bodies with words painted on them. Femen activists used slogans such as "Better naked than burka!" and "Muslim women let's get naked! Was this 'Islamophobic?'"[52] In their "topless jihad" in Paris, they burned the Salafist flag in front of the Grand Mosque.[53] Just as they deny that women can have the autonomy to give meaningful consent to sell sex, saying it's inherently and systematically bad for women everywhere regardless of individual choice, so too do they reject the idea that burkas and other Islamic women's clothing can be empowering.

In Qatar, abayas (the long black flowing cloaks women wear in public) are high fashion items. Women carefully select different fabric and silhouettes to express a range of personalities and tastes. Their faces and nails may be immaculately tended to. *Gulf News* quotes one abaya-wearing woman as explaining, "I take my child to school at 6 am, I do my errands, I get an unexpected call to go to a business meeting, I have a formal dinner at the end of the day and for all of which I'm wearing my abaya. . . . If you're in the west, you have to go and change or do your hair. I think the latter is more of a restriction."[54] The journalist Feyza Gumusluoglu notes the love of abaya fashion "speaks not to the women's desire to attract men's attention—far from the case for most Gulf women I have met. But rather it speaks to the desire of women to distinguish themselves from one another. . . . Today the black abaya of many young Qatari women hardly speaks to modesty. The quality of its fabric is eye catching."[55] She goes on to explain that "colorful designer bags, and expensive watches and sun glasses many Qatari women love to own attract even more attention against the background of a shimmering pitch-black abaya. Furthermore, the black gown looks extremely elegant worn with the high heels many young Qatari women wear as they regally walk Qatar's shopping malls."[56] A few young fashionistas have branched out into gray and even white abayas when in public spaces like universities. (White is typically the color of male dress, the thobe, in Qatar).[57]

Western feminists concern themselves with visibility but operate using an ethnocentric view of what constitutes visibility. Precisely because they ignore the cultural specificities of Qatar (to say nothing of other Arab countries), they fail to pick up the codes and signifiers that the Qatari women are putting down. Far from being rendered invisible, Qatari women are hypervisible, especially in the malls, and when there they intend to see and be seen. It's no wonder the migrant men look—or even "leer"—at the glamorous and wealthy fashionistas promenading dramatically through the malls.

In Edward Said's canonical work *Orientalism,* he describes a Western propensity for "dealing with the Orient" by "making *statements* about it, authorizing views of it, describing it, by teaching it, by ruling over it: in short, Orientalism as a Western style for dominating, restructuring, and having authority over the Orient."[58] This is much the same observation one might make about Western secular liberals' treatment of the Middle East or the Arab World, which is often perceived and rendered as monolithic. The Western liberal notion that somehow male bodies have free reign in public spaces in the Middle East, while women are cloistered, hidden, or invisible, has misapprehended the situation in Qatar. It's not the women who are absent from the hotels and malls and public life. It's the 60 percent of the population sequestered in (male) labor camps that is, in fact, invisible. Even the nightclubs in Doha's Western hotels have signs banning men from entering without being accompanied by a female companion (not the other way around). This is not the same as saying that women's rights are not imperiled, only that Western secular regimes of "visibility" are grossly inapplicable in Qatar.

THE HYPERINVISIBILITY OF SLAVERY

The Msheireb Downtown Doha is a US$5.5 billion real estate development project that includes community centers, hotels, schools, mosques, and shops. It is also the site of the Msheireb Museums, a quartet of museums devoted to somewhat niche topics. The Mohammed Bin Jassim House honors the past, present, and future of "sustainable elements" in Doha; the Company House is devoted to petroleum industry workers; the Radwani House showcases the history and evolution of "traditional Qatari family life"; and the Bin Jelmood House is devoted to the history of the global slave trade with an emphasis on the Indian Ocean region (which includes the Arabian Gulf). Bin Jelmood was a Saudi slave trader, and the museum is the site of his former home.

When I first visited the Msheireb Museums in 2016, they were not yet open to the public and required an appointment. I was looking for the Bin Jelmood House, but it did not have obvious signage and so I began to wander around looking for an entrance, wincing and sweating in the harsh sun. After ten or fifteen minutes, I was becoming increasingly confused and frustrated. Google Maps was no help, and as Doha has virtually no pedestrian foot traffic, there were no passersby to ask. As I circled what I thought were the museums, I saw about a dozen or so South Asian laborers hauling heavy supplies and wheelbarrows. They wore the neon yellow vests and hardhats of the construction companies. Nearby was a shuttle bus that would take them home to their labor camp at the end of the day. I wasn't sure whether they would speak English, but I figured it was worth a shot. I approached the men and asked about the Bin Jelmood House.

Before the men could respond, what I took to be a foreman—judging by his button-up shirt and the lack of dust on him—came running over and shouted at me in English: "You can't be here! You can't speak to them."

This admonishment struck me as curiously aggressive. When I said I was looking for the Bin Jelmood House he gestured to the building whose paving stones the workers were installing. "Yes, this is Bin Jelmood. You can go now."

It took a moment for the reality of the situation to fully sink in. Looking at the weary migrant workers, I couldn't help but think to myself, "Oh shit. The museum of slavery is being built by slaves."

Then again. *Of course it was.* How else is anything built in Qatar?

When I got inside, I was greeted enthusiastically by a charming young Arab woman in Western dress. She glided over to me, smiling. "Welcome, professor! We have been expecting you, Doctor Mitchell." She gave me a personal tour of the Bin Jelmood House, Company House, and Radwani House before turning me loose to photograph and explore the Bin Jelmood House in greater detail on my own.

The imperative to "make visible" is prominent in Bin Jelmood House. It is a gorgeous spectacle—perhaps too beautiful for its ugly subject matter. The museum does not just tell the history of slavery in Qatar but tells the history of Qatar as a history of enslavement. At times, it is unflinching; at other times, it acts as an apologist. There are stunning life-sized video panels in which models appear and disappear in their native garb, showing the diversity of enslaved people. The museum also highlights how Islam commands the humane treatment of the enslaved and ultimately implies that it is Islamic to abolish slavery.

Qatar is a young country, having emerged as an independent nation-state in 1971. Although inhabited long before, and a source of the pearl trade for many centuries, Qatar was conquered by Arab tribes in 1783 (along with Bahrain) and later came under Ottoman control in the late nineteenth century. During World War I, it became a protectorate of the British. The discovery of oil in the mid-twentieth century led to its development and increased wealth. As the museum tells the history of Qatar, it discusses the role of slaves in the country's various historical phases. Considerable space is given to the history of the pearl trade and the terrible conditions endured by the pearl divers, many of whom were Zanzibarians enslaved by the Qataris.

The museum also addresses "modern-day slavery" in Qatar head-on with a discussion about the kafala system and the World Cup. It's a PR-savvy bit of handwaving. In one panel, there is a sun-drenched landscape with half-built skyscrapers topped by construction cranes. In the foreground seven men in somewhat shabby clothes sit on a scrap of bricked sidewalk that cuts across a dusty median between two multilane highways. In both Arabic and English, the panel reads: "Workers having lunch in Doha: Throughout the Gulf states, the abuse of the kafala (sponsorship) system directly affects large numbers of foreign workers."

The most striking part of the museum, though, is a room full of large, vertically hung rectangular screens. Images of people, presumably enslaved, appear in them, one body per screen. Many of the bodies are Black, with touches of African attire barely visible. Some are fully clothed, with faces and heads covered. The renderings are shadowy, with cool blue tones. Direct lighting from above means that the contours of the bodies—chiseled muscles of the shirtless men and sumptuous curves of the women—are highlighted while the faces of the people are cloaked in shadow. The bodies are rendered as beautiful to gaze upon, perhaps even in the kind of aesthetic that could be erotic in another context. Periodically, the anonymous people disappear and other images such as maps and painted animations appear, only to ultimately revert back to the shadowy figures from the past. They are as stunning aesthetically as they are deeply problematic from a representational standpoint.

And yet despite the spectacularization of slavery in Qatar provided by the museum and its stated desire to make slavery visible, it's important to remember who it is building the Msheireb. The *Gulf Times* reports that Msheireb Properties is a subsidiary of the Qatar Foundation for Education, Science and Community Development (QF).[59] QF advertises itself as a defender of migrants' rights. It has been a major sponsor of conferences on labor rights protections marking International Workers Day (May 1, or May Day in the United States). It publicly disavows the kafala system and argues for best practices to be implemented in Qatar.[60]

Given this progressive stance, it's surprising to learn that shortly before I arrived the Msheireb project was halted by a workers' strike, an incredibly rare action in Qatar, which is good evidence of the severity of the situation. In late 2015, several hundred migrants from India, Nepal, Bangladesh, and the Philippines (estimated to be between two hundred and four hundred men) walked off the job in a labor dispute with subcontractor Drake & Scull, according to Doha News.[61] It is incredibly difficult to find media coverage online of the event because the security arm of the Qatari government shut down Doha News in 2016.

The *Columbia Journalism Review* notes that Doha News was the only reliable media source in the country, covering major issues ignored by sycophantic or government-run alternatives like al-Jazeera. Despite a culture of media blackouts, Doha News ran stories about food supply chain precarity, human rights abuses, and meager food allowances for migrant workers; stories about the availability of alcohol and hidden gay life in Qatar; quirky pieces about the introduction of chocolate-flavored camel milk; and coverage of current events such as a fire in a shopping mall that killed thirteen children and four adults. Reporters were sometimes detained, questioned, and intimidated.[62] Sometime after I gathered information and quotations from Doha News about the workers' strikes and protests against Msheireb properties, the Qatari government blocked the website and scrubbed it from the internet. What follows is information from Doha News that is only available thanks to the Wayback Machine, an internet archiving tool. It is unclear which story finally landed Doha News on the regime's permanent blacklist, but the chair of Msheireb Properties is none other than Sheikha Moza bint Nasser, the mother of Qatar's ruling emir, Sheikh Tamim bin Hamad Al-Thani.

The striking workers objecting to their treatment by Msheireb Properties had not been paid their US$440 monthly salary (a number that includes "a food allowance" from their employer). "While most described the incident as a peaceful protest, others said some individuals aggressively confronted their supervisors. Some men smashed air conditioning units and broke doors."[63] Police arrived and helped to mediate, eventually convincing the workers to return to their labor camp in the Industrial Area. Officials from an international trade union who had visited the site reported "disturbing evidence of wrong practices" and a general "climate of fear."[64] This kind of spontaneous and violent eruption signals a kind of unruly political action on the part of the workers. The men must have known what the consequences would be for their behavior, and yet they became unruly subjects acting outside of typical organizational tactics of the left. (I return to the importance of unruly politics in the next chapter.)

Strikes are practically unthinkable in Qatar, yet the Msheireb development experienced one on a massive scale. This may well explain why the foreman at the Mshreireb museums was so quick to intervene and prevent me from speaking to his employees. There is a high risk of punishment for offending management, including arrest and deportation. In this instance, the trade union monitoring the striking worker situation stated that the assumption was that all of the men who had walked off the job would be deported. In a statement to Doha News, Msheireb Properties declared that it "is taking this incident seriously and is firmly committed to stand against any form of exploitation, abuse or injustice."[65]

This was not the first time that Msheireb had harmed migrants, though. The project itself displaced workers from their housing, causing massive evictions. As reporter Victoria Baux explains, "Scores of migrant workers have been left homeless, some of them left to sleep on the streets of energy-rich Qatar's capital."[66] The news site quotes a construction worker as saying, "We were in our rooms when police arrived and gave us one hour to leave with all our belongings. . . . That night we slept on the road."[67] He had been living with fellow Bangladeshi workers crammed six people to a room. "They were told to never set foot inside the building again. But Furuq and his friends return every night to sit in front of their old home."[68] Another elderly worker added that the police came every night after *iftar* (the much cherished fast-breaking meal). "I would have thought they'd wait until the end of Ramadan at least," he said of his fellow Muslims, who reciprocated none of the basic religiosity Muslims expect of one another. After their long days working in the heat, the migrant men spent their afternoon searching for a place to sleep on the streets.[69]

The scholar Mariam Ibrahim-Al Mulla argues that Bin Jel-mood House is a show of soft power by Qatar in that it purports to be accountable for slavery in its various forms even as "the slaves' intangible history was carefully selected, manipulated and reinterpreted, thus reordering historical knowledge."[70] The museum furthers myths that slaves were satisfied with their lives and easily integrated into Qatari social life. By self-consciously making a spectacle of slavery through the museum, Qatar is able to misdirect attention from current abuses, including those of the showily progressive development company that has its own problematic business practices.

CONCLUSION

There are few easy solutions for the labor situation in Qatari. The kafala system, even in its somewhat reformed iteration, is deliberately and systematically abusive. However, as Christensen notes, there are a few possible policy changes that would yield improvements.[71] For one thing, effective labor courts could be established to receive and act on complaints. Fines and punishments for corporations could also be meaningfully increased. Workers should be allowed to unionize and engage in collective bargaining. Although FIFA did implement a human rights policy in 2017, it is, as Christensen notes, inadequate. "While FIFA is not directly responsible for the contractors who are operating with labor trafficked workers, FIFA could certainly select a host country whose regulatory scheme to prevent human trafficking is well developed."[72] In the future, FIFA should include as part of the bidding process a robust plane for maintaining good labor conditions.

Qatar contains an inversion of Western expectations about gender. While sex trafficking dominates policy, funding, and popular representations of human trafficking, Qatar is a location where labor trafficking of migrant men is beyond prominent. In Qatar, there are regimes of visibility that dictate who and what is visible. In this case, migrant sex workers in Qatar are hypervisible despite common Western refrains about sex trafficking being "hidden in plain sight." Conversely, male construction workers are actively restricted and erased, banned from public view; even their homes are removed from sight, and outsiders are prevented from ever seeing them. Meanwhile, Qatar has created other spectacles to distract from the abuses and deaths suffered by the migrants. Ultimately, the "beautiful games" playing out in the stadiums are part of this same reordering of visibility and serve to erase the plight of workers. The case of Qatar also provides an interesting opportunity to examine unexpected and unruly disruptions (a theme I take up in the next chapter), as in the case of the spontaneous protests and work stoppages that the government erased from the internet, rendering that spectacular display invisible. In denying the migrants' basic entitlement to care, Qatari regimes of visibility have serious consequences. The experiences of migrant workers in Qatar must be recentered.

CHAPTER 5

Let Come the Whore Assemblage

As the FIFA Confederations Cup began on a warm night in June 2013, the tear gas in the air was faint and painless, but we all recognized what it was immediately. It came from somewhere farther up in the procession on Avenida Presidente Vargas in Rio de Janeiro's downtown. A few people around me wore makeshift gas masks of bandanas or paper painter's masks laced with vinegar, bracing for a fight that had not yet begun. Global media coverage would briefly dub this mass uprising of millions of people protesting in cities across Brazil "The Vinegar Revolution," but the name never quite stuck. For now, though, the tear gas was a long way away. People cheered and smiled. My friend and former research assistant, Gustavo, looked at them nervously and took his usual cautious tone. "I think we shouldn't march near them," he said. "The masks will make them targets for the police."

Scattered throughout the crowd were other protestors wearing the white Guy Fawkes masks from the film *V for Vendetta*. A few of them were wrapped in black clothes for added anonymity, ostensibly part of the Black Bloc of anarchists who were often accused of arson, vandalism, and subverting the true aims of the protest (and almost as often alleged to be infiltrators paid by right-wing organizations, or by the government, as a way to delegitimize the protests).

A helicopter circled overhead, dipping down close to the crowd. The throng of protestors—visible to me as largely younger, whiter, and more middle class than the smaller, earlier protests of previous weeks—laughed at this show of police force. But they laughed nervously, drunk on adrenaline and *communitas*, that special spirit of unstructured community and unity social scientists pine for but seldom find. Some flashed green laser pointers at the windows of the helicopter, presumably to irritate or distract the pilot, though I couldn't see how making it crash on top of us was going to help our cause. Well, *any* of our causes—there wasn't a lot of rhetorical coherence at the protest, just a lot of affect. We weren't entirely in agreement about what we wanted (if we even knew ourselves), but we did agree that we were all pissed off, and that was sufficient for the moment.

Overhead, people in apartments looked down on the throng, which numbered 300,000 if you believe the political conservatives and over 1,000,000 according to various media reports and activists. Some of the audience above us waved cheerfully and shouted their support to those marching. Others glanced about nervously, aware of how dangerous the situation at their doorstep could become if police were to open fire.

The crowd saw the bystanders watching them and chanted at these people aloft in their apartments over and over again, "*Vem! Vem pra rua, vem!*" Come! Come to the street!

The expression came from a popular car commercial for Fiat that had been airing around this time. Given that the Confederations Cup was widely regarded as a rehearsal for the World Cup, the ad was tailored to the moment, featuring heartwarming and spectacular scenes of soccer in the run-up to the event. By co-opting a commercial slogan associated with the Cup, the protestors lobbed a critique at the celebratory and nationalistic spectacle of presumed solidarity around sports. YouTube has many parodies of this commercial featuring the familiar song but showing violent scenes of the 2013 Confederations Cup protests instead of the original images of happy, dancing, and soccer-playing Brazilians.

Vem pra rua, vem. Come to the street, all right. Come in protest. "Fuck FIFA!" someone cried. "Fora Cabral!" they shouted, calling for the ouster of the governor of the state of Rio de Janeiro, who had pushed for draconian police measures. My friend and I happily joined them. "Fora Cabral! Fora Cabral!" (Sérgio Cabral would later be convicted in 2016 on multiple charges of corruption, racketeering, and the embezzlement of US$80 million and sentenced to almost sixty years in prison.)

Then came a new chant: "Fora Dilma! Fora Dilma!" Out with Dilma!

"Oh no!" cried Gustavo, who was still in those days an avid supporter of the leftist Workers' Party (Partido dos Trabalhadores, PT) and President Dilma Rousseff, Brazil's first female president, who would later be impeached in what many on the left in Brazil call "the congressional coup" because there was no criminal charge. "This is terrible!" he hissed at me. "It's not her fault!"

Today, Brazilians remember these protests as the beginning of a wave of populism that would eventually result in the rise of the Far Right and of the authoritarian president Jair Bolsonaro. But in that initial moment, the unruly protestors did not see themselves as part of any such historical arc. The poor had sparked the original protest over a minor rise in bus and metro fares, but the movement had become something else. All around us, young people were snapping selfies and pictures of the protest, tweeting, posting on Facebook, and sending messages on WhatsApp. Sometimes the posts and messages wouldn't transmit, though, because of the amount of data bombarding the nearby cell towers. The protesting mass of smartphone users was not a crowd of *favelados* (residents of shanty towns) or working-class residents of the Zona Norte. These were young people with no memory of the dictatorship, youth from the consumer classes who grew up during the rise of what Goldman Sachs famously dubbed BRICs (Brazil, Russia, India, and China), a cluster of emerging economies whose growing clout would supposedly rival the United States. Brazil had even excelled during the aftermath of the 2008 financial crisis, benefiting from the hot money that fled the United States as investors poured into Brazil instead. But Brazil's emerging economic clout had ended owing to mismanagement, crashing commodity prices, and a resurgent United States. The protestors were disillusioned. People held up signs about corruption, but Gustavo scoffed and told me that this discourse about corruption was just a dog whistle for the political Right. It was unclear what politics this enormous uprising even had. This lack of clarity is part of how right-wing media, especially O Globo (a major Brazilian media network), manipulated coverage of the protests to give the sense that the entire nation had coalesced against leftist policies and practices. In reality, the Left was greatly disillusioned with the PT due to some shady dealings with certain politicians and issues around overhauling the tax system, as well as major corruption scandals.

The movement had begun in São Paulo with a student collective that was mostly Black, known as the Free Fare Movement (Movimento Passe Livre), which protested a small hike of a few cents in public transit fares. It grew quickly, and other social movements joined, mostly leftist groups representing progressive causes. Only after these groups had coalesced did the disaffected crowds concerned with anti-corruption begin to add their voices. As André Singer has noted, the initial demonstrators who first added their concerns onto those of the Free Fare Movement were largely young professionals who lamented their lost wealth and opportunities that had been gained under leftist president Luiz Inácio Lula da Silva.[1] As Leonardo Avritzer writes, over time the right-leaning elements of the movement began to call for the ouster of President Rousseff, Lula's successor, who was eventually impeached under the guise of "ending corruption." Ultimately, the once-leftist social movement grew into a populist force that may have laid the groundwork for the ultra-right-wing authoritarian Jair Bolsonaro's election.[2]

There were also many pro-gay signs denouncing Marco Feliciano, an evangelical Christian pastor who had become the head of the congressional human rights committee and used this position to advocate for homophobic policies such as gay conversion therapy. Some people congratulated those carrying these signs or flashed them a thumbs-up when they saw the placards. Armed with rainbow flags and defaced photos of Feliciano, the queer groups flowed through the streets alongside the rest of the demonstrators. The queers wended their way through crowds of kids with iPhones, the restless Left and some of the feckless Right, the Black Bloc and the wannabe anarchists, the bored, the curious, the hopeful and the malcontented, the people hoping to pick pockets, and the people who came to the street that historic night just to say they had been there—all one great unruly coalition.

Eventually the crowd stopped. Presumably those at the front of this kilometers-long procession had stopped at their final destination . . . or had they been stopped? We waited. Some time passed without movement. Uncertain what to do, people began to wander away from the crowd to head home. But the city government had closed the Praça Onze metro station, our nearest exit route, without warning. Police were suddenly everywhere. Unable to peacefully leave but afraid to stay where we were, some people began to panic, pushing one another and slowly becoming separated from friends and families. Gustavo and I escaped down a side street, where we parted ways; Gustavo fled on foot while I found a bus that got me as far as Glória, a neighborhood about halfway to where I was living. I arranged to meet some friends there who were academics and who had also been in the protest and were coming my way.

It was quiet in this neighborhood. I stood on the corner next to a little bar with outdoor seating. How anticlimactic, I thought. It was like a whole other world. Didn't these people know history was being made just ten minutes away? Why were they sitting here eating?

Mas as pessoas na sala de jantar são ocupadas em nascer e morrer, I thought. The old lyrics of the Tropicalia anti-dictatorship song from 1969, "Panis et Circensis" (Bread and Circuses) criticizing the bourgeoisie came to my mind. *But the people in the dining room are too busy being born and dying.* Brazil had always struggled with the question of middle-class inaction—and therefore complicity—with its right-wing governments. In this instance, the "revolution" of the right-wing Bolsonaro administration came about specifically because of a disillusioned middle class.

Then the tear gas rolled in thick. A handful of Black Bloc members came running fast, crashing into the diners, knocking over tables, sending food and drinks flying. Diners all along the street took refuge inside stores and restaurants. Others hid behind overturned tables. Proprietors began to lock doors and lower metal guards. Police roared through on foot and in cars, chasing the Bloc up the hill toward the winding streets around Santa Teresa. I wheezed and coughed, relying more on my somatic memories of the neighborhood than my vision as I retreated up the street past a sauna where I had spent some years interviewing rent boys. My colleagues arrived from the protest and led me to a little restaurant near the sauna, talking the owner into unlocking the door to let us inside, where they paid him back by entertaining his more respectable patrons with stories from the trenches. Not wanting to cooperate with or be detained by police, we and the other diners sealed ourselves inside to wait out the battle.

In thinking of these moments, I am reminded of the works of the theorist Maurice Blanchot, who wrote about the relationship between spectacle and protest. "We are no longer burdened by events, as soon as we behold their image with an interested, then simply curious, then empty but fascinated look. What good is it taking part in a street demonstration, since at the same moment, secure and at rest, we are at the demonstration itself, thanks to a television set?"[3] The people up above in the dining rooms could look out their windows at the protest below while also watching it on the televisions behind them. As Blanchot concludes, "The man of government who fears the street—because the man in the street is always on the verge of becoming political man—is delighted to be no more than an entrepreneur of spectacle, skilled at putting the citizen in us to sleep, the better to keep awake, in the half-light of a half-sleep, only the tireless voyeur of images."[4] These words capture the peculiarity of the political moment in Brazil that character-ized the shift from the spontaneous and unruly Confederations Cup protests in 2013 to the cheerfully conservative political behavior of the masses during the 2014 World Cup even as that event brought so much suffering to those on the margins of Brazilian society.

PREGAMING

I begin my exploration of social upheavals and policing with this first-hand account because I am interested in the shifting conditions for those on the margins of society during periods leading up to and including major sporting events. These are times of rapid change in terms of infra-structural development, gentrification, economic changes, and policing and surveillance. The protests were a huge spectacle, and nearly every major news site in the world showed powerful images of the millions of people in the streets facing down violent police. For many, Brazil's hosting of the World Cup and Olympic Games is most interesting in terms of representation and narratives. How should the country be rep-resented? Are the narratives triumphalist and laudatory or condescend-ing and skeptical? How does the government use spectacles—fallacious and otherwise—to incentivize particular performances of nationalism? However, I think that the spectacles of these games themselves and the co-opting of spectacular protests surrounding them present another op-portunity for scholars, which is to watch how an emergent form of governmentality shapes sexuality.

The Confederations Cup protests in 2013 were the first major show of popular force by the people in many years. I was curious about how those laboring on the sexual margins—people who are historically dis-empowered by the state—would fit into this present situation, in which the state and the Brazilian people seemed to be struggling to redefine the balance of shared power. By the time the World Cup arrived in 2014, however, the movement had been quelled. Sure, there was some cover-age of people who lived in the favelas who had attempted to fight their forced removal to make way for "FIFA-fication," and one could find oc-casional "FUCK FIFA" stamps and stencils on signs and sidewalks, but the millions of marchers were gone.

During the Confederations Cup protest in 2013, protests like that in Rio appeared in cities all over the country in a mass uprising. In the country's capital, Brasilia, angry demonstrators managed to crash through security barriers, bombard police, and overtake the capital in Brasilia.[5] They climbed on top of the congressional building and made a perimeter of burning tires around themselves. All across the country, Brazilians watched as these protesters danced in the flames atop the government building, their shadows looming impossibly large behind them. There was almost no widespread dissent during the 2014 World Cup.[6] And the populace performed their expected role: dancing samba, singing, smiling, and cheering their team (up until one of the most painful and humiliating losses in football history soured a lot of them on the whole thing). In 2016, Rousseff was ousted just days after the Olympics ended, and her right-wing vice president took power with a far-right Congress. Yet during the 2016 Olympics, the police were firmly in control.

Nationalistic spectacles like the World Cup create powerful opportunities for political leaders to advance their own agendas while the population is mollified, distracted by all the "bread and circus." Yet what has gone largely unexamined is what happens to those on the sexual margins of society—the queers, the hustlers, the streetwalkers, the gringo chasers looking for money and travel opportunities, the sexually unruly and undisciplined—during these moments of nationalist political reformation. These populations went from being part of the political sphere and generally (if tacitly) accepted as part of Brazilian society to being subordinated, denigrated, and rendered abject during the run-up to the World Cup. In fact, the condition of sex workers worsened as police raided brothels, closed bars and motels, and physically and sexually assaulted women in an effort to "clean up" red light areas before FIFA, tourists, and foreign journalists arrived.

After this experience, I wondered how Russia's World Cup would go. I traveled to Moscow and Saint Petersburg during the 2018 World Cup and met with members of the sex worker rights movement there. In particular, I was fortunate to get to spend time with Irina Maslova, the leader of Silver Rose, a sex worker rights group that has openly battled the Putin regime, even going so far as to sue the Putin government three times for the right to be recognized as an official NGO. Like Gabriela Leite in Brazil's sex worker rights movement, Irina is a charismatic figure. She is smart and witty and has a buzzy aura about her. She's petite, with perpetually wide eyes and an infectious energy when she speaks. She's a middle-aged woman who proudly boasted rainbow-colored hair when I interviewed her. As she spoke, she would periodically seize my pen and notebook to draw out illustrations of what she was saying or concepts she wanted to be sure I understood, a ferocious and indefatigable whirl-wind of activity.

Before the Russian World Cup, Irina was part of a delegation to the Joint United Nations Programme on HIV/AIDS (UNAIDS) Coordination Board. She explained to the board that in May 2016, a well-known former mixed-martial arts fighter leading an ultranationalist gang had "assaulted two brothels in St. Petersburg. They knocked down the door and forced the girls to undress and march naked in the streets. Police refused to intervene. We found there have been over fifty similar assaults against brothels in St. Petersburg recently."[7] She went on to recount a Nazi gang in the city throwing a Nigerian sex worker from a window.

The Global Fund for Women selected Maslova as one of its fourteen "Defenders," featuring her in its campaign. As she told the Fund, "Revolution starts from the bottom, when those who were excluded from this life have to fight for their right to get back in." She described how the right-wing vigilantes had filmed the sex workers as they marched them through the streets to the police station, posting the footage on You-Tube. "The police held more than fifty sex workers for a day—still without clothes—before Silver Rose intervened and provided clothing and legal aid."[8] The Silver Rose offices where I interviewed Maslova's staff had security systems installed, and Maslova herself carries a panic button because she has been threatened so many times. She has so far resisted hiring bodyguards or a security team but has had to move loved ones from her home for their own protection. "We fight until the end," she said. "We have nothing to lose."[9]

From there, the situation worsened. By May 2018, just before the World Cup guests arrived, she explained, "we have seen the work of law enforcement agencies intensifying in preparation for the World Cup. It looks like they are trying to cleanse the city and take 'unwanted people' away from the streets. They do this by intimidating people to ensure that the towns hosting the championship 'make a good impression' to the world. The majority of sex workers, understanding that they are in a no-win situation, have decided to stop working during the championship because pressure on them has become unbearable."[10]

Sex workers were not the only marginalized people to suffer. When I was in Russia, media began to report that the police were rounding up "undesirables" such as people experiencing homelessness, people with drug addiction, and sex workers and concentrating them in camps outside the city.[11] Amnesty International took notice of the increasing violence against sex workers related to the Cup. Maslova told Amnesty how, many years prior, she had been "arrested and taken to the Petrogradsky District police station where I spent 48 hours in solitary confinement. It was raining when I was taken in, and it was raining when I was released. It was the first time that I felt, in my own skin, what captivity was. This was not only about liberty. It was about that awful smell that penetrated my skin and my clothes, which I had to discard later."[12] Maslova's trauma was intense. "Even after three hours in the bathroom washing and scrubbing, I was not able to get rid of that smell. I felt like I was rubbing my skin off, until it bled, trying to remove it completely and regenerate a new one. I can still sense this smell when I hear other sex workers' stories or take up cases of crimes perpetrated against them. This smell is terrible, but it triggers my desire to fight."[13]

Maslova explained, "Defending the rights of sex workers is more than a job for me—it is my mission and my life's work. In preparation for the FIFA World Cup, the authorities started their 'cleansing' operations in Saint Petersburg. . . . I think soon they will proceed to more severe measures. Some sex worker businesses were told to close down for a very specific time frame. Those who have been in the business for a long time have already planned vacations during the World Cup. They will leave the city, and I think it is the right thing to do."[14]

The social scientist Alexander Kondakov interviewed forty-one sex workers in Saint Petersburg, and his findings corroborate Maslova's concerns. "The police are the centre of sex workers' fears. However, this is so not because sex work is illegal and sex workers could be arrested and convicted, but because anything can happen in a police department. The police officers have power over sex workers. The law reinforces and maintains this hierarchy as the police are representatives of the state, but also they are men, heterosexual, employed and powerful."[15] Kondakov goes on to explain how police are seen as representative of the law but also above it. "Sex workers talk about police actions with a very particular Russian word: *bespredel* (limitlessness or lawlessness). . . . This is an example of a particular technique of power which is mediated by law and establishes a hierarchy where police officers are positioned above other citizens. This leads to a situation where police officers may be the source of violence simply because of the power they have by law."[16] He explains that previously, the police would rape sex workers and force them to work in police stations cleaning floors and bathrooms in a system known as *subbotnik* (a not neatly translatable term here being used as something of a communist joke about citizens "giving back to the community"). Today, however, police have financial dealings with brothels and other sex businesses and so must exercise their power and orchestrate their abuses more carefully.

Although the West is fascinated by documentary accounts of sex trafficking in Russia, and media accounts abound with stereotypes about Russian mobsters, Kondakov's scholarly work and Maslova's years in the field of sex worker rights reveal that it is the police who instill widespread fear among the women. (This is consistent with the Brazilian context I've detailed at length and with the findings of the sex worker rights groups in South Africa whom I interviewed and whose work I describe in this book's introduction.)

While there is some major recognition from groups like UNAIDS and Amnesty International, the women's rights movement and the left in general have not rallied to Russian sex workers' side. There remains interest in Russian "sex trafficking," and there has been a lot of global interest in gay rights abuses in Russia owing to the draconian "gay propaganda" laws that forbid public displays of affection between same-sex couples on the grounds that it "promotes homosexuality" among children. There have been several news stories with widespread dissemination among gay audiences that detail (with horrifying video footage) gangs of Russian men luring gay men on Grindr, a sexual networking and dating app for gay men, to homes where they were brutally tortured.[17] However, the plight of sex workers has not captured the public imagination in the same way.

Perhaps no group has gotten more feminist attention than Pussy Riot, a ski mask–wearing group singing punk songs and staging protests who came to prominence in 2012 when they protested inside Moscow's main cathedral, an action that resulted in two members receiving prison sentences. Members have been persecuted and even poisoned by the Russian government.[18] Elsewhere, they have been invited on global speaking tours and showered with attention from celebrities, including Madonna and Sting.

Pussy Riot's members also saw the World Cup as an opportunity and entered the field during the final match, dressed as police officers. They high-fived French football star Kylian Mbappé. The stunt went viral, and the four activists were detained for around two weeks. Although many fans were put off by this protest, it did provide an opportunity for Pussy Riot to call attention to its demands to free political prisoners and allow political competition.[19] As Pussy Riot member Veronika Nikulshina explained to *Time Magazine*, it was significant to know that

Putin was watching them along with the rest of the world. "During the World Cup, a lot of foreigners came to Russia and thought how wonderful it seemed, and how great and friendly the police officers are. Actually, it is not like that. For the football fans saying that we ruined the field and ruined the game, maybe it is bad. But for us, it's totally not right to separate politics from FIFA and World Cup Final. It's all about politics, it's all about country. If we hadn't stopped the game, the message would not have been clear. We really wanted to show people that you can live your life, or you can play your own game, and at any time for no reason, the police will just ruin your life and do whatever they want—as we did to the field."[20]

I do not begrudge Pussy Riot its success. The group has mastered the art of using spectacle—both its theatrical performances/protests and media coverage of the group—to enact what I would describe as an "unruly sexual politics." The Brazilian theorist Sonia Corrêa defines unruly politics as "provocations in exploring the limits, caveats and pitfalls of crystallized notions of citizenship, civil society and justice."[21] Pussy Riot invokes the sexual nominally and considers itself feminist (and has done protests around LGBT rights), but its demands are less specifically feminist per se. They are diffuse and centered on disruption more than awareness raising or agenda setting. The FIFA stunt was about using the game to create a spectacle, offering the world an inverted reflection of police-citizen relations in Russia even as they, fake police, were taken into custody by real police. The protests I've described—widespread in the case of Brazil and microcosmic in the case of Russia—provide a useful opportunity for thinking about sexual politics and the roles of sex workers, queer theory, and the spectacular within them.

UNRULY SEXUAL POLITICS

During the protests during the 2013 Confederations Cup in Brazil, one of the more spectacular sights was the Pink Bloc, a radical queer collective. Members' pink costumes relied on both hyperfeminine and hypermasculine styles. For example, they donned frilly pink frocks coupled with gas masks and large water or bubble guns painted pink. Others copied the Black Bloc's makeshift balaclavas but used pink garments. Most were legible as young cisgender men, but they deliberately subverted gender norms by mixing masculine and feminine extremes. Some exposed their hairy chests. Others wore dresses and bared their legs. Factions of the Pink Bloc have surfaced at protest sites in Europe and

Latin America, often in response to International Monetary Fund structural adjustment programs and austerity measures. In Brazil, however, members tapped into the carnivalesque, using an aggressive sexual frivolity to taunt police and draw media attention to their objections to FIFA, Feliciano, and the economic conditions of Brazil. Armed with tactics like glitter and bubbles (dubbed *glittervandalismo* by Brazilian media), they genderfucked their way through the Confederations Cup and continued to appear as one of few visible protest groups during the World Cup.[22]

While the overall 2013 protests began out of unruliness, the political actions that eventually grew out of that tumult (in large part because of the renarrativization of that movement) became decidedly unliberatory and, indeed, became very much about re-entrenching the ruling class. Yet the Pink Bloc represents an unruly sexual politics within that messy mass of people in the initial giddy moments of the uprising. In recent years, scholars have become increasingly interested in the idea of "unruly politics." As mentioned earlier, for Corrêa they are embodied provocations; they move "beyond conventional state and law centered grammars underlining contradictions, fragmentations and erosion of public spheres."[23] They are not the politics of practicality; they are not oriented toward outcomes, goals, demands, or lists of action items; and they are extraneous to political parties, union formations, wildcat strikes, ballot initiatives, and legislation. They are fundamentally about demonstrations of affect that congeal, becoming events.

As Khanna and colleagues have developed their theorizing of this concept, unruly politics "is a broad conceptual space rather than a descriptive or nominal category. It is simultaneously the insistence on new languages of politics, the redefinition of spaces of politics, ruptures in the aesthetic regimes of power, and the creation of imaginaries of power beyond what is already intelligible."[24] Key case studies for unruly politics include the Occupy movements in the United States in 2008 and beyond and the uprising in Egypt's Tahrir Square in 2011. As Khanna and colleagues note, these "are events that are beyond the 'rules' of political action. Painting outside the lines, these phenomena are at their very core 'unruly.'"[25] They demand a new mode of political inquiry that spills outside of traditional notions of politics, and in which the relevance of acts and events is not reduced to the effect they have on formal structures of the political establishment.

Using the rubric of unruly politics, Lucy MacMahon examined protests in Recife, Brazil, in 2012 following the denial of licenses to street venders, as well as similar venders protesting in Salvador, Brazil, for the right to sell their wares in FIFA-controlled areas.[26] Sometimes they made concrete gains, such as the formation of a union to distribute more licenses, but the union leadership was quickly corrupted by the state. "A major challenge for political protest is to make changes that resist appropriation in service of the same old social hierarchies. Such an appropriation has a particularly bitter history in Brazil," where these efforts often "ended up as weak reformism."[27] MacMahon remains optimistic, though, focusing on "the affective experience of protest, rather than its limited outcomes . . . [suggesting] that the most powerful moments in the experience of street protest are where one's relationship with the state is altered."[28] Examples of such a shift in relation to the Brazilian state include "when middle class protesters branded as terrorists move from the category of citizen to that of criminal. Or when protest confers a citizen status on groups which were previously politically invisible."[29]

Corrêa turns to Foucault's treatment of Immanuel Kant, noting that for Foucault, revolution is not synonymous with progress. Instead, revolution is really about triggering "a sympathy of aspiration that merges into enthusiasm" precisely because "what matters is not the revolution per se, it is also what happens in the minds of those who have not done it. . . . [I]t is the relation they have with a revolution in which they have not been active actors."[30] In other words, *vem pra rua! vem!* The importance of the unruly politics in Brazil's uprising rested not in whether protesters could make coherent demands, but in the feelings that coalesced not only among disparate actors and also among the people looking down from their windows and the proverbial "people in the dining room."

Although I fully endorse these authors' engagement with unruly politics, my dilemma as an ethnographer of sexual economies is that I see very little space for understanding sexuality within the "unruly." That is, what might unruly *sexual* politics look like? The Pink Bloc is one direct example in the form of protest. But how do unruly sexual politics manifest in the quotidian?

During the World Cup in 2014, I watched the opening match in the middle-class Brazilian brothel 4 × 4 in Rio's Centro. I was accompanied by three other male members of the Observatóio da Prostituição. As I described in earlier chapters, women selling sex in Rio believed media reports that there would be a large increase in commercial sexual activity during the Cup and were ultimately sorely disappointed. In fact, business was so poor that brothel venues resorted to specials, such as giving away free beer during games, and then eventually resolved to close outright during matches. In the brothel 4 × 4, management required women to work during the match, but there were almost no clients. I sat with colleagues jotting field notes in the bar area on a bench directly across from a floor-length mirror, on top of which rested a TV.

The woman next to me, Alexa, is a blonde prostitute from the Zona Norte in her mid-twenties. She is pissed off. "I want to be at home watching this with my family . . . with my son . . . not sitting here. There isn't even any business! I am not even being paid to be here! But I am required to be here or [management] will give me a fine." She scratches her ankle idly, leaning over and fully revealing her breasts, which are hardly hidden by the green and yellow FIFA-themed bikini-style "uniforms" the women had been required to purchase from the house. She tells me that she would like to attend a technical school, but she needs to save up some money. She makes a good living working at 4 × 4. However, she knows that once she ages, she will lose the opportunity and will not make this amount of money again. As we watch the match, she screams and cheers so loudly that even the clients turn in surprise to look at her. When Brazil almost scores, she jumps to her feet, nearly losing her balance in her high-heeled shoes. She curses and plops back down. "The Cup is shit. Totally terrible for all the girls," she says. "Look!" she says, gesturing to the sparsely populated lounge. "Not even the gringos are here. Clients are just like me. They want to watch the Cup with friends and family and not with *putas*."

Then at one point the camera pans to Rousseff, and Alexa grips my leg suddenly, her nails digging in so sharply that I have to grab her hand. She pays no mind. Her eyes are fixed on the president. She stands up again, this time slowly. She towers in her high heels, shivering with rage, and slowly extends her arm toward the screen, middle finger raised defiantly. "Fuck you!" she roars at the president. She looks around the brothel and pumps her fists at the other patrons, who whoop in support of her. The camera returns to the players, and Alexa plops back down next to me, happily joining the other "putas" in cheering on their team.

In this moment, one can see the relationship between sexuality and the state symbolized through this act of defiance. Unlike the 2013 Confederations Cup, there was relatively little protest during the 2014 World Cup because of the massively increased police presence and the state's determination to squelch dissent. But Alexa's display of outrage at Rousseff points to the ways that sex workers also felt abandoned by the PT, which had not been as progressive economically or sexually as they had hoped. In place of a mass uprising like the previous year, one finds small moments of resistance such as "FUCK FIFA" or "FIFA GO HOME" stamps, stencils, and graffiti on sidewalks, walls, and streets. And in moments such as this, the people seek to reassert themselves in relationship to the state and its priorities. Indeed, Alexa is working as a prostitute in large part because of the failures of the state to provide her with better opportunities for employment and education. With the economy flailing; police crackdowns in favelas and red light areas; and cuts happening in education, infrastructure, and public services, Rousseff's government continued to spend on FIFA-related projects, many of which did not benefit the working classes that should have been championed by the PT.

Thus, there is a certain irony in Alexa's simultaneous enjoyment of the FIFA World Cup and denigration of Brazil's head of state. Importantly, unruly politics reorient the people vis-à-vis the state and renegotiate their relationship to it. But this assumes that the state is functioning as a run-of-the-mill neoliberal entity. In reality, scholars must consider unruly politics, including unruly sexual politics, as a reorienting of citizen-subjects in relation to the parastate.

As Paul Amar has shown in his extensive analysis of the Brazilian case that there has been a shift in governmentality. The parastate functions like a paramilitary; just as the military has expanded to include a variety of private contractors, government agencies, and even academics and NGOs working as consultants, so too has the state changed its structure, operations, and constitutive elements.[31] As I've noted throughout this book, the parastate is rooted in coalitions that wrap up government policy makers, governmental and nongovernmental organizations, property developers, religious groups, and both public and private security agencies who all perform *as a state*, but a state that has "outsourced its functions into a parallel realm of reduced accountability and unregulated power."[32] This shift is clearly evident in the protest movement described at the beginning of this chapter. What appears first as incoherence among protestors regarding whom they are targeting—Rousseff? Cabral? Feliciano? The PT? The police? FIFA?—is actually a diffusion that proves Amar's theory correct. The protests of 2013 were incoherent precisely because FIFA has joined the parastate along with a small army of consultants, NGOs, foreign observers, evangelical Christian groups, and neoliberal property developers. One of the demands of this parastate in 2013 was that certain areas not conducive to state interests—chief among them favelas, poor areas targeted for development, and red light areas—be rehabilitated. As Amar himself and others have demonstrated, this shift toward the parastatal in Brazil has had disastrous consequences for women like Alexa who work in Rio de Janeiro's sexual economy.

Unruly politics that reject the parastate and attempt to rethink the citizen-subject's place in this matrix of social power must also account for sexuality, and scholars must ask how certain sexual citizens come to be denigrated or valued. I argue that we must think through this question with special attention to spectacle precisely because spectacle is a language common to both the parastate and unruly political coalitions. As we see, however, the coalition that took to the streets in 2013 was perhaps not unruly enough, and those who are most sexually vulnerable ultimately suffered for it.

The parastate is keyed into the performative and rhetorical possibilities of spectacle. Its members are aware that the ideological battles they are fighting are being waged at the level of spectacle more so than on the actual ground. The state was keenly aware that the Confederations Cup protest was primarily a battle for public sympathies that were playing out in the media. The state even *thinks* in terms of the performative. In 2014, the FBI assembled teams in each of the host cities across Brazil, primarily to be on hand in the event that US "assets" like diplomats were compromised or threatened. As a courtesy, they also offered training for Brazilian police, including how to manage large-scale protests and demonstrations. The training sessions were over-enrolled and very much in demand.[33] The FBI teams were specialized around major events rather than country or region, so the agents did not have cultural competence or language skills. Predictably, this resulted in some problems; for one, visiting FBI agents did not appear to understand that Brazil has multiple police forces, with separate chains of command and funding sources, each of which famously despises the next. During an interview with the FBI in São Paulo during the World Cup, I asked a senior-ranking agent about the Black Bloc presence in the protests. He told me, "The Brazilian police that we are training have got the Black Bloc completely wrong. They keep insisting that the Black Bloc is a group, an organization that people join and become part of. It's not. The Black Bloc is a tactic. You can't think of it as a group of people, only as a tactic."

It's as if the FBI has added the writings of Judith Butler to their training manual. The FBI understands what the Brazilian police have failed to grasp: the Bloc is not a coherent group with a stable sense of identity.

People do not identify with the Bloc, go through a process of identification, and become a part of that community. The Bloc is a performance, an operation, a tactic, a behavior, a thing that one does. To don the theatrical costume, to burn a tire, to smash a bank window—these are performative tactics, but they are not the same as identity. This view is markedly different than how the Brazilian parastate had viewed the Bloc. The year prior to the World Cup and the FBI training, Brazil's own central intelligence agency (ABIN) and the army's cybersecurity command (CDCiber) had been surveilling citizens and politicians, even "arresting students suspected of curating Facebook pages associated with Black Bloc methods."[34] And anyone can participate in such a spectacle. The state uses spectacle and the people respond with spectacle. Thus, the dueling public performances forge a dialectic from which powerful discourses can emerge. The Brazilian people fought this battle of spectacles in 2013, but ultimately they receded into complacency. Many were genuinely swept up in the FIFA fervor in 2014. But the police were also out in full and visible force, looking meaner than ever. As the FBI agent explained, "Notice they all have the added 'armor' on now. But that's really just like plastic football padding. It doesn't do anything; it's just for show." Whether the Black Bloc, the Pink Bloc, Alexa shouting at the TV in the brothel, or the police playing dress-up, spectacle has become the battleground on which the sexual terrain of unruly politics plays out.

PUTA POLITICS

Few marginalized groups have capitalized on their abilities in the arena of spectacle like the prostitutes' rights movement in Brazil. Gabriela Leite, the founder of the movement, was famous for her tongue-in-cheek campaigns when she ran for "deputy" or congresswoman. *Uma puta deputada*, her posters read, which means something like a "deputy whore" but also "a bitchin' deputy." She founded a fashion line, Daspu, that used prostitutes and their allies on catwalks and did fashion shows in cafés, bookstores, and theatrical venues, on university steps, and in parks. Daspu means "from the whores" but was also a pun on "Daslu," a high-end fashion line whose owner promptly sued the group. The owner lost the suit (and eventually went to prison for unrelated financial crimes), but the story grabbed headlines and won over the public to the side of the self-described putas. Daspu was featured in *Brazil Vogue* and even got to perform on a popular evening telenovela watched by tens of millions of people. Known for dirty puns and provocative jokes, Daspu sells a variety of T-shirts and other items in pop-up shops.

The anthropologist Laura Murray has worked with the sex worker group Davida, which runs the Daspu project, for almost two decades and also made a documentary film about Gabriela. Through her extensive work with Gabriela and other activists, she formulated her theory of puta politics. Central to this was Gabriela and the prostitutes' rights movement's reclamation of the word *puta* as their ideal identification. She argues that biopolitical and neoliberal strategies that interact to produce "an ongoing and flexible politics of inclusion/exclusion" function as "tactics of exception."[35] These tactics of exception "exclude sex workers through political maneuvers couched in a language of inclusion."[36] For example, a prostitute named Cristina described working with a colleague in a shared room where they received clients. Citing laws that prevent "sexual exploitation" of women, police arrested Cristina and her friend, charging each of them with "exploiting" the other and remanding them to a maximum-security prison. Thus, the police use a law that is supposed to represent "women's rights" and is purportedly designed to prevent violence but actually functions as a way to exclude and harm women. Murray explains that "for sex workers, confronting tactics of exception involves the negotiation of boundaries established between pleasure derived from sex, money, and political power, and the danger of violence, arrest, and suffocating red tape. Through puta politics, sex worker activists operate at these boundaries, provocatively magnifying and embracing them as a way that obliterates the boundaries' existence."[37] Murray's notion of puta politics aligns with the kind of unruly eruptions to which Corrêa and others subscribe. As Murray explains, "What this means is that sex worker activists occupy a space of ambiguous moral status within these contested and fractured political fields. . . . Sex worker activists operate on the borders of the blurred lines between NGOs and government structures, and . . . it is precisely their history as putas, a group that has long eluded attempts at state control, abolition, and sanitization, that has been both their greatest strength and weakness."[38] That is, puta politics are *strategically unruly*, and putas draw on their own skill sets to advance their causes. This is why puta politics in Brazil proved less susceptible to co-optation by the Right, as the unruly political protests of 2013 did.

Melissa Gira Grant similarly outlines her thoughts on "whore solidarity," including her own choice to reclaim the word *whore* in order to "drain some of the hate off this word, to take up a little more space for ourselves in the world and to do it without shame."[39] She argues that "coming together around all the markers of who we are—where we come from, how we work, who we fuck—is how we produce the possibility of solidarity, no matter what we call it."[40]

Gabriela often discussed the importance of saying she was a puta. She found "sex worker" to be needlessly sanitizing and "politically correct." In the documentary *A Kiss for Gabriela*, she remarks that "if people didn't live with so much stigma in their heads, they would use this word [puta] . . . sons of putas should be a name of pride for our children. That is my thinking."[41] She goes on to say that she had attempted to attend university to study sociology but never finished. Still, she says, people in the media would describe her as a "sociologist and ex-prostitute."[42] In the film's interviews (recorded in 2013), she is visibly sick with cancer that would soon kill her. Still, she has a wry wit and liveliness to her that is inspiring. She laughs, "It's very funny because what I'm not, I am. And what I am, I'm not. . . . [I]t's absurd. I'm not a sociologist. I'm a puta . . . you don't need to call me a sociologist. I don't need or want to be one. If people come up and ask me what I am, I say, I'm a puta."[43]

Once when I interviewed her, she described herself as a classic whore, a puta from time immemorial. Perhaps remembering her brief time studying sociology in her youth, she made a passing reference to a "*puta ontológica*," meaning something like a "legendary whore" but a bit more literally, an ontological whore. Many years later, I think of that phrase often and regret not asking her what she meant. Perhaps she had misunderstood. Or perhaps I misheard her. Or perhaps she really did mean to suggest that there is an ontology of whoredom.

In my work, I am not especially interested in ontology itself. However, it is interesting that in the early 2000s, cultural anthropology had taken an "ontological turn" in which some scholars moved away from questions of culture and embraced ideas about multiple worlds and realities. Thus, anthropologists could attempt to answer questions such as the titular *How Forests Think: Toward an Anthropology beyond the Human*.[44] Anthropologists turned to thinking about animals and entire ecosystems. If I were to riff off Gabriela's passing comment, I wonder what might it mean to recognize puta or whore not just as a job title or a descriptor, but as another kind of entity completely. Certainly the puta is not a human creature; from a Deleuzian perspective, the whore's body would not be just a machine for sexual pleasure, but a body without organs.[45] More than the sum of its parts, the whore's body conjures up the idea of the relationship of the whore to her body. What, we might then ask, is it to *be* in the *puta world*? What is the experience of being in such a place?

In a lengthy, poetic, and stream-of-consciousness essay in Portuguese called "Puta Ontológica," the writers Hilan Bensusan and Fabiane Borges accuse an unspecified "you" (*tu*): "You never understood the ontology of the *putas*. The ontological desire that escapes the apprehension of class, of exploration and added value. Something of the talent and charisma of the *puta* exists in me. . . . The desire to be a whore, to be sustained by the pleasure I can have and to give, to give, to give, to be free and never to have a pimp has always been the target of your envy."[46] The authors go on to position the ontology of the whore within a cosmology drawing on Afro-Brazilian figures, including the Pomba-Gira, a patron spirit of putas. (Most Brazilian brothels I've done fieldwork in have an altar devoted to Pomba-Gira somewhere on the premises.) The elusive "whore's ontology" that emerges in their essay is an assemblage of affects with tenuous connections to other complex systems and sets of relations (such as the incarnations of Pomba-Gira), but central to their writing is the complexity of pleasure.

The possibility of pleasure is also central to Gabriela's puta politics.[47] Daspu shows are fun and celebratory. The putas show their bodies as they wish, and they publicly revel in them. Audiences cheer the prostitutes and their allies. (The shows usually end in a spontaneous dance party that breaks the fourth wall.) But Gabriela also emphasized in our interview that there is the real possibility of pleasure—sexual, emotional, and physical—in prostitution as a whole. Perhaps pleasure in and at the show, but also pleasure in the pride of work. The tagline from one controversial campaign—a partnership between the Ministry of Health and the prostitutes' rights movement—was "No shame, girl. You have a profession!" Another was: "I'm happy being a prostitute." Sure, it's not *always* pleasurable—it certainly wasn't for Gabriela, nor is it for any of the other sex workers I know. What job, even if you love it, is always a joy and always something you want to do all the time? But within puta politics, in sharp contrast to neo-abolitionism and anti-trafficking movements, prostitution is not always predetermined as a site of trauma and suffering—either already underway or threatening to erupt at any time.

Puta politics are about possibility and provocation. For example, when the National Prostitute Network meeting was convened in Rio in 2008, a conservative religious government was in power. The putas decided not to work quietly within the system by toning down their materials and instead confronted the religiosity head on. They created an enormous banner depicting Gabriela as Jesus at the Last Supper, with heads of prostitutes who were members of the network superimposed on the bodies of the disciples. They also designed the letters of the word *prostituta* (prostitute) in their title such that it could also be read as puta.[48]

As Grant observes in *Playing the Whore,* "The fear of the whore, or of being the whore, is the engine that drives the whole thing. That engine could be called 'misogyny,' but even that word misses something: the cheapness of the whore, how easily she might be discarded not only due to her gender but to her race, her class. Whore is maybe the original intersectional insult."[49] To support this analysis she argues that "to build a class [of whores] on this moves away from our perception of the whore as someone endangered principally by patriarchy to someone whose body is crossed by multiple points of prejudice and violence— oppression and exploitation not in the abstract hands of men but in the specific institutions that prop them up. . . . This is how we could reimagine whore as a class."[50] Grant's analysis aligns with Murray's notion of puta politics and with Gabriela's articulation of her "ontology of whores." Puta politics relate to the world of unruly sexual politics and offers a useful counter to the parastate's tactics of exception that seek to exclude the women even as they invoke the language of women's rights, human rights, equality, and diversity. In fact, puta politics serve as a useful intervention to the rise of another trend: the parastate's co-opting of feminism in order to whitewash the harms it perpetrates against vulnerable women.

FEMONATIONALISM

Throughout this book, I have argued that the crackdown on prostitution and sex trafficking globally is part of a parastatal pattern of land grabs that ejects sex workers so that development can occur, and that this is being undertaken in either good or bad faith by right-wing religious groups and liberal political actors in the name of women's rights because of an unfounded assumption that sex trafficking and exploitative prostitution are increasing as a result of the World Cup and Olympics. It is necessary to interrogate what the social consequences of this shift are vis-à-vis contemporary discourses about human sexuality and the rights of sexual minorities, offering a framework for how feminist and queer theorists might understand this situation not *only* as a set of colliding ideologies and economic interests, but as an assemblage of actors, events, and territorializations that reveal new aspects of parastatal governmentality.

The government holds up particular visions of normative sexuality at the expense of those on the sexual margins of society. One useful corollary is the queer theorist Jasbir Puar's groundbreaking work on homonationalism, building on Foucault (and Gilles Deleuze, among others).[51] However, some people have misunderstood Puar's concept as simply being shorthand for gay conservativism, gay racism, or valuing a particular vision of gay rights in such a way that one accepts or even promotes oppression. Specifically, Puar was talking about Israel and Zionists' lobbying efforts to curry favor as a champion of human rights by emphasizing Israel's regional role as the only outspoken protector of gay rights and freedoms, much as it had done for women's rights, thus obscuring the groups within Palestine fighting for LGBT rights and queer causes, diverting attention from Israel's own homophobia, and sidelining the question of its occupation and abuses. In this oversimplification, homonationalism became synonymous with *pinkwashing*.

A similar phenomenon happened with women's rights. In the example of Israel, the state prominently featured women's roles in the Israeli Defense Forces and lauded this participation as good for women's rights and as an example of inclusivity. It presented female Israeli fighters in contradistinction to the role of Palestinian women, whom it portrayed as oppressed within a misogynistic Muslim culture. Conservative governments, whether controlled by Benjamin Netanyahu in Israel, Vladimir Putin in Russia, Jair Bolsonaro in present-day Brazil, or Boris Johnson in a post-Brexit United Kingdom, make gestures toward protecting and defending women. They often frame their actions as being out of concern for "women and family issues" rather than feminism, but this is indicative of a larger pattern that is seen among a variety of feminists who would never outwardly ally themselves with such regimes. When feminists (be they radical or liberal or whatever other camp) take up the mantle of anti–sex trafficking and insist they know better than sex workers, they do this from a similar protectionist and condescending place. It is not surprising that there is substantial overlap among the radical feminists with anti-Muslim stances such as supporting the bans on hijab and veils, sowing panics about Sharia, and advocating limiting immigration from predominantly Muslim countries. They frame this as being about stopping misogyny from spreading in their countries, thereby emphasizing the importance of a particular type of womanhood to the project of shoring up the nation-state and national culture.

The sociologist Sara Farris takes up these questions in her book, *In the Name of Women's Rights: The Rise of Femonationalism*.[52] Femonationalism, in her formulation, includes both "feminist nationalism" and "femocratic nationalism." It is based on "the exploitation of feminist themes by nationalists and neoliberals" in anti-Islam and anti-immigration campaigns and often includes "the participation of certain feminists and femocrats in the stigmatization of Muslim men under the banner of gender equality."[53] For Farris, the convergences of "collusions" and "alliances" described by Puar have produced femonationalism.[54] She highlights the special role that the anti–sex trafficking movement has played in creating a special category for Muslim victims, whom it portrays as "coming from North and Sub-Saharan Africa, South Asia, and the Middle East" and as having "gained the reputation of being victims of specific forms of gendered violence (genital mutilations and honor killings, in particular)."[55]

Governmentality refers to the way the state produces citizens, especially the techniques used to create subjects most suited to its own ends. For Foucault, this is not hierarchical, but rather includes a complex and interlocuting collection of institutions, which in our present era include neoliberal actors from the market as embedded within the institutional apparatus.[56] However, Puar's notion of homonationalism was actually intended to mark far more than just pinkwashing. She later clarified that the analytic of homonationalism is not so much "an accusation, a problematic subject positioning, or something to oppose, but rather an assemblage of affect, bodily forces and discourses . . . a facet of modernity that is embedded in spatial logics of discipline and control that articulate an emergent form of neoliberal governmentality."[57]

Certain images of homosexuality may be acceptable to moderately conservative people who increasingly have accepted gay marriage, for example, as essentially a conservative and assimilationist practice that is less threatening than the idea of queers on the loose. These normative gays may be allowed a place within patria and even, in some locations, be seen as essential to the neoliberal (homonationalist) state. This does not mean homophobia has been eradicated; many of the global sports hosts I've mentioned have anti-gay public policies, which liberal democracies have used as an excuse to finger wag. For example, in the last chapter I mentioned criticisms from the West about Qatar's gay policies, policies which are almost never enacted but which serve as cover for Islamophobic dog whistling for Westerners unfamiliar with what gay life in Qatar is actually like irrespective of what laws are on the books.

Similarly, under femonationalism, certain women are rendered as essential to the state, whether they are good Israeli women fighting alongside men in the Israel Defense Forces or properly reproducing heteronormative mothers in Japan who will help the declining population. In this way, certain images of gender and sexuality are adjudicated and found to be acceptable to a vision of a progressive, tolerant, and diverse society.

Sex trafficking victims are acceptable to the extent that they inspire pity and bolster anti-immigrant nationalistic tendencies. They are an especially potent symbol during major sporting events because events like the World Cup and the Olympics are fundamentally *nationalistic* spectacles that represent countries to the world using the bodies of athletes who are presented as the finest specimens of their gender and sport. This is part of why the question of transgender and intersex athletes competing is so threatening: such athletes threaten the gender divisions that form the foundation of the sports and—by extension—the nation-states.

WHORES, ASSEMBLE!

The widespread misreading of her work is something that Puar herself has had to address publicly. As she explained in a Q & A published in Darkmatter, she is less interested in homonormative political formations, which she says are easy (but necessary) targets. Instead, she wants to know how "claims to oppositionality insidiously conceal . . . subterranean conservative proclivities."[58] Puar's titular move in *Terrorist Assemblages* is that we cast off intersectionality to move toward assemblage. She notes that intersectionality simply nods to and multiplies difference while failing to "articulate [difference] as a conceptual frame arising out of particular historical and activist contexts."[59] So we don't ever actually understand the "differing epistemological category formations" because intersectionality becomes a quick hit to gloss over a sort of ineffable difference.[60] The move to assemblage is "a reading practice . . . meaning that the implications for gay and lesbian activism is not that it needs to create assemblages but rather that contemporary and historical organizing practices need to be read as always already assemblages," which are going to open up new ways of "thinking, speaking, organizing, doing politics—lines of flight, affective eruptions, affect, energies, forces, temporalities, contagions, contingencies, and the inexplicable."[61] She says we can never know "how" to organize, and she will not provide a roadmap for resistance precisely because she dislikes a binary of "complicity-versus-resistance" and says we need to understand complicities much the same way scholars think of resistance: as slippery, multifarious, and unstable. For Deleuze and Guattari, assemblage allows us to access social complexity in a way that emphasizes the fluidity characterizing the connections between bodies within systems and bodies and their component parts, which is a view that is useful for thinking about the *unruliness* of puta politics.[62]

While Puar finds that intersectionality lacks the explanatory power that much of queer theory and leftist activism would find in it, Christen A. Smith finds assemblage to be useful for thinking about racialized performance, resistance, and anti-Black state violence. Noting that for Deleuze and Guattari, assemblages refer to lines of articulation, (de)territorializations, and flight, she argues that "genocide . . . is what we may call an assemblage."[63] Writing in the context of Brazil, where the police and parastatal actors commit thousands of murders of mostly Black and brown men, activist groups reacting and protesting spectacularly disrupt "heteronormative, patriarchal assumptions about race, gender, class and nation," thus recasting anti-Black genocide as "a deterritorialized concept that incorporates various, related forms of oppression [that are then viewable as] not only multivalent, multilayered, raced, gendered, sexualized, and classed but also resonant across time and space."[64] While she agrees with Puar that intersectionality cannot describe assemblages, she also argues that "assemblages imply transnational entangled time, connections, and clouds and clusters of interdependence and crossing. To talk about spectacular experiences with state terror in Bahia [Brazil] necessarily flows into other discussions of related, connected violence elsewhere at other times."[65] She concludes that "everyday experiences with racism and discrimination—violence in the 'quieter' hours—are extensions of the spectacular just as the spectacular is an extension of the everyday."[66] Thus, it is through the framework of assemblage (rather than intersectionality, or at least rather than intersectionality alone) that Smith feels the historical legacies of slavery and genocide may be connected to parastatal violence against marginalized and racialized subjects in the present.

The story of feminism for the last two centuries can be summarized as the idea that women must unite to fight their common oppression. But within puta politics we might frame this differently: women unite, but whores *assemble*. Assemblages theoretically position categories like race, gender, and sexuality as events, actions, and encounters between bodies rather than intersectional attributes of subjects. The body then is always in the process of being propelled into deterritorizalization and reterritorialization, being enunciated. Without a stable ontology, social formations can be seen as assemblages of various and extended configurations.[67] In the case of countries like Brazil, Russia, South Africa, and the United Kingdom that host global sporting events, parastatal alliances crack down on certain sexual subjectivities while valorizing others.

Parastatal alliances—including not only government ad campaigns but also international women's rights and anti-trafficking groups—create particular bodies. These bodies are racialized, sexualized, classed, and fetishized bodies, but the parastate creates bodies out of affects, desires, and other feelings, be they national pride, pleasure, abjection, and/or domination. And even as the state seeks to territorialize, form, constitute, and shape an assemblage in the host country that shores up gender conventions along particular self-serving axes, it seeks to deterritorialize, deform, deconstitute, and obliterate the whore assemblage, to rip out an ontology of whores, and to literally pave over the affective landscape and social geography of the red light areas that are so central to the territorialization of the whore in order to "develop" them into sites of national spectacle.

As Amanda De Lisio, Phil Hubbard, and Michael Silk have argued, Rio's mega-events served a site of "political and economic trajectories of neoliberal urbanism that seek to expropriate land and dispossess certain bodies."[68] In particular, Rio gave a major overhaul to its port area, adding museums and public spaces, new transportation, and infrastructure before the Olympics. It also displaced many brothel spaces and prostitutes in this process. "Development theory" is often the body of scholarship to which social scientists turn to examine mega-events and the attendant questions of gentrification and urban renewal. But as João Gabriel Rabello Sodré and Amanda De Lisio have argued, although Rio de Janeiro did follow the "entrepreneurial" approach to the Olympics, viewing the changing sexual landscape of the city through the lens of development leads to an "erasure of sexual diversity" and a lessened understanding of the "impact of FIFA/IOC-sanctioned urban renewal, and the manner in which local bodies (particularly those deemed sexually 'deviant') are repeatedly forced to circumvent these globally determined processes of development."[69]

When one examines the state's libidinal investments and its exaltation of gendered bodies—muscular athletes, vulnerable trafficking victims, good consumer families—and the denigration of the whore, one can see the full force of the state laid bare. In that view one can perhaps glimpse beyond just a Foucauldian disciplining and regulation of the body, instead seeing workings of power in terms of not only discipline but also the ability of the state to intervene at the level of affect while simultaneously revealing the state as also already imbricated as an extension of a broader geopolitical governmentality that demands an ontological sacrifice of the whore to sustain the emergence of a new consumer ethic and set of sexual relations and values.

The issue this form of femonational governmentality raises is not so much feminist versus misogynist, queer versus not queer, or oppositional versus complicit—with the whore as the new good/oppositional/marginalized/queer figure—but rather that this way of being in and apprehending the world is contingent and embedded in both complicities and resistances in ways that we may not have seen or known before.

CONCLUSION

At this critical juncture, I argue that we must understand the present crackdown on sex trafficking and prostitution as a fundamentally misguided effort. The shifting governmentality that is privileging certain forms of sexuality is not necessarily willful or deliberate. Yet the overall shift in the sexual landscape is important, and one can look at that sexual shift as one group of vulnerable and marginalized people—prostitutes who were once considered quite a normal part of many of the societies in question (and even, in the case of Brazil, quintessential to Brazilian-ness)—is persecuted. Meanwhile, other women—the victims and mothers and performers of sanctioned femininity—are suddenly brought into the fold and valorized.

There have also been meaningful attempts to push back against the parastatal oppression of sex workers and other marginalized people in many of these places. Pussy Riot is a good example of this in Russia. Brazil, like many countries, hosted events known as Slut Walks (*marchas das vadias*), which took on special cultural and geographic salience when nude, scantily clad, and disruptive bodies temporarily reclaimed contested territory from police and developers. However, Slut Walks in Brazil became a site of contestation as certain cities began to include "sex tourism and rape culture" as objects of protest, announcing on social media that "we scream that we are women and not World Cup souvenirs." The slogan of the Marchas das Vadias—*Nem Santa, Nem Puta* (Neither saint, nor whore)—showed the creeping whorephobia of that branch of feminism, although true to unruly politics, each march was its own independent show, and some aligned themselves with sex workers and worked with leaders of the trans rights movement.

Based on dozens of interviews with campaigners, the anthropologist Marie-Eve Carrier-Moisan argues that this contestation was yet another iteration of "sex panics" swirling around the mega-event.[70] In contrast to the unruly politics of the Confederations Cup uprising in 2013, the politics of protest in 2014 had snapped back into familiar feminist camps that were unaligned with puta politics. This demonstrates the influence of European and North American anti-prostitution activism. As Adriana Piscitelli bemoans in her skeptical treatment of the idea of "transnational sisterhood," "during the decades of 2000 and 2010, networks and coalitions of Brazilian feminists with transnational articulations have increasingly adopted an abolitionist position, denying the differences between prostitution and sex trafficking and refusing to listen to the voices of organized prostitutes" in Brazil.[71]

In contrast, Gabriela Leite's sex worker rights group, Davida, had a series of successful fashion shows in the 2000s featuring sex workers and allies on makeshift catwalks, including one in Praça Tiradentes, historically a red light area in the business district, held during rush hour to disrupt and reclaim space. During the Cup in Brazil, the scantily clad radical queer collective called the Pink Bloc protested wearing delightfully anarchic pink costumes and genderfuck gear, taunting police and bringing a carnivalesque but aggressive sexual frivolity to the streets. For its part, Daspu organized its own fashion show themed around the World Cup in protest against the police raids in Niteroí (described in the introduction), during which police had raped, robbed, and assaulted sex workers. Daspu's slogans included FIFA-related jokes such as "*Eu jogo pelada*," or "I play naked."

Importantly, all of these "unruly" groups operate on the idea of territorialization, disrupting normative and policed spaces with overt and nonnormative sexuality. They also are on the move, constantly marching, wandering, and circulating in a rhizomatic and often chaotic way, evoking Deleuzean views of sexuality as being in process, flux, and adrift. Per Corrêa's analysis, they may not be organized or pragmatic in function, but they also do not crystallize in their form and so are able to sustain their unruliness.

Despite these resistances, the ontological shift occurring in these host countries that denigrates the now abject ontology of the whore reveals a new governmentality predicated on human security as theorized by

Amar. It also shows that these governments, their politics, and their economies are critical to the process of subjugating and denigrating certain forms of sexuality and certain sexual subjects while simultaneously investing in shaping visions of countries as tolerant, open, and modern. In this way, these actors are helping to consolidate privileges that align with particular categories of race, class, gender, and sexuality. Much of this is ironically being done in the name of human rights, and these actors are therefore reliant on the promulgation of faulty information about sex trafficking and global sporting events.

Any attempt to provide redress must problematize discourses of sex trafficking and the concomitant manufacture of a moral panic around it, as these also mask class-based and racial prejudices as well as anti-immigrant and xenophobic modes of governance. One ought to understand this situation as not only an example of the revalorization and rebalancing of an ethics of sexuality but also a new kind of governmentality that is creating and destroying particular sexual ontologies, reshaping what it means to be a whore—that is, always and already in the process of becoming a victim—while promoting and producing sexual normativity as essential to the reinvention and rebranding of the nation-states in question.

Global sporting events are especially important and fleeting moments to study because it is during such events that otherwise skeptical audiences rejoice in nationalist narratives and propagandizing performances. The World Cup and Olympic Games represent moments when nation-states are free to remake their citizen-subjects in relationship to the state. It is clear the parastate's carceral feminist framing of prostitution recasts the whore as a victim whose body must always be available to the militarized state. In the case of Brazil, South Africa, and the United Kingdom, this invariably has meant the deterritorialization of the whore and the valorization of imperialist and carceral anti-trafficking regimes.

Throughout this book, I have shown how parastatal alliances—the strange bedfellows of NGOs, feminist groups, evangelical ministries, secular rescue projects, moral entrepreneurs, business developers, the police, and corrupt security apparatuses—have coalesced to produce sex trafficking. They create the *idea* of sex trafficking through their increasing reliance on fallacious spectacles that are bolstered by celebrification, virality, and social media. These spectacles rely on abstract, invisible, or missing girls and women, which is why the rescue industry so often focuses on raising awareness for its own sake.

The moral entrepreneurs in the rescue industry must continue to justify their own existence, so they have a perverse incentive to continue to whip up moral panics about sex trafficking. However, these would-be rescuers with their good intentions and noblesse oblige often lack the cultural competence they need, which means their operations during global mega-events fail. Only the very privileged can afford to say "fuck nuance" and rely on melodramatic narratives and the manufacture of perfect victims as they chase after funding and celebrity sponsorship. But all the smoke and mirrors of "awareness raising" have taught society to be constantly vigilant for any sign of sex trafficking, always in a state of hyperawareness and fear. This constant panic has consequences for marginalized groups such as sex workers, especially the lower-class and non-white ones, who are then made more susceptible to police violence, state surveillance, and carceral systems.

This transformation of the anti-trafficking industry into a parastatal alliance that exists to produce fallacious spectacles is but one part of a larger and perverse shift in governmentality. Those actors in the parastatal alliance, whether from the Left or the Right hand of the state, have harnessed the rhetoric of human rights and women's rights. To understand this shift and the realities of sexual economies, including their exploitative dimensions, requires deep local knowledge, true partnerships with women in the industry, and careful attention to ethnographic data and empirical research. This work must happen in multiple countries and sites, and ethnography must be from the top as well as the bottom. That is, we not only need ethnographic knowledge rooted in the lived realities of sex workers; we must turn our academic gaze toward the rescue industry itself and gain insights into how the organizations that comprise it came to be and how they are transforming even now. Researchers, activists, and allies striving for a politics based on putafeminismo must assemble themselves and work to discredit the discourses of the rescue industry while also materially supporting the sex workers on the front lines who are striving every day to resist the efforts of those who would rescue, collect, renarrativize, and commodify them in the production of the fallacious spectacle of sex trafficking.

Epilogue

I did not want to write a COVID-19 epilogue. When this book is released, all epilogues will be COVID-19 epilogues. There will be a whole cohort of books produced and written under its terrible shadow. I finished the very rough first draft—a thing that was mostly just words thrown forth without sourcing or notes or proofreading yet in place—just days before the first case of coronavirus was found at Princeton University (in my own program, no less). The world began contracting, retreating indoors. Donald Trump shut down flights from Europe and bellowed about closing the border with Mexico. What came next was months of self-isolation at home during which I did the mind-numbing tasks of compiling the bibliography and footnotes, rewriting, and additional sourcing and fact-checking. My various other trips to survey the building sites and neighborhoods of the 2024 Summer Olympics in Paris were canceled. The 2020 Olympics in Japan were postponed and foreign spectators eventually banned, blocking my ability to return to Japan for the games.

And yet there I sat, writing a book about things that, in that moment, seemed unthinkable: gatherings of millions of people who crowd into airplanes, cheer in crowded stadiums, and cram into bars where they shout in strangers' faces to be heard; sex between strangers—as much and as many as possible; and rapid and massive movement across borders.

By the time this book is in the hands of readers, the pandemic will be behind the rich world in many ways, but its effects—ranging from the absences left by the dead to jobs lost and businesses shuttered—will linger for decades. And it seems likely that COVID will continue to linger for many years, especially in the Global South.

I hope this book is birthed into a world where there are sporting events again; I hope this book is birthed into a world where there is sex work again . . . and in circumstances that are safe and crafted by the sex workers themselves rather than by the dictates of disaster capitalism, patriarchy, and tourist-dependent economies.

At the moment of writing, COVID-19 is tearing through labor camps in Qatar, but the men are still made to work on the stadiums for an event that the Qataris are determined to will into existence. The virus sweeps the camps; the men are crammed into their quarters (usually eight to a room in bunk beds) and share unsanitary kitchen and bathroom areas. The government attempts to deport the infected; their home countries refuse them. A few months ago, the evangelicals at Exodus Cry were planning for a moral panic tour of Japan to stir up outrage about the sex trafficking they imagined would happen there during the Olympics. It appears that is no longer a concern. Colleges are closed, and the UN Gift Box is no longer touring their campuses. In Brazil, the right-wing president continues to deny that COVID-19 is a problem. The sex tourist bars are all closed. Domestic work and cleaning, the only other jobs available to most of the women, are much less viable, as middle-class families fear letting favela-dwelling "vectors of transmission" into their homes. (The first coronavirus case in Brazil is widely believed to have been a domestic worker who then infected the family employing her.) Prostitutes from Davida, many of whom work in Vila Mimosa, are organizing fundraisers and seeking donations to survive, running a characteristically cheeky campaign called It's Your Turn to Put Out.

And yet, I hope that someday soon after this book is released people will return to something resembling "normal"—the good parts of the old world, not the bad. I want to see a triumphal gathering in Paris in 2024 where people can enjoy sports again. I want to see the jointly hosted World Cup in 2026 across Mexico, the United States, and Canada happen in a world where people do not fear international travel and instead believe it to be paramount for cultural understanding and empathy. And I hope that everyone—migrants as well as tourists—can cross the Mexican border with equal ease.

Despite mass gatherings being banned, 2020 also saw the rise of global anti-racist protest movements in response to the murders of George Floyd and Breonna Taylor at the hands of police. Demonstrations in Minneapolis and Louisville spread to many cities and at least eighteen different countries. The shape and nature of the protests felt like an unruly political uprising, including things such as the establishment of the "Capitol Hill Autonomous Zone" in Seattle. Meanwhile, presidential primary candidates called for investigations into the impacts of FOSTA-SESTA on sex workers, a promising move that shows that some Democrats see the harms they helped cause. A few progressives such as Alexandria Ocasio-Cortez observed International Sex Workers Day and advocated openly for decriminalization of prostitution. And to conclude with the image I invoked at the beginning of this book, the world saw the effects of the moral panic about sex trafficking help launch QAnon to power, resulting in an insurrection and assault on the US Capitol. The sex trafficking panic continues. OnlyFans and Just for Fans, subscription sites for pornography and camming, exploded during the pandemic as thousands of entrepreneurial sex workers (many of whom had lost their jobs and were new to the industry) attempted to replace income streams. It's unclear what sexual economies will look like in a post-COVID world, but the desire of people to gather (whether in protest or for leisure) is strong. Neither sex nor sport is gone forever, but they are perhaps forever changed.

Acknowledgments

One accrues a lot of personal and professional debts to colleagues, friends, and collaborators over the many years it takes to write a book. I first need to thank the original members of the 2014 Observatório who conducted fieldwork with me at various times, especially Laura Murray, Amanda (Gringa) De Lisio, Yaa Sarpong, Soraya Simões, Guilherme Alef, and Gonçalo Zuquete. In 2007, Ana Paula da Silva and Thad Blanchette selflessly took me in and have been the best comrades and co-conspirators for which one could hope. Alongside the Observatório were other important allies in Brazil, including Indianara Siqueira, Flavio Lenz, Thayane Brêtas, Julie Ruvolo, Tiago de Aquino Tamborino, Richard Parker, Vagner Almeida, Adriana Piscitelli, Sonia Corrêa, Robson Cruz, Steve Berg, Marcos Coutinho, Sadakne Baroudi, and Jake Milnor. I owe a special debt of gratitude to João Gabriel Rabello Sodré, who has been a longtime friend and the most helpfully critical "native informant" in all of Brazil. João also read an early draft of this book and provided helpful commentary.

Research requires money. After I defended my dissertation at Northwestern University, my mentors there encouraged me to use the resources available to explore options for what would become "book two." Therefore, I continue to owe E. Patrick Johnson, my adviser and closest mentor, a huge debt of gratitude. Similarly, I have benefited from the training and friendship of my original committee members from the first book project, Soyini Madison, Ramón Rivera-Servera, Mary Weismantel, and Don Kulick. Also at Northwestern, Héctor Carillo and Steve Epstein provided funding through their sexuality studies project (SPAN) for the South Africa portion of the research.

At Williams, I benefited from significant funding from the Hellman Fellowship, the Class of 1945 World Fellowship, and the Dean of Faculty's Office. A Global Initiatives Venture Fund grant also allowed me to bring students to Brazil for two class trips, where we visited many of my field sites. At Williams, I especially benefited from the counsel and mentoring of Katie Kent, Sara Dubow, Lucie Schmidt, Ondine Chavoya, and Roger Kittleson. My Williams folks are too numerous to list, but I must thank Matt Martin, Rashida Braggs, Rhon Manigault-Bryant, Corinna Campbell, Julie Cassiday, Amy Holzapfel, Vivian Huang, Mérida Rua, Greta Snyder, Alison Case, Kiaran Honderich, Marshall Green, Julie Blackwood, and Phoebe Cohen. The Oakley Center for the Humanities & Social Sciences also provided assistance and support for me on numerous occasions, and I thank Krista Birch, Jana Sawicki, Gage McWeeny, and Leyla Rouhi. Their Center hosted a lengthy manuscript workshop, and I thank the participants who guided this work through their extensive engagement: Kimberly Kay Hoang, Laura Murray, and Christina Simko.

This project would not have been possible without the support of The National Science Foundation program in cultural anthropology, which funded the research during the Brazilian World Cup. I thank Jeff Mantz and Deborah Wilson for their firm commitment to my work. They are true defenders of academic freedom and represent all that is good about the NSF. However, let it be officially be disclaimed: material in this book is based on work supported by the NSF under Grant Number 1450870. Any opinions, findings, and conclusions or recommendations expressed in this material are those of the author and do not necessarily reflect the views of the National Science Foundation.

I also thank the American Council of Learned Societies (ACLS), which provided me with an ACLS Burkhardt Fellowship at Princeton University. My year at Princeton was invaluable, and the ACLS provided a wonderful opportunity to finally focus on the craft of writing. I especially need to thank Regina Kunzel for sponsoring and mentoring me, as well as Dara Strolovitch, Niina Vuolajarvi, Greta LaFleur, Kira Thurman, Brian Herrera, Anne McClintock, Anisha Thomas, Anthony Petro, Jackie Wasneski, James Lee, and Maria Papadakis. I also thank Princeton University for providing additional research funding and support.

I also must thank the Rockefeller Foundation for providing me a month-long writing residency in Bellagio, Italy, at a critical juncture as well as Pilar Palacia, Taylor Royle, and my cohort there for igniting connections and conversations.

Myriad other colleagues and friends have helped to support me and further my research in recent years, including Nico Amador, Matt Kluk, Pavi Prasad, Kareem Khubchandani, Evren Savci, Mitch Katz, Jenn Tyburczy, Sandra L. Richards, Megan Geigner, Sarah Luna, Mark Butler, Heather Berg, Ben Junge, Bryan Pitts, Ron Weitzer, Brandon Fischer, George Paul Meiu, Thad Dowad, Marcia Ochoa, Paul Amar, Svati Shah, Elizabeth Bernstein, Kerwin Kaye, Mireille Miller-Young, Carole Vance, Mindy Chateauvert, Jennifer Musto, Elena Shih, Kamala Kempadoo, Ghassan Moussawi, Nayan Shah, Katie Zien, Reed Mettler, and Mal Harrison. Nic Mai was especially influential in steering me toward this project at a critical early juncture. I also thank my mother, Darlene Halm, for her many years of encouragement.

I must also thank audiences and workshop attendees who gave critical feedback on my work during the years I wrote this book. These include wonderful colleagues at presentations I gave at Yale University, McGill University, Harvard University, Princeton University, the University of Chicago, University of Cambridge, Bennington College, SUNY-New Paltz, and The University of Wyoming.

Many leaders of the sex worker movement helped to educate and include me, providing valuable insights and mentorship. Chief among these has been Carol Leigh, whom I am proud to have fought alongside for fifteen years. I must also thank Irina Maslova and her team in Russia; Cris Sardina and her team at Desiree Alliance; Norma Jean Almodovar, Audacia Ray, Bella Robinson, and everyone at COYOTE; and Ceyenne Doroshow, among many others. Nothing would have been possible without the late Gabriela Leite, the longtime leader of Brazil's prostitutes and a self-avowed *puta* to the very end.

My students at Williams College were also extremely helpful to me over the years, particularly those in my Sexual Economies seminars. Alex Pear provided a great deal of helpful feedback. Several worked as full-time research assistants and deserve special thanks. These include Olivia Goodheart and Bee Sachsse, who spent a summer drowning in bibliography, annotations, and media reports in several languages. Essence Perry was an invaluable asset to me in thinking through the shape and structure of the book and serving as an early reader. Roxana Rodriguez worked for the Observatório and also assisted me for several months in Brazil during the 2016 Olympics. Ryan Buggy provided grounding and *caiprinhas* in Brazil whenever shit got real. And Josh Buznitsky at Brown University also worked for many months, serving as a reader, fact checker, and editor. He also helped me with interviews and translation on-site in Tokyo. Danil Zhaivoronok and Viktoriya Krutsch helped me with translations and logistics in Russia.

I owe a debt of gratitude to the late Doug Mitchell (no relation) at the University of Chicago Press, who mentored me through my first book and had hours of discussion with me about this project over many a fine meal. The good folks at the University of California Press have been no less kind, and I thank Naomi Schneider, Marlon Bailey, and Jeffrey McCune for their support and wisdom. I am honored to be part of their new series. I also thank the peer reviewers of both the proposal and the draft of the manuscript for their invaluable feedback. Keisha-Khan Y. Perry, Erica L. Williams and Susan Dewey "outed" themselves as manuscript reviewers, and so I am happy to name and thank them directly for their deep engagement and support.

During the years we spent adventuring, Austin Eklund was the best support system for which I could have ever hoped. Certainly this book would not exist without him. He also provided excellent copyediting and feedback on the first draft. Nor would this book have come into being it had not been for my dog, Dexter, who kept me sane and tolerated my long absences into the field.

Notes

PREFACE

1. Kevin Roose, "How 'Save the Children' Is Keeping QAnon Alive," *New York Times*, September 28, 2020.

2. Roose, "How 'Save the Children' Is Keeping QAnon Alive."

3. Matthew Brown, "Fact Check: Mask-Wearing Not Connected to Child Trafficking," *USA Today*, August 11, 2020.

4. Laura María Agustín, *Sex at the Margins: Migration, Labour Markets and the Rescue Industry* (New York: Palgrave, 2007).

5. Kimberly Kay Hoang, "Perverse Humanitarianism and the Business of Rescue: What's Wrong with NGOs and What's Right about the 'Johns,'" *Political Power & Social Theory* 30, no. 1 (2016): 22–23.

6. David Mikkelson, "Super Bowl Prostitution Increase," Snopes, February 6, 2012.

7. Shannon Blackler, "Sex Trafficking Made Easier, Thanks to the World Cup in Russia," *New York Minute*, July 12, 2018; and Laura Dean, "A Stage for Human Trafficking: The World Cup in Russia," *The Russia File: A Blog of the Keenan Institute*, June 18, 2018.

8. Jeremy Armstrong, "England Fans Warned over Fake Russian Bride Scams at the FIFA World Cup," *Mirror*, January 9, 2018.

9. Perez Hilton, "The Nightmare Side of Sports: World Cup Expected to Cause Rise in Prostitution and Sexual Assault in Brazil," June 11, 2014.

INTRODUCTION: THE MYTH OF THE 40,000 MISSING GIRLS

1. A portion of this chapter was previously published as Gregory Mitchell, "Evangelical Ecstasy Meets Feminist Fury," *GLQ* 22, no. 3 (2016): 325–57.

2. Eliane Trindade, "Sonhos de Belém," *Folha de São Paulo*, Fevereiro 2011.

3. For more on the complexity of Brazilian migrant women selling sex, see Adriana Piscitelli, "Sujeição ou subversão? Migrantes brasileiras na indústria do sexo na Espanha," *História & Perspectivas* 35 (Agosto–Dezembro 2006): 13–55.

4. Bruno Lupion, "Polícia descobre esquema de tráfico de travestis em SP," *Estadão*, February 2011.

5. Trindade, "Sonhos de Belém."

6. Paul Amar, *The Security Archipelago: Human-Security States, Sexuality Politics, and the End of Neoliberalism* (Durham, NC: Duke University Press, 2013), 18.

7. Janet Halley et al., "From the International to the Local in Feminist Legal Responses to Rape, Prostitution/Sex Work and Sex Trafficking: Four Studies in Contemporary Governance Feminism," *Harvard Journal of Law & Gender* 29 (2006): 336–423.

8. Elizabeth Bernstein, *Temporarily Yours: Intimacy, Authenticity, and the Commerce of Sex* (Chicago: University of Chicago Press, 2007).

9. See, for example, Kamala Kempadoo and Jo Doezema, eds., *Global Sex Workers: Rights, Resistance, and Redefinition* (New York: Routledge, 1998).

10. Janie A. Chuang, "Rescuing Trafficking from Ideological Capture: Prostitution Reform and Anti-Trafficking Law and Policy," *University of Pennsylvania Law Review* 158 (2010): 1–74.

11. Laura María Agustín, *Sex at the Margins: Migration, Labour Markets and the Rescue Industry* (New York: Palgrave, 2007).

12. Brigitte Suhr, *Funding the Fight against Modern Slavery: Mapping Private Funds in the Ant-Slavery and Anti-Trafficking Sector: 2012–2014*, 2016.

13. Janie A. Chuang, "Exploitation Creep and the Unmaking of Human Trafficking Law," *American Journal of International Law* 108, no. 4 (2014): 611.

14. Chuang, "Exploitation Creep."

15. Stuart Forrest, *Down, Out, and Under Arrest: Policing and Everyday Life in Skid Row* (Chicago: University of Chicago Press, 2016), 20.

16. Kimberly Kay Hoang, "Perverse Humanitarianism and the Business of Rescue: What's Wrong with NGOs and What's Right about the 'Johns,'" *Political Power & Social Theory* 30, no. 1 (2016): 23.

17. Jamie Peck, "Zombie Neoliberalism and the Ambidextrous State," *Theoretical Criminology* 14, no. 1 (2010): 104–10.

18. Jules Boykoff, *Celebration Capitalism and the Olympic Games* (London: Taylor and Francis, 2013), 3.

19. Boykoff, *Celebration Capitalism*.

20. See, for example, Danielle Lama, "Local Groups Work to Spread Awareness about Sex Trafficking Ahead of Derby," WDRB, June 14, 2017.

21. Jeff Bahr, "State Fair, Eclipse May Bring in Sex Trafficking," *Grand Island Independent*, June 14, 2017; Tonya S. Grace, "Ahead of Eclipse, Warn-

ings about Potential Human Trafficking," *Washington Times*, July 9, 2017; Joy Greenwald, "Wyoming Solar Eclipse a Hotbed for Sex Trafficking," K2 Radio, August 1, 2017; and Julia Shumway, "Human Trafficking Expected during Solar Eclipse," *Bend Bulletin*, August 10, 2017.

22. Tom Morton, "Wyoming Department of Family Services Will Be in Full Force for Eclipse," August 17, 2017.

23. Elizabeth Bernstein, *Brokered Subjects: Sex, Trafficking & the Politics of Freedom* (Chicago: University of Chicago Press, 2018), 25.

24. Bernstein, *Brokered Subjects*, 25.

25. Jo Doezema, *Sex Slaves and Discourse Masters: The Construction of Trafficking* (London: Zed Books, 2010), 9–10.

26. Michel Foucault, *Archaeology of Knowledge and the Discourse of Language* (London: Routledge, 2002), 54.

27. M. Jacqui Alexander, *Pedagogies of Crossing: Meditations on Feminism, Sexual Politics, Memory, and the Sacred* (Durham, NC: Duke University Press, 2005), 5.

28. Alexander, *Pedagogies of Crossing*.

29. Andrea Cornwall, Sonia Corrêa, and Susie Jolly, *Development with a Body: Sexuality, Human Rights, and Development* (London: Zed Books, 2008).

30. All conversions of exchange rates are at the approximate time in question. Some of the currencies in question, especially the Brazilian real, experienced extreme volatility over the years during which events described took place.

31. Kimberly Kay Hoang, *Dealing in Desire: Asian Ascendancy, Western Decline, and the Hidden Currencies of Global Sex Work* (Oakland: University of California Press, 2015), 104–25.

32. Maurício Simionato, "Levantamento indica que gays são mais agredidos por policies," *Folha de São Paulo*, June 19, 2010.

33. UPI, "Brazil Campaigning for Permanent U.N. Security Council Seat," *United Press International*, October 16, 2009.

34. Marina Pereira Pires de Oliveira, "Sobre armadilhas e cascas de banana: Uma análise crítica da Administração de Justiça em temas associados aos direitos humanos," *Cadernos Pagu* 31 (2008): 125–49.

35. Jim Kouri, "Giuliani Named Security Chief for 2016 Rio Olympic Games," *Examiner*, December 4, 2009.

36. Amar, *Security Archipelago*, 66.

37. Elizabeth Bernstein, "Militarized Humanitarianism Meets Carceral Feminism: The Politics of Sex, Rights, and Freedom in Contemporary Antitrafficking Campaigns," *Signs: Journal of Women in Culture and Society* 36, no. 1 (2010): 45–71.

38. Bernstein, "Militarized Humanitarianism," 60.

39. Denise Brennan, *Life Interrupted: Trafficking into Forced Labor in the United States* (Durham, NC: Duke University Press, 2014), 63–65.

40. For a fuller elaboration, see Gregory Mitchell, "A Camel Walks into a Brothel, or: Passing Anxieties in Brazil's Sexual Economies," in *Sex: Ethnographic Encounters*, ed. Richard Joseph Martin and Dieter Haller (London: Bloomsbury, 2018), 47–58. For more on the subjectivity of the researcher, see also other contributions to this same edited volume.

41. Soyini Madison, *Critical Ethnography: Method, Ethics, and Performance*, 2nd ed. (Newbury Park, CA: Sage, 2011).

42. Julie Ruvolo, "Brazil's Most Wanted Prostitute," July 24, 2014.

43. Laura Murray, "Entre 'fazer direito' e 'direitinho': Gestão de vítimas e as políticas de proteção," *Revista Ártemis* 18, no. 1 (2014): 28–41.

44. For the more detailed report, see Prostitution Policy Watch, *O Observatório Da Prostituição*, 2014.

45. Prostitution Policy Watch, *O Observatório Da Prostituição*.

46. Jornal Naçional, "Imagens mostram prostituição infantil e tráfico de drogas em Copacabana," *O Globo*, April 26, 2012.

47. Alexandra de Vries and Shawn Blore, *Frommer's Brazil* (Hoboken, NJ: John Wiley & Sons, 2012).

48. Julie Ham, *What's the Cost of a Rumour: A Guide to Sorting out the Myths and the Facts about Sporting Events and Trafficking* (Bangkok: Global Alliance Against Trafficking in Women, 2011).

49. For examples of hyperbole, see "The Sold Project: Super Bowl Sex for Sale." Ham, *What's the Cost of a Rumour*.

50. Jessica Huseman, "Top FBI Agent in Dallas Praises Super Bowl Security Effort, Sees No Evidence of Expected Spike in Child Sex Trafficking," *Dallas Morning News*, March 2, 2011; and Eddie Lee, "Super Bowl Hyperbole and Prostitution," *Toronto Star*, February 3, 2011.

51. For more on this, see Peter Kotz, "Super Bowl Prostitution: 100,000 Hookers Didn't Show, but America's Latest Political Scam Did," *Dallas Observer*, March 3, 2011.

52. Cory Zurowski, "Minnesota Ramps Up for a Mythical Super Bowl Sex Trafficking Rampage," City Pages, June 27, 2017.

53. Zurowski, "Minnesota Ramps Up."

54. Felicia Kelley, "I Spent 15 Hours at QC's 2020 Stripper Bowl—the Fyre Festival for Dancers," OK Player, February 3, 2020.

55. Kirsten Isgro, Maria Stehle, and Beverly Weber, "From Sex Shacks to Mega-Brothels: The Politics of Anti-Trafficking and the 2006 Soccer World Cup," *European Journal of Cultural Studies* 16, no. 2 (2013): 171–93.

56. Reid Cherner, "A Billion Condoms May Not Be Enough," *USA Today*, June 15, 2010.

57. Ana Campoy, "The Rio Olympics Organizers Are Giving out Enough Condoms for Each Athlete to Have Sex 84 Times," Quartz, June 14, 2017.

58. Campoy, "Rio Olympics Organizers."

59. Chandre Gould, "Moral Panic, Human Trafficking and the 2010 Soccer World Cup," *Agenda: Empowering Women for Gender Equity* 85 (2010): 31–44.

60. Savious Kwinika, "Prostitutes Flock to South Africa Ahead of World Cup 2010," *Christian Science Monitor*, June 15, 2010.

61. Ham, *What's the Cost of a Rumour*.

62. Gould, "Moral Panic."

63. Giedre Steikunaite, "Olympic Sex-Trafficking Myth Creates Climate of Fear," New Internationalist, February 1, 2012.

64. Jana Hennig et al., *Trafficking in Human Beings and the 2006 World Cup in Germany* (Geneva: International Organization for Migration, 2007), 2.

65. Hennig et al., *Trafficking in Human Beings*, 11–12.

66. Hennig et al., *Trafficking in Human Beings*, 14.

67. Hennig et al., *Trafficking in Human Beings*, 14.

68. Hennig et al., *Trafficking in Human Beings*, 21.

69. Kashiefa Ajam, "Trafficking of People, the Cup Crisis That Never Was," *IOL News*, July 17, 2010.

70. Courtney Campbell, dir., *Don't Shout Too Loud* (Changing Directions Films, 2011).

71. Campbell, *Don't Shout Too Loud*.

72. Marlise Richter and Wim Delva Richter, *"Maybe It Will Be Better Once This World Cup Has Passed": Research Findings Regarding the Impact of the 2010 Soccer World Cup on Sex Work in South Africa*, 2010.

73. Richter and Richter, *"Maybe It Will Be Better,"* 18.

74. Richter and Richter, *"Maybe It Will Be Better,"* 18.

75. Richter and Richter, *"Maybe It Will Be Better,"* 25.

76. Andrew Boff, *Silence on Violence: Improving the Safety of Women: The Policing of Off-Street Sex Work and Sex Trafficking in London*, March 2012, https://maggiemcneill.files.wordpress.com/2012/04/silence-on-violence.pdf.

77. For more on London, see The International Union of Sex Workers, "Harm Was Done: Prostitution, Politics and Power in the Run up to the 2012 London Olympics," IUSW, 2012, 17.

78. César Teixeira Castilho et al., "Turismo sexual infanto-juvenil em Zeque no contexto da Copa do Mundo de 2014," *Revista Estudos Feministas* 26, no. 2 (2018): 16.

79. Annie Hill, "How to Stage a Raid: Police, Media and the Master Narrative of Trafficking," *Anti-Trafficking Review* 7 (2016): 55.

80. Kate Cooper and Sue Branford, *Exploitation and Trafficking of Women: Critiquing Narratives during the London Olympics 2012* (Central America Women's Network, 2013), 7.

81. Ko-Lin Chin and James O. Finckenauer, "Chickenheads, Agents, Mommies, and Jockeys: The Social Organization of Transnational Commercial Sex," *Crime, Law and Social Change* 56 (2011): 463–84.

82. Cooper and Branford, *Exploitation and Trafficking of Women*, 7.

83. Carl Bialik, "Suspect Estimates of Sex Trafficking at the World Cup," *Wall Street Journal*, June 19, 2010.

84. Ham, *What's the Cost of a Rumour*.

85. NPR News, "World Cup Avoids Flood of Sex Workers," *All Things Considered*, July 6, 2010.

86. Thabiso Thakali and Candice Bailey, "No 'Boom Boom' for Joburg's Sex Workers," *IOL News*, June 19, 2010.

87. Frankie Mullin, "Sex Workers Reveal What Cops Took from Them During Police Raids," Broadly, June 14, 2017.

88. Laura María Agustín, "Getting Money to Prevent Sex Trafficking Even If There Isn't Any: London Olympics," *Naked Anthropologist* (blog), October 5, 2012.

89. Stanley Cohen, *Folk Devils and Moral Panics* (New York: Routledge, 2011).

90. Erich Goode and Nachman Ben-Yehuda, *Moral Panics: The Social Construction of Deviance*, 2nd ed. (Malden, MA: Wiley-Blackwell, 2009), 22.

91. Goode and Ben-Yehuda, *Moral Panics*, 23–31.

92. Goode and Ben-Yehuda, *Moral Panics*, 37–43.

93. Sreyasi Pal, "Bengal: Mob Lynches Mentally Ill Woman after Branding Her a Child Trafficker," *Hindustan Times*, June 27, 2017.

94. Gayle Rubin, *Deviations: A Gayle Rubin Reader* (Durham, NC: Duke University Press, 2012), 26.

95. Jeffrey Weeks, *Sex, Politics, and Society: The Regulation of Sexuality since 1800*, 3rd ed. (New York: Routledge, 2012), 20.

96. Rubin, *Deviations*, 168.

97. Janice Raymond, *Not a Choice, Not a Job: Exposing the Myths about Prostitution and the Global Sex Trade* (Washington, DC: Potomac Books, 2013), 16–17.

98. Ron Weitzer, *Legalizing Prostitution: From Illicit Vice to Lawful Business* (New York: NYU Press, 2012).

99. Ron Weitzer and Melissa Ditmore, "Sex Trafficking Facts and Fictions," in *Sex for Sale: Prostitution, Pornography, and the Sex Industry*, 2nd ed. (New York: Routledge, 2010), 335.

100. Weitzer and Ditmore, "Sex Trafficking Facts and Fictions.".

101. Sally Engle Merry, "How Big Is the Trafficking Problem? The Mysteries of Quantification," openDemocracy, June 14, 2017.

102. Glenn Kessler, "The False Claim That Human Trafficking Is a '$9.5 Billion Business' in the United States," *Washington Post*, June 14, 2017.

103. Janice Raymond, *The Transsexual Empire: The Making of the She-Male* (Boston: Beacon Press, 1979).

104. Bernstein, *Brokered Subjects*, 17.

105. Bernstein, *Brokered Subjects*, 18.

106. Bernstein, *Brokered Subjects*, 18.

107. Bernstein, *Brokered Subjects*, 74–76.

108. Bernstein, *Brokered Subjects*, 79–80.

109. For more on the International House of Prayer and Christian dominionists' involvement in Uganda's antigay policies, see Roger Ross Williams, "Gospel of Intolerance," *New York Times*, January 22, 2013.

110. Joe Robertson and Donald Bradley, "Secrets of Tyler Deaton's Prayer Group Emerge," *Kansas City Star*, November 17, 2012.

111. Brian Tashman, "Anti-Gay Leaders Call for Prayer Movement to Stop 'Homosexual Tornado' Coming to 'Destroy America," Right Wing Watch, April 23, 2012.

112. Exodus Cry, "All Eyes on Brazil."

113. See Exodus Cry, "Exodus Cry: Liberdade."

114. Exodus Cry, "Exodus Cry: Liberdade."

115. Exodus Cry, "Exodus Cry Facebook."

116. Roger Lancaster, *Sex Panic and the Punitive State* (Berkeley: University of California Press, 2011), 24.

117. Lancaster, *Sex Panic*, 24.

118. BBC News Brasil, "Quem é Sara Winter, a ex-feminista e atual militante radical bolsonarista presa pela PF a mando do STF," June 15, 2020.

119. BBC News, "Anger in Brazil as 10-Year-Old Rape Victim's Name Put On-Line," August 18, 2020.

120. BBC News, "Anger in Brazil.".

121. Sonia Corrêa, "Dialoguing with the (Im)Possibilities of Unruly Politics," in *The Changing Faces of Citizen Action: A Mapping Study through an 'Unruly' Lens*, ed. Akshay Khanna et al. (N.p.: International Development Institute, 2013), 44.

122. Corrêa, "Dialoguing with the (Im)Possibilities of Unruly Politics," 44.

CHAPTER 1. SEX TRAFFICKING DISCOURSE
AS WHITE SUPREMACY

1. A small portion of this article appeared in Gregory Mitchell and Thaddeus Blanchette, "Tricks of the Light: Refractive Masculinity in Heterosexual and Homosexual Middle-Class Brothels in rio de Janeiro," *South Atlantic Quarterly* 120, no 3 (2021): 609–30.

2. Many activists have begun to group *pardos* (mixed-race) people and *pretos* (an official census term that is otherwise largely offensive) into the broader category of *negro* for political purposes. However, many Brazilians will delineate between *pardos* and *negros*, observing more distinctions between these and other categories such as *morenos, caboclos,* and other racial identifications indicating various mixtures of white, Black, and indigenous ancestry.

3. Thaddeus Blanchette and Ana Paula da Silva, "A mistura clássica: Misegenação e o apelo do Rio de Janeiro como destino para o turismo sexual,"*Bagoas: Revista de Estudos Gays* 4 (2010): 221–44.

4. James Scott, *Weapons of the Weak: Everyday Forms of Peasant Resistance* (New Haven, CT: Yale University Press, 1987).

5. Thaddeus Blanchette and Ana Paula da Silva, "Men in Brothels: (Homo)Sexuality in Rio de Janeiro Commercial Sexual Venues," in *Routledge Handbook of Sex Industry Research*, ed. Susan Dewey, Chimaraoke Izugbara, and Isabel Crowhurst (London: Routledge, 2019), 331–41.

6. For more on this dynamic, see Donna Goldstein, *Laughter Out of Place: Race, Class, Violence, and Sexuality in a Rio Shantytown*, 2nd ed. (Berkeley: University of California Press, 2013).

7. For more on sexscapes, see Denise Brennan, *What's Love Got to Do with It? Transnational Desires and Sex Tourism in the Dominican Republic* (Durham, NC: Duke University Press, 2004); and Émile Durkheim, "As Regras Do Método Sociológico," in *Os Pensadores: Durkheim*, ed. José Giannotti (São Paulo: Abril Cultural, 1978).

8. Robert Alun Jones, *Émile Durkheim: An Introduction to Four Major Works* (Beverly Hills: Sage, 1986), 60–81.

9. Edward Telles, *Race in Another America: The Significance of Skin Color in Brazil* (Princeton, NJ: Princeton University Press, 2004).

10. Lilia Moritz Schwarcz, *Nem Preto, Nem Branco, Muito Contrário* (São Paulo: ClaroEnigma 2013).

11. For example, see Gail Dines, *Pornland: How Porn Has Hijacked Our Sexuality* (Boston: Beacon Press, 2010).

12. Lin Chew, "Reflections by an Anti-Trafficking Activist," in *Trafficking and Prostitution Reconsidered: New Perspectives on Migration, Sex Work, and Human Rights*, ed. Kamala Kempadoo, 2nd ed. (Philadelphia: Taylor and Francis, 2017), 65.

13. Jo Doezema, "Ouch! Western Feminists' 'Wounded Attachment' to the 'Third World Prostitute,'" *Feminist Review* 67, no. 1 (2001): 16–38.

14. Carole S. Vance, "Innocence and Experience: Melodramatic Narratives of Sex Trafficking and Their Consequences for Law and Policy," *History of the Present* 2, no. 2 (2012): 200–218.

15. Tryon Woods, "Surrogate Selves: Notes on Anti-Trafficking and Anti-Blackness," *Social Identities* 19, no. 1 (2013): 120–34.

16. Brian Donovan, *White Slave Crusades: Race, Gender & Anti-Vice Activism, 1887–1917* (Champaign: University of Illinois Press, 2010), 2.

17. Jo Doezema, *Sex Slaves and Discourse Masters: The Construction of Trafficking* (London: Zed Books, 2010), 55.

18. Erich Goode and Nachman Ben-Yehuda, *Moral Panics: The Social Construction of Deviance*, 2nd ed. (Malden, MA: Wiley-Blackwell, 2009), 5.

19. Mark Thomas Connelly, *The Response to Prostitution in the Progressive Era* (Chapel Hill: University of North Carolina Press, 2018), 84.

20. Doezema, *Sex Slaves and Discourse Masters*, 91–92.

21. Doezema, *Sex Slaves and Discourse Masters*, 91–92.

22. Donovan, *White Slave Crusades*, 18, 30–31.

23. Donovan, *White Slave Crusades*, 30.

24. Ernest Bell, *Fighting the Traffic in Young Girls; or, the War on the White Slave Trade* (n.p.: publisher unknown, 1910).

25. Carole S. Vance, "Thinking Trafficking, Thinking Sex," *GLQ* 17, no. 1 (2011): 139.

26. Roxana Galusca, "Slave Hunters, Brothel Busters, and Feminist Interventions: Investigative Journalists as Anti-Sex Trafficking Humanitarians," *Feminist Formations* 24, no. 2 (2012): 3.

27. Jennifer Tyburczy, "Sex Trafficking Talk: Rosi Orozco and the Neoliberal Narrative of Empathy in Post-NAFTA Mexico," *Feminist Formations* 31, no. 3 (2019): 96.

28. Goode and Ben-Yehuda, *Moral Panics*, 5–6.

29. PBS, "The Mann Act," *Unforgivable Blackness: The Rise and Fall of Jack Johnson* (blog).

30. Donovan, *White Slave Crusades*, 14.

31. Doezema, *Sex Slaves and Discourse Masters*, 85.

32. Donovan, *White Slave Crusades*, 13.

33. Donovan, *White Slave Crusades*.

34. Christen A. Smith, *Afro-Paradise: Blackness, Violence, and Performance in Brazil* (Urbana: University of Illinois Press, 2016), 172.

35. Luciane de Oliveira Rocha, "Black Mothers' Experiences of Violence in Rio de Janeiro," *Cultural Dynamics* 24, no. 1 (2012): 59.

36. Kathleen Williamson and Anthony Marcus, "Black Pimps Matter: Racially Selective Identification and Prosecution of Sex Trafficking in the United States," in *Third Party Sex Work and Pimps in the Age of Anti-Trafficking*, ed. Amber Horning and Anthony Marcus (New York: Springer International, 2017), 177–95.

37. Linda Tucker-Smith, *Lock Step and Dance: Images of Black Men in Popular Culture* (Jackson: University of Mississippi Press, 2007), 138.

38. Donovan, *White Slave Crusades*, 14–15.

39. Donovan, *White Slave Crusades*, 49.

40. Donovan, *White Slave Crusades*, 51.

41. "For Stanton, All Women Were Not Created Equal," *NPR's Morning Edition*, July 13, 2011.

42. Brent Staples, "How the Suffrage Movement Betrayed Black Women," *New York Times*, July 28, 2018.

43. Staples, "How the Suffrage Movement Betrayed Black Women."

44. Rudyard Kipling, "The White Man's Burden: The United States & the Philippine Islands, 1899," in *Rudyard Kipling's Verse* (Garden City, NY: Doubleday, 1929).

45. Lisa Duggan and Nan Hunter, *Sex Wars: Sexual Dissent and Political Culture* (New York: Routledge, 2006).

46. Susan Brownmiller, *Against Our Will: Men, Women, and Rape* (New York: Simon and Schuster, 1975).

47. Andrea Dworkin, *Pornography: Men Possessing Women* (New York: Plume, 1989), xvii.

48. Robin Morgan, "Theory and Practice: Pornography and Rape," in *Take Back the Night: Women on Pornography*, ed. Laura Lederer (New York: William Morrow, 1980), 134–40.

49. Catharine MacKinnon, "Not a Moral Issue," *Yale Law & Policy Review* 2, no. 2 (1984): 325–26.

50. Laura Lederer, ed., *Take Back the Night: Women on Pornography* (New York: William Morrow, 1980).

51. Dustin Daniels, "The Real Victims of Pornography," interview with Laura Lederer, December 26, 2012, in *God, Sex & You!* (podcast).

52. Charles Moser, *Sadomasochism: Powerful Pleasures* (New York: Harrington Park Press, 2006), 211.

53. Audrey Lorde, "Sadomasochism: Not about Condemnation," in *A Burst of Light: Essays by Audrey Lorde* (Ithaca, NY: Firebrand Books, 1988).

54. Lorde, "Sadomasochism: Not about Condemnation."

55. Lorde, "Sadomasochism: Not about Condemnation."

56. Donald Downs, "The Attorney General's Commission and the New Politics of Pornography," *American Bar Foundation Research Journal* 12, no. 4 ([1987]): 639–79.

57. Mireille Miller-Young, *A Taste for Brown Sugar: Black Women in Pornography* (Durham, NC: Duke University Press, 2014), 20.

58. Ariane Cruz, *The Color of Kink: Black Women, BDSM, and Pornography* (New York: NYU Press, 2016).

59. Cruz, *Color of Kink*, 18.

60. Jennifer Nash, *The Black Body in Ecstasy: Reading Race, Reading Pornography* (Durham, Nc: Duke University Press, 2014), 10–11.

61. Nash, *Black Body in Ecstasy*, 12.

62. Janice Raymond, *The Transsexual Empire: The Making of the She-Male* (Boston: Beacon Press, 1979), 104.

63. Raymond, *Transsexual Empire*, 178.

64. Tarpley Hitt, "Why Are HBO and Melissa McCarthy Raising Money for an Anti-LGBTQ Group?," *Daily Beast*, November 12, 2020.

65. Exodus Cry, "Exodus Cry Receives a Flood of Support after Melissa McCarthy Cancels Donation," November 18, 2020.

66. Exodus Cry, "Myths vs. Truths about Exodus Cry," August 20, 2020.

67. Hitt, "Why Are HBO and Melissa McCarthy Raising Money for an Anti-LGBTQ Group?"

68. Exodus Cry, "Myths vs. Truths about Exodus Cry."

69. Melissa Gira Grant, "Nick Kristof and the Holy War on Pornhub," *New Republic*, December 10, 2020.

70. Grant, "Nick Kristof and the Holy War on Pornhub."

71. Drew Fox, "How Radical Anti-Porn Zealots Became the Media's Sex-ploitation 'Experts,'" XBIZ: The Industry Source, November 26, 2019.

72. Kipling, "White Man's Burden."

73. Destiny Rescue, "Destiny Rescue: Rescuing Children," Short Term Trips.

74. "Rahab's Rope," Go! Venture India.

75. "Rahab's Rope," Go! Venture India.

76. Crossroads Church, "India: Mumbai/November."

77. Crossroads Church, "India: Mumbai/November."

78. Crossroads Church, "India: Mumbai/November."

79. Elizabeth Bernstein and Elena Shih, "Travels of Trafficking," in *Brokered Subjects: Sex, Trafficking, and the Politics of Freedom* (Chicago: University of Chicago Press, 2018), 98–127.

80. Natasha Rausch, "I AM Freedom Heads to World Cup," *Norfolk Daily News*, June 6, 2014.

81. University of Wisconsin, "UW Global Health and Human Rights Training in Spain and Morocco to Combat Sex-Trafficking."

82. University of Wisconsin, "UW Global Health and Human Rights Training."

83. University of Wisconsin, "UW Global Health and Human Rights Training."

84. University of Wisconsin, "UW Global Health and Human Rights Training."

85. Bernstein and Shih, "Travels of Trafficking," 109.

86. Bernstein and Shih, "Travels of Trafficking," 112.

87. Galusca, "Slave Hunters, Brothel Busters, and Feminist Interventions," 13.

88. Galusca, "Slave Hunters, Brothel Busters, and Feminist Interventions," 13.

89. Bronislaw Malinowski, *Sexual Lives of Savages* (Boston: Beacon Press, 1987).

90. Robert Rydell, "In Sight and Sound with the Other Senses All Around: Racial Hierarchies at America's World's Fairs," in *The Invention of Race* (New York: Routledge, 2006), 209–21.

91. Bianca Freire-Medeiros, *Touring Poverty* (New York: Routledge, 2014); and Erika Robb Larkins, *The Spectacular Favela: Violence in Modern Brazil* (Oakland: University of California Press, 2015).

92. Fabian Frenzel, *Slumming It: The Valorization of Urban Poverty* (London: Zed Books, 2016).

93. Kimberly Pendleton, "The Other Sex Industry: Narratives of Feminism and Freedom in Evangelical Discourses of Human Trafficking," *New Formations* 91 (2017): 102.

94. Pendleton, "Other Sex Industry."

95. Elena Shih, "Duplicitous Freedom: Moral and Material Care Work in Anti-Trafficking Rescue and Rehabilitation," *Critical Sociology* 44, nos. 7–8 (2018): 1077.

96. Elizabeth Bernstein, "Militarized Humanitarianism Meets Carceral Feminism: The Politics of Sex, Rights, and Freedom in Contemporary Antitrafficking Campaigns," *Signs: Journal of Women in Culture and Society* 36, no. 1 (2010): 45–71.

97. Tryon Woods, "The Antiblackness of 'Modern-Day Slavery' Abolitionism," openDemocracy, October 10, 2014.

98. Woods, "Antiblackness of 'Modern-Day Slavery' Abolitionism."

99. Woods, "Antiblackness of 'Modern-Day Slavery' Abolitionism."

100. Gospel for Asia, "Thousands of Girls in Asia Saved from Possible 'Fate Worse Than Death,'" Standard Newswire, October 1, 2019.

101. Woods, "Antiblackness of 'Modern-Day Slavery' Abolitionism."

102. Lyndsey Beutin, "Black Suffering for/from Anti-Trafficking Advocacy," *Anti-Trafficking Review* 9, no. 1 (2017): 14–30.

103. Julia O'Connell Davidson, *Modern Slavery: The Margins of Freedom* (New York: Palgrave Macmillan, 2015), 81.

104. O'Connell Davidson, *Modern Slavery*.

105. Julieta Hua, *Trafficking Women's Human Rights* (Minneapolis: University of Minnesota Press, 2011), 97.

106. Hua, *Trafficking Women's Human Rights*, 96.

107. Laura Lederer, "Human Trafficking and the Law" (speech presented at the Library of Congress Law Day, May 1, 2001).

108. Lederer, "Human Trafficking and the Law."

109. Lederer, "Human Trafficking and the Law."

110. Woods, ".Antiblackness of 'Modern-Day Slavery' Abolitionism."

111. Woods, ".Antiblackness of 'Modern-Day Slavery' Abolitionism."

112. Kamala Kempadoo, "From Moral Panics to Global Justice: Changing Perspectives on Trafficking," in *Trafficking and Prostitution Reconsidered: New Perspectives on Migration, Sex Work, and Human Rights*, ed. Kamala Kempadoo (London: Paradigm Publishers, 2005), xii–xxxiv.

113. See Denise Brennan, *Life Interrupted: Trafficking into Forced Labor in the United States* (Durham, NC: Duke University Press, 2014).

114. Carol Leigh, *Just Sign on the Dotted Line: The Anti-Prostitution Loyalty Oath* (Sex Worker Media Library, n.d.).

115. Larry Rohter, "Prostitution Puts U.S. and Brazil at Odds on AIDS Policy," *New York Times*, July 24, 2005.

116. Adam Liptak, "Justices Say U.S. Cannot Impose Antiprostitution Condition on AIDS Grants," *New York Times*, June 20, 2013.

117. Sonia Corrêa and José Miguel Nieto Olivar, "The Politics of Prostitution in Brazil: Between 'State Neutrality' and 'Feminist Troubles,'" in *The Global HIV Epidemics among Sex Workers*, ed. Deanna Kerrigan et al. (Washington, DC: World Bank Publications, 2012), 7.

118. Corrêa and José Miguel Nieto Olivar, "Politics of Prostitution in Brazil," 7.

119. Crystal Jackson, Jennifer Reed, and Barbara Brents, "Strange Confluences: Radical Feminism and Evangelical Christianity as Drivers of US Neo-Abolitionism," in *Feminism, Prostitution, and the State: The Politics of Neo-Abolitionism*, ed. Eilís Ward and Gillian Wylie (New York: Routledge, 2017), 76.

120. Laura María Agustín, "Well-Meaning Interference," *Philadelphia Inquirer*, July 1, 2007.

121. Laura María Agustín, "TIP: Trafficking in Persons, the No-Methodology Report," *Naked Anthropologist* (blog), June 26, 2009.

122. Kudakwashe P. Vanyoro, "'Skeptics' and 'Believers': Anti-Trafficking, Sex Work, and Migrant Rights Activism in South Africa," *Gender and Development* 27, no. 1 (2019): 127.

123. Vanyoro, "'Skeptics' and 'Believers,'" 125.

124. Agustín, "TIP: Trafficking in Persons, the No-Methodology Report."

125. Jay Levy, *Criminalising the Purchase of Sex: Lessons from Sweden* (London: Routledge, 2014).

126. Niina Vuolajärvi, "Governing in the Name of Caring—The Nordic Model of Prostitution and Its Punitive Consequences for Migrants Who Sell Sex," *Sexuality Research and Social Policy* 16, no. 2 (2019): 160–61.

127. Boglárka Fedorkó, "'Send Them Back': Migrant Sex Workers Deported from Europe," openDemocracy, August 19, 2019.

128. Fedorkó, "'Send Them Back': Migrant Sex Workers Deported from Europe."

129. Sine Plambech, "Sex, Deportation and Rescue: Economies of Migration among Nigerian Sex Workers," *Feminist Economics* 23, no. 1 (2017): 134–59.

130. Plambech, "Sex, Deportation and Rescue," 151–52.

131. Levy, *Criminalising the Purchase of Sex*, 33.

132. Levy, *Criminalising the Purchase of Sex*, 34.

133. Levy, *Criminalising the Purchase of Sex*, 225.

134. Yvonne Svanström, "From Contested to Consensus: Swedish Politics on Prostitution and Trafficking," in *Feminism, Prostitution, and the State: The Politics of Neo-Abolitionism*, ed. Eilís Ward and Gillian Wylie (New York: Routledge, 2017), 29.

135. Anita Heber, "The Hunt for an Elusive Crime—an Analysis of Swedish Measures to Combat Sex Trafficking," *Journal of Scandinavian Studies in Criminology and Crime Prevention* 19, no. 1 (2018): 4.

136. Lynzi Armstrong, "Decriminalising Sex Work Is the Only Way to Protect Women—and New Zealand Has Proved That It Works," *Independent*, May 29, 2017.

137. Armstrong, "Decriminalising Sex Work."

138. Brennan, *What's Love Got to Do with It?*.

CHAPTER 2. PANIC AT THE GRINGO

1. Don Kulick, "Causing a Commotion: Public Scandal as Resistance among Brazilian Transgendered Prostitutes," *Anthropology Today* 12, no. 6 (1996): 3–7.

2. Eleanor Goldberg, "Children Sold for Sex at World Cup for Few Dollars, Pack of Cigarettes," *Huffington Post*, June 12, 2014.

3. Michelle Lillie, "Sex Trafficking at the FIFA World Cup in Brazil," Human Trafficking Search, July 14, 2014.

4. Jarbas Aragão, "Missionários fazem protesto acorrentados em frente a hotel," *CPAD News: Gospel Prime*, June 16, 2014.

5. "Tourism: Not Germany, but Rio de Janeiro Hit the Jackpot," *eTurbo-News: Global Travel Industry News*, June 27, 2014.

6. Ewan Mackenna, "Brazil's Sex Trade: How the Country's One Million Prostitutes Are Preparing for the World Cup," *Independent*, June 14, 2014.

7. Melissa Gira Grant, "Sex Work at the Super Bowl: The Myth and Its Makers," *Guardian*, June 14, 2017.

8. Grant, "Sex Work at the Super Bowl."

9. Thaddeus Blanchette, "'Fariseus' e 'gringos bons': Masculinidade e turismo sexual em copacabana," in *Gênero, sexo, afetos e dinheiro: Mobilidades transnacionais envolvendo o Brasil* (Campinas, Brazil: EDUNICAMP/PAGU, 2011), 57–103.

10. Blanchette, "'Fariseus' e 'gringos bons,'" 75 (author's translation). Blanchette's original text stated, "para as prostitutas de Copacabana, 'gringo bom' é aquele recém-chegado que fala pouco ou nenhum português e paga os programas sem pechinchar."

11. Thaddeus Blanchette and Ana Paula da Silva, "A mistura clássica: Misegenação e o apelo do Rio de Janeiro como destino para o turismo sexual," *Bagoas: Revista de Estudos Gays* 4 (2010): 221–44.

12. Renata Melo Rosa, "Vivendo um conto de fadas: Ensaio sobre cor e 'fantasia' entre mulheres cariocas e homens estrangeiros" (mestrado [master's thesis], Instituto de Filosofia e Ciências Sociais, Universidade Federal do Rio de Janeiro, 1999).

13. Blanchette, "'Fariseus' e 'gringos bons,'" 73 (author's translation). Blanchette's original states, "Fariseu é aquele gringo que se acha melhor que a gente. Ele fala português e sabe agir como brasileiro. Nem fode, nem sai de cima: ele gosta de ter a garota em torno de sua mesa, fazendo mis en scène, fazendo-o se sentir o máximo, mas na hora do programa, não quer pagar."

14. Jeremy Armstrong and Andy Lines, "Brazilian Women Turning to Prostitution for World Cup—and England Fans Are Their Biggest Goal," *Mirror*, June 12, 2014.

15. M. Jacqui Alexander, *Pedagogies of Crossing: Meditations on Feminism, Sexual Politics, Memory, and the Sacred* (Durham, NC: Duke University Press, 2005), 56.

16. Alexander, *Pedagogies of Crossing.*

17. Alexander, *Pedagogies of Crossing.*

18. Erica Lorraine Williams, *Sex Tourism in Bahia: Ambiguous Entanglements* (Urbana: University of Illinois Press, 2013), 65.

19. Williams, *Sex Tourism in Bahia,* 68.

20. "Tourism: Not Germany, but Rio de Janeiro Hit the Jackpot."

21. Clarissa Thomé and Thaise Constâncio, "Hotel é fechado no Rio por envolvimento em exploração sexual," *Estadão,* June 13, 2014.

22. See Anthony Marcus et al., "Conflict and Agency among Sex Workers and Pimps: A Closer Look at Domestic Minor Sex Trafficking," *ANNALS of the American Academy of Political and Social Science* 653, no. 1 (2014): 225–46.

23. Tom Phillips, "Rio Nightclub Closure Leaves Prostitutes Helpless," *Guardian,* August 17, 2009.

24. Carolina Benevides et al., "Aliciadores já atuam em cidades da Copa do Mundo," *O Globo,* April 27, 2014. The original text reads, "Daqui a menos de 50 dias começa a Copa do Mundo, e 600 mil estrangeiros deverão desembarcar no país e se somar aos três milhões de brasileiros que, segundo o Ministério do Turismo, se deslocarão entre as 12 cidades-sede durante o evento. O campeonato vai aquecer a economia e mudar a rotina do país, mas também deve deixar crianças e adolescentes brasileiros ainda mais vulneráveis à exploração sexual. Em diversas cidades do Brasil, já há sinais da ação de aliciadores de menores—pessoas dispostas a montar pequenos exércitos capazes de saciar a demanda por sexo."

25. Waleska Borges, "Três pessoas são presas na zona sul acusadas de incentivar a prostituição," *O Globo,* June 15, 2012.

26. Coburn Palmer, "Even Rio Prostitutes Think Olympics Will Be a Failure, Sex Workers Offer 'Supermarket Sale,'" Inquisitr, July 4, 2016, 3.

27. David Williams, "'I Want to Win Olympic Gold for Sex': Rio Escort Wants to Use Games to Find a Boyfriend 'Just like a Julia Roberts in Pretty Woman,'" *Daily Mail,* August 3, 2016, 21.

28. Thaddeus Blanchette, "'Almost a Brazilian': Gringos, Immigration and Irregularity in Brazil," in *In Global Migration: Old Assumptions, New Dynamics,* ed. D. A. Acarazo and A. Weisbrock (Santa Barbara, CA: Praeger, 2015), 171.

29. Gregory Mitchell, *Tourist Attractions: Performing Race and Masculinity in Brazil's Sexual Economy* (Chicago: University of Chicago Press, 2015).

30. De Maio and Andrea Dip, *Meninas em jogo,* Repórter Brasil, VII Concurso Tim Lopes de Jornalismo Investigativo (Brasília: Agência de reportagem e jornalismo investigativo, 2013).

31. Ramón Spaaij, "Men Like Us, Boys Like Them: Violence, Masculinity, and Collective Identity in Football Hooliganism," *Journal of Sport and Social Issues* 32, no. 4 (2008): 369–92. See also Ramón Spaaij, "Football Hooliganism as a Transnational Phenomenon: Past and Present Analysis; A Critique—More

Specificity and Less Generality," *International Journal of the History of Sport* 24, no. 4 (2007): 411–31.

32. Spaaij, "Men Like Us, Boys Like Them," 372.

33. Patrick Reevell, "Russian Hooligans' Toughest Opponents? Russia's Police," *New York Times*, June 14, 2017.

34. Mary Weismantel, "Race Rape: White Masculinity in Andean Pishtaco Tales," *Identities: Global Studies in Culture and Power* 7, no. 3 (2000): 408.

35. Weismantel, "Race Rape," 410.

36. Mary Weismantel, *Cholas and Pishtacos: Stories of Race and Sex in the Andes* (Chicago: University of Chicago Press, 2001).

37. Louise Ridley, "Rio Child Sex Trafficking 'Epidemic' Could Rocket during the 2016 Olympics—Here's Why," *HuffPost*, June 14, 2017.

38. Roger Lancaster, *Sex Panic and the Punitive State* (Berkeley: University of California Press, 2011).

CHAPTER 3. FALLACIOUS SPECTACLES AND THE CELEBRIFICATION OF SEX TRAFFICKING

1. ECPAT USA, "Gift Box."

2. ECPAT USA, "Gift Box."

3. Lilie Chouliaraki, *The Ironic Spectator: Solidarity in the Age of Post-Humanitarianism* (Cambridge, NY: Polity Press, 2013), 60.

4. Chouliaraki, *Ironic Spectator*, 60.

5. Guy Debord, *Society of the Spectacle* (New York: Zone Books, 1995).

6. Marcia Ochoa, *Queen for a Day: Transformistas, Beauty Queens, and the Performance of Femininity in Venezuela* (Durham, NC: Duke University Press, 2014), 203–4.

7. Ochoa, *Queen for a Day*, 221.

8. Debord, *Society of the Spectacle*, 24.

9. John Simi, "Rio Carnival 2013: Topless Activists Stage Sex Protest at Airport," *International Business Times*, February 10, 2013.

10. Femen, "Femen: About Us."

11. Femen, "Femen: About Us."

12. Femen, "Femen: About Us."

13. Laura María Agustín, "Becoming Aware of Awareness-Raising as Anti-Trafficking Tactic," *Naked Anthropologist* (blog), July 1, 2015.

14. Theresa Flores, "SOAP Project."

15. Flores, "SOAP Project."

16. James Pilcher and Kimball Perry, "Using Soap to Fight Sex Trafficking for All-Star Game," July 5, 2015, updated July 10, 2015.

17. Paul Strand, "Rescuing Sex Slaves with Soap and Paper," *CBN News: The Christian Perspective*, June 5, 2017, 2.

18. SA Foundation, "Calgary Ice Breaker—It's Cool to Be Cold!"

19. Human Trafficking Task Force, "Run for Freedom," January 19, 2019.

20. Red Sand Project, home page.

21. Oasis of Hope, "Shine a Light on Slavery Day."

22. Oasis of Hope, "Shine a Light on Slavery Day."

23. End It Movement, home page.

24. End It Movement, home page.

25. Charlotte Lapp, "CNN Freedom Project #FlytoFreedom," McCain Institute, November 19, 2015.

26. Lapp, "CNN Freedom Project #FlytoFreedom."

27. Samantha Majic, "Real Men Set Norms? Anti-Trafficking Campaigns and the Limits of Celebrity Norm Entrepreneurship," *Crime, Media, Culture* 14, no. 2 (2018): 289–309.

28. Dina Francesca Haynes, "The Celebritization of Human Trafficking," *Annals of the American Academy of Political and Social Science* 653 (May 2014): 25–45.

29. Chouliaraki, *Ironic Spectator*, 6.

30. Chouliaraki, *Ironic Spectator*, 6.

31. Denise Brennan, *Life Interrupted: Trafficking into Forced Labor in the United States* (Durham, NC: Duke University Press, 2014).

32. Brennan, *Life Interrupted*, 65.

33. Wendy Hesford, *Spectacular Rhetorics: Human Rights Visions, Recognitions, Feminisms* (Durham, NC: Duke University Press, 2011), 133.

34. Hesford, *Spectacular Rhetorics*.

35. Emily Bazelon, "Should Prostitution Be a Crime?," *New York Times Magazine*, May 5, 2016.

36. "CATW Responds: Amnesty International Turned Its Back on Women," Coalition Against Trafficking in Women, August 11, 2015.

37. Donor Direct Action, "Meryl Streep Speaks in Support of Sex Trade Survivors," Sisterhood Is Global Institute, July 11, 2016.

38. Donor Direct Action, "Meryl Streep Speaks in Support of Sex Trade Survivors."

39. Marcia Stepanek, "Emma Thompson's 'Journey' into Sexual Slavery," *NBC News*, November 13, 2009.

40. Stepanek, "Emma Thompson's 'Journey' into Sexual Slavery."

41. Edward Davis, "Anne Hathaway on Channeling Her Tears, Emotions & Cutting Her Hair for Harrowing 'Les Misérables' Scene," *Indie Wire*, December 26, 2012.

42. Amnesty International, "Q & A: Policy to Protect the Human Rights of Sex Workers," May 26, 2016.

43. Rupert Everett, "Rupert Everett in Defence of Prostitutes: 'There Is a Land Grab Going On,'" *Guardian*, June 14, 2017.

44. MSN Take Part, "Demi Moore: Why I Joined the Fight against Child Trafficking," Celebrities, March 17, 2013.

45. Marlow Stern, "Sean Penn's Horrifying History of Alleged Abuse," *Daily Beast*, September 19, 2018.

46. Global News, "Ashton Kutcher Testifies before U.S. Congress on Ending Modern Slavery," February 15, 2017.

47. Global News, "Ashton Kutcher Testifies before U.S. Congress."

48. Dan MacGuill, "Did Ashton Kutcher's Software Help Rescue 6,000 Children from Sex Trafficking?," Snopes, September 4, 2018.

49. Global News, "Ashton Kutcher Testifies before U.S. Congress."

50. Global News, "Ashton Kutcher Testifies before U.S. Congress."

51. MeiMei Fox, "How Thorn Is Fighting to Eliminate Child Sexual Abuse from the Internet," *Forbes*, August 14, 2019.

52. Tierney Sneed, "How Big Data Battles Human Trafficking," *US News*, January 14, 2015, 16.

53. Violet Blue, "Sex, Lies, and Surveillance: Something's Wrong with the War on Sex Trafficking," Engadget, May 31, 2019.

54. Elise Conklin, Martin Cizmar, and Kristen Hinman, "Real Men Get Their Facts Straight," *Village Voice*, June 29, 2011.

55. Caitlin Dickson, "Ashton Kutcher Calls Out Village Voice for Sex Trafficking Charges," *Atlantic*, June 30, 2011.

56. Thorn, "Wea Are Thorn."

57. See Jamie Peck, "Zombie Neoliberalism and the Ambidextrous State," *Theoretical Criminology* 14, no. 1 (2010): 104–10.

58. Irin Carmon, "Nick Kristof to the Rescue!," *Salon*, November 8, 2011.

59. Carmon, "Nick Kristof to the Rescue!"

60. Carmon, "Nick Kristof to the Rescue!"

61. Carmon, "Nick Kristof to the Rescue!"

62. Carmon, "Nick Kristof to the Rescue!"

63. Maro Chermayeff, *Half the Sky* (PBS Independent Lens, 2012).

64. Chermayeff, *Half the Sky.*

65. Chermayeff, *Half the Sky.*

66. Chermayeff, *Half the Sky.*

67. Chermayeff, *Half the Sky.*

68. Dorinda Elliott, "Somaly Mam and Susan Sarandon Give Shelter to Former Sex Slaves," *Condé Nast Traveler*, August 20, 2012.

69. Simon Marks, "Somaly Mam: The Holy Saint (and Sinner) of Sex Trafficking," *Newsweek*, May 21, 2014.

70. Marks, "Somaly Mam."

71. Marks, "Somaly Mam."

72. Marks, "Somaly Mam."

73. Marks, "Somaly Mam."

74. Marks, "Somaly Mam."

75. Nicholas Kristof, "When Sources May Have Lied," *On the Ground* (blog), *New York Times*, New York Times, June 7, 2014; Nicholas Kristof, "A Woman I Regarded as a Hero, and New Doubts," *On the Ground* (blog), *New York Times*, June 14, 2017.

76. Melissa Mendes and Anne Elizabeth Moore, "'Unraveling': Anti-Trafficking NGOs and the Garment Industry," Truth Out, August 19, 2014, 4.

77. Nicholas Kirstof, "Where Sweatshops Are a Dream," *New York Times*, January 14, 2009.

78. David Adams and Josie Swantek, dirs., *The Wrong Light* (Shine Global, 2017).

79. Adams and Swantek, *Wrong Light.*

80. Adams and Swantek, *Wrong Light.*

81. Adams and Swantek, *Wrong Light.*

82. Adams and Swantek, *Wrong Light.*

83. Adams and Swantek, *Wrong Light*.

84. Noah Berlatsky, "The Lies about Sex Trafficking That Brought down Backpage," *Salon*, April 15, 2018.

85. Berlatsky, "Lies about Sex Trafficking."

86. David Schmader, "Chong Kim, the Woman Whose Allegedly True Story Served as the Basis for Megan Griffith's Film *Eden*, Denounced as a Fraud," *Stranger*, June 4, 2014.

87. Schmader, "Chong Kim."

88. Noah Berlatsky, "Hollywood's Dangerous Obsession with Sex Trafficking," *Salon*, June 10, 2014.

89. Berlatsky, "Hollywood's Dangerous Obsession with Sex Trafficking."

90. Asia Pacific Regional Correspondent, "Swedish NGO under Investigation for Creating Fake 'Rescue' Stories to Solicit Donations," NSWP: Global Network of Sex Work Projects, August 28, 2017.

91. Asia Pacific Regional Correspondent, "Swedish NGO under Investigation."

92. Asia Pacific Regional Correspondent, "Swedish NGO under Investigation."

93. "Anti-Trafficking Group 'Saved In America' Losing Support," *NBC San Diego*, October 2019.

94. Marjie Lundstrom and Sam Stanton, "This Charity Keeps Raising Money to Help Young Sex-Trafficking Victims: But Where Are the Victims?," *Sacramento Bee*, June 26, 2017.

95. Lundstrom and Stanton, "This Charity Keeps Raising Money."

96. Lundstrom and Stanton, "This Charity Keeps Raising Money."

97. Matt Keeley, "DOJ Gave $500K Grant to 'Hookers for Jesus' Instead of Established Anti-Trafficking Groups: Report," *Newsweek*, February 10, 2020.

98. Keeley, "DOJ Gave $500K Grant to 'Hookers for Jesus' Instead."

99. Elizabeth Nolan Brown, "NYC Councilman Completely Fabricates Child Sex-Trafficking Ring," *Reason*, July 6, 2016.

100. Brown, "NYC Councilman Completely Fabricates Child Sex-Trafficking Ring,"

101. Brown, "NYC Councilman Completely Fabricates Child Sex-Trafficking Ring."

102. Cecilia Kang, "Fake News Onslaught Targets Pizzeria as Nest of Child-Trafficking," *New York Times*, November 21, 2016.

103. Felicia Sonmez and Mike DeBonis, "Believer in QAnon Conspiracy Theory Wins Republican Senate Nomination in Oregon," *Washington Post*, May 20, 2020.

104. Ryan Mink, "Benjamin Watson's Next Crusade Is Against Sex Trafficking in the Dominican Republic," June 21, 2017.

105. It's a Penalty, home page.

106. It's a Penalty, home page.

107. Breeana Edwards, "Asian Woman Says Federal Agents Harassed Her after Mistaking Her for Human Trafficking Victim," *Root*, November 28, 2017.

108. Kalhan Rosenblatt, "Flight Attendants Train to Spot Human Trafficking," *NBC News*, June 14, 2017.

109. Ira Glass, "Save the Girl," *This American Life*, July 12, 2019,.

110. Glass, "Save the Girl."

111. Glass, "Save the Girl."

112. Glass, "Save the Girl."

113. It's a Penalty, home page.

114. It's a Penalty, home page.

115. It's a Penalty, home page.

116. It's a Penalty, home page.

117. It's a Penalty, home page.

118. Andréa Cardarello, "The Movement of the Mothers of the Courthouse Square: 'Legal Child Trafficking,' Adoption and Poverty in Brazil," *Journal of Latin American and Caribbean Anthropology* 14, no. 1 (2009): 140–61.

119. Carol Glatz, "Tourists Must Blow Whistle on Trafficking during Olympics, Religious Say," *[Boston] Pilot*, June 14, 2017.

120. Fiona Keating, "Nuns Take on Brazil's Child Sex Gangs in Run-up to World Cup," *International Business Times*, May 24, 2014.

121. Keating, "Nuns Take on Brazil's Child Sex Gangs."

122. Ary Sperling, "A carinho da verdade," August 22, 2011.

123. Glória Perez, "Salve Jorge," *O Globo*, 2012.

124. Jo Doezema, *Sex Slaves and Discourse Masters: The Construction of Trafficking* (London: Zed Books, 2010); and Carole S. Vance, "Innocence and Experience: Melodramatic Narratives of Sex Trafficking and Their Consequences for Law and Policy," *History of the Present* 2, no. 2 (2012): 200–218.

125. Julie Bindel, *The Pimping of Prostitution: Abolishing the Sex Work Myth* (London: Palgrave, 2019).

126. Alison Phipps, "Sex Wars Revisited: A Rhetorical Economy of Sex Industry Opposition," *Journal of International Women's Studies* 18, no. 4 (2017): 312.

127. Phipps, "Sex Wars Revisited," 313.

128. Phipps, "Sex Wars Revisited," 314.

129. Claudia Cojocaru, "Sex Trafficking, Captivity, and Narrative: Constructing Victimhood with the Goal of Salvation," *Dialectical Anthropology* 39 (2015): 184.

130. Cojocaru, "Sex Trafficking, Captivity, and Narrative," 184.

131. Cojocaru, "Sex Trafficking, Captivity, and Narrative," 185.

132. Christine M. Jacobsen and May-Len Skilbrei, "Reproachable Victims? Representations and Self-Representations of Russian Women Involved in Transnational Prostitution," *Ethnos* 75, no. 2 (2010): 194.

133. Jacobsen and Skilbrei, "Reproachable Victims?"

134. Colin Campbell, *The Romantic Ethic and the Spirit of Modern Consumerism*, 3rd ed. (London: Alcuin Academics, 2005).

135. Campbell, *Romantic Ethic*, 131.

136. Campbell, *Romantic Ethic*, 132.

137. Campbell, *Romantic Ethic*, 132.

138. Campbell, *Romantic Ethic*, 132.

139. Campbell, *Romantic Ethic*, 132.

140. Miriam Ticktin, *Casualties of Care: Immigration and the Politics of Humanitarianism in France* (Berkeley: University of California Press, 2011), 3.

141. Ticktin, *Casualties of Care*, 3.

CHAPTER 4. EAT—PRAY—LABOR

1. Sarah Hamill, "The 2022 World Cup: Forced Labor of Migrant Workers," *Trafficking Matters*, January 15, 2019.

2. Pete Pattisson and Roshan Sedhai, "Covid-19 Lockdown Turns Qatar's Largest Migrant Camp into a 'Virtual Prison,'" *Guardian*, March 20, 2020.

3. Human Rights Watch, "Qatar: Take Urgent Action to Protect Construction Workers," September 27, 2017.

4. Mark Lobel, "Arrested for Reporting on Qatar's World Cup Labourers," *BBC News*, May 18, 2015.

5. Nick Anderson, "In Qatar's Education City, US Colleges Are Building an Academic Oasis," *Washington Post*, December 6, 2015.

6. Human Rights Watch, "Qatar: Censorship Ignores Rights, FIFA Rules: 2022 World Cup Host Should Reform Anti-LGBT Laws," August 3, 2018.

7. Sarah McLaughlin, "Northwestern University in Qatar Partner Claims Controversial Event Was Canceled Due to 'Qatari Laws', 'Cultural and Social Customs,'" FIRE: Foundation for Individual Rights in Education, February 5, 2020.

8. Pete Pattisson, "Qatar's Ambitious Future Driven on by North Korean 'Forced Labour,'" *Guardian*, June 14, 2017.

9. Pattisson, "Qatar's Ambitious Future."

10. Pattisson, "Qatar's Ambitious Future."

11. Maureen Callahan, "Eat, Pray, Loathe," *New York Post*, December 23, 2007; and Lindy West, "Pay. Sit. Barf," *Stranger*, September 14, 2010.

12. Haley Christenson, "For the Game. For the World. But What about for the Workers? Evaluating FIFA's Human Rights Policy in Relation to International Standards," *San Diego International Law Journal* 20, no. 1 (2018): 94.

13. Parvis Mahdavi, "Gender, Labour and the Law: The Nexus of Domestic Work, Human Trafficking and the Informal Economy in the United Arab Emirates," *Global Networks* 13, no. 4 (2013): 425–40.

14. Parvis Mahdavi and Christine Sargent, "Questioning the Discursive Construction of Trafficking and Forced Labor in the United Arab Emirates," *Journal of Middle East Women's Studies* 7, no. 3 (2011): 16.

15. Mahdavi and Sargent, "Questioning the Discursive Construction," 17.

16. Rhacel Parreñas, *Illicit Flirtations: Labor, Migration, and Sex Trafficking in Tokyo* (Redwood City, CA: Stanford University Press, 2011).

17. Pete Pattisson, "Revealed: Qatar's World Cup 'Slaves,'" *Guardian*, September 25, 2013.

18. Pattisson, "Qatar's Ambitious Future."

19. Pattisson, "Revealed: Qatar's World Cup 'Slaves.'"

20. Paula Renkiewicz, "Sweat Makes the Green Grass Grow: The Precarious Future of Qatar's Migrant Workers in the Run Up to the 2022 FIFA World Cup under the Kafala System and Recommendations for Effective Reform," *American University Law Review* 65, no. 1 (2017): 723–24.

21. Hamill, "2022 World Cup."

22. Claudia Müller-Hoff and Zarah Baur, "Compliance Alert: Forced Labour in Qatar," *International Union Rights* 25, no. 2 (2018): 22–28.

23. Hamill, "2022 World Cup."

24. Hamill, "2022 World Cup."

25. Christenson, "For the Game," 97.

26. Müller-Hoff and Baur, "Compliance Alert."

27. Sarath K. Ganji, "Leveraging the World Cup: Mega Sporting Events, Human Rights Risk, and Worker Welfare Reform in Qatar," *Journal on Migration and Human Security* 4, no. 4 (2016): 221.

28. Ganji, "Leveraging the World Cup," 225.

29. Bhaskar Sunkara, "Soccer in Sun and Shadow," *In These Times*, January 1, 2014.

30. Adam Sobel, dir., *The Workers Cup* (Autlook Filmsales, 2017).

31. Freedom House, "Freedom of the Press: Qatar," 2015.

32. Lobel, "Arrested for Reporting on Qatar's World Cup Labourers."

33. Lobel, "Arrested for Reporting on Qatar's World Cup Labourers."

34. Lobel, "Arrested for Reporting on Qatar's World Cup Labourers."

35. Alex Sabino, "Gays devem respeitar cultura do Qatar, diz Organizador da Copa," *Folha de São Paulo*, January 5, 2020.

36. George Vecsey, "Views That Soccer Can Do Without," *New York Times*, December 17, 2010.

37. Christopher Gaffney, *Temples of the Earthbound Gods: Stadiums in the Cultural Landscapes of Rio de Janeiro and Buenos Aires* (Austin: University of Texas Press, 2008).

38. Christenson, "For the Game," 99.

39. Sobel, *Workers Cup*.

40. Stephen Bijan, "In Praise of the Flâneur," *Paris Review*, October 17, 2013.

41. Pavithra Prasad and Anjana Raghavan, "Dark Looks: Sensory Contours of Racism in India," in *De-Whitening Intersectionality: Race, Intercultural Communication, and Politics*, ed. Shinsuke Eguchi, Shadee Abdi, and Bernadette Marie Calafell (Lanham, MD: Lexington Books, 2020).

42. Prasad and Raghavan, "Dark Looks."

43. Prasad and Raghavan, "Dark Looks."

44. Kate Conger, "Uber Says 3,045 Sexual Assaults Were Reported in US Rides Last Year," *New York Times*, December 5, 2019.

45. Conger, "Uber Says 3,045 Sexual Assaults Were Reported."

46. Soo Youn, "Uber Announces 21 Categories of Sexual Misconduct to Report," *ABC News*, November 12, 2018.

47. Youn, "Uber Announces 21 Categories of Sexual Misconduct."

48. Mary Douglas, *Purity and Danger: An Analysis of the Concepts of Pollution and Taboo* (London: Ark Paperbacks, 1966).

49. Quoted in Carol Wical, "Matter Out of Place: Reading Dirty Women," *M/C Journal* 9, no. 5 (November 2006).

50. Wical, "Matter Out of Place."

51. Mahdavi and Sargent, "Questioning the Discursive Construction," 21.

52. Jeffrey Tayler, "Femen's Inna Shevchenko: Fear of Causing Offense Has Cost Too Many Innocent Lives," *Quillette*, December 30, 2017.

53. Tayler, "Femen's Inna Shevchenko."

54. Elizabeth Day, "Can Abaya Become a Style Choice?," *Gulf News*, November 1, 2013.

55. Feyza Gumusluoglu, "Women in White: The Changing Abaya Fashion in Qatar," Arab Gulf States Institute in Washington, January 17, 2017.

56. Gumusluoglu, "Women in White."

57. Gumusluoglu, "Women in White."

58. Edward Said, *Orientalism* (London: Routledge, 1978), 3.

59. GPCC, "Msheireb Properties' Initiative Promotes Community Spirit," *Gulf Times*, December 14, 2016.

60. Qatar Foundation, "Qatar Marks International Workers' Day with Conference on Labour Rights Protection, Ending Kafala," April 27, 2016.

61. Peter Kovessy, "Strike Temporarily Halts Work on Part of Qatar's Msheireb Project," *Doha News*, November 24, 2015.

62. Buhrhan Wazir, "Mysterious Shutdown Plagues Popular News Site in Qatar," *Columbia Journalism Review*, December 9, 2016.

63. Kovessy, "Strike Temporarily Halts Work."

64. Kovessy, "Strike Temporarily Halts Work."

65. Kovessy, "Strike Temporarily Halts Work."

66. Victoria Baux, "Doha Facelift Dumps Migrant Workers on the Streets," *AFP News*, July 17, 2014.

67. Baux, "Doha Facelift Dumps Migrant Workers."

68. Baux, "Doha Facelift Dumps Migrant Workers."

69. Baux, "Doha Facelift Dumps Migrant Workers."

70. Mariam Ibrahim Al-Mulla, "History of Slaves in Qatar: Social Reality and Contemporary Political Vision," *Journal of History Culture and Art Research* 6, no. 4 (2017): 85–111.

71. Christenson, "For the Game."

72. Christenson, "For the Game," 100.

CHAPTER 5. LET COME THE WHORE ASSEMBLAGE

1. André Singer, "Brasil, junho de 2013, Classes e ideologias cruzadas," *Novos Estudos—CEBRAP* 97 (November 2013): 23–40.

2. Leonardo Avritzer, "Participation in Democratic Brazil: From Popular Hegemony and Innovation to Middle-Class Protest," *Opinão Pública* 23, no. 1 (2017): 43–59.

3. Maurice Blanchot and Susan Hanson, "Everyday Speech," *Yale French Studies* 73 (1987): 14–15.

4. Blanchot and Hanson, "Everyday Speech,"15.

5. BBC News, "Brazil Protests Spread in São Paulo, Brasilia, and Rio," June 18, 2013.

6. Donna Bowater, "Whatever Happened to Brazil's World Cup Protests?," *Al Jazeera America*, July 10, 2014.

7. Irina Maslova, "NGO Delegation to the United Nations Programme Coordinating Board," Facebook, June 30, 2016.

8. Global Fund for Women, "Defend Her: Irina Maslova," 2016.

9. Global Fund for Women, "Defend Her."

10. Amnesty International, "Irina Maslova, Saint Petersburg," June 8, 2018.

11. Will Stewart, "New Gulags? Russia 'Cleanses World Cup 2018 Cities of Homeless People' by 'Forcefully Bussing Them to Special Camps,'" *Sun*, June 8, 2018.

12. Amnesty International, "Irina Maslova, Saint Petersburg."

13. Amnesty International, "Irina Maslova, Saint Petersburg."

14. Amnesty International, "Irina Maslova, Saint Petersburg."

15. Alexander Kondakov, "Spatial Justice: How the Police Craft the City by Enforcing Law on Prostitution," in *Understanding Sex for Sale: Meanings and Moralities of Sexual Commerce*, ed. May-Len Skilbrei and Marlene Spanger (New York: Routledge, 2019), 210.

16. Kondakov, "Spatial Justice."

17. Cavan Sieczkowski, "Russian Neo-Nazis Allegedly Lure, Torture Gay Teens with Online Dating Scam," *Huffington Post*, July 26, 2013.

18. Masha Gessen, "We Now Know More about the Apparent Poisoning of the Pussy Riot Member Pyotr Verzilov," *New Yorker*, September 19, 2018.

19. Suyin Haynes, "'It's Not Putin's Russia—It's Our Russia': Pussy Riot Members on Protests, Poisonings and Politics," *Time Magazine*, November 2, 2018.

20. Haynes, "'It's Not Putin's Russia."

21. Sonia Corrêa, "Dialoguing with the (Im)Possibilities of Unruly Politics," in *The Changing Faces of Citizen Action: A Mapping Study through an 'Unruly' Lens*, ed. Akshay Khanna et al. (n.p.: International Development Institute, 2013), 44.

22. Roberta Pennafort, "Glittervandalismo do Pink Bloc toma as ruas do Rio," *Estadão*, October 14, 2013.

23. Corrêa, "Dialoguing with the (Im)Possibilities of Unruly Politics," 44.

24. Akshay Khanna et al., *The Changing Faces of Citizen Action: A Mapping Study through an "Unruly" Lens. International Development Institute* (n.p.: International Development Institute, 2013), 3.

25. Khanna et al., *Changing Faces of Citizen Action*, 11.

26. Lucy MacMahon, "The Right to (Sell in) the City: Street Vending and Protest in Rio de Janeiro and Recife" (presented at the "Bread, Freedom and Social Justice": Organised Workers and Mass Mobilizations in the Arab World, Europe and Latin America conference, Cambridge University, July 10, 2014).

27. MacMahon, "The Right to (Sell in) the City," 2.

28. MacMahon, "The Right to (Sell in) the City," 2.

29. MacMahon, "The Right to (Sell in) the City," 2.

30. MacMahon, "The Right to (Sell in) the City," 48.

31. Paul Amar, *The Security Archipelago: Human-Security States, Sexuality Politics, and the End of Neoliberalism* (Durham, NC: Duke University Press, 2013).

32. Amar, *Security Archipelago*, 18.

33. James Masters, "World Cup 2014: Can the FBI Help Stop Brazil's World Cup Protesters?," *CNN*, May 13, 2014, 8.

34. Nathan B. Thompson, "Brazil's Digital Protests Spell Trouble on the Street," openDemocracy, January 28, 2016.

35. Laura Murray, "Not Fooling Around: The Politics of Sex Worker Activisim in Brazil" (PhD thesis, Columbia University, 2015), 11.

36. Murray, "Not Fooling Around," 11.

37. Murray, "Not Fooling Around," 12.

38. Murray, "Not Fooling Around," 17–18.

39. Melissa Gira Grant, *Playing the Whore: The Work of Sex Work* (New York: Verso, 2014), 126.

40. Grant, *Playing the Whore*, 127.

41. Laura Murray, dir., *A Kiss for Gabriela* (Rattapallax, 2020).

42. Murray, *Kiss for Gabriela*.

43. Murray, *Kiss for Gabriela*.

44. Eduardo Kohn, *How Forests Think: Toward an Anthropology Beyond the Human* (Berkeley: University of California Press, 2013).

45. Gilles Deleuze and Félix Guattari, *A Thousand Plateaus* (Minneapolis: University of Minnesota Press, 1993).

46. Hilan Bensusan and Fabiane Borges, "Praia de Xangri-Lá: Puta Ontológica," *Le Monde Diplomatique*, January 9, 2009.

47. Laura Murray, Deanna Kerrigan, and Vera Silvia Paiva, "Rites of Resistance: Sex Workers' Fight to Maintain Rights and Pleasure in the Centre of the Response to HIV in Brazil," *Global Public Health* 14, no. 6–7 (2019): 939–53.

48. Murray, Kerrigan, and Paiva, "Rites of Resistance."

49. Grant, *Playing the Whore*, 127–28.

50. Grant, *Playing the Whore*, 128.

51. Jasbir Puar, *Terrorist Assemblages: Homonationalism in Queer Times* (Durham, NC: Duke University Press, 2007).

52. Sara Farris, *In the Name of Women's Rights: The Rise of Femonationalism* (Durham, NC: Duke University Press, 2017).

53. Farris, *In the Name of Women's Rights*, 4.

54. Farris, *In the Name of Women's Rights*, 6.

55. Farris, *In the Name of Women's Rights*, 27.

56. Michel Foucault, "Governmentality," in *The Foucault Effect: Studies in Governmentality with Two Lectures by and an Interview with Michel Foucault*, ed. Graham Burchell, Colin Gordon, and Peter Miller (Chicago: University of Chicago Press, 1991).

57. Jasbir Puar, *Homonationalism Gone Viral: Discipline, Control, and the Affective Politics of Sensation* (Portland Center for Public Humanities, May 21, 2012).

58. Jasbir Puar, Ben Pitcher, and Gunkel, "Q & A with Jasbir Puar," *Darkmatter*, May 2, 2008.

59. Puar, Pitcher, and Gunkel, "Q & A with Jasbir Puar."

60. Puar, Pitcher, and Gunkel, "Q & A with Jasbir Puar."

61. Puar, Pitcher, and Gunkel, "Q & A with Jasbir Puar."

62. Deleuze and Guattari, *Thousand Plateaus*.

63. Christen A. Smith, *Afro-Paradise: Blackness, Violence, and Performance in Brazil* (Urbana: University of Illinois Press, 2016), 17.

64. Smith, *Afro-Paradise*, 18.

65. Smith, *Afro-Paradise*, 87.

66. Smith, *Afro-Paradise*.

67. For an excellent and fairly accessible overview of assemblage theory, see Dan Little, "Assemblage Theory," *Understanding Society* (blog), November 15, 2012.

68. Amanda De Lisio, Philip Hubbard, and Michael Silk, "Economies of (Alleged) Deviance: Sex Work and the Sport Mega-Event," *Sexuality Research and Social Policy* 16, no. 2 (2018): 179.

69. Amanda De Lisio and João Gabriel Rabello Sodré, "FIFA/IOC-Sanctioned Development and the Imminence of Erotic Space," *Journal of Latin American Research* 38, no. 3 (2018): 1.

70. Marie-Eve Carrier-Moisan, "'A Red Card against Sex Tourism': Sex Panics Public Emotions, and the 2014 World Cup in Brazil," *Feminist Formations* 31, no. 2 (2019): 126.

71. Adriana Piscitelli, "Transnational Sisterhood? Brazilian Feminisms Facing Prostitution," *Latin American Policy* 5, no. 2 (2014): 221.

Bibliography

Adams, David, and Josie Swantek, dirs. *The Wrong Light*. Shine Global, 2017.

Agustín, Laura María. "Becoming Aware of Awareness-Raising as Anti-Trafficking Tactic." *Naked Anthropologist* (blog), July 1, 2015. www.laura agustin.com/becoming-aware-of-awareness-raising-as-anti-trafficking-tactic.

———. "Getting Money to Prevent Sex Trafficking Even If There Isn't Any: London Olympics." *Naked Anthropologist* (blog), October 5, 2012. www .lauraagustin.com/getting-money-to-prevent-sex-trafficking-even-if-there -isnt-any-london-olympics.

———. *Sex at the Margins: Migration, Labour Markets and the Rescue Industry*. New York: Palgrave, 2007.

———. "TIP: Trafficking in Persons, the No-Methodology Report." *Naked Anthropologist* (blog), June 26, 2009. www.lauraagustin.com/tip-trafficking -in-persons-the-no-methodology-report.

———. "Well-Meaning Interference." *Philadelphia Inquirer*, July 1, 2007. www .inquirer.com/philly/opinion/20070701_Well-meaning_interference.html.

Ajam, Kashiefa. "Trafficking of People, the Cup Crisis That Never Was." *IOL News*, July 17, 2010. www.iol.co.za/news/south-africa/trafficking-of-people -the-cup-crisis-that-never-was-490109#.UVDCD1sjr-A.

Alexander, M. Jacqui. *Pedagogies of Crossing: Meditations on Feminism, Sexual Politics, Memory, and the Sacred*. Durham, NC: Duke University Press, 2005.

Amar, Paul. *The Security Archipelago: Human-Security States, Sexuality Politics, and the End of Neoliberalism*. Durham. NC: Duke University Press, 2013.

Amnesty International. "Irina Maslova, Saint Petersburg," June 8, 2018. www
.amnesty.org/en/latest/news/2018/06/irina-maslova-human-rights-defender
-in-russia/.

———. "Q & A: Policy to Protect the Human Rights of Sex Workers." May 26,
2016. www.amnesty.org/en/qa-policy-to-protect-the-human-rights-of-sex
-workers/.

Anderson, Nick. "In Qatar's Education City, US Colleges Are Building an Academic Oasis." *Washington Post*, December 6, 2015. www.washingtonpost
.com/local/education/in-qatars-education-city-us-colleges-are-building-an
-academic-oasis/2015/12/06/6b538702-8e01-11e5-ae1f-af46b7df8483
_story.html.

"Anti-Trafficking Group 'Saved in America' Losing Support." NBC San Diego,
October 25, 2019. www.nbcsandiego.com/news/local/anti-trafficking
-organization-saved-in-america-losing-key-support/2035414/.

Aragão, Jarbas. "Missionários fazem protesto acorrentados em frente a
hotel." *CPAD News: Gospel Prime*, June 16, 2014. https://cpadnews.com
.br/universo-cristao/22604/missionarios-fazem-protesto-acorrentados-em
-frente-a-hotel.html.

Armstrong, Jeremy. "England Fans Warned over Fake Russian Bride Scams at
the FIFA World Cup." *Mirror*, January 9, 2018. www.mirror.co.uk/news/uk
-news/england-fans-warned-over-fake-11824593.

Armstrong, Jeremy, and Andy Lines. "Brazilian Women Turning to Prostitution for World Cup—and England Fans Are Their Biggest Goal." *Mirror*, June 12, 2014. www.mirror.co.uk/news/world-news/brazilian-women
-turning-prostitution-world-3677902.

Armstrong, Lynzi. "Decriminalising Sex Work Is the Only Way to Protect
Women—and New Zealand Has Proved That It Works." *Independent*,
May 29, 2017. www.independent.co.uk/voices/sex-workers-decriminal
isation-of-prostitution-new-zealand-new-law-works-research-proves-sex
-workers-safer-justice-a7761426.html.

Asia Pacific Regional Correspondent. "Swedish NGO under Investigation for
Creating Fake 'Rescue' Stories to Solicit Donations." NSWP: Global Network of Sex Work Projects. August 28, 2017. www.nswp.org/news/swedish
-ngo-under-investigation-creating-fake-rescue-stories-solicit-donations.

Avritzer, Leonardo. "Participation in Democratic Brazil: From Popular Hegemony and Innovation to Middle-Class Protest." *Opinão Pública* 23, no. 1
(2017): 43–59.

Bahr, Jeff. "State Fair, Eclipse May Bring in Sex Trafficking." *Grand Island
Independent*, June 14, 2017. www.theindependent.com/news/local/state
-fair-eclipse-may-bring-in-sex-trafficking/article_c17a7aa6-53cf-11e7-b867
-a339162ee295.html.

Baux, Victoria. "Doha Facelift Dumps Migrant Workers on the Streets."
AFP News, July 17, 2014. www.yahoo.com/news/doha-facelift-dumps
-migrant-workers-streets-104746520.html?guccounter=1&guce_referrer=
aHR0cHM6Ly93d3cuZ29vZ2xlLmNvbS8&guce_referrer_sig=AQAAAJtK08
N8094ULp9VLyC8ImR5DUa6FRRtmoOg3suyS575OaWyAmmhupVjnQvcu

__jeqfDaus4RmoeveYNBHO_rWXg2rsotqYzP3y7hSuKeAzJ8kLQBw-SS4 ZPKgG3Ar7coMy9jKfw2CsxM3U2BdDDTJmCup9MRmv5i7nASCNGk4SR.

Bazelon, Emily. "Should Prostitution Be a Crime?" *New York Times Magazine*, May 5, 2016. www.nytimes.com/2016/05/08/magazine/should-prostitution -be-a-crime.html.

BBC News. "Anger in Brazil as 10-Year-Old Rape Victim's Name Put On-Line." August 18, 2020. www.bbc.com/news/world-latin-america-53820497.

———. "Brazil Protests Spread in São Paulo, Brasilia, and Rio." June 18, 2013. www.bbc.com/news/world-latin-america-22946736.

BBC News Brasil. "Quem é Sara Winter, a ex-feminista e atual militante radical bolsonarista presa pela PF a mando do STF." June 15, 2020. www.bbc.com /portuguese/brasil-53053329?SThisFB&fbclid=IwAR3WwwcKWdIBDo MCMa-2ra1LaDfXzIuhWzx4PGlTKba9pP_vf63tkjqEPHw.

Bell, Ernest. *Fighting the Traffic in Young Girls; or, the War on the White Slave Trade.* n.p.: publisher unknown, 1910.

Benevides, Carolina, Renato Onofre, Anselmo Carvalho Pinto, and Thays Lavor. "Aliciadores já atuam em cidades da Copa do Mundo." *O Globo*, April 27, 2014. http://oglobo.globo.com/brasil/aliciadores-ja-atuam-em-cidades-da -copa-do-mundo-12310760#ixzz3dik5oJDN.

Bensusan, Hilan, and Fabiane Borges. "Praia de Xangri-Lá: Puta Ontológica." *Le Monde Diplomatique*, January 9, 2009. http://praiadexangrila.com.br /2009/01/page/25/.

Berlatsky, Noah. "Hollywood's Dangerous Obsession with Sex Trafficking." *Salon*, June 10, 2014. www.salon.com/2014/06/10/hollywoods_dangerous _obsession_with_sex_trafficking/.

———. "The Lies about Sex Trafficking That Brought down Backpage." *Salon*, April 15, 2018. www.salon.com/2018/04/15/the-lies-about-sex-trafficking -that-brought-down-backpage/.

Bernstein, Elizabeth. *Brokered Subjects: Sex, Trafficking & the Politics of Freedom.* Chicago: University of Chicago Press, 2018.

———. "Militarized Humanitarianism Meets Carceral Feminism: The Politics of Sex, Rights, and Freedom in Contemporary Antitrafficking Campaigns." *Signs: Journal of Women in Culture and Society* 36, no. 1 (2010): 45–71.

———. *Temporarily Yours: Intimacy, Authenticity, and the Commerce of Sex.* Chicago: University of Chicago Press, 2007.

Bernstein, Elizabeth, and Elena Shih. "Travels of Trafficking." In *Brokered Subjects: Sex, Trafficking, and the Politics of Freedom*, 98–127. Chicago: University of Chicago Press, 2018.

Beutin, Lyndsey. "Black Suffering for/from Anti-Trafficking Advocacy." *Anti-Trafficking Review* 9, no. 1 (2017): 14–30.

Bialik, Carl. "Suspect Estimates of Sex Trafficking at the World Cup." *Wall Street Journal*, June 19, 2010. http://on.wsj.com/8YsG25.

Bijan, Stephen. "In Praise of the Flâneur." *Paris Review*, October 17, 2013. www.theparisreview.org/blog/2013/10/17/in-praise-of-the-flaneur/.

Bindel, Julie. *The Pimping of Prostitution: Abolishing the Sex Work Myth.* London: Palgrave, 2019.

Blackler, Shannon. "Sex Trafficking Made Easier, Thanks to the World Cup in Russia." *New York Minute*, July 12, 2018. www.newyorkminutemag.com /sex-trafficking-made-easier-thanks-to-the-world-cup-in-russia/.

Blanchette, Thaddeus. "'Almost a Brazilian': Gringos, Immigration and Irregularity in Brazil." In *In Global Migration: Old Assumptions, New Dynamics*, edited by D. A. Acarazo and A. Weisbrock, 167–94. Santa Barbara, CA: Praeger, 2015.

———. "'Fariseus' e 'gringos bons': Masculinidade e turismo sexual em copacabana." In *Gênero, sexo, afetos e dinheiro: Mobilidades transnacionais envolvendo o Brasil*, 57–103. Campinas, Brazil: EDUNICAMP/PAGU, 2011.

Blanchette, Thaddeus, and Ana Paula da Silva. "A mistura clássica: Misegenação e o apelo do Rio de Janeiro como destino para o turismo sexual." *Bagoas: Revista de estudos gays* 4 (2010): 221–44.

———. "Men in Brothels: (Homo) Sexuality in Rio de Janeiro Commercial Sexual Venues." In *Routledge Handbook of Sex Industry Research*, edited by Susan Dewey, Chimaraoke Izugbara, and Isabel Crowhurst, 331–41. London: Routledge, 2019.

Blanchot, Maurice, and Susan Hanson. "Everyday Speech." *Yale French Studies* 73 (1987): 12–20.

Blue, Violet. "Sex, Lies, and Surveillance: Something's Wrong with the War on Sex Trafficking." Engadget, May 31, 2019. www.engadget.com/2019-05-31 -sex-lies-and-surveillance-fosta-privacy.html.

Boff, Andrew. *Silence on Violence: Improving the Safety of Women: The Policing of Off-Street Sex Work and Sex Trafficking in London*. March 2012. https://maggiemcneill.files.wordpress.com/2012/04/silence-on-violence.pdf.

Borges, Waleska. "Três pessoas são presas na zona sul acusadas de incentivar a prostituição." *O Globo*, June 15, 2012. http://oglobo.globo.com /rio/tres-pessoas-sao-presas-na-zona-sul-acusadas-de-incentivar-prostituicao -5213176.

Bowater, Donna. "Whatever Happened to Brazil's World Cup Protests?" *Al Jazeera America*, July 10, 2014. http://america.aljazeera.com/articles/2014/7 /10/brazil-protests-worldcup.html.

Boykoff, Jules. *Celebration Capitalism and the Olympic Games*. London: Taylor and Francis, 2013.

Brennan, Denise. *Life Interrupted: Trafficking into Forced Labor in the United States*. Durham. NC: Duke University Press, 2014.

———. *What's Love Got to Do with It? Transnational Desires and Sex Tourism in the Dominican Republic*. Durham, NC: Duke University Press, 2004.

Brown, Elizabeth Nolan. "The Biggest Sex-Trafficking Bust in FBI History Was Totally Bogus." *Reason*, March 4, 2016. https://reason.com/2016/03/04/the -somali-sex-slave-ring-that-wasnt/.

———. "NYC Councilman Completely Fabricates Child Sex-Trafficking Ring." *Reason*, July 6, 2016. https://reason.com/2016/07/06/child-sextrafficking -fear-in-bronx-bogus/.

Brown, Matthew. "Fact Check: Mask-Wearing Not Connected to Child Trafficking." *USA Today*, August 11, 2020. www.usatoday.com/story/news/factcheck

/2020/08/11/fact-check-mask-wearing-not-connected-child-trafficking/331 8642001/.

Brownmiller, Susan. *Against Our Will: Men, Women, and Rape.* New York: Simon and Schuster, 1975.

Callahan, Maureen. "Eat, Pray, Loathe." *New York Post*, December 23, 2007. https://nypost.com/2007/12/23/eat-pray-loathe/.

Campbell, Colin. *The Romantic Ethic and the Spirit of Modern Consumerism.* 3rd ed. London: Alcuin Academics, 2005.

Campbell, Courtney, dir. *Don't Shout Too Loud.* Changing Directions Films, 2011.

Campoy, Ana. "The Rio Olympics Organizers Are Giving out Enough Condoms for Each Athlete to Have Sex 84 Times." Quartz, June 14, 2017. https://qz.com/689356/the-rio-olympics-organizers-are-giving-out-enough -condoms-for-each-athlete-to-have-sex-84-times/.

Cardarello, Andréa. "The Movement of the Mothers of the Courthouse Square: 'Legal Child Trafficking,' Adoption and Poverty in Brazil." *Journal of Latin American and Caribbean Anthropology* 14, no. 1 (2009): 140–61.

Carmon, Irin. "Nick Kristof to the Rescue!" *Salon*, November 8, 2011. www .salon.com/2011/11/08/nick_kristof_to_the_rescue/.

Carrier-Moisan, Marie-Eve. "'A Red Card against Sex Tourism:' Sex Panics Public Emotions, and the 2014 World Cup in Brazil." *Feminist Formations* 31, no. 2 (2019): 125–54.

"CATW Responds: Amnesty International Turned Its Back on Women." Coalition Against Trafficking in Women. August 11, 2015. https://catwinter national.org/press/amnesty-international-turned-its-back-on-women/.

Chermayeff, Maro. *Half the Sky.* PBS Independent Lens, 2012.

Cherner, Reid. "A Billion Condoms May Not Be Enough." *USA Today*, June 15, 2010. http://content.usatoday.com/communities/gameon/post/2010 /06/world-cup-a-billion-condoms-may-not-be-enough/1#.YjH9t3rMKM9.

Chew, Lin. "Reflections by an Anti-Trafficking Activist." In *Trafficking and Prostitution Reconsidered: New Perspectives on Migration, Sex Work, and Human Rights*, 2nd ed., edited by Kamala Kempadoo, 65–82. Philadelphia: Taylor and Francis, 2017.

Chin, Ko-Lin, and James O. Finckenauer. "Chickenheads, Agents, Mommies, and Jockeys: The Social Organization of Transnational Commercial Sex." *Crime, Law and Social Change* 56 (2011): 463–84.

Chouliaraki, Lilie. *The Ironic Spectator: Solidarity in the Age of Post-Humanitarianism.* Cambridge, UK: Polity Press, 2013.

Christenson, Haley. "For the Game. For the World. But What about for the Workers? Evaluating FIFA's Human Rights Policy in Relation to International Standards." *San Diego International Law Journal* 20, no. 1 (2018): 93–126.

Chuang, Janie A. "Exploitation Creep and the Unmaking of Human Trafficking Law." *The American Journal of International Law* 108, no. 4 (2014): 609–49.

———. "Rescuing Trafficking from Ideological Capture: Prostitution Reform and Anti-Trafficking Law and Policy." *University of Pennsylvania Law Review* 158 (2010): 1–74.

Cohen, Stanley. *Folk Devils and Moral Panics*. New York: Routledge, 2011.

Cojocaru, Claudia. "Sex Trafficking, Captivity, and Narrative: Constructing Victimhood with the Goal of Salvation." *Dialectical Anthropology* 39 (2015): 183–94.

Conger, Kate. "Uber Says 3,045 Sexual Assaults Were Reported in US Rides Last Year." *New York Times*, December 5, 2019. www.nytimes.com/2019/12/05/technology/uber-sexual-assaults-murders-deaths-safety.html.

Conklin, Elise, Martin Cizmar, and Kristen Hinman. "Real Men Get Their Facts Straight." *Village Voice*, June 29, 2011. www.villagevoice.com/2011/06/29/real-men-get-their-facts-straight/.

Connelly, Mark Thomas. *The Response to Prostitution in the Progressive Era*. Chapel Hill: University of North Carolina Press, 2018.

Cooper, Kate, and Sue Branford. *Exploitation and Trafficking of Women: Critiquing Narratives during the London Olympics 2012*. Central America Women's Network, 2013.

Cornwall, Andrea, Sonia Corrêa, and Susie Jolly. *Development with a Body: Sexuality, Human Rights, and Development*. London: Zed Books, 2008.

Corrêa, Sonia. "Dialoguing with the (Im)Possibilities of Unruly Politics." In *The Changing Faces of Citizen Action: A Mapping Study through an "Unruly" Lens*, edited by Akshay Khanna, Priyashri Mani, Zachary Patterson, Maro Pantazidou, and Maysa Shqerat, 44–50. N.p.: International Development Institute, 2013. www.sxpolitics.org/wp-content/uploads/2013/06/ids-working-paper-on-unruly-politics.pdf.

Corrêa, Sonia, and José Miguel Nieto Olivar. "The Politics of Prostitution in Brazil: Between 'State Neutrality' and 'Feminist Troubles.'" In *The Global HIV Epidemics among Sex Workers*, edited by Deanna Kerrigan, Andrea Wirtz, N'Della N'jie, Stefan Baral, Anderson Stanciole, Jenny Butler, Robert Oelrichs, and Chris Beyer, 101–26. Washington, DC: World Bank Publications, 2012.

Crossroads Church. "India: Mumbai/November." Accessed February 22, 2020. www.crossroads.net/reachout/go/india/november-mumbai-2020/.

Cruz, Ariane. *The Color of Kink: Black Women, BDSM, and Pornography*. New York: NYU Press, 2016.

Daniels, Dustin. "The Real Victims of Pornography," interview with Laura Lederer, December 6, 2017. *God, Sex & You!* (podcast), episode 237. www.podomatic.com/podcasts/dustindaniels/episodes/2017-12-06T01_00_00-08_00.

Davis, Edward. "Anne Hathaway on Channeling Her Tears, Emotions & Cutting Her Hair for Harrowing 'Les Misérables' Scene." *Indie Wire*, December 26, 2012. www.indiewire.com/2012/12/anne-hathaway-on-channeling-her-tears-emotions-cutting-her-hair-for-harrowing-les-miserables-scene-249973/.

Day, Elizabeth. "Can Abaya Become a Style Choice?" *Gulf News*, November 1, 2013.

De Lisio, Amanda, Philip Hubbard, and Michael Silk. "Economies of (Alleged) Deviance: Sex Work and the Sport Mega-Event." *Sexuality Research and Social Policy* 16, no. 2 (2018): 179–89.

De Lisio, Amanda, and João Gabriel Rabello Sodré. "FIFA/IOC-Sanctioned Development and the Imminence of Erotic Space." *Journal of Latin American Research* 38, no. 3 (2018): 1–14.

de Vries, Alexandra, and Shawn Blore. *Frommer's Brazil*. Hoboken, NJ: John Wiley & Sons, 2012).

Dean, Laura. "A Stage for Human Trafficking: The World Cup in Russia." *The Russia File: A Blog of the Keenan Institute* (blog), June 18, 2018. www.wilsoncenter.org/blog-post/stage-for-human-trafficking-the-world-cup-russia.

Debord, Guy. *Society of the Spectacle*. New York: Zone Books, 1995.

Deleuze, Gilles, and Félix Guattari. *A Thousand Plateaus*. Minneapolis: University of Minnesota Press, 1993.

Destiny Rescue. "Destiny Rescue: Rescuing Children." Short Term Trips. Accessed February 22, 2020 (no longer accessible). www.destinyrescue.org/us/get-involved/teams/short-term-trips/.

Dickson, Caitlin. "Ashton Kutcher Calls Out Village Voice for Sex Trafficking Charges." *Atlantic*, June 30, 2011. www.theatlantic.com/culture/archive/2011/06/village-voice/352374/.

Dines, Gail. *Pornland: How Porn Has Hijacked Our Sexuality*. Boston: Beacon Press, 2010.

Doezema, Jo. "Ouch! Western Feminists' 'Wounded Attachment' to the 'Third World Prostitute.'" *Feminist Review* 67, no. 1 (2001): 16–38.

———. *Sex Slaves and Discourse Masters: The Construction of Trafficking*. London: Zed Books, 2010.

Donelli, Eva. "'Don't Look Away' from Sexual Exploitation of Minors in Brazil." *Devex*, June 13, 2014, 2. www.devex.com/news/eu-don-t-look-away-from-sexual-exploitation-of-minors-in-brazil-83684.

Donor Direct Action. "Meryl Streep Speaks in Support of Sex Trade Survivors." Sisterhood Is Global Institute. July 11, 2016. https://donordirectaction.org/2016/07/meryl-streep-speaks-support-sex-trade-survivors/.

Donovan, Brian. *White Slave Crusades: Race, Gender & Anti-Vice Activism, 1887–1917*. Champaign: University of Illinois Press, 2010.

Douglas, Mary. *Purity and Danger: An Analysis of the Concepts of Pollution and Taboo*. London: Ark Paperbacks, 1966.

Downs, Donald. "The Attorney General's Commission and the New Politics of Pornography." *American Bar Foundation Research Journal* 12, no. 4 ([1987]): 639–79.

Duggan, Lisa, and Nan Hunter. *Sex Wars: Sexual Dissent and Political Culture*. New York: Routledge, 2006.

Durkheim, Émile. "As Regras Do Método Sociológico." In *Os Pensadores: Durkheim*, edited by José Giannotti, 355–84. São Paulo: Abril Cultural, 1978.

Dworkin, Andrea. *Pornography: Men Possessing Women*. New York: Plume, 1989.

ECPAT USA. "Gift Box." Accessed April 3, 2020. https://www.ecpatusa.org/giftbox.

Edwards, Breeana. "Asian Woman Says Federal Agents Harassed Her after Mistaking Her for Human Trafficking Victim." *Root*, November 28, 2017.

www.theroot.com/asian-woman-says-federal-agents-harassed-her-after-mist
-1820806591.

Elliott, Dorinda. "Somaly Mam and Susan Sarandon Give Shelter to Former Sex Slaves." *Condé Nast Traveler*, August 20, 2012. www.cntraveler.com /stories/2012-08-20/somaly-mam-susan-sarandon.

End It Movement. Home page. Accessed April 3, 2020. https://enditmovement .com/.

Everett, Rupert. "Rupert Everett in Defence of Prostitutes: 'There Is a Land Grab Going On.'" *Guardian*, June 14, 2017. www.theguardian.com/film /2014/jan/19/rupert-everett-in-defence-of-prostitutes.

Exodus Cry. "All Eyes on Brazil." Accessed March 23, 2013. http://exoduscry .com/blog/all-eyes-on-brazil/.

———. "Exodus Cry Facebook." Accessed March 21, 2022. www.facebook .com/exoduscry/.

———. "Exodus Cry: Liberdade." Accessed August 23, 2018. http://exoduscry .com/liberdade.

———. "Exodus Cry Receives a Flood of Support after Melissa McCarthy Cancels Donation," November 18, 2020. https://exoduscry.com/blog/shifting culture/exodus-cry-receives-a-flood-of-support-after-melissa-mccarthy -cancels-donation/.

———. "Myths vs. Truths about Exodus Cry." August 20, 2020. https:// exoduscry.com/blog/general/myths-vs-truths-about-exodus-cry/.

Farris, Sara. *In the Name of Women's Rights: The Rise of Femonationalism.* Durham, NC: Duke University Press, 2017.

Fedorkó, Boglárka. "'Send Them Back': Migrant Sex Workers Deported from Europe." Open Democracy. August 19, 2019. www.opendemocracy.net /en/beyond-trafficking-and-slavery/send-them-back-migrant-sex-workers -deported-from-europe/.

Femen. "Femen: About Us." Accessed April 3, 2020. https://femen.org/about-us/.

Flores, Theresa. "SOAP Project." Accessed April 3, 2020. https://www.soap project.org/.

"For Stanton, All Women Were Not Created Equal." Interview. *NPR's Morning Edition*, July 13, 2011. www.npr.org/2011/07/13/137681070/for-stanton -all-women-were-not-created-equal.

Forrest, Stuart. *Down, Out, and Under Arrest: Policing and Everyday Life in Skid Row.* Chicago: University of Chicago Press, 2016.

Foucault, Michel. *Archaeology of Knowledge and the Discourse of Language.* London: Routledge, 2002.

———. "Governmentality." In *The Foucault Effect: Studies in Governmentality with Two Lectures by and an Interview with Michel Foucault*, edited by Graham Burchell, Colin Gordon, and Peter Miller, 87–104. Chicago: University of Chicago Press, 1991.

Fox, Drew. "How Radical Anti-Porn Zealots Became the Media's Sexploitation 'Experts.'" XBIZ: The Industry Source. November 26, 2019. https://www .xbiz.com/news/248603/how-radical-anti-porn-zealots-became-the-medias -sexploitation-experts.

Fox, MeiMei. "How Thorn Is Fighting to Eliminate Child Sexual Abuse from the Internet." *Forbes*, August 14, 2019. www.forbes.com/sites/meimeifox /2019/08/14/how-thorn-is-fighting-to-eliminate-child-sexual-abuse-from -the-internet/#39b13d3e2495.

Freedom House. "Freedom of the Press: Qatar." 2015. https://freedomhouse .org/country/qatar/freedom-world/2022.

Freire-Medeiros, Bianca. *Touring Poverty*. New York: Routledge, 2014.

Frenzel, Fabian. *Slumming It: The Valorization of Urban Poverty*. London: Zed Books, 2016.

Gaffney, Christopher. *Temples of the Earthbound Gods: Stadiums in the Cultural Landscapes of Rio de Janeiro and Buenos Aires*. Austin: University of Texas Press, 2008.

Galusca, Roxana. "Slave Hunters, Brothel Busters, and Feminist Interventions: Investigative Journalists as Anti-Sex Trafficking Humanitarians." *Feminist Formations* 24, no. 2 (2012): 1–24.

Ganji, Sarath K. "Leveraging the World Cup: Mega Sporting Events, Human Rights Risk, and Worker Welfare Reform in Qatar." *Journal on Migration and Human Security* 4, no. 4 (2016): 221–59.

Gessen, Masha. "We Now Know More about the Apparent Poisoning of the Pussy Riot Member Pyotr Verzilov." *New Yorker*, September 19, 2018. www.newyorker.com/news/our-columnists/we-now-know-more-about-the -apparent-poisoning-of-the-pussy-riot-member-pyotr-verzilov.

Glass, Ira. "Save the Girl." *This American Life*, July 12, 2019. www.this americanlife.org/679/save-the-girl.

Glatz, Carol. "Tourists Must Blow Whistle on Trafficking during Olympics, Religious Say," *[Boston] Pilot*, June 14, 2017. www.thebostonpilot.com /article.asp?ID=176778.

Global Fund for Women. "Defend Her: Irina Maslova." 2016. www.global fundforwomen.org/irina-maslova/.

Global News. "Ashton Kutcher Testifies before U.S. Congress on Ending Modern Slavery." February 15, 2017. www.youtube.com/watch?v=ZTT-_tbZf10.

Goldberg, Eleanor. "Children Sold for Sex at World Cup for Few Dollars, Pack of Cigarettes." *Huffington Post*, June 12, 2014. www.huffingtonpost.com /2014/06/12/world-cup-child-prostitution_n_5474716.html.

Goldstein, Donna. *Laughter Out of Place: Race, Class, Violence, and Sexuality in a Rio Shantytown*. 2nd ed. Berkeley: University of California Press, 2013.

Goode, Erich, and Nachman Ben-Yehuda. *Moral Panics: The Social Construction of Deviance*. 2nd ed. Malden, MA: Wiley-Blackwell, 2009.

Gospel for Asia. "Thousands of Girls in Asia Saved from Possible 'Fate Worse Than Death.'" Standard Newswire, October 1, 2019. www.christiannews wire.com/news/5076283058.html.

Gould, Chandre. "Moral Panic, Human Trafficking and the 2010 Soccer World Cup." *Agenda: Empowering Women for Gender Equity* 85 (2010): 31–44.

GPCC. "Msheireb Properties' Initiative Promotes Community Spirit." *Gulf Times*, December 14, 2016. www.gulf-times.com/story/524658/Msheireb -Properties-initiative-promotes-community-spirit.

Grace, Tonya S. "Ahead of Eclipse, Warnings about Potential Human Trafficking." *Washington Times*, July 9, 2017. https://m.washingtontimes.com/news /2017/jul/9/ahead-of-eclipse-warnings-about-potential-human-tr/.

Grant, Melissa Gira. "Nick Kristof and the Holy War on Pornhub." *New Republic*, December 10, 2020. https://newrepublic.com/article/160488/nick -kristof-holy-war-pornhub.

———. *Playing the Whore: The Work of Sex Work*. New York: Verso, 2014.

———. "Sex Work at the Super Bowl: The Myth and Its Makers." *Guardian*, June 14, 2017. www.theguardian.com/commentisfree/2013/feb/07/sex -work-super-bowl-myth.

Greenwald, Joy. "Wyoming Solar Eclipse a Hotbed for Sex Trafficking." K2 Radio. August 1, 2017. https://k2radio.com/wyoming-solar-eclipse-a-hotbed -for-sex-trafficking/.

Gumusluoglu, Feyza. "Women in White: The Changing Abaya Fashion in Qatar." Arab Gulf States Institute in Washington. January 17, 2017. https:// agsiw.org/women-white-changing-abaya-fashion-qatar/.

Halley, Janet, Prabha Kotiswaran, Hila Shamir, and Chantal Thomas. "From the International to the Local in Feminist Legal Responses to Rape, Prostitution/ Sex Work and Sex Trafficking: Four Studies in Contemporary Governance Feminism." *Harvard Journal of Law & Gender* 29 (2006): 336–423.

Ham, Julie. *What's the Cost of a Rumour: A Guide to Sorting out the Myths and the Facts about Sporting Events and Trafficking*. Bangkok: Global Alliance Against Trafficking in Women, 2011. www.gaatw.org/publications /WhatstheCostofaRumour.11.15.2011.pdf.

Hamill, Sarah. "The 2022 World Cup: Forced Labor of Migrant Workers." Trafficking Matters. January 15, 2019. https://traffickinginstitute.org/tag /migrant-workers/.

Haynes, Dina Francesca. "The Celebritization of Human Trafficking." *Annals of the American Academy of Political and Social Science* 653 (May 2014): 25–45.

Haynes, Suyin. "'It's Not Putin's Russia—It's Our Russia': Pussy Riot Members on Protests, Poisonings and Politics." *Time Magazine*, November 2, 2018. https://time.com/5442791/pussy-riot-russia-poisoning-olga-kyrachyova -veronika-nikulshina/.

Hearth, Katey. "2014 World Cup to Cause Human Trafficking Spike." *Mission Network News*, March 17, 2014, 3. www.mnnonline.org/news/2014-world -cup-cause-human-trafficking-spike/.

Heber, Anita. "The Hunt for an Elusive Crime—an Analysis of Swedish Measures to Combat Sex Trafficking." *Journal of Scandinavian Studies in Criminology and Crime Prevention* 19, no. 1 (2018): 3–21.

Hennig, Jana, Sarah Craggs, Frank Laczko, and Fred Larsson. *Trafficking in Human Beings and the 2006 World Cup in Germany*. Geneva: International Organization for Migration, 2007. www.iom.int/sites/default/files/our_work /ICP/IDM/mrs29THBWCG.pdf.

Hesford, Wendy. *Spectacular Rhetorics: Human Rights Visions, Recognitions, Feminisms*. Durham, NC: Duke University Press, 2011.

Hill, Annie. "How to Stage a Raid: Police, Media and the Master Narrative of Trafficking." *Anti-Trafficking Review* 7 (2016): 39–55.

Hilton, Perez. "The Nightmare Side of Sports: World Cup Expected to Cause Rise in Prostitution and Sexual Assault in Brazil." June 11, 2014. https://perezhilton.com/world-cup-brazil-expecting-rise-in-prostitution-sexual -assault-due-to-tourism/.

Hitt, Tarpley. "Why Are HBO and Melissa McCarthy Raising Money for an Anti-LGBTQ Group?" *Daily Beast*, November 12, 2020. www.thedailybeast .com/why-are-hbo-and-melissa-mccarthy-raising-money-for-exodus-cry-an -anti-abortion-group.

Hoang, Kimberly Kay. *Dealing in Desire: Asian Ascendancy, Western Decline, and the Hidden Currencies of Global Sex Work*. Oakland: University of California Press, 2015.

———. "Perverse Humanitarianism and the Business of Rescue: What's Wrong with NGOs and What's Right about the 'Johns.'" *Political Power & Social Theory* 30, no. 1 (2016): 19–43.

Hua, Julieta. *Trafficking Women's Human Rights*. Minneapolis: University of Minnesota Press, 2011.

Human Rights Watch. "Qatar: Censorship Ignores Rights, FIFA Rules: 2022 World Cup Host Should Reform Anti-LGBT Laws." August 3, 2018. www .hrw.org/news/2018/08/03/qatar-censorship-ignores-rights-fifa-rules#.

———. "Qatar: Take Urgent Action to Protect Construction Workers." September 27, 2017. shorturl.at/IKV56. www.hrw.org/news/2017/09/27/qatar -take-urgent-action-protect-construction-workers.

Human Trafficking Task Force. "Run for Freedom" (January 19, 2019). Accessed April 3, 2020. https://runsignup.com/Race/CA/VISALIA/JUSTICE RUNRUNFORFREEDOM.

Huseman, Jessica. "Top FBI Agent in Dallas Praises Super Bowl Security Effort, Sees No Evidence of Expected Spike in Child Sex Trafficking." *Dallas Morning News*, March 2, 2011. www.dallasnews.com/sports/2011/03/02/top -fbi-agent-in-dallas-praises-super-bowl-security-effort-sees-no-evidence-of -expected-spike-in-child-sex-trafficking/.

Ibrahim Al-Mulla, Mariam. "History of Slaves in Qatar: Social Reality and Contemporary Political Vision." *Journal of History Culture and Art Research* 6, no. 4 (2017): 85–111.

The International Union of Sex Workers. "Harm Was Done: Prostitution, Politics and Power in the Run up to the 2012 London Olympics." IUSW, 2012, 17. www.iusw.org/2012/12/policing-and-policy-on-prostitution-during-london -2012-olympics-%E2%80%9Charm-was-done%E2%80%9D/.

Isgro, Kirsten, Maria Stehle, and Beverly Weber. "From Sex Shacks to Mega-Brothels: The Politics of Anti-Trafficking and the 2006 Soccer World Cup." *European Journal of Cultural Studies* 16, no. 2 (2013): 171–93.

It's a Penalty. Home page. Accessed April 4, 2020. https://itsapenalty.org/.

Jackson, Crystal, Jennifer Reed, and Barbara Brents. "Strange Confluences: Radical Feminism and Evangelical Christianity as Drivers of US Neo-Abolitionism." In *Feminism, Prostitution, and the State: The Politics of*

Neo-Abolitionism, edited by Eilís Ward and Gillian Wylie, 66–85. New York: Routledge, 2017.

Jacobsen, Christine M., and May-Len Skilbrei. "Reproachable Victims? Representations and Self-Representations of Russian Women Involved in Transnational Prostitution." *Ethnos* 75, no. 2 (2010): 190–212.

Jones, Robert Alun. *Émile Durkheim: An Introduction to Four Major Works.* Beverly Hills, CA: Sage, 1986.

Jornal Naçional. "Imagens mostram prostituição infantil e tráfico de drogas em Copacabana." *O Globo*, April 26, 2012. https://g1.globo.com/rio-de -janeiro/noticia/2012/04/imagens-mostram-prostituicao-infantil-e-trafico-de -drogas-em-copacabana.html.

Jornalistas Livres. "'Mulheres contra Cunha' param o Rio de Janeiro em protesto." Medium, October 28, 2015, 4. https://medium.com/@jornalistaslivres /mulheres-contra-cunha-param-o-rio-de-janeiro-em-protesto-2eeac97 do7de.

Kang, Cecilia. "Fake News Onslaught Targets Pizzeria as Nest of Child-Trafficking." *New York Times*, November 21, 2016. www.nytimes.com/2016 /11/21/technology/fact-check-this-pizzeria-is-not-a-child-trafficking-site.html.

Keating, Fiona. "Nuns Take on Brazil's Child Sex Gangs in Run-up to World Cup." *International Business Times*, May 24, 2014. www.ibtimes.co.uk /nuns-take-brazils-child-sex-gangs-run-world-cup-1449900.

Keeley, Matt. "DOJ Gave $500K Grant to 'Hookers for Jesus' Instead of Established Anti-Trafficking Groups: Report." *Newsweek*, February 10, 2020. www.newsweek.com/doj-gave-500k-grant-hookers-jesus-instead-established -anti-trafficking-groups-report-1486596.

Kelley, Felicia. "I Spent 15 Hours at QC's 2020 Stripper Bowl—the Fyre Festival for Dancers." OK Player, February 3, 2020. www.okayplayer.com /culture/stripper-bowl-issues-2020.html.

Kempadoo, Kamala. "From Moral Panics to Global Justice: Changing Perspectives on Trafficking." In *Trafficking and Prostitution Reconsidered: New Perspectives on Migration, Sex Work, and Human Rights*, edited by Kamala Kempadoo, xii–xxxiv. London: Paradigm, 2005.

Kempadoo, Kamala, and Jo Doezema, eds. *Global Sex Workers: Rights, Resistance, and Redefinition.* New York: Routledge, 1998.

Kessler, Glenn. "The False Claim That Human Trafficking Is a '$9.5 Billion Business' in the United States." *Washington Post*, June 14, 2017. www .washingtonpost.com/news/fact-checker/wp/2015/06/02/the-false-claim -that-child-sex-trafficking-is-a-9-5-billion-business-in-the-united-states/.

Khanna, Akshay, Mani Privashri, Zachary Patterson, Maro Pantiazidou, and Maysa Shqera. *The Changing Faces of Citizen Action: A Mapping Study through an "Unruly" Lens. International Development Institute.* Brighton, UK: Institute of Development Studies, 2013. www.sxpolitics.org/wp-content /uploads/2013/06/ids-working-paper-on-unruly-politics.pdf.

Kipling, Rudyard. "The White Man's Burden: The United States & the Philippine Islands, 1899." In *Rudyard Kipling's Verse.* Garden City, NY: Doubleday, 1929.

Kohn, Eduardo. *How Forests Think: Toward an Anthropology beyond the Human*. Berkeley: University of California Press, 2013.

Kondakov, Alexander. "Spatial Justice: How the Police Craft the City by Enforcing Law on Prostitution." In *Understanding Sex for Sale: Meanings and Moralities of Sexual Commerce*, edited by May-Len Skilbrei and Marlene Spanger, 199–214. New York: Routledge, 2019.

Kotz, Peter. "Super Bowl Prostitution: 100,000 Hookers Didn't Show, but America's Latest Political Scam Did." *Dallas Observer*, March 3, 2011. www.dallasobserver.com/news/super-bowl-prostitution-100-000-hookers -didnt-show-but-americas-latest-political-scam-did-6421853.

Kouri, Jim. "Giuliani Named Security Chief for 2016 Rio Olympic Games." Renew America, December 4, 2009. www.renewamerica.com/columns/kouri /091204.

Kovessy, Peter. "Strike Temporarily Halts Work on Part of Qatar's Msheireb Project." *Doha News*, November 24, 2015. https://web.archive.org/web/20 191031142238/https://dohanews.co/strike-temporarily-halts-work-on-paert -of-msheireb-project/.

Kristof, Nicholas. "When Sources May Have Lied." *On the Ground* (blog), *New York Times*, June 7, 2014. https://kristof.blogs.nytimes.com/2014/06 /07/when-sources-may-have-lied/.

———. "Where Sweatshops Are a Dream." *On the Ground* (blog), *New York Times*, January 14, 2009. www.nytimes.com/2009/01/15/opinion/15kristof .html.

———. "A Woman I Regarded as a Hero, and New Doubts." *On the Ground* (blog), *New York Times*, June 14, 2017. https://kristof.blogs.nytimes.com /2014/06/02/a-woman-i-regarded-as-a-hero-and-new-doubts/.

Kulick, Don. "Causing a Commotion: Public Scandal as Resistance among Brazilian Transgendered Prostitutes." *Anthropology Today* 12, no. 6 (1996): 3–7.

Kwinika, Savious. "Prostitutes Flock to South Africa Ahead of World Cup 2010." *Christian Science Monitor*, June 15, 2010. www.csmonitor.com /World/Africa/2010/0512/Prostitutes-flock-to-South-Africa-ahead-of-World -Cup-2010.

Lama, Danielle. "Local Groups Work to Spread Awareness about Sex Trafficking Ahead of Derby." WDRB. June 14, 2017. www.wdrb.com/story /28783198/local-groups-work-to-spread-awareness-about-sex-trafficking -ahead-of-derby.

Lancaster, Roger. *Sex Panic and the Punitive State*. Berkeley: University of California Press, 2011.

Lapp, Charlotte. "CNN Freedom Project #FlytoFreedom." McCain Institute. November 19, 2015. www.mccaininstitute.org/blog/cnn-freedom-project-fly tofreedom/.

Larkins, Erika Robb. *The Spectacular Favela: Violence in Modern Brazil*. Oakland: University of California Press, 2015.

Lederer, Laura. "Human Trafficking and the Law." Speech presented at the Library of Congress Law Day, May 1, 2001.

————, ed. *Take Back the Night: Women on Pornography*. New York: William Morrow, 1980.

Lee, Eddie. "Super Bowl Hyperbole and Prostitution." *Toronto Star*, February 3, 2011. www.thestar.com/sports/football/2011/02/03/super_bowl _hyperbole_and_prostitution.html.

Leigh, Carol. *Just Sign on the Dotted Line: The Anti-Prostitution Loyalty Oath*. Sex Worker Media Library. N.d. https://vimeo.com/434961052.

Levy, Jay. *Criminalising the Purchase of Sex: Lessons from Sweden*. London: Routledge, 2014.

Lillie, Michelle. "Sex Trafficking at the FIFA World Cup in Brazil." Human Trafficking Search. July 14, 2014. http://humantraffickingsearch.net/wp/sex -trafficking-at-the-fifa-world-cup-in-brazil/.

Liptak, Adam. "Justices Say U.S. Cannot Impose Antiprostitution Condition on AIDS Grants." *New York Times*, June 20, 2013. www.nytimes.com/2013 /06/21/us/court-finds-aids-programs-rules-violate-free-speech.html.

Little, Dan. "Assemblage Theory." *Understanding Society* (blog), November 15, 2012. https://understandingsociety.blogspot.com/2012/11/assemblage -theory.html.

Lobel, Mark. "Arrested for Reporting on Qatar's World Cup Labourers." *BBC News*, May 18, 2015. www.bbc.com/news/world-middle-east-32775563.

Lorde, Audrey. "Sadomasochism: Not about Condemnation." In *A Burst of Light: Essays by Audrey Lorde*. Ithaca, NY: Firebrand Books, 1988.

Lundstrom, Marjie, and Sam Stanton. "This Charity Keeps Raising Money to Help Young Sex-Trafficking Victims: But Where Are the Victims?" *Sacramento Bee*, June 26, 2017. www.sacbee.com/news/investigations/the-public -eye/article158151789.html.

Lupion, Bruno. "Polícia descobre esquema de tráfico de travestis em SP." *Estadão*, February 2011. www.estadao.com.br/noticias/geral,policia-descobre -esquema-de-trafico-de-travestis-em-sp,674716.

MacGuill, Dan. "Did Ashton Kutcher's Software Help Rescue 6,000 Children from Sex Trafficking?" Snopes, September 4, 2018. www.snopes.com/fact -check/kutcher-software-child-trafficking/.

Mackenna, Ewan. "Brazil's Sex Trade: How the Country's One Million Prostitutes Are Preparing for the World Cup." *Independent*, June 14, 2014. www .independent.co.uk/news/world/americas/brazil-s-sex-trade-how-the-country -s-one-million-prostitutes-are-preparing-for-the-world-cup-9457494.html.

MacKinnon, Catharine. "Not a Moral Issue." *Yale Law & Policy Review* 2, no. 2 (1984): 321–45.

MacMahon, Lucy. "The Right to (Sell in) the City: Street Vending and Protest in Rio de Janeiro and Recife." Presented at the "Bread, Freedom and Social Justice": Organised Workers and Mass Mobilizations in the Arab World, Europe and Latin America conference, Cambridge University, July 10, 2014.

Madison, Soyini. *Critical Ethnography: Method, Ethics, and Performance*. 2nd ed. Newbury Park, CA: Sage, 2011.

Mahdavi, Parvis. "Gender, Labour and the Law: The Nexus of Domestic Work, Human Trafficking and the Informal Economy in the United Arab Emirates." *Global Networks* 13, no. 4 (2013): 425–40.

Mahdavi, Parvis, and Christine Sargent. "Questioning the Discursive Construction of Trafficking and Forced Labor in the United Arab Emirates." *Journal of Middle East Women's Studies* 7, no. 3 (2011): 6–35.

Maio, De, and Andrea Dip. *Meninas em jogo*. Repórter Brasil. VII Concurso Tim Lopes de Jornalismo Investigativo. Brasília: Agência de reportagem e jornalismo investigativo, 2013.

Majic, Samantha. "Real Men Set Norms? Anti-Trafficking Campaigns and the Limits of Celebrity Norm Entrepreneurship." *Crime, Media, Culture* 14, no. 2 (2018): 289–309.

Malinowski, Bronislaw. *Sexual Lives of Savages*. Boston: Beacon Press, 1987.

Marcus, Anthony, Amber Horning, Ric Curtis, Jo Sanson, and Efram Thompson. "Conflict and Agency among Sex Workers and Pimps: A Closer Look at Domestic Minor Sex Trafficking." *ANNALS of the American Academy of Political and Social Science* 653, no. 1 (May 2014): 225–46.

Marks, Simon. "Somaly Mam: The Holy Saint (and Sinner) of Sex Trafficking." *Newsweek*, May 21, 2014. www.newsweek.com/2014/05/30/somaly-mam -holy-saint-and-sinner-sex-trafficking-251642.html.

Maslova, Irina. "NGO Delegation to the United Nations Programme Coordinating Board." Facebook, June 30, 2016. https://m.facebook.com/ngo delegationpcb/posts/1731591860447392.

Masters, James. "World Cup 2014: Can the FBI Help Stop Brazil's World Cup Protesters?" *CNN*, May 13, 2014. http://edition.cnn.com/2014/05/13/sport /football/world-cup-brazil-security-football/index.html.

McLaughlin, Sarah. "Northwestern University in Qatar Partner Claims Controversial Event Was Canceled Due to 'Qatari Laws', 'Cultural and Social Customs.'" FIRE: Foundation for Individual Rights in Education. February 5, 2020. www.thefire.org/northwestern-university-in-qatar-partner-claims -controversial-event-was-canceled-due-to-qatari-laws-cultural-and-social -customs/.

Mendes, Melissa, and Anne Elizabeth Moore. "'Unraveling': Anti-Trafficking NGOs and the Garment Industry." Truth Out. August 19, 2014. https:// truthout.org/art/unraveling-anti-trafficking-ngos-and-the-garment-industry/.

Merry, Sally Engle. "How Big Is the Trafficking Problem? The Mysteries of Quantification." openDemocracy. January 26, 2015. www.opendemocracy .net/beyondslavery/sally-engle-merry/how-big-is-trafficking-problem -mysteries-of-quantification.

Mikkelson, David. "Super Bowl Prostitution Increase." Snopes. February 6, 2012. www.snopes.com/fact-check/super-bowl-prostitution-increase/.

Miller-Young, Mireille. *A Taste for Brown Sugar: Black Women in Pornography*. Durham, NC: Duke University Press, 2014.

Mink, Ryan. "Benjamin Watson's Next Crusade Is against Sex Trafficking in the Dominican Republic." June 21, 2017. www.baltimoreravens.com/news /benjamin-watson-s-next-crusade-is-against-sex-trafficking-in-the-domini -18986716.

Mitchell, Gregory. "A Camel Walks into a Brothel, or: Passing Anxieties in Brazil's Sexual Economies." In *Sex: Ethnographic Encounters*, edited by Richard Joseph Martin and Dieter Haller, 47–58. London: Bloomsbury, 2018.

———. "Evangelical Ecstasy Meets Feminist Fury: Sex Trafficking, Moral Panics, and Homonationalism during Global Sporting Events." *GL* 22, no. 3. (2016): 325–57.

———. *Tourist Attractions : Performing Race and Masculinity in Brazil's Sexual Economy*. Chicago: University of Chicago Press, 2015.

Mitchell, Gregory, and Thaddeus Blanchette. "Tricks of the Light: Refractive Masculinity in Heterosexual and Homosexual Middle-Class Brothels in Rio de Janeiro." *South Atlantic Quarterly* 120, no 3. (2021). 609–30.

Morgan, Robin. "Theory and Practice: Pornography and Rape." In *Take Back the Night: Women on Pornography*, edited by Laura Lederer, 134–40. New York: William Morrow, 1980.

Morton, Tom. "Wyoming Department of Family Services Will Be in Full Force for Eclipse." K2 Radio. August 7, 2017. https://k2radio.com/wyoming -department-of-family-services-will-be-in-full-force-for-eclipse/.

Moser, Charles. *Sadomasochism: Powerful Pleasures*. New York: Harrington Park Press, 2006.

MSN Take Part. "Demi Moore: Why I Joined the Fight against Child Trafficking." Celebrities. March 17, 2013. https://web.archive.org/web/201303 17194144/http://causes.msn.com/human_trafficking/.

Müller-Hoff, Claudia, and Zarah Baur. "Compliance Alert: Forced Labour in Qatar." *International Union Rights* 25, no. 2 (2018): 22–28.

Mullin, Frankie. "Sex Workers Reveal What Cops Took from Them During Police Raids." Broadly. June 14, 2017. https://broadly.vice.com/en _us/article/nz888d/sex-workers-reveal-what-cops-took-from-them-during -police-raids.

Murray, Laura. "Entre 'fazer direito' e 'direitinho': Gestão de vítimas e as políticas de proteção." *Revista Ártemis* 18, no. 1 (2014): 28–41.

———, dir. *A Kiss for Gabriela*. Rattapallax, 2020.

———. "Not Fooling Around: The Politics of Sex Worker Activisim in Brazil." PhD thesis, Columbia University, 2015.

Murray, Laura, Deanna Kerrigan, and Vera Silvia Paiva. "Rites of Resistance: Sex Workers' Fight to Maintain Rights and Pleasure in the Centre of the Response to HIV in Brazil." *Global Public Health* 14, nos. 6–7 (2019): 939–53.

Nash, Jennifer. *The Black Body in Ecstasy: Reading Race, Reading Pornography*. Durham, NC: Duke University Press, 2014.

NPR News. "World Cup Avoids Flood of Sex Workers." *All Things Considered*, July 6, 2010. www.npr.org/templates/story/story.php?storyId=128342077.

Oasis of Hope. "Shine a Light on Slavery Day." Accessed April 3, 2020. www .oasisofhopeusa.org/event/shine-a-light-on-slavery-day/.

Ochoa, Marcia. *Queen for a Day: Transformistas, Beauty Queens, and the Performance of Femininity in Venezuela*. Durham, NC: Duke University Press, 2014.

O'Connell Davidson, Julia. *Modern Slavery: The Margins of Freedom*. New York: Palgrave Macmillan, 2015.

Oliveira Rocha, Luciane de. "Black Mothers' Experiences of Violence in Rio de Janeiro." *Cultural Dynamics* 24, no. 1 (2012): 59–73.

Pal, Sreyasi. "Bengal: Mob Lynches Mentally Ill Woman after Branding Her a Child Trafficker." *Hindustan Times*, June 27, 2017. www.hindustantimes .com/kolkata/bengal-mob-lynches-mentally-ill-woman-after-branding-her-a -child-trafficker/story-xMcNPNb6oatfnrrUM7D3HP.html.

Palmer, Coburn. "Even Rio Prostitutes Think Olympics Will Be a Failure, Sex Workers Offer 'Supermarket Sale.'" Inquisitr. July 4, 2016. www.inquisitr .com/3274920/even-rio-prostitutes-think-olympics-will-be-a-failure-sex -workers-offer-supermarket-sale/.

Parreñas, Rhacel. *Illicit Flirtations: Labor, Migration, and Sex Trafficking in Tokyo*. Redwood City, CA: Stanford University Press, 2011.

Pattisson, Pete. "Qatar's Ambitious Future Driven on by North Korean 'Forced Labour.'" *Guardian*, June 14, 2017. www.theguardian.com/global -development/2014/nov/07/qatar-north-korean-forced-labour.

———. "Revealed: Qatar's World Cup 'Slaves.'" *Guardian*, September 25, 2013. www.theguardian.com/world/2013/sep/25/revealed-qatars-world-cup-slaves.

Pattisson, Pete, and Roshan Sedhai. "Covid-19 Lockdown Turns Qatar's Largest Migrant Camp into a 'Virtual Prison.'" *Guardian*, March 20, 2020. www .theguardian.com/global-development/2020/mar/20/covid-19-lockdown -turns-qatars-largest-migrant-camp-into-virtual-prison.

PBS. "The Mann Act." *Unforgivable Blackness: The Rise and Fall of Jack Johnson* (blog). Accessed March 25, 2020. www.pbs.org/kenburns/unforgivable -blackness/mann-act.

Peck, Jamie. "Zombie Neoliberalism and the Ambidextrous State." *Theoretical Criminology* 14, no. 1 (2010): 104–10.

Pendleton, Kimberly. "The Other Sex Industry: Narratives of Feminism and Freedom in Evangelical Discourses of Human Trafficking." *New Formations* 91 (2017): 102–15.

Pennafort, Roberta. "Glittervandalismo do Pink Bloc toma as ruas do Rio." *Estadão*, October 14, 2013. www.estadao.com.br/noticias/geral,glitter vandalismo-do-pink-bloc-toma-as-ruas-do-rio,1085743.

Pereira Pires de Oliveira, Marina. "Sobre armadilhas e cascas de banana: Uma análise crítica da Administração de Justiça em temas associados aos direitos humanos." *Cadernos Pagu* 31 (2008): 15–149.

Perez, Glória. "Salve Jorge." *O Globo*, 2012. https://globoplay.globo.com /salve-jorge/t/PqbGyWsY8F.

Phillips, Tom. "Rio Nightclub Closure Leaves Prostitutes Helpless." *Guardian*, August 17, 2009. www.theguardian.com/world/2009/aug/17/rio-help -nightclub-closure.

Phipps, Alison. "Sex Wars Revisited: A Rhetorical Economy of Sex Industry Opposition." *Journal of International Women's Studies* 18, no. 4 (2017): 306–20.

Pilcher, James, and Kimball Perry. "Using Soap to Fight Sex Trafficking for All-Star Game." *Enquirer*, July 5, 2015; updated July 10, 2015. www.cincinnati .com/story/news/2015/07/05/using-soap-fight-sex-trafficking-star-game /29640265/.

Piscitelli, Adriana. "Sujeição ou subversão? Migrantes brasileiras na indústria do sexo na Espanha." *História & Perspectivas* 35 (Agosto–Dezembro 2006): 13–55.

———. "Transnational Sisterhood? Brazilian Feminisms Facing Prostitution." *Latin American Policy* 5, no. 2 (2014): 221–35.

Plambech, Sine. "Sex, Deportation and Rescue: Economies of Migration among Nigerian Sex Workers." *Feminist Economics* 23, no. 1 (2017): 134–59.

Prasad, Pavithra, and Anjana Raghavan. "Dark Looks: Sensory Contours of Racism in India." In *De-Whitening Intersectionality: Race, Intercultural Communication, and Politics,* edited by Shinsuke Eguchi, Shadee Abdi, and Bernadette Marie Calafell, 223–42. Lanham, MD: Lexington Books, 2020.

Prostitution Policy Watch. *O Observatório Da Prostituição.* 2014. https://observatoriodaprostituicao.wordpress.com/.

Puar, Jasbir. *Homonationalism Gone Viral: Discipline, Control, and the Affective Politics of Sensation.* Portland Center for Public Humanities. May 21, 2012.

———. *Terrorist Assemblages: Homonationalism in Queer Times.* Durham, NC: Duke University Press, 2007.

Puar, Jasbir, Ben Pitcher, and Gunkel. "Q & A with Jasbir Puar." *Darkmatter.* May 2, 2008. No longer accessible. www.darkmatter101.org/site/2008/05/02/qa-with-jasbir-puar/.

Qatar Foundation. "Qatar Marks International Workers' Day with Conference on Labour Rights Protection, Ending Kafala." April 27, 2016. www.business-humanrights.org/en/latest-news/qatar-marks-international-workers-day-with-conference-on-labour-rights-protection-ending-kafala/.

"Rahab's Rope." Go! Venture India. Accessed February 22, 2020. www.rahabsrope.com/venture-india/.

Rausch, Natasha. "I AM Freedom Heads to World Cup." *Norfolk Daily News,* June 6, 2014. https://norfolkdailynews.com/news/i-am-freedom-heads-to-world-cup/article_eb65df34-ed81-11e3-8063-001a4bcf6878.html.

Raymond, Janice. *Not a Choice, Not a Job: Exposing the Myths about Prostitution and the Global Sex Trade.* Washington, DC: Potomac Books, 2013.

———. *The Transsexual Empire: The Making of the She-Male.* Boston: Beacon Press, 1979.

Red Sand Project. Home page. Accessed April 3, 2020. https://redsandproject.org/.

Reevell, Patrick. "Russian Hooligans' Toughest Opponents? Russia's Police." *New York Times,* June 14, 2017. www.nytimes.com/2017/04/28/sports/soccer/russian-hooligans-toughest-opponents-russias-police.html.

Renkiewicz, Paula. "Sweat Makes the Green Grass Grow: The Precarious Future of Qatar's Migrant Workers in the Run Up to the 2022 FIFA World Cup under the Kafala System and Recommendations for Effective Reform." *American University Law Review* 65, no. 1 (2017): 721–61.

Richter, Marlise. "Serious Soccer, Sex (Work) and HIV—Will South Africa Be Too Hot to Handle during the 2010 World Cup." *South African Medical Journal* 100, no. 4 (2010): 222–23.

Richter, Marlise, and Wim Delva. *"Maybe It Will Be Better Once This World Cup Has Passed": Research Findings Regarding the Impact of the 2010 Soccer World Cup on Sex Work in South Africa.* United Nations Population Fund. 2010. www.migration.org.za/wp-content/uploads/2017/08/%E2%80

%9CMaybe-it-will-be-better-once-this-World-Cup-has-passed%E2%80 %9D.pdf.

Ridley, Louise. "Rio Child Sex Trafficking 'Epidemic' Could Rocket during the 2016 Olympics—Here's Why." *HuffPost*, June 14, 2017. www .huffingtonpost.co.uk/entry/rio-olympics-2016-child-sex-trafficking_uk _57a9a7efe4b089961b85468b.

Robertson, Joe, and Donald Bradley. "Secrets of Tyler Deaton's Prayer Group Emerge." *Kansas City Star*, November 17, 2012. www.icyte.com/system/snap shots/fs1/1/0/7/d/107d819a545761ba34ebdbf69f815d1252ef5202/index.html.

Rohter, Larry. "Prostitution Puts U.S. and Brazil at Odds on AIDS Policy." *New York Times*, July 24, 2005. www.nytimes.com/2005/07/24/world/americas /prostitution-puts-us-and-brazil-at-odds-on-aids-policy.html.

Roose, Kevin. "How 'Save the Children' Is Keeping QAnon Alive." *New York Times*, September 28, 2020. www.nytimes.com/2020/09/28/technology/save -the-children-qanon.html.

Rosa, Renata Melo. "Vivendo um conto de fadas: Ensaio sobre cor e 'fantasia' entre mulheres cariocas e homens estrangeiros." Mestrado [master's thesis], Instituto de Filosofia e Ciências Sociais, Universidade Federal do Rio de Janeiro, 1999.

Rosenblatt, Kalhan. "Flight Attendants Train to Spot Human Trafficking." *NBC News*, June 14, 2017. www.nbcnews.com/news/us-news/flight-attendants -train-spot-human-trafficking-n716181.

Rubin, Gayle. *Deviations: A Gayle Rubin Reader*. Durham, NC: Duke University Press, 2012.

Ruvolo, Julie. "Brazil's Most Wanted Prostitute." Red Light Rio. July 24, 2014. https://redlightr.io/brazils-most-wanted-prostitute/.

Rydell, Robert. "In Sight and Sound with the Other Senses All Around: Racial Hierarchies at America's World's Fairs." In *The Invention of Race*, 209–21. New York: Routledge, 2006.

SA Foundation. "Calgary Ice Breaker—It's Cool to Be Cold!" Accessed April 3, 2020. https://calgaryicebreaker.com/.

Sabino, Alex. "Gays devem respeitar cultura do Qatar, diz Organizador da Copa." *Folha de São Paulo*, January 5, 2020. www1.folha.uol.com.br/esporte/2020 /01/gays-devem-aceitar-cultura-do-qatar-diz-organizador-da-copa.shtml.

Said, Edward. *Orientalism*. London: Routledge, 1978.

Schmader, David. "Chong Kim, the Woman Whose Allegedly True Story Served as the Basis for Megan Griffith's Film *Eden*, Denounced as a Fraud." *Stranger*, June 4, 2014. www.thestranger.com/slog/archives/2014/06/04 /chong-kim-the-woman-whose-allegedly-true-story-served-as-the-basis-for -megan-griffiths-film-eden-revealed-to-be-a-fraud.

Scott, James. *Weapons of the Weak: Everyday Forms of Peasant Resistance*. New Haven, CT: Yale University Press, 1987.

Schwarcz, Lilia Moritz. *Nem Preto, Nem Branco, Muito Contrário*. São Paulo: ClaroEnigma 2013.

Shih, Elena. "Duplicitous Freedom: Moral and Material Care Work in Anti-Trafficking Rescue and Rehabilitation." *Critical Sociology* 44, nos. 7–8 (2018): 1077–86.

Shumway, Julia. "Human Trafficking Expected during Solar Eclipse." *Bend Bulletin*, August 10, 2017. www.bendbulletin.com/localstate/human -trafficking-expected-during-solar-eclipse/article_a80f2cda-aaa2-5439-872c -6c97185a2e84.html.

Sieczkowski, Cavan. "Russian Neo-Nazis Allegedly Lure, Torture Gay Teens with Online Dating Scam." *Huffington Post*, July 26, 2013. www.huffpost .com/entry/russian-nazi-torture-gay-teens_n_3658636.

Simi, John. "Rio Carnival 2013: Topless Activists Stage Sex Protest at Airport." *International Business Times*, February 10, 2013. www.ibtimes.co.uk/rio -carnival-2013-femen-topless-activists-photos-433414.

Simionato, Maurício. "Levantamento indica que gays são mais agredidos por policies." *Folha de São Paulo*, June 19, 2010. www1.folha.uol.com.br /cotidiano/753714-levantamento-indica-que-gays-sao-mais-agredidos-por -policiais.shtml.

Singer, André. "Brasil, junho de 2013, Classes e ideologias cruzadas." *Novos Estudos—CEBRAP* 97 (November 2013): 23–40.

Smith, Christen A. *Afro-Paradise: Blackness, Violence, and Performance in Brazil*. Urbana: University of Illinois Press, 2016.

Sneed, Tierney. "How Big Data Battles Human Trafficking." *US News*, January 14, 2015. www.usnews.com/news/articles/2015/01/14/how-big-data-is -being-used-in-the-fight-against-human-trafficking.

Sobel, Adam, dir. *The Workers Cup*. Autlook Filmsales, 2017.

"The Sold Project: Super Bowl Sex for Sale." Accessed March 26, 2013. http:// thesoldproject.wordpress.com/2011/01/27/super-bowl-sex-for-sale/.

Sonmez, Felicia, and Mike DeBonis. "Believer in QAnon Conspiracy Theory Wins Republican Senate Nomination in Oregon." *Washington Post*, May 20, 2020. www.washingtonpost.com/politics/believer-in-qanon-conspiracy-theory-wins -republican-senate-nomination-in-oregon/2020/05/20/bf2d910a-9aaa-11ea -89fd-28fb313d1886_story.html.

Spaaij, Ramón. "Football Hooliganism as a Transnational Phenomenon: Past and Present Analysis; A Critique—More Specificity and Less Generality." *International Journal of the History of Sport* 24, no. 4 (2007): 411–31.

———. "Men Like Us, Boys Like Them: Violence, Masculinity, and Collective Identity in Football Hooliganism." *Journal of Sport and Social Issues* 32, no. 4 (2008): 369–92.

Sperling, Ary. "A carinho da verdade." August 22, 2011. www.youtube.com /watch?v=QcH26K8RPaY.

Staples, Brent. "How the Suffrage Movement Betrayed Black Women." *New York Times*, July 28, 2018. www.nytimes.com/2018/07/28/opinion/sunday /suffrage-movement-racism-black-women.html.

Steikunaite, Giedre. "Olympic Sex-Trafficking Myth Creates Climate of Fear." New Internationalist. February 1, 2012. https://newint.org/blog/2012/02/01 /sex-trafficking-rumours-at-olympics/.

Stepanek, Marcia. "Emma Thompson's 'Journey' into Sexual Slavery." *NBC News*, November 13, 2009. www.nbcnews.com/id/33913920/ns/us_news -giving/t/emma-thompsons-journey-sex-slavery/#.XqoE7lNKg1I.

Stern, Marlow. "Sean Penn's Horrifying History of Alleged Abuse." *Daily Beast*, September 19, 2018. www.thedailybeast.com/sean-penns-horrifying -history-of-alleged-abuse.

Stewart, Will. "New Gulags? Russia 'Cleanses World Cup 2018 Cities of Home-less People' by 'Forcefully Bussing Them to Special Camps.'" *Sun*, June 8, 2018. www.thesun.co.uk/world-cup-2018/6484499/russia-cleanse-world-cup -2018-cities-homeless-people-camps/.

Strand, Paul. "Rescuing Sex Slaves with Soap and Paper." *CBN News: The Christian Perspective*, June 5, 2017. www1.cbn.com/cbnnews/us/2017/june /rescuing-sex-slaves-with-soap-and-paper.

Suhr, Brigitte. *Funding the Fight against Modern Slavery: Mapping Private Funds in the Ant-Slavery and Anti-Trafficking Sector: 2012–2014.* 2016. http://freedomfund.org/wp-content/uploads/Donor-Mapping-Report-for -web-FINAL-30March16-1.pdf.

Sunkara, Bhaskar. "Soccer in Sun and Shadow." *In These Times*, January 1, 2014. https://inthesetimes.com/article/soccer-in-sun-and-shadow.

Svanström, Yvonne. "From Contested to Consensus: Swedish Politics on Pros-titution and Trafficking." In *Feminism, Prostitution, and the State: The Poli-tics of Neo-Abolitionism*, edited by Eilís Ward and Gillian Wylie, 29–45. New York: Routledge, 2017.

Tashman, Brian. "Anti-Gay Leaders Call for Prayer Movement to Stop 'Homo-sexual Tornado' Coming to 'Destroy America.'" Right Wing Watch. April 23, 2012. www.rightwingwatch.org/post/anti-gay-leaders-call-for-prayer-movement -to-stop-homosexual-tornado-coming-to-destroy-america/.

Tayler, Jeffrey. "Femen's Inna Shevchenko: Fear of Causing Offense Has Cost Too Many Innocent Lives." *Quillette*, December 30, 2017. https://quillette .com/2017/12/30/femens-inna-shevchenko-fear-causing-offense-cost-many -innocent-lives/.

Teixeira Castilho, César, Barbara Evrard, Leonardo Turchi Pacheco, and Dom-inique Charrier. "Turismo sexual infanto-juvenil em Zeque no contexto da Copa do Mundo de 2014." *Revista Estudos Feministas* 26, no. 2 (2018): 1–20.

Telles, Edward. *Race in Another America: The Significance of Skin Color in Brazil.* Princeton, NJ: Princeton University Press, 2004.

Thakali, Thabiso, and Candice Bailey. "No 'Boom Boom' for Joburg's Sex Workers." *IOL News*, June 19, 2010. www.iol.co.za/capeargus/sport/no -boom-boom-for-joburgs-sex-workers-490629.

Thomé, Clarissa, and Thaise Constâncio. "Hotel é fechado no Rio por envolvi-mento em exploração sexual." *Estadão*, June 13, 2014. https://brasil.estadao .com.br/noticias/rio-de-janeiro,hotel-e-fechado-no-rio-por-envolvimento-em -exploracao-sexual,1511430.

Thompson, Nathan B. "Brazil's Digital Protests Spell Trouble on the Street." openDemocracy. January 28, 2016. www.opendemocracy.net/nathan -bthompson/brazils-digital-protests-spell-trouble-on-street.

Thorn. "We Are Thorn." Accessed April 4, 2020. www.thorn.org/about-our -fight-against-sexual-exploitation-of-children/.

Ticktin, Miriam. *Casualties of Care: Immigration and the Politics of Humanitarianism in France*. Berkeley: University of California Press, 2011.

"Tourism: Not Germany, but Rio de Janeiro Hit the Jackpot." *eTurboNews: Global Travel Industry News*, June 27, 2014. www.eturbonews.com/48139/tourism-not-germany-rio-de-janeiro-hit-jackpot.

Trindade, Eliane. "Sonhos de Belém." *Folha de São Paulo*, February 7, 2011. www1.folha.uol.com.br/fsp/cotidian/ff0702201119.htm.

Tucker-Smith, Linda. *Lock Step and Dance: Images of Black Men in Popular Culture*. Jackson: University of Mississippi Press, 2007.

Tyburczy, Jennifer. "Sex Trafficking Talk: Rosi Orozco and the Neoliberal Narrative of Empathy in Post-NAFTA Mexico." *Feminist Formations* 31, no. 3 (2019): 95–117.

University of Wisconsin. "UW Global Health and Human Rights Training in Spain and Morocco to Combat Sex-Trafficking." Accessed February 22, 2020. https://studyabroad.wisc.edu/program/?programId=524.

UPI. "Brazil Campaigning for Permanent U.N. Security Council Seat." *United Press International*, October 16, 2009. www.upi.com/Top_News/Special/2009/10/16/Brazil-campaigning-for-permanent-UN-Security-Council-seat/71131255711794/?u3L=1#ixzz2OHYjX7dl.

Vance, Carole S. "Innocence and Experience: Melodramatic Narratives of Sex Trafficking and Their Consequences for Law and Policy." *History of the Present* 2, no. 2 (2012): 200–218.

———. "Thinking Trafficking, Thinking Sex." *GLQ* 17, no. 1 (2011): 135–43.

Vanyoro, Kudakwashe P. "'Skeptics' and 'Believers': Anti-Trafficking, Sex Work, and Migrant Rights Activism in South Africa." *Gender and Development* 27, no. 1 (2019): 123–37.

Vecsey, George. "Views That Soccer Can Do Without." *New York Times*, December 17, 2010. www.nytimes.com/2010/12/18/sports/soccer/18vecsey.html.

Vries, Alexandra de, and Shawn Blore. *Frommer's Brazil*. Hoboken, NJ: John Wiley & Sons, 2012.

Vuolajärvi, Niina. "Governing in the Name of Caring—The Nordic Model of Prostitution and Its Punitive Consequences for Migrants Who Sell Sex." *Sexuality Research and Social Policy* 16, no. 2 (2019): 151–65.

Wazir, Buhrhan. "Mysterious Shutdown Plagues Popular News Site in Qatar." *Columbia Journalism Review*, December 9, 2016. www.cjr.org/watchdog/doha_news_censorship_journalism.php.

Weeks, Jeffrey. *Sex, Politics, and Society: The Regulation of Sexuality Since 1800*. 3rd ed. New York: Routledge, 2012.

Weismantel, Mary. *Cholas and Pishtacos: Stories of Race and Sex in the Andes*. Chicago: University of Chicago Press, 2001.

———. "Race Rape: White Masculinity in Andean Pishtaco Tales." *Identities: Global Studies in Culture and Power* 7, no. 3 (2000): 407–40.

Weitzer, Ron. *Legalizing Prostitution: From Illicit Vice to Lawful Business*. New York: NYU Press, 2012.

Weitzer, Ron, and Melissa Ditmore. "Sex Trafficking Facts and Fictions." In *Sex for Sale: Prostitution, Pornography, and the Sex Industry*, 2nd ed. New York: Routledge, 2010.

West, Lindy. "Pay. Sit. Barf." *Stranger*, September 14, 2010. www.thestranger
.com/slog/archives/2010/09/14/pay-sit-barf.

Wical, Carol. "Matter Out of Place: Reading Dirty Women." *M/C Journal* 9,
no. 5 (2006). https://journal.media-culture.org.au/mcjournal/article/view
/2673.

Williams, David. "'I Want to Win Olympic Gold for Sex': Rio Escort Wants to
Use Games to Find a Boyfriend 'Just Like a Julia Roberts in Pretty Woman.'"
Daily Mail, August 3, 2016, 21. www.dailymail.co.uk/news/article-3718345
/I-want-win-Olympic-gold-sex-Rio-escort-wants-use-Games-boyfriend-just
-like-Julia-Roberts-Pretty-Woman.html.

Williams, Erica Lorraine. *Sex Tourism in Bahia: Ambiguous Entanglements*.
Urbana: University of Illinois Press, 2013.

Williams, Roger Ross. "Gospel of Intolerance." *New York Times*, January 22,
2013. www.nytimes.com/2013/01/23/opinion/gospel-of-intolerance.html.

Williamson, Kathleen, and Anthony Marcus. "Black Pimps Matter: Racially
Selective Identification and Prosecution of Sex Trafficking in the United
States." In *Third Party Sex Work and Pimps in the Age of Anti-Trafficking*,
edited by Amber Horning and Anthony Marcus, 177–95. New York:
Springer International, 2017.

Woods, Tryon. "The Antiblackness of 'Modern-Day Slavery' Abolitionism."
openDemocracy. October 10, 2014. www.opendemocracy.net/en/beyond
-trafficking-and-slavery/antiblackness-of-modernday-slavery-abolitionism/.

———. "Surrogate Selves: Notes on Anti-Trafficking and Anti-Blackness."
Social Identities 19, no. 1 (2013): 120–34.

Youn, Soo. "Uber Announces 21 Categories of Sexual Misconduct to Report."
ABC News, November 12, 2018. https://abcnews.go.com/Business/uber
-announces-21-categories-sexual-misconduct-report/story?id=59139591.

Zurowski, Cory. "Minnesota Ramps Up for a Mythical Super Bowl Sex Trafficking Rampage," City Pages. June 27, 2017. www.citypages.com/news
/minnesota-ramps-up-for-a-mythical-super-bowl-sex-trafficking-rampage
/430883973. www.policeprostitutionandpolitics.com/pdfs_all/Superbowl
_sex_trafficking_hysteria/2017%20Minnesota%20ramps%20up%20for
%20a%20mythical%20Super%20Bowl%20sex%20trafficking%20
rampage%20%7C%20City%20Pages.pdf.

Index

4 × 4 (bathhouse brothel), 50–53, 54, 55, 209–210
40,000 myth. *See* myth of 40,000
2014 World Cup. *See* World Cup 2014 in Brazil
2016 Olympics. *See* Olympics 2016 in Brazil

abayas, 189–190
abolitionist term, 8, 57–58, 82
academic researchers, 167
accountability, lack of, 2–3, 170–171
Adams, Dave, 150
Addams, Jane, 67
Against Our Will (Brownmiller), 69
Agustín, Laura María, 4, 36, 87, 88, 89, 133
aid agencies, expansion of, 139
Airline Ambassadors, 158
Ajam, Kashiefa, 31
A Kiss for Gabriela (2013), 215
Alexa, 210
Alexander, M. Jacqui, 12, 105
Al Jazeera, 173, 193
Amar, Paul, 2, 16, 211, 212, 224–225
Amnesty International, 140, 141, 165, 204–205, 206
Amoah, Jewel D., 72
Anthony, Susan B., 66

anthropology, 79, 120
anti-Blackness, 64, 65
anti-prostitution loyalty oath (APLO), 3–4, 85, 86, 87
anti-prostitution movement, 40, 65, 166–167
anti-prostitution radical feminists, 39, 188–189. *See also* feminism
anti-sex trafficking movement: awareness raising as goal of, 133–134; carceral focus of, 81; celebrity activists in, 63; coalitions in, 40–41; discourses in, 80; harm of legislation, 129; inoculating against skepticism, 164–168; neo-colonialism of, 84–89; origins of, 53; programs and tours of, 75; racism in, 34–35, 65; roots in anti-pornography, 73; roots in white supremacy, 57–68, 93–94; term co-option of, 82, 83; unintended consequences of, 161–162; white fragility of, 74
antislavery movement, 66
anti-trafficking laws in Brazil, 14
Arizona State University, 137
Armstrong, Linzi, 92
Asian immigrants, 58
Asia Pacific Regional Correspondent for the Network of Sex: Work Projects, 153

Founded in 1893,
UNIVERSITY OF CALIFORNIA PRESS
publishes bold, progressive books and journals
on topics in the arts, humanities, social sciences,
and natural sciences—with a focus on social
justice issues—that inspire thought and action
among readers worldwide.

The UC PRESS FOUNDATION
raises funds to uphold the press's vital role
as an independent, nonprofit publisher, and
receives philanthropic support from a wide
range of individuals and institutions—and from
committed readers like you. To learn more, visit
ucpress.edu/supportus.